Interpretation and Application of IPSAS

Interpretation and Application of IPSAS

Caroline Aggestam-Pontoppidan
Isabelle Andernack

WILEY

Library of Congress Cataloging-in-Publication Data

Names: Aggestam-Pontoppidan, Caroline, 1975– Andernack, Isabelle, 1972–
Title: Interpretation and application of IPSAS / Caroline Aggestam-Pontoppidan.
Description: Hoboken : Wiley, 2016. Series: Wiley regulatory reporting
   Includes bibliographical references and index.
Identifiers: LCCN 2015037506 (print) ISBN 9781119010296 (paperback)
Subjects: LCSH: Finance, Public–Accounting–Standards. International public sector accounting
standard.
Classification: LCC HJ9733 .A34 2016 (print) LCC HJ9733 (ebook) DDC
   657/.8350218–dc23
LC record available at http://lccn.loc.gov/2015037506

A catalogue record for this book is available from the British Library.

ISBN 978-1-119-01029-6 (pbk) ISBN 978-1-119-01031-9 (ebk)
ISBN 978-1-119-01030-2 (ebk) ISBN 978-1-119-17032-7 (ebk)

Cover Design & Image: Wiley

Set in 11/12pt Times by Aptara Inc., New Delhi, India
Printed in Great Britain by TJ International Ltd, Padstow, Cornwall, UK

CONTENTS

FOREWORD

It is with pleasure that I am writing this foreword to *Interpretation and Application of IPSAS*, which has been authored by Caroline Aggestam-Pontoppidan and Isabelle Andernack.

International Public Sector Accounting Standards (IPSASs) are issued by the IPSAS Board (IPSASB) for use by public sector entities around the world in the preparation of their financial statements, and are intended to improve the quality of financial reporting.

However, although an entirely accurate picture is difficult to obtain, it would appear that adoption and implementation of IPSAS around the world has been slower than expected. It is hopefully the case that the next few years will see many more public sector organizations on all continents embracing IPSAS, and thereby upgrading the reporting, the accountability and the transparency of their organizations.

Relatively few publications dealing with the practical adoption of IPSAS have been available to implementers and other interested parties so far, and it is to everybody's benefit to see this work, entitled *Interpretation and Application of IPSAS*, being published.

In particular, I am pleased to see a text that includes examples and mini-case studies that help to illustrate how IPSAS is applied – this will be very helpful for training and education purposes. This book also provides useful insights into navigation of the transition to IPSAS, either under the accrual basis or cash basis of accounting.

I am confident that this important work will be of significant benefit to the relevant communities, and congratulate the authors on their achievement.

By Marc Gardiner BSc (Econ) CPA, Chief Executive
Officer of IASeminars Ltd., London

IASeminars is an independent global financial training company specialising in international accounting seminars (IFRS & US GAAP & IPSAS) and other financial training events.

ACKNOWLEDGEMENTS

The process of writing this book has been enabled by the inspiration and support of a number of individuals from the global "IPSAS-community", who have taken time out to help us.

Firstly, we are sending our sincere appreciation to the commissioning team at John Wiley & Sons Ltd. We have had the pleasure of being supported by wonderful, encouraging and helpful people, such as Stephen Mullaly, Gemma Valler and Tessa Allen.

Secondly, we would like to thank the knowledgeable IPSAS practitioners who have granted us permission to use IPSAS compliant financial statements. We are particularly thankful to Ms. Nutan Wozencroft (UNESCO) and Mr. Uday Dayal (formerly at the IAEA). We send special appreciation to Melissa Dias Buerbaumer, Ph.D., CPA, and Chief of Accounts at the OSCE, who has lent us her expertise and has let us include two practical case studies, based on her experiences of adopting IPSAS. For this we are grateful.

In addition to those who have directly contributed to this book, we would like to mention that a number of organizations, such as the CIPFA and IASeminars, have been valuable resources in the writing of this book. We are also thankful to the well-maintained website of the IPSASB, which allows any public sector accountant to stay fully abreast of the developments in IPSAS and other work related to the IPSASB.

Also, we send our special thanks to Gary Bandy for his review of the manuscript and invaluable suggestions for improvements hereof.

Thirdly, we want to thank former and present colleagues, both in the academic and the practice communities, who, through conversations about public sector accounting and IPSAS, have provided insight and inspiration that has helped to shape this book. Specifically, we thank our respective departments at the Copenhagen Business School and Sorbonne University for supporting us with the writing of this book.

Finally, we both thank our respective families, who have endured us spending many long days and nights in front of our computers.

Any errors or flaws in the book remain the authors' responsibility.

ABOUT THE AUTHORS

CAROLINE AGGESTAM PONTOPPIDAN

Caroline Aggestam Pontoppidan (Ph.D) works as an Associate Professor at the Department of Accounting and Auditing at the Copenhagen Business School (CBS). She earned her Ph.D in auditing in 2005. Caroline is an experienced educator and researcher who today specializes in International Public Sector Accounting Standards (IPSAS) and other international accounting and auditing issues in the public sector as well as the education of public sector accountants.

Since completing her Ph.D, she has carried out research on the development of public sector accounting at the global level as well as providing training services for various public sector entities on International Standards of Auditing (ISA) as well as on the interpretation and application of IPSAS.

Caroline previously spent three years in Japan teaching and researching emerging accounting and auditing issues. In addition, she has practical work experience from having served a number of United Nations agencies for more than eight years in total. Her work within international organizations has included, for example, business process re-engineering and the provision of technical advice on accounting and internal control systems.

ISABELLE ANDERNACK

Isabelle Andernack is a French Chartered Accountant (Diplômée d'expertise comptable) and Financial Auditor (Commissaire aux comptes), and a Member of the French financial analysts' institution (Société française des analystes financiers, SFAF).

She has nearly 20 years of professional experience in both the private and public sectors, including training, accounting, managing transitions to new accounting systems, planning and implementation. and specifically International Financial Reporting Standards (IFRS) and International Public Sector Accounting Standards (IPSAS).

She has worked on many high-profile accounting and audit training and consulting engagements, both in the public as well as in the private sector. Recently Isabelle has been implementing an ERP (enterprise resource planning) system for an international organization that she had previously converted from cash accounting to the accrual basis of accounting under IPSAS, in order to improve its management and long-term financial and business strategy.

Isabelle is a lecturer at Paris I Panthéon-Sorbonne University and at CFAF (Training Centre for French Financial Analysts). To follow the work of Caroline and Isabelle on IPSAS please visit www.ipsasapplied.com.

LIST OF IPSAS WITH CORRESPONDING IFRS

FULL LISTING OF ALL IPSAS AND IFRS "EQUIVALENT" AS AT 2 MARCH 2015

IPSAS	IFRS "equivalent" (if applicable)
IPSAS 1—Presentation of Financial Statements	IAS 1
IPSAS 2—Cash Flow Statements	IAS 7
IPSAS 3—Accounting Policies, Changes in Accounting Estimates and Errors	IAS 8
IPSAS 4—The Effects of Changes in Foreign Exchange Rates	IAS 21
IPSAS 5—Borrowing Costs	IAS 23
IPSAS 6—Consolidated and Separate Financial Statements[1]	IAS 27 (replaced)
IPSAS 7—Investments in Associates[2]	IAS 28 (replaced)
IPSAS 8—Interests in Joint Ventures[3]	IAS 31 (replaced)
IPSAS 9—Revenue from Exchange Transactions	IAS 18
IPSAS 10—Financial Reporting in Hyperinflationary Economies	IAS 29
IPSAS 11—Construction Contracts	IAS 11
IPSAS 12—Inventories	IAS 2
IPSAS 13—Leases	IAS 17
IPSAS 14—Events after the Reporting Date	IAS 10
IPSAS 15— (withdrawn)[4]	
IPSAS 16—Investment Property	IAS 40
IPSAS 17—Property, Plant, and Equipment	IAS 16
IPSAS 18—Segment Reporting	IAS 14 (replaced)
IPSAS 19—Provisions, Contingent Liabilities and Contingent Assets	IAS 37
IPSAS 20—Related Party Disclosures	IAS 24
IPSAS 21—Impairment of Non-Cash-Generating Assets	N/A[5]
IPSAS 22—Disclosure of Information about the General Government Sector	N/A
IPSAS 23—Revenue from Non-Exchange Transactions (Taxes and Transfers)	N/A
IPSAS 24—Presentation of Budget Information in Financial Statements	N/A
IPSAS 25—Employee Benefits	IAS 19
IPSAS 26—Impairment of Cash-Generating Assets	IAS 36
IPSAS 27—Agriculture	IAS 41
IPSAS 28—Financial Instruments: Presentation	IAS 32
IPSAS 29—Financial Instruments: Recognition and Measurement	IAS 39

[1]To be replaced by IPSAS 34 and IPSAS 35.
[2]To be replaced by IPSAS 36.
[3]To be replaced by IPSAS 37.
[4]Replaced by IPSAS 28, IPSAS 29, and IPSAS 30 for accounting periods beginning on or after 1 January 2013.
[5]N/A: not applicable.

IPSAS 30—Financial Instruments: Disclosures   IFRS 7

IPSAS 31—Intangible Assets   IAS 38

IPSAS 32—Service Concession Arrangements: grantor   N/A

IPSAS 33—First-Time Adoption of Accrual Basis IPSASs   IFRS 1
An entity shall apply those amendments for annual financial statements covering periods beginning on or after 1 January 2017. Earlier application is permitted. If an entity applies IPSAS 33 for a period beginning before 1 January 2017, the amendments shall also be applied for that earlier period.

IPSAS 34—Separate Financial Statements   IAS 27 (2011)
An entity shall apply this Standard for annual financial statements covering periods beginning on or after 1 January 2017. Earlier application is encouraged. If an entity applies this Standard for a period beginning before 1 January 2017, it shall disclose that fact and apply IPSAS 35, IPSAS 36, IPSAS 37, and IPSAS 38 at the same time.

IPSAS 35—Consolidated Financial Statements   IFRS 10
An entity shall apply this Standard for annual financial statements covering periods beginning on or after 1 January 2017. Earlier application is encouraged. If an entity applies this Standard for a period beginning before 1 January 2017, it shall disclose that fact and apply IPSAS 34, Separate Financial Statements, IPSAS 36, IPSAS 37, and IPSAS 38 at the same time.

IPSAS 36—Investments in Associates and Joint Ventures   IAS 28 (2011)
An entity shall apply this Standard for annual financial statements covering periods beginning on or after 1 January 2017. Earlier application is encouraged. If an entity applies this Standard for a period beginning before 1 January 2017, it shall disclose that fact and apply IPSAS 34, IPSAS 35, IPSAS 37, and IPSAS 38, Disclosure of Interests in Other Entities, at the same time.

IPSAS 37—Joint Arrangements   IFRS 11
An entity shall apply this Standard for annual financial statements covering periods beginning on or after 1 January 2017. Earlier application is encouraged. If an entity applies this Standard for a period beginning before 1 January 2017, it shall disclose that fact and apply IPSAS 34, IPSAS 35, IPSAS 36, and IPSAS 38, Disclosure of Interests in Other Entities, at the same time.

IPSAS 38—Disclosure of Interests in Other Entities   IFRS 12
An entity shall apply this Standard for annual financial statements covering periods beginning on or after 1 January 2017. Earlier application is encouraged.

LIST OF IPSAS WITH BRIEF DESCRIPTION

IPSAS 1 Presentation of Financial Statements sets out the overall considerations for the presentation of financial statements, guidance for their structure and minimum requirements for the content of financial statements prepared under the accrual basis of accounting.

IPSAS 2 Cash Flow Statements requires the provision of information about the changes in cash and cash equivalents during the financial period from operating, investing and financing activities.

IPSAS 3 Accounting Policies, Changes in Accounting Estimates and Errors specifies the accounting treatment for changes in accounting estimates, changes in accounting policies and the correction of material errors.

IPSAS 4 The Effects of Changes in Foreign Exchange Rates deals with accounting for foreign currency transactions and foreign operations, sets out the requirements for determining which exchange rate to use for the recognition of certain transactions and balances, and prescribes how to recognize the financial effect of changes in exchange rates within the financial statements.

IPSAS 5 Borrowing Costs prescribes the accounting treatment for borrowing costs and requires either the immediate expensing of borrowing costs or, as an allowed alternative treatment, the capitalization of borrowing costs that are directly attributable to the acquisition, construction, or production of a qualifying asset.

IPSAS 6 Consolidated and Separate Financial Statements requires all controlling entities to prepare consolidated financial statements, which consolidate all controlled entities on a line-by-line basis.

IPSAS 7 Investments in Associates requires all such investments to be accounted for in the consolidated financial statements using the equity method of accounting.

IPSAS 8 Interests in Joint Ventures requires proportionate consolidation to be adopted as the benchmark treatment, and the equity method of accounting as an allowed alternative to account for joint ventures.

IPSAS 9 Revenue from Exchange Transactions establishes the conditions for the recognition of revenue arising from exchange transactions, and requires such revenue to be measured at the fair value of the consideration received or receivable.

IPSAS 10 Financial Reporting in Hyperinflationary Economies describes the characteristics of a hyperinflationary economy and requires financial statements of entities that operate in such economies to be restated so that the financial information provided is meaningful.

IPSAS 11 Construction Contracts defines construction contracts and establishes requirements for the recognition of revenues and expenses arising from such contracts.

IPSAS 12 Inventories establishes the measurement requirements for inventories (including those held for distribution at no or nominal charge), and provides guidance on the assignment of costs.

IPSAS 13 Leases establishes requirements for the accounting treatment of operating and finance leases by lessees and lessors.

IPSAS 14 Events After the Reporting Date establishes requirements for the treatment of certain events that occur after the reporting date, and distinguishes between adjusting and non-adjusting events.

IPSAS 15 Financial Instruments: Disclosure and Presentation *has been superseded* by IPSAS 28 Financial Instruments: Presentation, IPSAS 29 Financial Instruments: Recognition and Measurement, and IPSAS 30 Financial Instruments: Disclosures.

IPSAS 16 Investment Property establishes the accounting treatment and related disclosures for investment property, providing for application of either a fair value or historical cost model.

IPSAS 17 Property, Plant and Equipment (PPE) establishes the accounting treatment for property, plant and equipment, including the basis and timing of their initial recognition, and the determination of their ongoing carrying amounts and related depreciation.

IPSAS 18 Segment Reporting establishes requirements for the disclosure of financial information of the distinguishable activities of reporting entities.

IPSAS 19 Provisions, Contingent Liabilities and Contingent Assets establishes requirements for the recognition and measurement of provisions, and the disclosure of contingent liabilities and contingent assets.

IPSAS 20 Related Party Disclosures establishes requirements for the disclosure of transactions with parties that are related to the reporting entity.

IPSAS 21 Impairment of Non-Cash-Generating Assets prescribes the procedures that apply to determine whether a non-cash-generating asset is impaired and to ensure that impairment losses are recognized.

IPSAS 22 Disclosure of Financial Information About the General Government Sector prescribes disclosure requirements for governments that elect to present information about the general government sector in their consolidated financial statements.

IPSAS 23 Revenue from Non-Exchange Transactions deals with issues that need to be considered in recognizing and measuring revenue from non-exchange transactions.

IPSAS 24 Presentation of Budget Information in Financial Statements sets out the requirement for a comparison of budget amounts and the actual amounts arising from execution of the budget to be included in the financial statements, and a reconciliation of the actual amounts in the budget to actual amounts in the financial statements.

IPSAS 25 Employee Benefits prescribes the accounting treatment and disclosure requirements of employee benefits, including the timing of recognition of liabilities and expenses.

IPSAS 26 Impairment of Cash-Generating Assets prescribes the procedures that apply to determine whether a cash-generating asset is impaired and to ensure that impairment losses are recognized.

IPSAS 27 Agriculture prescribes the accounting treatment and disclosures for biological assets and agricultural produce at the point of harvest when they relate to agricultural activity.

IPSAS 28 Financial Instruments: Presentation establishes principles for presenting financial instruments as liabilities or net assets/equity and for offsetting financial assets and financial liabilities.

IPSAS 29 Financial Instruments: Recognition and Measurement establishes principles for recognizing and measuring financial assets, financial liabilities, and some contracts to buy or sell non-financial items.

IPSAS 30 Financial Instruments: Disclosures requires entities to provide disclosures in their financial statements that enable users to evaluate (a) the significance of financial instruments for the entity's financial position and performance; and (b) the nature and extent of risks arising from financial instruments to which the entity is exposed during the period and at the end of the reporting period, and how the entity manages those risks.

IPSAS 31 Intangible Assets prescribes the accounting treatment for recognizing and measuring intangible assets.

IPSAS 32 Service Concession Arrangements prescribes the accounting for service concession arrangements by the grantor, a public sector entity.

IPSAS 33 First-Time Adoption of Accrual Basis IPSASs. An entity shall apply those amendments for annual financial statements covering periods beginning on or after 1 January 2017.

IPSAS 34 Separate Financial Statements. An entity shall apply this Standard for annual financial statements covering periods beginning on or after 1 January 2017.

IPSAS 35 Consolidated Financial Statements. An entity shall apply this Standard for annual financial statements covering periods beginning on or after 1 January 2017.

IPSAS 36 Investments in Associates and Joint Ventures. An entity shall apply this Standard for annual financial statements covering periods beginning on or after 1 January 2017.

IPSAS 37 Joint Arrangements. An entity shall apply this Standard for annual financial statements covering periods beginning on or after 1 January 2017.

IPSAS 38 Disclosure of Interests in Other Entities. An entity shall apply this Standard for annual financial statements covering periods beginning on or after 1 January 2017.

DISCLAIMER

This book should not be used as a substitute for obtaining professional advice and input when adopting either cash based or accrual based IPSAS. The brief summaries of IPSAS requirements and principles provided in this book should be read in conjunction with the IPSASs and other guidance materials as promulgated by the IPSASB, which are copyrighted by the IFAC. The IPSASB website will provide a reader with updates on all new developments.

It should also be noted that this book does not contain advice on accounting treatments and does not consider the particular legal or other regulatory requirements of specific countries.

Readers of this book who are working on the implementation of IPSAS are encouraged to contact IPSAS specialists to obtain advice and support specific to their circumstances and requirements.

PART 1

INTRODUCING PUBLIC SECTOR ACCOUNTING

1 INTRODUCTION

International Public Sector Accounting Standards (IPSAS) are gaining increasing acceptance globally (see Table 1.1 for a full listing of all IPSAS). Public administrators are today encountering important challenges in reducing the distance between accounting systems within countries as well as across borders. This entails a move towards harmonization[1] of accounting practices in the public sector and thus requires choosing an appropriate set of accounting and financial reporting standards (see also Caperchione, 2015).

The focus on creating one common set of standards at the global level is relatively new, in comparison to what we have witnessed for the private sector, with the global spread and institutionalization of International Financial Reporting Standards (IFRS) (see also for example Ball, 2012).

Many governments across the globe operate on a cash basis (or modified cash basis[2]) and do not account for many significant items, such as liabilities for public sector pensions and financial instruments. Accrual accounting is a fundamental tenet of strong accounting and reporting for public companies, and so it should be for governments as well. This is why the adoption of accrual accounting by public sector entities should result in a more comprehensive and accurate view of the financial position, and help to ensure that governments and other public sector entities are transparent and accountable. It should also be noted, however, that in some cases, governments do not have standardized practices for applying cash-basis accounting and, in such cases, applying cash-basis IPSAS could be a first step towards transparency and accountability.

The International Public Sector Accounting Standards Board (IPSASB) and the IPSAS that it establishes have increasingly become a point for international standardization and reference within the area of public sector accounting. The IPSASB is, today, an independent standard-setting board under the auspices of the International Federation of Accountants (IFAC). It has been said that the issuing of the complete Conceptual Framework in 2014 has served as a "landmark document that firmly

---

[1] Harmonization refers to a "process of increasing the compatibility of accounting practices by setting bounds to their degree of variation" (Nobes, 1991: 70).

[2] A *modified cash accounting* system recognizes transactions on a cash basis during the year, but it also incorporates the unpaid accounts and/or receivables at year's end (Christiaens, Reyniers, and Rollé, 2010: 539).

places IPSASB alongside its private sector counterpart, the International Accounting Standards Board (IASB), as an international standard setter" (Cain, 2014).

AIM OF THE BOOK

The aim of this book is to provide the reader with an overview of IPSAS with a focus on their practical application and interpretation. With this in mind, the book includes numerous examples of their application by governments and public sector entities that are issuing IPSAS-compliant financial statements. By drawing on examples, practice highlights on specific accounting and reporting issues, and IPSAS, this book seeks to be a comprehensive guide on how to apply accrual-based IPSAS as well as cash basis. The book thus aims to serve as a practical implementation guide for IPSAS for practitioners, policy makers, academics, and students. Nevertheless, we would like to emphasize that this book is not a replacement for reading the standards themselves. We therefore recommend reading this book in conjunction with the full suite of IPSAS[3] in order to ensure that knowledge of all aspects of IPSAS is gained.

Readers will be able to find the answers to questions such as:

- What is the role and history of IPSASB?
- What is the scope of accrual-based IPSAS?
- What is prescribed in the suite of IPSAS for accrual basis accounting?
- What options do accrual-based IPSAS provide for measurement and recognition for each of the standards?
- What are some of the key practical implementation issues when preparing IPSAS-compliant financial statements?
- What options are provided within IPSAS when determining key accounting policy issues?
- What is prescribed in cash-basis IPSAS?
- How does one prepare a transition to cash-basis IPSAS or to accrual-based IPSAS?

IPSAS AND PUBLIC SECTOR ENTITIES

International Public Sector Accounting Standards (IPSAS) apply to public sector entities. Public sector entities can seem to be an obvious concept, but it is worth defining the key characteristics of public sector entities (see also Annex 2 at the end of this book).

As with applying any set of accounting standards, the first issue is to ensure that the scope is well defined and the preselected set of standards is really the one adapted to the current situation and entity.

---

[3] The standards are available in full at IFACs website (www.ifac.org): see under the section on IPSASB. It should be noted that the approved text of IPSAS is that published in the English language by the IPSASB. The IPSASB Handbook has been translated from English into a number of languages, including French, Spanish, German, Russian, and Chinese. The Arab Society of Certified Accountants (ASCA) of Jordan has issued an Arabic version of the IPSASB Handbook.

The Conceptual Framework of IPSAS states that it applies to financial reporting by public sector entities, i.e.:

- National, state/provincial and local governments;
- Government ministries, departments, programs, boards, commissions, and agencies;
- Public sector social security funds, trusts, and statutory authorities; and
- International governmental organizations. (Conceptual Framework § 1.8).

The Conceptual Framework states: "The objectives of financial reporting by public sector entities are to provide information about the entity that is useful to users of GPFR (general purpose financial reporting) for accountability purposes and for decision-making purposes (hereafter referred to as "useful for accountability and decision-making purposes")" (Conceptual Framework, § 2.1).

It also states that "the primary objective of governments and other public sector entities is to deliver services to constituents rather than to generate profits" (Conceptual Framework, BC 2.18), which constitutes a major difference with entities (usually companies) the purpose of which is to generate profits. In fact, governments around the world are entrusted by their populations with managing their financial resources in a sensible and cost-effective way. They collect revenues, largely through taxation, and in return are expected to deliver a wide range of public services such as education, health, infrastructure, and social transfers for the benefit of current and future generations. It is not a matter of profitability.

Another key characteristic is that: "[c]itizens and other eligible residents are dependent on governments and other public sector entities to provide a wide range of services on an ongoing basis over the long term. The activities of, and decisions made by, governments and other public sector entities in a particular reporting period can have significant consequences for future generations of service recipients and future generations of taxpayers and other involuntary resource providers" (Conceptual Framework, BC 2.18). In other words, the timescale of public sector entities is much longer than the timescale of companies preoccupied by their year-end result. In public sector entities, decisions can have impacts on the long run, even on future generations of taxpayers.

"Most governments and other public sector entities operate within spending mandates and financial constraints established through the budgetary process. Monitoring implementation of the approved budget is the primary method by which the legislature exercises oversight, and citizens and their elected representatives hold the government's management financially accountable" (Conceptual Framework, BC 2.18). Budget is another characteristic of public sector entities.

All these specificities make public sector entities different from private sector entities.

At the same time, though, there are entities where it is not so easy to distinguish whether they are public or private sector entities. Following IPSAS, government business enterprises (GBEs) are not included within the scope of IPSAS. The scope section of each standard within IPSAS specifically excludes GBEs and includes a reference to the Preface to International Public Sector Accounting Standards (Preface), which states that GBEs apply International Financial Reporting Standards (IFRS) issued by the International Accounting Standards Board (IASB).

Currently the term GBE is defined in IPSAS 1, Presentation of Financial Statements. A GBE is defined as an entity that has all of the following characteristics:

(a) Is an entity with the power to contract in its own name;
(b) Has been assigned the financial and operational authority to carry on a business;
(c) Sells goods and services, in the normal course of its business, to other entities at a profit or full cost recovery;
(d) Is not reliant on continuing government funding to be a going concern (other than purchases of outputs at arm's length); and
(e) Is controlled by a public sector entity (IPSAS 1.7).

In substance GBEs are no different from entities carrying out similar activities in the private sector.[4] GBEs typically operate to make a profit. GBEs may however also have limited community service obligations under which they are required to provide some individuals and organizations in the community with goods and services either at no charge or at a significantly reduced charge (IPSAS 1.12).

There is a wide range of entities being described as GBEs. In some cases, entities clearly do not meet the IPSASB definition of a GBE. In other cases there are different interpretations of the components of the definition of a GBE. In order to clarify the definition of a GBE, the IPSASB issued the Consultation Paper "The Applicability of IPSASs to Government Business Enterprises and Other Public Sector Entities" in August 2014, in which they sought comments by 31 December 2014.

In this Consultation Paper, the IPSASB acknowledges the role of regulators and other relevant authorities in each jurisdiction in determining which entities should be required to prepare general purpose financial statements (GPFSs) and the suite of accounting standards to be applied. In its role as the international standard setter for the public sector, the IPSASB considers that it has a responsibility to be transparent about the types of public sector entities for which it is developing IPSAS.

This ongoing debate shows how important it is to define the scope of the application of IPSAS in the public sector, and illustrates some of the complexities that can be identified in the debate on financial information within the public sector.

STRUCTURE OF THE BOOK

This book is divided into four key parts. The first part provides an introduction to global developments within public sector accounting more broadly as well as IPSAS. It introduces the IPSASB and its expanding role.

The second part provides an overview of cash-basis IPSAS. It addresses the key technical issues and provides practical examples of the application of cash-basis IPSAS.

---

[4] GBEs can comprise both trading enterprises, such as utilities, and financial enterprises, such as financial institutions.

The third, and main, part of the book is devoted to a full review and explanation of accrual-based IPSAS as well as the conceptual framework underlying these standards. This is currently a suite of 38 standards[5] (however IPSAS 35–37 will replace the existing IPSAS 6–8). A number of IPSAS have been updated, and as a result we will see some changes in IPSAS over the coming few years. These changes are highlighted where each standard subject to change is covered. In addition a specific chapter is devoted to describing and discussing IPSASB work-in-progress.

Table 1.1 Full listing of all IPSAS and IFRS "equivalent" as at 1 March 2015

IPSAS	**IFRS "equivalent" (if applicable)**
IPSAS 1—Presentation of Financial Statements	IAS 1
IPSAS 2—Cash Flow Statements	IAS 7
IPSAS 3—Accounting Policies, Changes in Accounting Estimates and Errors	IAS 8
IPSAS 4—The Effects of Changes in Foreign Exchange Rates	IAS 21
IPSAS 5—Borrowing Costs	IAS 23
IPSAS 6—Consolidated and Separate Financial Statements[6]	IAS 27 (replaced)
IPSAS 7—Investments in Associates[7]	IAS 28 (replaced)
IPSAS 8—Interests in Joint Ventures[8]	IAS 31 (replaced)
IPSAS 9—Revenue from Exchange Transactions	IAS 18
IPSAS 10—Financial Reporting in Hyperinflationary Economies	IAS 29
IPSAS 11—Construction Contracts	IAS 11
IPSAS 12—Inventories	IAS 2
IPSAS 13—Leases	IAS 17
IPSAS 14—Events after the Reporting Date	IAS 10
IPSAS 15— (withdrawn)[9]	
IPSAS 16—Investment Property	IAS 40
IPSAS 17—Property, Plant, and Equipment	IAS 16
IPSAS 18—Segment Reporting	IAS 14 (replaced)
IPSAS 19—Provisions, Contingent Liabilities and Contingent Assets	IAS 37
IPSAS 20—Related Party Disclosures	IAS 24
IPSAS 21—Impairment of Non-Cash-Generating Assets	N/A[10]
IPSAS 22—Disclosure of Information about the General Government Sector	N/A
IPSAS 23—Revenue from Non-Exchange Transactions (Taxes and Transfers)	N/A

(continued)

[5] Please note that IPSAS 33–38 are only required to be applied as of 1 January 2017. See also Table 1.1 at the end of this chapter, which provides a full listing of the accrual-based IPSAS and the corresponding IFRS (where applicable).
[6] To be replaced by IPSAS 34 and IPSAS 35.
[7] To be replaced by IPSAS 36.
[8] To be replaced by IPSAS 37.
[9] Replaced by IPSAS 28, IPSAS 29, and IPSAS 30 for accounting periods beginning on/after 1 January 2013.
[10] N/A: not applicable.

Table 1.1   *(Continued)*

IPSAS	IFRS "equivalent" (if applicable)
IPSAS 24—Presentation of Budget Information in Financial Statements	N/A
IPSAS 25—Employee Benefits	IAS 19
IPSAS 26—Impairment of Cash-Generating Assets	IAS 36
IPSAS 27—Agriculture	IAS 41
IPSAS 28—Financial Instruments: Presentation	IAS 32
IPSAS 29—Financial Instruments: Recognition and Measurement	IAS 39
IPSAS 30—Financial Instruments: Disclosures	IFRS 7
IPSAS 31—Intangible Assets	IAS 38
IPSAS 32—Service Concession Arrangements: grantor	N/A
IPSAS 33—First-Time Adoption of Accrual Basis IPSASs	IFRS 1
An entity shall apply those amendments for annual financial statements covering periods beginning on or after 1 January 2017. Earlier application is permitted. If an entity applies IPSAS 33 for a period beginning before 1 January 2017, the amendments shall also be applied for that earlier period.	
IPSAS 34—Separate Financial Statements	IAS 27 (2011)
An entity shall apply this Standard for annual financial statements covering periods beginning on or after 1 January 2017. Earlier application is encouraged. If an entity applies this Standard for a period beginning before 1 January 2017, it shall disclose that fact and apply IPSAS 35, IPSAS 36, IPSAS 37, and IPSAS 38 at the same time.	
IPSAS 35—Consolidated Financial Statements	IFRS 10
An entity shall apply this Standard for annual financial statements covering periods beginning on or after 1 January 2017. Earlier application is encouraged. If an entity applies this Standard for a period beginning before 1 January 2017, it shall disclose that fact and apply IPSAS 34, Separate Financial Statements, IPSAS 36, IPSAS 37, and IPSAS 38 at the same time.	
IPSAS 36—Investments in Associates and Joint Ventures	IAS 28 (2011)
An entity shall apply this Standard for annual financial statements covering periods beginning on or after 1 January 2017. Earlier application is encouraged. If an entity applies this Standard for a period beginning before 1 January 2017, it shall disclose that fact and apply IPSAS 34, IPSAS 35, IPSAS 37, and IPSAS 38, Disclosure of Interests in Other Entities, at the same time.	
IPSAS 37—Joint Arrangements	IFRS 11
An entity shall apply this Standard for annual financial statements covering periods beginning on or after 1 January 2017. Earlier application is encouraged. If an entity applies this Standard for a period beginning before 1 January 2017, it shall disclose that fact and apply IPSAS 34, IPSAS 35, IPSAS 36 and IPSAS 38, Disclosure of Interests in Other Entities, at the same time.	
IPSAS 38—Disclosure of Interests in Other Entities	IFRS 12
An entity shall apply this Standard for annual financial statements covering periods beginning on or after 1 January 2017. Earlier application is encouraged.	

The fourth and final part of the book focuses on the practical aspects of transitioning to IPSAS. This section includes information on change management and governance of an accounting change project.

In addition, at the end of the book there is an annex that provides the readers with additional support information to the book as a whole.

All parts of the book are characterized by the inclusion of multiple examples and practice highlights borrowed from financial statements that are IPSAS-compliant. The inclusion of a number of real examples of how IPSAS is applied serve as a basis for enhancing our understanding of this.

2 WHY CONVERGE PUBLIC SECTOR ACCOUNTING PRACTICES?

This chapter considers the trend of global convergence within the arena of public sector accounting. Convergence of accounting practices and systems across borders should establish a largely homogenous basis for underlying assumptions for accounting and financial reporting. IPSAS serves as a mechanism for enabling increased homogeneity between public sector financial reporting in different countries.

The adoption of IPSAS in a variety of different countries and standard-setting bodies has gained increasing attention on the part of nation states and some countries have initiated processes for adopting or converging with IPSAS (see for example Deloitte, 2013; Jensen and Smith, 2013). At the same time, academics, regulators, and policy makers are increasingly devoting attention to recent developments in the global convergence of public sector accounting (Ball, 2014; Brusca et al., 2015; Christiaens et al., 2010; Mason, 2012).

In debates on global, regional, and local convergence of accounting practices, accountability and transparency often stand out as critical components; in particular, during the last decade, where the impact of the global financial crisis on government funds has been seen to be significant, with squeezed budgets having to satisfy ever-increasing demands for public services (Bandy, 2015).

This chapter therefore looks at some of the key definitions of transparency and accountability, as these are two terms that recur when debating accrual accounting in the public sector. A link will then be provided between transparency and accountability and the current debates on financial transparency of nation states and the role of the global spread of IPSAS.

TRANSPARENCY

Transparency can be defined in many ways depending on the context in which it is used. Transparency is a key concept, both in terms of getting the right information, and in enabling stakeholders to hold managers/decision makers accountable to their actions. Barth and Schipper (2008) do note that transparency is not well defined in a financial reporting context. Yet, in times of financial crisis, there are a growing number of calls for increased transparency in financial reporting for the public sector.

Transparency International[1] state that one of the objectives of transparency is that it "[...] ensures that public officials, civil servants, managers, board members and businessmen act visibly and understandably, and report on their activities. And it means that the general public can hold them to account" (Transparency International, 2014). Transparency International thus signals the critical link between transparency and accountability.

Other definitions of transparency in terms of financial reporting include:[2]

[...] the extent to which financial reports reveal an entity's underlying economics in a way that is readily understandable by those using the financial reports. (Barth and Schipper, 2008: 173)

a standard that requires transparency mandates statements that reveal the events, transactions, judgments and estimates underlying financial statements, and their implications. (Pownall and Schipper, 1999: 262)

There is agreement in the literature that the key elements of transparency enable accountability (see also Bovens, 2007).

The accounting literature highlights the importance not only of transparency, but also that the information provided shall be "readily understandable." This very much depends on who is reading the financial report. Professional accountants and regular users of financial reports have a much greater knowledge and understanding of financial reporting information, whereas the individual without accounting knowledge has only a limited ability to understand an annual report (Norton and Porter, 2011: 61). Consequently, it is essential that the reporting entity considers who the users of their financial reports are and what their knowledge of accounting is.

Many examples of increased transparency can be found when studying the financial statements of public sector entities that have adopted IPSAS. Below is an example from the first set of IPSAS-compliant financial statements of the World Food Programme (WFP).

Under IPSAS, all purchases of food commodities and in-kind donations are added to inventory, together with the cost of transportation to the country where the food becomes distributable and any other relevant costs, such as milling or bagging. In 2008, the value of food and associated costs added to existing stock of US$ 0.5 billion was US$ 2.7 billion. When commodities are issued for beneficiaries, the value of the inventory issued is expensed through the statement of financial performance. In 2008 the total value of food commodities issued was US$ 2.2 billion. At the year end, the inventory in warehouses controlled by the WFP was valued at US$ 1.0 billion and has been reported in the financial statements for the first time. This new information gives the Board visibility on the value of inventories. (WFP, 2008: 74)

---

[1] See http://www.transparency.org/ (last accessed 26 February 2015).
[2] The accounting literature that discusses transparency focuses primarily on discussing financial reporting and transparency in the context of the private sector.

The Financial Reporting in Practice 2.1 highlight from WFP illustrates the change in the value of their inventory in their statement of financial position at the time of first adoption of IPSAS.[3]

IPSAS Financial Reporting in Practice 2.1 WFP Statement of Financial Position etc.

WORLD FOOD PROGRAMME
STATEMENT I
STATEMENT OF FINANCIAL POSITION
AT 31 DECEMBER 2008
(US$ millions)

	Note	2008	Opening Balance 01.01.2008 (Restated)
ASSETS			
Current assets			
Cash and cash equivalents	2.1	972.3	548.7
Short-term investments	2.2	460.1	673.1
Contributions receivable	2.3	1991.2	1185.5
Inventories	2.4	1021.8	515.9
Other receivables	2.5	127.9	162.5
		4573.3	**3085.7**

Source: WFP, 2008, p. 17.

ACCOUNTABILITY

At the most basic level, accountability is based on the notion of authorization. There is an actor in authority (a "principal"), who delegates to a subordinate actor (an "agent") the responsibility for carrying out specific tasks, with the expectation that the agent will achieve the goals defined by the principal (Elgie, 2001: 3).

It is difficult to make governments and other public sector entities accountable for their actions if there is no transparency. Consequently, transparency is a crucial element of accountability (Bovens, 2007). The (IPSASB) has highlighted this importance on several occasions. They have stated, for example, that: "[s]trong and transparent financial reporting has the potential to improve public sector decision making and make governments *more* accountable to their constituents" (International Federation of Accountants, 2013). The concept of accountability can thus be understood as an umbrella consisting of several aspects, where transparency is one of the key elements

---

[3] Alesani et al. (2012) wrote an article on the adoption of WFP IPSAS which will provide further insight into that entity's accounting reform.

(cf. Bovens, 2007). It is important to note that accountability is more complex in the public sector than it is in the private sector (Parker and Gould, 1999; Mulgan, 1997; Sinclair, 1995).

Important questions to ask when reflecting on "accountability" are: (a) accountability to whom and (b) accountability for what? (cf. Valentinov, 2011). Lack of clarity on both these questions can highlight the absence of blueprints or even general guidelines on how public sector and nonprofit accountability mechanism should be designed and implemented.

UN General Assembly Elaboration on Accountability within the United Nations

Accountability is the *obligation of the Secretariat* and its staff members to be *answerable for all decisions* made and actions Accountability in the United Nations taken by them, and to be *responsible for honouring their commitments*, without qualification or exception. Accountability includes *achieving objectives and high-quality results in a timely and cost-effective manner*, in fully implementing and delivering on all mandates to the Secretariat approved by the United Nations intergovernmental bodies and other subsidiary organs established by them in *compliance with all resolutions*, regulations, rules and ethical standards; truthful, objective, accurate and timely *reporting on performance results*; responsible stewardship of funds and resources, all aspects of performance, including a *clearly defined system of rewards and sanctions*; and with due recognition to the important role of oversight bodies and in full compliance with accepted recommendations. (emphasis added) (UN, 2010)

One can distinguish between two different forms of accountability, both of which are relevant when considering the move towards IPSAS. One form is "process" accountability, or "compliance." The focus here is on *how* a public sector entity accomplishes something rather than on *what* is actually accomplished. Process accountability involves traditional conceptions of accountability, such as adhering to rules and regulations, including principles of due process.

A second form is *performance accountability*, which is of more recent vintage and focuses not on the "how" but on the "what": results, outputs, and outcomes. Performance accountability has been central to the new public management reforms (NPM) that have been undertaken within the public sector arena over the last decades.

WHY IS THERE AN INTEREST IN GLOBAL CONVERGENCE OF PUBLIC SECTOR ACCOUNTING?

Concerns over the financial transparency of nation states, globally, have been increasing during the last decade. This strong critique has been echoed in regards to governments' financial reporting, and in 2012 Ian Ball (former Chief Executive Officer of IFAC) published an article entitled: "Government Accounting – Making Enron look good." In this article he argues strongly for strengthened public sector financial reporting, disclosure, and financial management. Transparency and accountability in the public sector have increasingly become a matter of global concern. Accounting and financial reporting are increasingly looked upon as a part of the solution for better management of public money.[4]

The financial and sovereign debt crises that we have witnessed over the last decade have accentuated the need for better financial reporting by governments worldwide, and for improvements in the management of public sector resources (see for example Ball and Pflugrath, 2012; EC, 2013; Müller-Marques Berger, 2012). As argued by the European Commission, the crisis has highlighted the need for a clear demonstration by governments of their financial stability and a more rigorous and transparent account of their balance sheet data[5] (EC, 2013).

> [...] it is time for sovereign debt issues to be addressed and considered from an accounting perspective, as well as the more traditional economic and political perspectives [...] (Ball and Pflugrath, 2012: 17)

In a similar vein, Soll (2015)[6] linked concerns on weaknesses in the transparency of the financial reporting of governments to the case of Greece:

> Greece is back as a focal point of the world financial crisis. While coming elections are spooking the markets, the supposed cause of the crisis has not changed. Greece has a declared debt of 319 billion euros, or about $369 billion, 175 percent of its 182-billion-euro ($210 billion) gross domestic product. This sounds like a nearly impossible task for any government: to govern effectively, spur economic growth and avoid default. The shackles of the declared Greek debt have effectively paralyzed the country. Yet maybe all of this debt drama is unnecessary.

> The brutal and counterproductive response has been austerity.

> [...] Without real accounting, we also can't evaluate the claims of Prime Minister Antonis Samaras's government – as well as those of numerous commentators – that Greece has made improvement in its fiscal position over the last two years. If the European Commission, the International Monetary Fund and the European Central Bank (known as the troika) are giving Greece 283 billion euros ($327 billion) of financing in return for good economic indicators – and credit ratings agencies like Moody's shake Greek and Eurozone economies with pronouncements made on these numbers – one would think they would want to verify the numbers, using IPSAS, which would be much more transparent and something people outside the troika could realistically evaluate.[...]

Nevertheless, despite harsh criticism of government financial reporting, it should be highlighted that we have, during last two decades, witnessed significant developments in public sector accounting and accountability systems. In a number of countries such developments have culminated in the implementation and/or consideration of

---

[4] See Bandy (2015) for comprehensive coverage of the management of public money, concentrating on an increased focus on post-crisis austerity.
[5] The European Commission ran a public consultation on the assessment of the suitability of the International Public Sector Accounting Standards (IPSAS) for EU Member States (Eurostat, 2012).
[6] Professor of history and accounting at the University of Southern California, presented an analysis of the present financial crisis in the 21 January 2015 issue of the *New York Times*.

advanced accounting ideas such as that of preparing accruals based public sector financial reports. Accounting practices that result in comprehensive and reliable reporting of the financial performance as well as the financial position of the government, and that are audited, enhance accountability and transparency.

Today there is a rather broad consensus in debates on public sector financial reporting and management that better transparency and accountability require robust financial information in the public sector.

CONCLUSION

The financial crises of a number of nation states, which we have witnessed during the last decade, have forced the role of financial reporting of the public sector into the spotlight. Financial crises have placed increasing importance on the role of transparency and accountability, which act as two key drivers in the global spread of IPSAS. The implementation of accrual-based IPSAS is thus seen as one of the stepping stones towards enabling better accountability across nation states.

This move is keenly pursued by international standard setter, the International Public Sector Accounting Standards Board (IPSASB), which is the issuer of IPSAS. The International Federation of Accountants (IFAC) issued a series of recommendations for consideration by the G20 countries at their meeting in June 2010. IFAC specifically points out that:

> … many governments adhere to the cash basis of accounting, IFAC and the [IPSASB] encourage the adoption of accrual-based accounting as it reinforces the principles of transparency and accountability. Under the accrual basis of accounting, transactions and other events are recognized when they occur (and not only when cash or its equivalent is received or paid). Therefore, transactions and events are recognized and reported in the financial statements of the periods to which they relate.

In addition, the Organisation for Economic Co-operation and Development (OECD) has stated that accrual accounting is critical to enable accounting and reporting on the allocation and use of total economic resources at the disposal of managers. Recently, Ian Ball of IFAC strongly re-emphasized the message of the incoming chairman of the International Accounting Standards Board (IASB), Hans Hoogervorst, that "without transparency, there can be no enduring stability" at a 2011 international conference on "Trust and Accountability in Public Financial Management."

3 THE IPSASB

During the last two decades the International Public Sector Accounting Standards Board (IPSASB) and the IPSAS that it establishes have increasingly become a point for international standardization and reference within the area of public sector accounting. The IPSASB is, today, an independent standard-setting board under the auspices of the International Federation of Accountants (IFAC). IFAC and its standard-setting boards are becoming an increasingly integral player in global financial governance processes (Humphrey et al., 2006).

IFAC is an international organization, a private standard-setting organization, for the accounting profession that was established back in 1977 (see Humphrey and Loft, 2008; 2007; Rocher, 2010, for detailed historical accounts). The original constitution of the IFAC presented stated that the role of the IFAC was the development and enhancement of a co-ordinated worldwide accounting profession with harmonized standards (Rocher, 2010; Dye, 1988; Humphrey et al., 2006).

To enable it to reach its target objectives, the IFAC established four committees in the year of its foundation.[1] The committees were supporting IFACs objectives through developing international guidelines, standards, and application notes. At that time, however, none of these four committees was devoted to public sector accounting. It was not until June 1986 that the IFAC created a fifth committee dedicated to accountancy issues in the public sector, namely the Public Sector Committee (PSC).

---

[1] (1) The International Auditing Practices Committee (today the International Auditing and Assurance Standards Board); (2) the Education Committee (today the International Accounting Education Standards Board); (3) the Ethics Committee (today the International Ethics Standards Board for Accountants); (4) the Management Accounting Committee (today the Professional Accountants in Business Committee).

A REVIEW OF EVENTS THAT HAVE SHAPED TODAY'S IPSASB

The Establishment of the Public Sector Committee (PSC) of IFAC

The need for international harmonization in the area of accounting and financial reporting in the private context started developing as early as the late 1960s and early 1970s.[2] As a result the then International Accounting Standards Committee (IASC) (today IASB) was formed in 1973 and became the first international standard-setting body in accountancy.

The idea of facilitating a process of international harmonization in the area of public sector accounting materialized approximately a decade later. The need to undertake harmonization in the area of public sector accounting, and thus the origin of the PSC, has been linked to what was, at the time, increasing problematization of the fact that little financial data existed for public sector entities and governmental organizations. An increasing awareness of the large amount of funds held and managed in the public sector resulted in a growing need for better financial accountability within the public sector (Dye, 1988; Rocher, 2010).

Rocher (2010) documents that the first meeting of the PSC was held in January 1987 in London, where its role and the direction of its work were defined. More specifically it was agreed that "the Committee is charged with the task of developing accounting and auditing standards and promoting their voluntary acceptance" (Dye, 1988: 17). The scope of the PSC's work was not limited to accounting aspects, but also auditing and reporting in the public sector. The PSC had a wide-ranging mandate to develop programs aimed at strengthening public sector financial management and accountability. During its first decade of existence, the PSC strived to establish itself and its output consisted largely of one-off studies on specialized accounting matters in the public sector (IPSASB Governance Group, 2014).

Advancing the Work of the PSC (1990s)

During the 1990s the world witnessed financial restraints on public expenditure which resulted in increased accountability requirements for limited resources and continuous efforts to improve the efficiency and effectiveness of public services. During that time there was, as a result, increasing financial and political pressure contributing to significant restructuring of governments and the privatization of services provided by the public sector (see for example: Pollanen and Pollanen, 2009; Guthrie and English, 1997). This movement was instituted based on the principles of New Public Management (NPM) (Hood, 1995). The term NPM was established in the late 1980s to denote a new emphasis on the importance of management and "production engineering" in public service delivery, often linked to principles of economic rationalism (see Hood, 1989; Pollitt, 1993). Accounting practices became an integral part of the NPM movement from the 1990s onwards (see Hood, 1995).

---

[2] The concept of convergence arose even earlier (i.e., in the late 1950s) in response to post World War II economic integration and subsequent increases in cross-border capital flows.

In line with the NPM movement, the starting point for the work of the PSC on accounting standards was a consideration of where existing private sector accounting could be applied within the public sector. Subsequently, in 1996, the PSC started its standards development program and moved beyond its early work on providing guidance in various forms to work towards international standard-setting in accounting for the public sector (see IPSASB Governance Group, 2014). The PSC received joint funding from the World Bank, IMF, Asian Development Bank, and United Nations Development Program (UNDP), organizations which considered it important for their borrowers to keep good public sector accounts (Humphrey and Loft, 2008). The initial draft reporting guidelines were issued for comment in 1998, with then IFAC President, Frank Harding, noting: "IFAC will be carrying out a similar role with respect to governments and government agencies that the International Accounting Standards Committee undertakes with respect to private sector entities"[3] (ibid. quoting Platt).

The PSC Becomes the IPSASB

The first International Public Sector Accounting Standards (IPSAS) were published in May 2000. They were primarily based on International Accounting Standards (IAS) and incorporated the accrual method of accounting. The then Chairman of the PSC (Ian Ball) acknowledged that IFAC had no authority to mandate compliance, and stated that the "main force for adoption" was "increased pressure on governments to account for and measure how well they improve their economies' competitiveness"[4] (Humphrey and Loft, 2008: 15). The OECD (Organisation for Economic Co-operation and Development) was an early adopter of IPSAS (issuing its first set of IPSAS-compliant financial statements in 2000) followed by NATO (North Atlantic Treaty Organization) in 2008. The work of the PSC was increasingly seen as an important component to enhance the quality as well as the consistency of public sector financial reporting, where financial information reported to internal and external users was in many cases limited (Adhémar, 2002).

In 2003, IFAC commissioned a review of the PSC by an externally chaired review panel. The review became known as the "Likierman Review"[5] (IFAC, 2004). To serve as an input basis for the review, a questionnaire was distributed to actors with an interest in the improvement of public sector financial reporting and management, such as governments and their agencies, national and international standard-setters, intra-governmental institutions, external funders of the PSC's activities, etc. (IFAC, 2004a). The key areas that the questionnaire sought to cover included: the role of the PSC, its governance, organization, the accounting standards translation, and due

---

[3] *Journal of Commerce Week*, 2 April 1998, "Accountants issue global guidelines aimed at greater transparency" by Gordon Platt.
[4] *Journal of Accountancy*, 1 August 2000, 190(2): 15–16.
[5] After the external chairman Sir Andrew Likierman. In addition to Likierman, the panel was composed of Ian Ball (representing IFAC), Ian Mackintosh (retiring PSC chair), Philippe Adhémar (incoming PSC chair), Simon Bradbury of the World Bank (representing external funders), Tom Allen, Chairman of the US Governmental Accounting Standards Board and Blandina Nyoni, Accountant-General of Tanzania (IFAC, 2004a: 30).

Table 3.1   Key factors justifying private international standard-setting for public sector accounting and financial reporting

The need to enhance and improve the quality of public sector financial reporting and build on recent improvements.

The improvement of international consistency and comparison.

The significance, often neglected, of public sector debt in global capital markets.

The fact that few countries have independent standard-setters with public sector responsibility.

The need for a standard-setter independent of national governments.

The global economies of scale that can be achieved through an international independent standard-setter.

The improvement of the quality of financial management in the public sector.

process.[6] Based on the data and analysis collected, the "Likierman Review" raised a number of reasons for justifying the establishment of an independent accounting standard-setter in the public sector (see Table 3.1).

The recommendations of the Likierman Review led the IFAC to re-establish the PSC as the IPSASB in 2004 with revised terms of reference to reflect that the mandate of the IPSASB would focus on developing and issuing IPSAS.

Recently a study by the Institute of the Chartered Accountants Australia (2013: 7), commenting on the change from PSC to IPSASB, noted:

> With a new name and a renewed mandate the IPSASB set about bringing its body of standards up to date with those of the IASB as well as continuing to develop standards of particular significance to the public sector. With the benefit of increased funding the IPSASB has been able to improve the currency and comprehensiveness of its body of standards, but has struggled to keep pace with the IASB which has been undertaking an extensive work program of issuing new IFRSs and revising and updating existing IFRSs. Moreover, notwithstanding the elevated status of the IPSASB, its improved productivity and the significant progress that has been made in a relatively short period, the take-up of IPSASs around the world while now taking place at an increasing rate has to date been limited.

CURRENT OBJECTIVES, STRUCTURE, AND MEMBERS OF THE IPSASB

Since 2004 the IPSASB has been operating as an independent standard-setting board dedicated to developing high-quality IPSAS, guidance papers, and other resources for the use by public sector entities around the world for general purpose financial reporting. In 2011, the terms of reference of the IPSASB were expanded. The IPSASB was, as of November 2011, not only to set standards for the general purpose financial statements, but also to work towards strengthening general purpose financial reports (GPFRs) (see Müller-Marqués Berge, 2012). GPFRs denotes all financial reports that are intended to meet the information needs of users who are unable to

---

[6] See Rocher (2010) for a detailed discussion on the questionnaire.

require the preparation of financial reports and are thus designed to meet these users' specific information needs. This means that the role of the IPSASB today embraces developing and issuing, in the public interest and under its own authority, high-quality accounting standards and other publications for use by public sector entities across the globe in the preparation of GPFRs.

The objective of the IPSASB is:

> … to serve the public interest by developing high-quality accounting standards and other publications for use by public sector entities around the world in the preparation of general purpose financial reports.
>
> This is intended to enhance the quality and transparency of public sector financial reporting by providing better information for public sector financial management and decision making. In pursuit of this objective, the IPSASB supports the convergence of international and national public sector accounting standards and the convergence of accounting and statistical bases of financial reporting where appropriate; and also promotes the acceptance of its standards and other publications. (IPSASB, 2014[7])

More specifically, in order to fulfill its objective, the IPSASB carries out the following work agenda:

- International Public Sector Accounting Standards (IPSAS) as the standards to be applied by members of the profession in the preparation of general purpose financial reports of public sector entities.
- Recommended Practice Guidelines (RPGs) to provide guidance that represents good practice that public sector entities are encouraged to follow.
- Studies to provide advice on financial reporting issues in the public sector. They are based on study of the best practices and most effective methods for dealing with the issues being addressed.
- Other papers and research reports to provide information that contributes to the body of knowledge about public sector financial reporting issues and developments. They are aimed at providing new information or fresh insights and generally result from research activities such as: literature searches, questionnaire surveys, interviews, experiments, case studies, and analysis.

The current form of the IPSASB is made up of 18 volunteer members. Fifteen members come from IFAC member bodies and there are three public members, with experience and expertise in public sector financial reporting. Members include representatives from ministries of finance, government audit institutions, public practice, and academia. All members of the IPSASB, including the chair and deputy chair, are appointed by the IFAC Board upon recommendations from the IFAC Nominating Committee.[8] The selection process is based on the individual qualities and abilities of the nominee in relation to the available board position. The IPSASB strives to cultivate members who possess the knowledge, insight, and geographical footprint necessary to

---

[7] http://www.ifac.org/public-sector/about-ipsasb/terms-reference (last accessed 26 August 2014).
[8] A complete listing of IPSASB members and their bios can be accessed at www.ifac.org/PublicSector/CommitteeMembers.php.

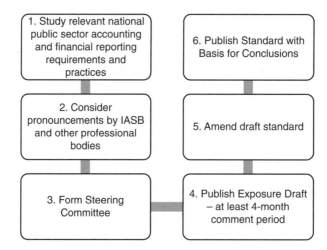

Figure 3.1   Step-by-step due process for the development of IPSAS

best serve the public interest. The IPSASB receives support (both direct financial and in-kind) from the World Bank, the Asian Development Bank, the United Nations, and the governments of Canada, China, New Zealand, and Switzerland (IPSASB, 2013).

The standards (the IPSAS) set by the IPSASB, follow public due process (see Figure 3.1). This process provides the opportunity for all those interested in financial reporting in the public sector to make their opinions known to the IPSASB, and ensure that their opinions are taken into account in the standard-setting development process. Exposure drafts (ED) of all proposed IPSAS are developed, typically, with the input of a task-based group of IPSASB members. Exposure drafts are usually preceded by a consultation paper that explores the subject in detail and provides the basis for further discussion, development, and policy formation. All exposure drafts have open and finite comment periods (see IPSASB, 2013).

RELATIONSHIP BETWEEN THE IASB AND THE IPSASB

In November 2011 the IFAC and the IASB publicized an agreement aimed at strengthening their co-operation in developing private and public accounting and financial reporting standards (Müller-Marques Berger, 2012). To formalize their co-operation a Memorandum of Understanding (MoU) was established between the IFAC and the IASB[9] that refers to both organizations striving towards high-quality financial reporting standards (see MoU[10]). The MoU specifically addresses the relationship between the IPSASB and the IASB and it defines the following key characteristics of the co-operation and communication between the two bodies (see Figure 3.2):

---

[9] International Accounting Standards Board (IASB), see www.iasb.org.
[10] The MoU is available here at http://www.ifrs.org/Use-around-the-world/Documents/IFACIASBMOU. pdf (last accessed 15 August 2014).

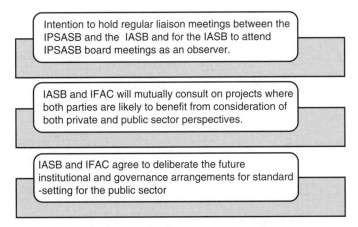

Figure 3.2 IPSASB and IASB co-operation

In addition, the MoU emphasizes that the sovereign debt and global financial crisis has placed additional emphasis on sound and transparent financial reporting in the public sector, which the IASB will underline to its stakeholders.

To develop its IPSAS, the IPSASB actively draws on extant IFRS/IAS as a basis. More specifically, the accrual-based IPSAS addresses public sector accounting and financial reporting issues in two different ways:

- By attending to public sector accounting and financial reporting issues (1) that have not been comprehensively or appropriately dealt with in existing International Financial Reporting Standards (IFRS) issued by the International Accounting Standards Board (IASB), or (2) for which there is no related IFRS; and
- By developing IPSAS that are converged with IFRS by adapting them to the public sector context.

To support the process of convergence between the IPSASB documents and IASB documents, the IPSASB issued a paper, in October 2008, that concerns (and is entitled) the "Process for reviewing and modifying IASB documents" (IPSASB, 2008). Figure 3.3 illustrates the process in practice.

OVERSIGHT AND GOVERNANCE OF THE IPSASB

The IPSASB governance issues have been debated for more than a decade. The subject was addressed back in 2003 as part of the IFAC reform. Following that, the IPSASB governance arrangements were also considered in a report prepared by an externally chaired review panel (the Likierman Review) in 2004. In 2009, IPSASB governance was underscored as a key agenda item, when the IPSASB initiated its discussion on the strategies and work plans for 2010–2012. IPSASB has since prioritized its own governance arrangements as an imperative issue.

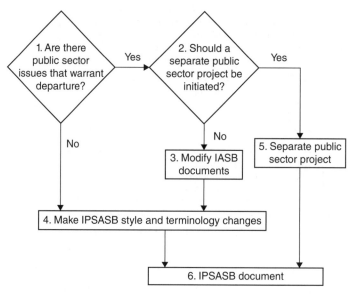

Figure 3.3   Process for the IPSASB for reviewing and modifying IASB documents (IPSASB, 2008)

During this period the Monitoring Group (MG) of IFAC consulted on two options to improve IPSASB oversight and governance and thus to enhance the credibility of IPSAS: (1) using the existing Public Interest Oversight Board (PIOB) structure, or (2) setting up an ad hoc body. This consultation revealed widespread support for public interest oversight of IPSASB and for strengthening the IPSASB; however, the responses were split between the two options. Following these developments, the IPSASB Governance Review Group ("the Review Group") was established. Its role is to propose future governance and oversight arrangements for the IPSASB. The Review Group is chaired by representatives from the World Bank, International Monetary Fund (IMF), and Organisation for Economic Co-operation and Development (OECD), and includes representatives from the Financial Stability Board (FSB), the International Organization of Securities Commissions (IOSCO), and the International Organization of Supreme Audit Institutions (INTOSAI). Subsequently the Review Group launched the public consultation on the governance of the IPSASB with the aim of collecting views from stakeholders and the public at large on the governance and oversight of the setting of accounting standards for the public sector (see IPSASB Governance Group, 2014a).

The IPSASB Governance Review Group proposes three options for improving public interest oversight of the IPSASB:

> OPTION A: Monitoring and oversight of the IPSASB by the IFRS Foundation's Monitoring Board and Trustees the IPSASB.
> OPTION B: Separate monitoring and oversight boards for the IPSASB, while it remains under the auspices of the IFAC.
> OPTION C: Re-establishing the IPSASB outside of IFAC with its own monitoring and oversight bodies.

Table 3.2   Proposed governance models for the IPSASB as per the Governance Consultation

OPTION A. Monitoring and oversight of the IPSASB by the IFRS Foundation's Monitoring Board and Trustees	OPTION B. Separate monitoring and oversight boards for the IPSASB, while it remains under the auspices of the IFAC	OPTION C. Re-establishing the IPSASB outside of IFAC with its own monitoring and oversight bodies
11 responses supported option A as their first choice	25 responses supported option B. Out of these 23, however, 8 preferred to see this solution only as a short-to-medium-term solution and then favoured opting for either option A or C as the long-term governance model.	4 responses supported option C.

3 responses took a neutral approach

The consultation paper also allowed for any other governance alternatives to be included in the responses to its consultation (compare the fact that it stated that one could elaborate on "[a]nother approach, including some combination or sequenced implementation (e.g., short-term/long-term approaches)" of the three listed options).

An Overview of the Responses Received

In total 43 responses were published at the Review Group's site (see Table 3.2).[11] Responses were submitted from a rather wide range of countries and stakeholders. Nevertheless, the number of responses seems somewhat low considering how many countries could potentially be applying IPSAS globally and thus have an interest in the future governance of IPSAS.

In total 19 countries were represented in the consultation responses. In addition international standard-setters, regional and national accounting associations, accounting firms, and other stakeholders contributed with their views.

Overall, option B on establishing separate monitoring and oversight boards for the IPSASB, while it remains under the auspices of the IFAC, was the option that attracted most support in the short to medium term. It was seen in the stakeholders' responses that some of them (eight out of the 23 who opted for option B) chose that option only as a short-term solution while preferring to see either IFRS Foundation take over at a later stage or the re-establishment of IPSASB outside the IFAC.

At first glance it looks as though option B would be likely to be the most viable solution. However the majority of support for option B only advocated this model of governance in the short to medium term. The pie charts published by the IPSASB Governance Review Group (Figure 3.4) illustrate this.

Some stakeholders, such as FEE, stated in their response: "All these options have their pros and cons. A more innovative approach might be required." When taking

---

[11] See http://www.oecd.org/gov/budgeting/IPSASB-Governance-Review.htm, last accessed 15 August 2014.

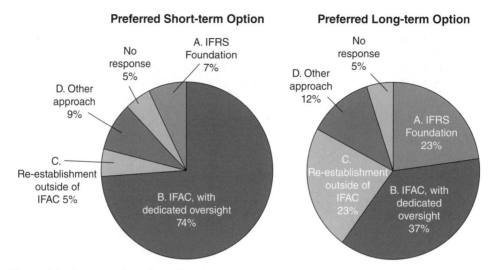

Figure 3.4   Summary view of responses in favor of IPSAS governance modalities in the long term vs. short term Source: IPSASB governance review group, 2014c: 3.

into account the result of respondents' selection of either option A, B, or C, for the long term, it might be suggested that the desired long-term outcome for a new model for IPSASB governance, outside IFAC was for option C.

Primary support for moving towards governance under the IFRS Foundation came from stakeholders in Australia and the UK as well as the "big 4" accounting firms. Stakeholders in these Anglo-Saxon countries seem to favour a stronger interlinking between private and public accounting, and this is underlies their support for IFRS governance modality. Most other countries indicated support for convergence between IFRS and IPSAS while at the same time highlighting the importance of keeping private and public sector accounting standards separate. It was, for example, stated in one of the responses that "the convergence between IFRS and IPSAS is to be maintained and enhanced, however, both the private and public sectors have their own peculiarities which require specific guidance. Thus, the distinction between the two bodies is important because of sector specific issues."

Key Issue Raised in the Responses: Funding

The governance issues of the IPSASB (and any standard-setter for that matter) are closely related to fundraising in order to cover the cost of the standard-setting and oversight activities. The funding sources for the IPSASB to date have been relying heavily on IFAC and external contributors. The discussions on IPSASB governance need to carefully and clearly address the funding arrangements for future governance modalities. It has been suggested in a number of the responses that a wider pool of funding should be investigated to reduce the risk and perception of conflicts of interest.

Final Outcome of the Governance Review

Based on the responses to a public consultation that was conducted from 17 January to 30 April 2014 and discussions held at the time of its meetings on 31 May 2013 and 22 September 2014 in Paris, the Review Group has compiled a set of recommendations regarding the future governance of the International Public Sector Accounting Standards (IPSAS).

The table (see IPSASB Governance Group, 2014b: 3–4) below outlines the recommendations made by the Review Group, based on the outcomes of the consultation. In an effort to strengthen the governance arrangements the key recommendation of the Review Group was that the IPSASB should continue to operate under the auspices of the International Federation of Accountants (IFAC). In addition, for the further strengthening of IPSASB governance the following recommendations were made:

A single governance body, the **Public Interest Committee (the "Committee")**, should be established to ensure that the public interest is served by the standard-setting activities of the IPSASB.

The Committee should be independent from IFAC and distinct from the existing governance bodies overseeing the IFAC's private sector standard-setting activities – that is the Public Interest Oversight Board (PIOB) and Monitoring Group (MG).

The Committee's objectives should be to review and advise the IFAC and IPSASB on the (1) terms of reference of the IPSASB; (2) arrangements for nomination and appointment of IPSAB members; and (3) procedures and processes for the formulation of the IPSASB's strategy and work plan and development of standards to ensure that all are consistent with the public interest. The Committee should not have a direct role in the development, adoption, and implementation of accounting standards.

The Committee should conduct a first review of the IPSASB terms of reference, nomination procedures, and standard-setting arrangements no later than the first semester of 2015, and provide advice to the IFAC and IPSASB on any potential improvements.

The Committee should meet at least annually thereafter to review progress against their recommendations and provide further guidance where necessary.

The initial membership of the Committee should include individuals with expertise in public sector financial reporting, and professional engagement in organizations that have an interest in promoting high-quality and internationally comparable financial information. Members will serve the Committee for a maximum of three years per period.[12]

The public Terms of Reference specify the functioning of the Committee. Functioning rules should ensure at least that (1) the Committee will meet annually and with an appropriate quorum; (2) a chairperson will be in charge of organizing the Committee's

---

[12] Members should not accept any honoraria or other compensation for any work done in this capacity. Members should work for a limited period, which should not exceed three years and be renewable for an additional three years. Additional members or observers, including other international and national bodies, may be admitted by consensus of the existing Committee members, taking into account the need to ensure balanced representation.

meetings and performing secretariat activities – that is keeping minutes of meetings and records of opinions and decisions of the Committee – to ensure an appropriate transparency of the Committee's operations.

To carry out its activities, the Committee should receive reports from the IFAC and the IPSASB regarding the procedures and processes followed in the appointment of IPSASB members, formulation of the IPSASB strategy and work plan, and development of individual accounting standards.

IFAC shall establish a separate Consultative Advisory Group (CAG) for the IPSASB. The role of the CAG should be to enable the IPSASB to receive direct feedback from interested public and private sector institutions, especially those engaged in the preparation, audit, or evaluation of public sector financial statements, on their strategy, work program, and standard-setting activities. The CAG would also provide an opportunity for IFAC and IPSASB to hear from government representatives about the technical issues that may have impeded their adoption of IPSAS.

The final recommendation stated that a next public consultation on the improvements to the IPSASB's governance arrangements shall be undertaken no later than 2020.

IPSASB WORK IN PROCESS

The IPSASB's goals and objectives are to enhance the quality and transparency of public sector financial reporting by:

- Establishing high-quality accounting standards for use by public sector entities;
- Promoting the adoption of, and international convergence to, IPSAS;
- Providing comprehensive information for public sector financial management and decision making; and
- Providing guidance on issues and experiences in financial reporting in the public sector.

In order to achieve these goals and objectives, the IPSASB is developing, in an ongoing process, high-quality International Public Sector Accounting Standards (IPSAS), guidance, and resources for use by public sector entities around the world for general purpose financial reporting.

It can be observed that the work of the IPSASB has been intensifying somewhat of late, with the release of the Conceptual Framework on 31 October 2014 as well a suite of new IPSAS in January 2015. In addition, as this chapter illustrates, the IPSASB has a rather comprehensive work agenda for the coming years.

NEW PRONOUNCEMENTS

The IPSASB Conceptual Framework released on 31 October 2014 is explained in Chapter 4 "The IPSASB Conceptual Framework and Key Accrual Accounting Concepts."

The IPSASB released the following standards on 29–30 January 2015:

- IPSAS 33, First-time Adoption of Accrual Basis IPSASs;
- IPSAS 34, Separate Financial Statements;
- IPSAS 35, Consolidated Financial Statements;
- IPSAS 36, Investments in Associates and Joint Ventures;
- IPSAS 37, Joint Arrangements; and
- IPSAS 38, Disclosure of Interests in Other Entities.

It should be noted that the impact of these new standards is discussed in the forthcoming technical chapters, where applicable.

IPSAS 33, First-time Adoption of Accrual Basis IPSAS

IPSAS 33, First-time Adoption of Accrual Basis IPSASs, applicable to first-time adopters for their first IPSAS financial statements for periods beginning on or after 1 January 2017, grants transitional exemptions to entities adopting accrual basis IPSAS for the first time, providing a major tool to help entities on their journey to implement IPSAS. IPSAS 33 allows first-time adopters three years to recognize specified assets and liabilities, to allow them sufficient time to develop reliable models for recognizing and measuring assets and liabilities during the transition period (see Chapter 20).

"With IPSAS 33, the IPSASB has developed a comprehensive standard that provides guidance and exemptions for entities that are transitioning to accrual basis IPSAS. IPSAS 33 meets the needs of both preparers and users of financial statements during the transition period. Its publication is a further incentive for entities to make the decision to apply IPSASs" said IPSASB Chair Andreas Bergmann when he announced the release of this new IPSAS on 29 January 2015.[13]

New IPSAS

The IPSASB published the following five IPSAS during 2014 (these IPSAS are covered in Chapter 16 of this book):

- IPSAS 34, Separate Financial Statements;
- IPSAS 35, Consolidated Financial Statements;
- IPSAS 36, Investments in Associates and Joint Ventures;
- IPSAS 37, Joint Arrangements; and
- IPSAS 38, Disclosure of Interests in Other Entities.

These are intended, by 1 January 2017, to replace current requirements in:

- IPSAS 6, Consolidated and Separate Financial Statements;
- IPSAS 7, Investments in Associates; and
- IPSAS 8, Interests in Joint Ventures.

A key part of the IPSASB's strategy to develop high-quality public sector financial reporting standards is to maintain and update existing IPSAS. IPSAS 6–8 are based

---

[13] See http://www.ifac.org/news-events/2015-01/ipsasb-publishes-standard-first-time-adoption-accrual-basis-ipsass.

on former versions of IFRS. Since the underlying IFRS have changed, the IPSASB has developed IPSAS 34–38 so that convergence with the related IFRS is maintained to the appropriate extent. These new IPSAS also incorporate important guidance to make them appropriate for application in the public sector.

"These five IPSASs establish requirements for how public sector entities, including governments, should account for their interests in other entities. Accrual-based accounting practices provide a comprehensive picture of the financial performance and position of public sector entities. Appropriate accounting for interests in other entities is an important aspect of this comprehensive picture" noted IPSASB Chair Andreas Bergmann when he announced the release of the new IPSAS on 30 January 2015.[14]

WORK-IN-PROGRESS

The IPSASB Strategy Consultation, published on 31 March 2014, had a comment deadline of 31 July 2014. It had the objective of seeking the views of IPSASB stakeholders on the priority of individual projects on the IPSASB's work program for the five-year period from 2015–2019: "to give our stakeholders an opportunity to provide their views on the strategic direction of the IPSASB for the period from 2015 forward" (IPSASB Strategy Consultation:[15] 2).

The timetable of the approved and committed IPSASB projects is as follows:

- Public sector combinations – completion 2015;
- Government business enterprises – completion 2015;
- Public sector specific financial instruments – completion 2016;
- Emissions trading schemes – completion 2017;
- Social benefits – completion 2017;
- Various projects on IPSAS – reducing differences – ongoing activities, timing to be determined;
- Update of financial instruments (IPSAS 28–30) – completion to be determined based on IASB work on IFRS 9.

Public sector combinations: The objective is to prescribe the accounting treatment for public sector combinations and to set out the classification and measurement of such combinations (i.e., transactions or other events that bring two or more separate operations into a single public sector entity).

Government business enterprises: The objective of the project is to explore issues within the current definition of Government Business Enterprises (GBEs) and to consider whether the current accounting requirements are adequate.

---

[14] See http://www.ifac.org/news-events/2015-01/ipsasb-publishes-ipsass-accounting-interests-other-entities.
[15] ISBN 978-1-60815-180-6.

Public sector specific financial instruments: The objective of the project is to focus on issues related to public sector specific financial instruments which are outside the scope of those covered under current IPSAS 28–30. Issues the project intends to consider include (but are not necessarily limited to):

- Monetary gold;
- Currency and coin in circulation;
- Special Drawing Rights;
- Memberships/investments in international organizations (such as the International Monetary Fund);
- Statutory receivables and payables.

The IPSASB is also considering potential new projects to be added to the IPSASB work program for 2015–2019 (see Table 3.3):

Table 3.3   IPSASB Strategy Consultation

Projects to address public sector specific issues	Projects to maintain existing IPSAS	Projects to converge with IFRS	Other projects
Biological assets held for the provision or supply of services	*Borrowing Costs IPSAS 5*	*Extractive Industries (IFRS 6 interim standard but no comparable IPSAS)*	*Differential Reporting*
Heritage assets	*Construction Contracts IPSAS 11*		*Integrated Reporting*
Infrastructure assets	*Disclosure of Financial*		*Interim Financial Reporting*
Public sector specific intangible assets	*Information about the General Government Sector IPSAS 22*	*Insurance Contracts (IFRS 4 interim standard but no comparable IPSAS)*	
Measurement, public sector specific	*Employee Benefits IPSAS 25*		
Military assets		*Non-current Assets Held for Sale and Discontinued*	
Natural resources	*Improvements to IPSAS 23*		
Non-exchange expenses	*Non-Exchange Revenues*	*Operations (IFRS 5 but no comparable IPSAS)*	
Role of government as owner rather than government	*Leases IPSAS 13*	*Rate Regulated Industries*	
Sovereign powers and their impact on financial reporting	*Presentation of Financial Statements IPSAS 1*		
Trust funds	*Related Party Transactions IPSAS 20*		
	Revenue IPSAS 9		
	Segment Reporting IPSAS 18		

The IPSASB Strategy and Work Program is expected to be published in March 2015, but none of these potential projects should reasonably result in new IPSAS before at least 2018–2019.

CONCLUSION

It may be considered that, today, the corpus of IPSAS (IPSAS 1–38) together with the IPSASB Conceptual Framework constitute a rather accomplished platform for public sector accounting and financial reporting.

PART 2

ACCRUAL-BASED IPSAS

4 THE IPSASB CONCEPTUAL FRAMEWORK AND KEY ACCRUAL ACCOUNTING CONCEPTS

This chapter focuses on explaining the key accrual accounting concepts embedded within the IPSASB Conceptual Framework. Principles-based accrual accounting standards, such as IPSAS, are underpinned by a conceptual framework that provides the broad principles on which the accounting standards can be built. An understanding of the Conceptual Framework is essential for anyone who wants to understand the basis of the requirements in IPSAS. In addition, when developing IPSAS-compliant accounting policies, an understanding of the Framework is necessary.

Chapter 4 is the first of the 15 chapters (Chapter 4 to Chapter 18) that consider the essential requirements of the accrual-based IPSAS. It should be noted that these chapters are supported by question and answer boxes, IPSAS financial reporting in practice highlights, and explanations as well as mini-cases, where relevant throughout the chapters. However, not all chapters will include all types of illustrations.

PRINCIPLES-BASED ACCRUAL ACCOUNTING

Accrual-based IPSAS embeds what is referred to as the principles-based approach. The principles-based approach is set out within the IPSASB Conceptual Framework.

Concept highlight: Principles- vs. rules-based accounting

Principles-based accounting is often discussed in comparison with rules-based accounting standards. To make the contrast US accounting standards are described as rules based. In the US the Federal Accounting Standards Advisory Board (FASAB) is the national government standard-setter, while the Governmental Accounting Standards Board (GASB) provides the standards for state and local level.

Key to the principles-based approach is the exercise of professional judgment, while, in contrast, the rules-based approach will include a rule that directs how a transaction should be recorded.

Accrual-based accounting shows the effects of transactions and other events and circumstances on a reporting entity's economic resources and claims are accounted for in the periods in which those effects occur, even if the resulting cash receipts and payments occur in a different period.

BACKGROUND AND PURPOSE OF THE IPSASB CONCEPTUAL FRAMEWORK

The Conceptual Framework of the IPSASB has been developed over an eight-year period and was published in full on 31 October 2014 with the title "The Conceptual Framework for General Purpose Financial Reporting by Public Sector Entities." The Framework explains that IPSAS are developed to apply across countries and jurisdictions with diverse political systems, different forms of government, and varying institutional and administrative arrangements for the delivery of services to citizens. The IPSASB recognizes these numerous differences in the form of government, social and cultural traditions, and service delivery mechanisms that exist in the many nation states that may adopt IPSAS. In establishing the Conceptual Framework, the IPSASB has sought to consider and respond to, and embrace, this diversity.

The role of the Framework is to establish the concepts that underpin general purpose financial reporting ("financial reporting") by public sector entities that adopt the accrual basis of accounting. Having these concepts established in the Framework will assist the IPSASB in the development of future IPSAS and Recommended Practice Guidelines (RPGs). The Framework will also assist preparers of financial statements, auditors, and users of the financial statements to better understand IPSAS.

THE CONTENT OF THE CONCEPTUAL FRAMEWORK

This section will cover the key content of the Framework. Practical examples will serve as illustrative examples of some of the main concepts. The Framework includes a preface which describes and explains features and factors that distinguish public sector entities from private sector entities.

The Framework is structured into eight chapters with the following titles:

Chapter 1: Role and Authority of the Conceptual Framework;
Chapter 2: Objectives and Users of General Purpose Financial Reporting;
Chapter 3: Qualitative Characteristics;
Chapter 4: Reporting Entity;
Chapter 5: Elements in Financial Statements;
Chapter 6: Recognition in Financial Statements;
Chapter 7: Measurement of Assets and Liabilities in Financial Statements;
Chapter 8: Presentation of Information in General Purpose Financial Statements.

Chapters 1–4 relate to the role, authority, and scope of general purpose financial reporting, the objectives and users as well as the qualitative characteristics and the reporting entity. The chapters will play a role in ensuring that accounting policies developed, based on individual IPSAS, will be compatible with the four available chapters of the Conceptual Framework. Nevertheless, the Conceptual Framework is not an accounting standard, and as such it should be noted that requirements stipulated in an individual IPSAS standard or Recommended Practice Guidelines (RPGs) will prevail over the Conceptual Framework. For financial reporting issues that are not dealt with by IPSAS or RPGs the Conceptual Framework can serve an important role in providing guidance. In these circumstances, preparers and others can refer to and consider the applicability of the definitions, recognition criteria, measurement principles, and other concepts identified in the Conceptual Framework (cf. paragraphs 1.2–1.3, Chapter 1 of the Conceptual Framework).

Chapters 5–8 define the elements, qualified as "building blocks" that together establish the financial statements, the criteria for elements to be recognized in financial statements, how assets and liabilities should be measured in financial statements, and how financial statements should be presented. These chapters of the Conceptual Framework are not IPSAS, and should not be applied as such. However they settle the principles which are developed in IPSAS, which means that preparers and others may refer to these chapters when they want to understand the underlying concepts in applying specific requirements of IPSAS.

Preface

The preface provides a sound introduction on matters that are specific to the public sector and of which it is important to be aware before reading the Framework in full. The preface thus highlights the topics shown in Table 4.1.

The preface of the Framework makes reference of the notion of "going concern"[1] (see para. 13). It is stated that when preparing financial statements management need to consider whether an entity can continue as a going concern or not. Financial statements are normally prepared on a going concern basis unless management intends to liquidate the entity or cease trading or has no realistic alternative but to do so.

---

[1] This is also covered in IPSAS 1, para. 38.

Table 4.1   Conceptual Framework preface

Non-exchange transactions	In a non-exchange transaction, an entity receives value from another party without directly giving approximately equal value in exchange. These types of transaction are frequent in the public sector.
	The nature of non-exchange transactions may influence how they are recognized, measured, and presented to best support assessments of the entity by service recipients and resource providers.
	Chapter 11 on revenue in this book will cover "IPSAS 23 Revenue from non-exchange revenue" in detail.
Role of the approved budget	Most governments and other public sector entities prepare budgets. In stark contrast to the private sector, there is, for many public sector entities, a constitutional requirement to prepare and make publicly available a budget approved by the legislature.
	The approved budget is therefore of great significance within the public sector. Information that enables users to compare financial results with the budget thus assists an assessment of the extent to which a public sector entity has met its financial objectives. Chapter 14 in this book includes coverage of IPSAS 24 on the "Presentation of budget information in the financial statements."
Public sector programs and the longevity of the public sector	Public sector programs are often long term and the ability to meet commitments depends upon future taxation and contributions.
Assets and liabilities in the public sector	The primary reason, within the public sector, for holding property, plant, and equipment and other assets is for their service potential rather than their ability to generate cash flows.
Public sector entities' regulatory role	It is often seen that governments and other public sector entities have powers to regulate entities operating in certain sectors of the economy. The principle, behind the public policy rationale, is for such regulation to safeguard the public interest in accordance with specified public policy objectives.
Link to statistical reporting	A very specific feature of the public sector is that many governments produce two types of ex-post financial information: (a) government finance statistics (GFS) on the general government sector (GGS) for the purpose of macroeconomic analysis and decision-making, and (b) general purpose financial statements ("financial statements") for accountability and decision-making at an entity level. The preface specifically highlights that: "IPSAS financial statements and GFS reports have much in common. Both reporting frameworks are concerned with (a) financial, accrual-based information, (b) a government's assets, liabilities, revenue, and expenses, and (c) comprehensive information on cash flows. There is considerable overlap between the two reporting frameworks that underpin this information" (para. 22, p. 9).

Chapter 1. Role and Authority of the Conceptual Framework

Chapter 1 defines the role of the Conceptual Framework and thus states that the Framework will identify the concepts that the IPSASB will draw upon in developing the IPSAS and RPGs. Thus the Conceptual Framework will underpin the development of IPSAS.

Chapter 2. Objectives and Users of General Purpose Financial Reporting

Chapter 2 outlines the objectives of financial reporting, the users of GPFRs, accountability, and decision-making as well as the information needs of users and information provided by the GPFR. The GPFR encompasses financial statements and the presentation of information that enhances and supplements the financial statements. Examples include: information on service delivery achievements, prospective financial and non-financial information, as well as other narrative explanations (i.e., explanatory information).

Service recipients and resource providers are defined as the primary users of the GPFRs. The provision of useful information for accountability and decision-making is the ultimate target objective of the GPFRs.

Chapter 3. Qualitative Characteristics

The qualitative characteristics of information to be included in GPFRs are: relevance, faithful representation, understandability, timeliness, comparability, and verifiability.

In addition to the qualitative characteristics, Chapter 3 of the Conceptual Framework also addresses constraints on information included in the GPFRs.

1. **Materiality.** Information is material if its omission or misstatement could influence the discharge of accountability by the entity or the decisions that users make on the basis of the entity's GPFRs prepared for the reporting period.
2. **Cost–Benefit.** The benefits of the financial report should justify the costs.
3. **Balance between the qualitative characteristics.** As a preparer of GPFRs consideration has to be given to the balance between qualitative characteristics. The qualitative characteristics should work together to contribute to the usefulness of the information.

Example 4.1   Relevance

A public sector entity is a scientific intergovernmental organization.
A broad analysis shows that expenses are split as follows:

- 70% staff cost
  - 30% scientific staff cost
  - 20% support staff cost
  - 20% pension fund contribution
- 13% depreciation of assets
- 10% operating expenses
- 5% laboratory expenses
- 2% site maintenance

Would you suggest presenting expenses classified by nature or by function, considering that useful information would help the management pilot costs?

In the present case, an analysis of expenses using a classification based on the nature of expenses is more useful to management because what they intend to do is to manage costs which are under their control, and prioritize expenses. For instance, it may be useful to follow up the evolution of support staff costs and compare it to scientific staff costs. It may also be useful to monitor operating and site maintenance expenses.

Example 4.2.   Substance over form

Under the section on faithful representation (para. 3.10) IPSAS embeds the principle of substance over form. This means that when accounting for a transaction it should be according to its transactional substance rather than its legal form. A practical example of this could be illustrated by considering a leasing scenario where a public sector entity leases medical equipment. The entity does not legally own this asset, as the title is held by the leasing company. However, the business will use the machine to produce goods in the same manner as any equipment which it legally owns.

An international organization has a grant of tenure signed with its host country. This contract requires it to maintain the assets that have been granted as long as the international organization operates on the site. It has the right to erect new buildings on the granted site. If a decision to relocate the organization were taken, the organization should return these buildings to the host country. No such decision has been taken so far, therefore the organization considers that it can use these buildings, and possibly build new ones, for the purpose of its activities, behaving as the owner of these buildings. Even though the organization is not legally the owner of these buildings, it recognizes all of its buildings in tangible assets, considering, in accordance with IPSAS 17, that they are identifiable assets, controlled by the organization as a result of past events and which provide future economic benefits or service potential to the organization.

The transactional substance of the lease arrangement is that the public sector entity has a resource (an asset) from which it will generate service potential. Therefore the financial statements should reflect the asset on its statement of financial position.

Note. Accounting for Leases according to IPSAS 13 is discussed in detail in Chapter 10.

Chapter 4. Reporting Entity

A public sector entity is an entity that raises economic resources from, or on behalf of, constituents and/or uses economic resources to undertake activities for the benefit of, or on behalf of, those constituents, and whose service recipients or resource providers are dependent on the GPFRs of the entity for information for accountability or decision-making purposes.

Chapter 5. Elements in Financial Statements

Following the Framework, elements in financial statements serve to group the financial effects of transactions and other events into broad classes that share common economic characteristics. The IPSASB has referred to these as "building blocks" that together establish the financial statements. The table below provides the high-level definition of the key elements recognized in Chapter 5 (see also EY, 2014).

The elements thus serve a role in recording, classifying, and aggregating economic data and activity. They structure the data in a way that provides users with information that achieves the objectives and meets the qualitative characteristics of financial reporting.

Defined elements are assets, liabilities, revenues, expenses, ownership contributions, and ownership distributions (see Table 4.2).[2] Other resources and obligations may need to be recognized to meet the objectives of financial reporting.

Each of the elements then has definitions as well as recognition and measurement criteria specified in each of the IPSAS applicable to the elements (Figure 4.1 provides an illustration of this).

Chapter 6: Recognition in Financial Statements

Recognition is described as the process of incorporating and including amounts shown on the face of the appropriate financial statement. An item that is recognized is one that meets the definition of an element and can be measured in a way that achieves the qualitative characteristics provided for in the Framework.

---

[2] Deferred inflows and deferred outflows are no longer defined as elements.

Table 4.2   Elements of GPFRs

Term	Definition	Additional description
Asset	A resource presently controlled by the entity as a result of a past event (5.6).	An asset is a resource with service potential or the ability to generate economic benefits. Service potential is a concept that is specific to the public sector, and refers to the capacity to provide services that contribute to achieving the entity's objectives. Service potential enables an entity to achieve its objectives without necessarily generating net cash inflows.
Liability	A present obligation of the entity for an outflow of resources that results from a past event (5.14).	A present obligation may or may not be legally binding. A liability must be settled by an outflow of resources from the entity. The Framework explains that the obligation must be to an external party, to be considered a liability. For a liability to exist, it is not necessary to know the identity of the external party before the time of settlement. An entity however, cannot be obligated to itself, even where it has publicly announced an intention to behave in a certain way.
Revenue	Increases in the net financial position of the entity, other than increases arising from ownership contributions (5.29).	Revenue and expenses can arise from a wide range of transactions. Examples include: exchange or non-exchange transactions and depreciation. In addition revenue and expenses can arise from individual transactions or groups of transactions.
Expenses	Decreases in the net financial position of the entity, other than decreases arising from ownership distributions (5.30).	Surplus and deficit for the period are not defined as elements in the Framework. An entity's surplus or deficit for the period is defined as the difference between revenue and expenses presented in the statement of financial performance.
Ownership contributions and distributions	Inflows of resources to an entity, contributed by external parties in their capacity as owners, which establish or increase an interest in the net financial position of the entity (5.33).	The Framework underlines that inflows of resources from owners and outflows of resources to owners in their capacity as owners need to be distinguished from revenue and expenses. For example, transactions where an entity transfers assets and liabilities to another public sector entity may fall into the definitions of ownership contributions or ownership distributions.

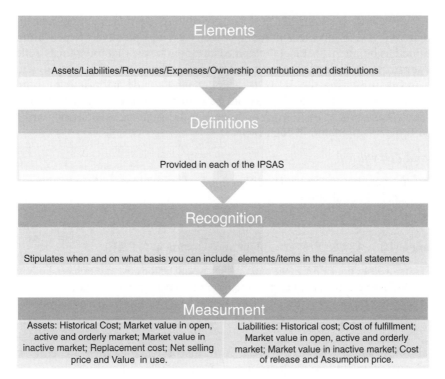

Figure 4.1   IPSAS elements

The criteria for an element to be recognized in financial statements include: (1) the item needs to meet the definition of an element, and (2) the item can be measured in a way that achieves the qualitative characteristics. When an item meets the recognition criteria, it must be recognized in the financial statements. The process of recognizing an item includes an assessment of uncertainty related to the existence and to the measurement of the element. Public sector entities may, at any point in time, be exposed to conditions that lead to uncertainty and change. Subsequently, any recognition uncertainties are required to be assessed at each reporting date

It should however be noted that there may be cases were an IPSAS stipulates that, in order to meet the objectives of financial reporting, other resources or other obligations have to be recognized in the financial statements (even if they do not meet the definition of an element). In such cases though, there will be a requirement for such items to be able to be measured in a way that meets the qualitative characteristics.

Chapter 7: Measurement of Assets and Liabilities in Financial Statements

When a transaction, event, or economic phenomenon is deemed to be recognized, the subsequent step in the process is to assign a monetary value to the item for the financial statements. Assigning a monetary value to a transaction requires the selection of an appropriate measurement basis and ensuring that the measurement is sufficiently relevant and faithfully representative of the item.

The Framework explains that it is not possible to identify a single measurement basis that best meets the measurement objective. The objective of measurement is thus defined as being "[t]o select those measurement bases that most fairly reflect the cost of services, operational capacity and financial capacity of the entity in a manner that is useful in holding the entity to account, and for decision-making purposes" (para. 7.2). Subsequently, the Framework provides for more than one measurement basis. The measurement of items recognized in the financial statements will follow the requirements stipulated in each IPSAS.

Entry and exit values

Measurement bases can lead to either entry or exit values. For assets, entry values reflect the cost of acquisition.

Example 4.3.   Assets: Property, plant and equipment (PP&E)

Entry value: For PPE&E, the entry values would be the cost of purchase. Following IPSAS 17 on PP&E historical cost and replacement cost are entry values.
Exit value: Exit values for the PP&E would be the economic benefits from sale.

Liabilities can also be categorized in terms of whether they are entry or exit values. Entry values relate to the transaction under which an obligation is received or the amount that an entity would accept to assume a liability. The amount required to meet an obligation or the amount required to release the entity from an obligation would be the exit value.

Entity-specific and non-entity-specific measures

Entity-specific measurement bases reflect the economic and current policy constraints that affect the possible uses of an asset and the settlement of a liability by an entity. Economic opportunities that are not obtainable by other entities and risks that are not experienced by other entities can be reflected in entity-specific measures.

Non-entity-specific measures reflect general market opportunities and risks. The Framework explains that the judgment on whether to use an entity-specific or non-entity-specific measure shall refer to the measurement objective and the qualitative characteristics.

Observable and unobservable measures

Measures can be categorized according to whether they are observable in an open, active, and orderly market or not. Measures that are observable in a market are likely to be more understandable and verifiable than measures that are not observable.

For instance, the best evidence of fair value of a financial instrument, as explained in IPSAS 29.51, is quoted prices in an active market. If the market for a financial instrument is not active, IPSAS 29 requires that an entity establishes fair value by using a valuation technique, in order to establish what the transaction price would have been on the measurement date in an arm's length exchange motivated by normal operating considerations. If there is a valuation technique commonly used by market participants to price the instrument and that technique has been demonstrated to provide reliable estimates of prices obtained in actual market transactions, the entity should use that technique. IPSAS 29 recommends that the chosen valuation technique makes maximum use of market inputs and relies as little as possible on entity-specific inputs. The underlying idea is to refer, as much as possible, to observable measures.

Reflecting time value of money

The Framework explains that, where cash flows will not take place for an extended period, the asset or liability has to be discounted to reflect its value at the reporting date.

Types of measurement bases for assets

Historical cost

Historical cost is defined as: "[t]he consideration given to acquire or develop an asset, which is the cash or cash equivalents or the value of the other consideration given, at the time of its acquisition or development" (para. 7.13).

The Framework highlights that, for public sector entities, where historical cost is used "the cost of services reflects the amount of resources expended to acquire or develop assets consumed in the provision of services."

When public sector entities acquire assets in an exchange transaction, historical cost provides information about the resources available to the acquirer to provide services in the future.

Current value measurements

The Framework explains that current value measurements reflect the economic environment prevailing at the reporting date. There are four current value measurements available for assets:

Market value	Replacement cost	Net selling price	Value in use
• *"The amount for which an asset could be exchanged between knowledgeable, willing parties in an arm's length transaction"* (para. 7.24)	• *"The most economic cost required for the entity to replace the service potential of an asset (including the amount that the entity will receive from its disposal at the end of its useful life) at the reporting date."* (para. 7.37)	• *"The amount that the entity can obtain from sale of the asset, after deducting the costs of sale."* (para. 7.49)	• *"The present value to the entity of the asset's remaining service potential or ability to generate economic benefits if it continues to be used, and of the net amount that the entity will receive from its disposal at the end of its useful life."* (para. 7.58)

Market value

The use of market values permits a return on assets to be determined. It is defined as: "[t]he amount for which an asset could be exchanged between knowledgeable, willing parties in an arm's length transaction" (para. 7.24). It is however important to note that public sector entities do not commonly carry out activities where the main objective is that of generating profits, and services are often provided in non-exchange transactions or on subsidized terms. As a result, there may be limited relevance in market prices, except for financial assets such as commodities, currencies, and securities where prices are publicly available (EY, 2014).

Replacement cost (or optimized depreciated replacement cost)

The replacement cost is defined as: "[t]he most economic cost required for the entity to replace the service potential of an asset (including the amount that the entity will receive from its disposal at the end of its useful life) at the reporting date" (para. 7.37).

The Framework states that this is the cost of replacing an asset's service potential, which is different from reproduction cost, which is the cost of acquiring an identical asset. However, in many instances, the most economically relevant replacement of the service potential will be by purchasing an asset that is similar to that which is controlled; replacement cost is based on an alternative asset (if that alternative would provide the same service potential) but more inexpensively (EY, 2014). For financial reporting purposes, it is thus required to reflect the difference in service potential between the existing and the replacement asset. The appropriate service potential is that which the entity is capable of using or expects to use, having considered the necessity of holding sufficient service capacity to deal with contingencies.

Example 4.4   Replacement cost

Therefore, the replacement cost of an asset reflects reductions in required service capacity. For example, if an entity owns a kindergarten that accommodates 400 children but, because of demographic changes since its construction, a kindergarten for 150 children would be adequate for current and reasonably foreseeable requirements, the replacement cost of the asset is that of a kindergarten for 150 children.

In principle, replacement cost provides a suitable measure of the resources available to provide services in future periods, since its focus is on the current value of assets and their service potential to the entity.

Net selling price

This is defined as "the amount that the entity can obtain from sale of the asset, after deducting the costs of sale" (para. 7.49). The net selling price differs from the market value as it does not require an open, active, and orderly market or the estimation of a price in such a market, and it includes the entity's costs of sale. It is therefore entity specific and reflects constraints on sale. The potential usefulness of measuring assets at net selling price is that an asset cannot be worth less to the entity than the amount the entity could obtain on its sale. However, it is not appropriate as a measurement basis if the entity is able to use its resources more efficiently by employing the asset in another way, for example, by using it in the delivery of services.

Value in use

This is defined as "the present value to the entity of the asset's remaining service potential or ability to generate economic benefits if it continues to be used, and of the net amount that the entity will receive from its disposal at the end of its useful life" (para. 7.58).

Value in use reflects the amount that can be derived from an asset through its operation and its disposal at the end of its useful life. The value in use is thus an entity-specific value. The value that will be derived from an asset is often greater than its replacement cost; it is also frequently greater than its historical cost. Where this is the case, reporting an asset at its value in use is of limited usefulness as, by definition, the entity is able to secure equivalent service potential at replacement cost. Value in use is also not an appropriate measurement basis when the net selling price is greater than the value in use as, in this case, the most resource-efficient use of the asset is to sell it, rather than continue to use it (see also EY, 2014). It can therefore be argued that value in use is suitable to apply where it is less than the replacement cost and greater than the net selling price.[3]

A majority of assets within the public sector are held with the primary objective of contributing to the provision of services, rather than to the generation of profits. To accommodate this public sector specific feature of assets, IPSAS embraces the concept of "non-cash-generating assets." It should be noted that since value in use for cash-generating assets is normally derived from expected cash flows, using the concept in such a context can be problematic. As explained by EY (2014) it can be inappropriate to calculate value in use on the basis of expected cash flows, since such a measure would not be faithfully representative of the value in use of such an asset to the entity. Consequently, it would be required to use replacement cost as a surrogate for financial reporting purposes.

Types of measurement bases for liabilities

Historical cost

Historical cost is suitable where liabilities are likely to be settled at stated terms. This means that it will not be appropriate for long-term liabilities. Historical cost, however, cannot be applied for liabilities that do not arise from a transaction.

---

[3] This kind of scenario is observable when an asset is not worth replacing, but the value of its service potential or ability to create economic benefits is greater than its net selling price. In such cases, value in use represents the value of the asset to the entity. Applying value in use as a measurement basis for the assessment of certain impairments is considered appropriate, since it is used in the determination of the recoverable amount for an asset or group of assets.

Cost of fulfilment

This is "the costs that the entity will incur in fulfilling the obligations represented by the liability, assuming that it does so in the least costly manner" (para. 7.74). Where fulfilment necessitates work to be done, the relevant costs are those that the entity will incur.[4]

Example 4.5   Cost of fulfilment

In order to attract and to retain staff, an entity has granted health insurance coverage to active staff and also as pensioners. The entity is committed to this obligation and is to record as a provision the expected cost of fulfilling this obligation taking into account parameters such as mortality tables and medical inflation.

Market value

The advantages and disadvantages of market value for liabilities are the same as those for using market value for assets.

Using market values as a measurement basis may be appropriate, for example, where the liability is attributable to changes in a specified rate, price, or index quoted in an open, active, and orderly market, which is the case for derivatives.

However, where the ability to transfer a liability is restricted and the terms on which such a transfer might be made are unclear, the case for market values (even if they exist) is significantly weaker. This is particularly true when there is no active market or when it is unlikely that there is an open, active, and orderly market, for instance for liabilities arising from obligations in non-exchange transactions. In general, except for some financial instruments, market value is difficult to assess for liabilities.

Cost of release

"Cost of release" is a more appropriate measure of the current burden of a liability, just as, for an asset, net selling price is more relevant when it is higher than value in use (see para. 7.79).

Cost of release reflects the amount of an instant exit from the obligation. Cost of release is therefore the amount that the creditor will accept in settlement of its claim, or that a third party would charge to accept the transfer of the liability from the obligor. If there is more than one way of securing release from the liability, the cost of release shall be the lowest amount.

---

[4]This could include the cost to the entity of doing the corrective work itself, or the cost of contracting with an external party to carry out the work. It should however be noted that the costs of contracting with an external party are only appropriate to include when employing a contractor is the least costly means of fulfilling the obligation (EY, 2014).

Assumption price

"Assumption price" is the term used in the context of liabilities to refer to the same concept as replacement cost for assets (para. 7.87). In the same manner as replacement cost represents the amount that an entity would rationally pay to acquire an asset, the assumption price is the amount which the entity would rationally be willing to accept in exchange for assuming an existing liability.

Summary

For a summary of measurement bases for assets and liabilities see Table 4.3.

Chapter 8: Presentation of Information in General Purpose Financial Statements

Presentation is defined in the Framework as "the selection, location and organization of information that is reported in the GPFRs" (para. 8.4). Chapter 8 focuses on the comprehensive scope of financial reporting, and describes the concepts applicable to financial statements in greater detail. The key objective of decisions regarding the presentation is to provide information that supports the objectives and meets the qualitative characteristics of financial reporting. Decisions about information selection, location, and organization are interlinked and are often to be considered together.

Presentation in GPFRs describes the concepts that are applicable to both the financial statements and additional information that enhances, complements, and supplements the financial statements. It should be highlighted that Chapter 8 does not stipulate a list of factors that ought to be included in a financial statement or the notes.

Information selection

The selection of information should reflect what information is reported: (a) in the financial statements, and (b) in GPFRs outside the financial statements.

The users of GPFRs need information about the financial position, financial performance, and cash flows of an entity. The information derived from the financial statements will enable users to identify the resources and claims on an entity and make informed assessments about the efficiency and effectiveness of an entity's service delivery as well as its financial performance, liquidity, and solvency (see also EY, 2014).

In GPFRs, information is selected for display or disclosure (see Figure 4.2).

For information that is to be displayed or disclosed, the Framework advises that the following considerations are made:

- The objectives of the financial reporting;
- The qualitative characteristics and constraints on information included in GPFRs;
- The relevant economic or other phenomena about which information may be necessary;
- Decisions about information selection involve information prioritization and summarization. In addition, the benefit to users of receiving the information is

Table 4.3 Summary of measurement bases for assets and liabilities

Measurement Bases for Assets

Measurement basis	Entry or exit	Observable or unobservable in a market	Entity- or non-entity-specific	Examples
Historical cost	Entry	Generally observable	Entity-specific	Equipment[5] and externally acquired intangible assets
Historical cost	Entry	Generally observable	Entity-specific	Internally developed intangible assets, such as internally developed software
Market value in open, active, and orderly market	Entry & exit	Observable	Non-entity-specific	Investments such as equity securities, bonds
Market value in inactive market	Exit	Dependent on valuation technique	Dependent on valuation technique	Financial instruments, e.g., embedded derivatives
Replacement cost	Entry	Observable	Entity-specific	Infrastructure assets, e.g., railway tracks, water pipes, heating system pipes; Inventories distributed at no cost
Replacement cost	Entry	Unobservable	Entity-specific	Historical buildings used as offices
Net selling price	Exit	Observable	Entity-specific	Inventories
Value in use[6]	Exit	Unobservable	Entity-specific	Infrastructure assets, e.g., music schools, schools, public libraries, prisons. Assessing impairment of assets

Measurement Bases for Liabilities

Measurement basis	Entry or exit	Observable or unobservable in a market	Entity- or non-entity-specific	Examples
Historical cost	Entry	Generally observable	Entity-specific	Trade payables
Cost of Fulfillment	Exit	Unobservable	Entity-specific	Rehabilitation costs, healthcare for pensioners
Market value in open, active, and orderly market	Entry & exit	Observable	Non-entity-specific	Derivative instruments
Market value in inactive market	Exit	Dependent on valuation technique	Dependent on valuation technique	Financial instruments, e.g., embedded derivatives
Cost of Release	Exit	Observable	Entity-specific	Settlement of claims
Assumption Price	Entry	Observable	Entity-specific	Financial guarantees

Source: Conceptual Framework with added examples.

[5] Depending on the accounting policy adopted, IPSAS 17 Property, Plant and Equipment and IPSAS 31 Intangible Assets allow an entity to choose between the cost or revaluation model.

[6] For non-cash-generating assets the calculation of value in use may require the use of replacement cost as a surrogate.

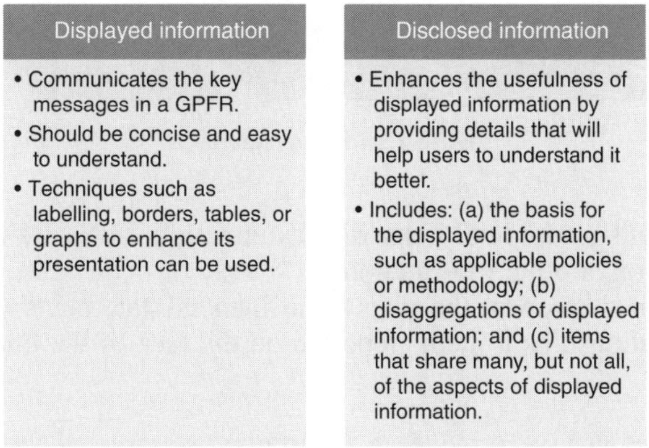

Displayed information	Disclosed information
• Communicates the key messages in a GPFR. • Should be concise and easy to understand. • Techniques such as labelling, borders, tables, or graphs to enhance its presentation can be used.	• Enhances the usefulness of displayed information by providing details that will help users to understand it better. • Includes: (a) the basis for the displayed information, such as applicable policies or methodology; (b) disaggregations of displayed information; and (c) items that share many, but not all, of the aspects of displayed information.

Figure 4.2 GPFRs information: display or disclosure

needed to justify the cost to entities of collecting and presenting that information.

• Information needs to be presented on a timely basis to enable users to hold management accountable and to inform users' decisions.

Information location

Information location decisions focus on the allocation of information between different reports and on locating information within a report.

The Framework defines the following factors for allocating information between different reports:

1. Nature of the information;
2. Jurisdiction-specific factors;
3. Linkages between information.

The Framework explains that displayed information should be presented prominently in a report. The location of information in the financial statements is intended to communicate a comprehensive financial picture of an entity.

Information organization

Information organization considers and describes the arrangement, grouping, and ordering of information, which includes decisions about: (a) how information is arranged within a GPFR, and (b) the overall structure of a GPFR.

Information organization considers important relationships between information and whether it is for display or disclosure. Key relationships include, but are not restricted to, the following (see Figure 4.3).

In sum, information organization within the financial statements includes decisions about:

• The type and number of statements;
• Disaggregation of totals into meaningful subcategories;

Figure 4.3   Key relationships

- Ordering and grouping of items displayed within each statement;
- Identification of other information;
- Information disclosed in the notes to the financial statements which is organized so that relationships to items reported on the face of the financial statements are clear.

To finalize this chapter we provide an illustrative example of the table of content of the World Health Organization (WHO) Financial Report and Audited Financial Statements for the year ended 31 December 2013.

Financial Reporting in Practice 4.1. WHO – Financial Report and Audited Financial Statements for the year ended 31 December 2013

The above table of contents clearly discloses the type and number of statements forming part of the WHO Financial Statements. Information disclosed in the notes to the financial statements is organized so that relationships to items reported on the face of each element of the financial statements are clear, since notes to the financial statements are classified as notes:

- Supporting information to the Statement of Financial Position;
- Supporting information to the Statement of Financial Performance;
- Supporting information to the Statement of Net Assets/Equity;
- Supporting information to the Statement of Comparison of Budget and Actual Amounts.

5 FINANCIAL STATEMENTS

The objective of general purpose financial reports (GPFRs) are to provide information that is useful to a wide range of users and stakeholders. Note that Chapter 2 in the Conceptual Framework for GPFR by public sector entities (released in October 2014) is dedicated to the objectives and users of GPFR (in this book this is covered in detail in Chapter 4).

Example 5.1   Examples of users of GPFRs

Service recipients
Resource providers
External auditors

Regulators
Governments
Stakeholders in society such as the voters.

GPFRs more specifically provide information to users for both accountability and decision-making purposes (see IPSASB, 2014 Conceptual Framework).[1] The usefulness of the financial statements to the users thereof is enhanced if they are comparable and understandable. Comparability and understandability of the financial statements is underpinned by consistency, from year to year, in the presentation of the financial statements of public sector entities. IPSAS 1 Presentation of Financial Statements provides the basic framework for preparing the statement of financial position, statement of financial performance, and statement of changes in net assets/equity. IPSAS 1 also provides public sector entities with the flexibility to adapt formats and headings to present their information in a way that aids understanding of the specific entity. It should be noted that IPSAS 1 does not apply to condensed interim financial information nor does it apply to Government Business Enterprises (GBEs).

This chapter focuses on explaining and illustrating the key standards applied for the presentation of IPSAS-compliant financial statements. It therefore includes IPSAS 1 Presentation of Financial Statements, IPSAS 2 Cash Flow Statements, IPSAS 18 Segment Reporting, and IPSAS 14 Events After the Reporting Date.

PRESENTATION OF FINANCIAL STATEMENTS

To meet the requirement of providing users and stakeholders with relevant and reliable information a number of key statements have been identified which allow users to assess the financial performance, financial position, and liquidity of an entity. The structure of financial statements is standardized in order to ensure that this information is presented in a similar manner by all entities applying IPSAS, allowing meaningful comparisons to be made across different entities. It should however be noted that comparative information may not be provided in the first set of IPSAS-compliant financial statements. Although IPSAS 1 Presentation of Financial Statements provides the basic framework for the structure of the statements, public sector entities do have the flexibility to adapt formats and headings to present their information in a way that aids understanding of the specificities of the entity.

Fair Presentation

In the previous chapter on the Conceptual Framework, the meaning of fair value was explained and it was highlighted that a number of the IPSAS include fair value either as a potential or required measurement basis. IPSAS 1 states that "[f]inancial statements shall present fairly the financial position, financial performance, and cash flows of an entity" (IPSAS 1.27).

---

[1] Bandy (2014) elaborates further on different types of usage of the financial statements and highlights that each individual user or user group can or will have their unique reasons for being interested in the financial statements (pp. 199–200).

The phrase "present fairly" has broadly been equated with the notion of "true and fair view."[2] The requirement of IPSAS 1 on fair presentation requires public sector entities to provide a faithful representation of the effects of transactions, other conditions and events, in accordance with the definitions and recognition criteria established for assets, liabilities, revenue, and expenses, as provided in the Conceptual Framework.

A true and fair view will, in the vast majority of cases, be attained by compliance with IPSAS and, where necessary, by additional disclosure to fully explain an issue. IPSAS 1 does however in extremely rare circumstances allow for departure (override) from the application of particular requirement of an IPSAS, if the alternative accounting treatment or disclosure ensures the achievement of a fair presentation (cf. IPSAS 1.32a).

The external auditors following International Standards on Auditing (ISA) (ISA 200)[3] will issue, where the financial reporting framework is a fair presentation framework, as is IPSAS and as is generally the case for general purpose financial statements, an audit opinion (as required by the ISAs) on whether the financial statements are presented fairly, in all material respects, or give a true and fair view.

Where the auditor expresses an opinion on whether the financial statements are presented fairly, in all material respects, or give a true and fair view, misstatements also include those adjustments of amounts, classifications, presentation, or disclosures that, in the auditor's judgment, are required for the financial statements to be presented fairly, in all material respects, or to provide a true and fair view (cf. ISA 200, para. 13i).

Going Concern

Those responsible[4] for the preparation of financial statements of the public sector entity need to consider whether the entity can continue as a going concern or not (IPSAS 1.38). Financial statements are normally prepared on a going concern basis, unless the preparers of the financial statements intend to liquidate the entity or cease activities, or has no realistic alternative but to cease activities.

Example 5.2   Accounting policy – IPSAS 1 and Going Concern

IPSAS 1. Presentation of financial statements

"UNOPS prepares its corporate financial statements on **an accrual and going concern basis** in compliance with the requirements of International Public Sector Accounting Standards (IPSAS).

---

[2] See for example Kirk's (2001) discussion paper on "True and fair view" versus "present fairly" in conformity with Generally Accepted Accounting Principles.
[3] International Standard on Auditing (ISA) 200, "Overall objectives of the independent auditor and the conduct of an audit in accordance with international standards on auditing."
[4] Examples of functions which may have the responsibility to prepare the financial statements of individual entities (such as government departments or their equivalent) include the individual who heads the entity, the head of the central finance agency (or the senior finance official, such as the controller or accountant-general), as well as the president or the director of the entity.

These financial statements include a complete set of notes providing additional narrative descriptions or disaggregations on the items disclosed.

All items of revenue and expense recognized in a financial period are included in the UNOPS statement of financial performance unless a specific IPSAS standard requires otherwise. Wherever possible, revenue is matched with the expenses incurred in the period."

Source: UNOPS (2014). IPSAS compliant accounting policies, p. 4.

Materiality and Aggregation

On a daily basis public sector entities process large numbers of transactions which they need to account for. This necessitates the aggregation of transactions into classes following their nature or function. IPSAS 1 stipulates that each material class of similar items shall be shown separately in the financial statements and that items of a dissimilar nature or function are to be presented separately, unless they are immaterial (see IPSAS 1.45).

Example 5.3   Aggregation of transactions

Some public sector entities have a large number of and different types of assets (non-current assets). Following IPSAS 17 on Property, Plant and Equipment (PP&E) these assets are **aggregated** into different classes, such as buildings, vehicles, and equipment.

Information regarding the value of each class of PP&E is useful for the reader of the financial statements; nevertheless, it is not deemed necessary on the face of the statement of financial position, and is therefore disclosed in the notes instead. This means that the statement of financial position will include the total value of non-current assets while disclosure notes on PP&E will cater for a breakdown of the values per class of PP&E.

It should be noted that the materiality threshold that applies to the notes is generally lower than the threshold that applies to the other components of the financial statements. This means that an item that is not sufficiently material to warrant separate presentation on the face of those statements may nevertheless be sufficiently material for it to be presented separately in the notes (see IPSAS 1.46).[5]

Assessing whether an omission or misstatement is material involves the consideration of whether the omission or misstatement could influence decisions of users, and therefore be material. This requires attention to the characteristics of the users of the financial statements. The users are assumed to have a reasonable knowledge of

[5] From an auditor's perspective, the external auditor shall (following ISA 320) include in the audit documentation the following amounts and the factors considered in their determination: (a) Materiality for the financial statements as a whole; (b) If applicable, the materiality level or levels for particular classes of transactions, account balances or disclosures, and (c) Performance materiality […] (para. 14).

the public sector and economic activities and accounting, and to be prepared to study the information with reasonable attentiveness. Therefore, the assessment of whether something is material or not has to take into account how users with such attributes could reasonably be expected to be influenced in making and evaluating decisions (see IPSAS 1.13).

It should be highlighted that what is considered "material" in public sector entities can be very different from that in private sector companies. One reason for this divergence is that the financial statements of a public sector entity can be relied upon in making significant public policy decisions that have political, social, and security, implications. This means that public sector entities must be concerned about the nature of transactions and the level of detail in their disclosure. Therefore the "qualitative significance"[6] of information regarding the entity is essential.

Example 5.4   Responsibility for the financial statements and materiality

Management's responsibility for the financial statements

"Management's responsibility for the financial statements The Comptroller of UNICEF is responsible for the preparation and fair presentation of these financial statements in accordance with the International Public Sector Accounting Standards (IPSAS). This responsibility includes: designing, implementing and maintaining internal control relevant to the preparation and fair presentation of financial statements that are **free from material misstatement**, whether due to fraud or error; selecting and applying appropriate accounting policies; and making accounting estimates that are reasonable in the circumstances."

Source: UNICEF (2012) Financial Statements, p. 1.

Offsetting[7]

To ensure that readers of financial statements can understand the substance of transactions and other events, sufficient information has to be shown. This means that when a transaction gives rise to both a material asset and a liability, these are to be presented separately and are thus not allowed to offset each other. Offsetting is also not allowed for revenue and expense transactions. Offsetting as such is therefore not permitted under IPSAS unless a certain standard permits this (IPSAS 1.48).

---

[6] Qualitative significance refers to the nature of transactions that, independent of their value, can influence the decisions of a user of the financial statements.

[7] Note that offsetting will also be discussed where relevant in other chapters of this book.

Example 5.5   Where offsetting is not allowed versus where it is allowed

Where offsetting is not allowed

A public sector entity has acquired a non-current asset under a finance lease agreement. The substance of this transaction is that the company has a resource, i.e., an asset and a liability for the amounts due under the lease agreement.

Despite the fact that the asset and the liability are associated, they are shown separately and not allowed to be netted off on the statement of financial position. Both transactions have independent implications for the entity's cash flow. Therefore readers of the financial statements must be able to understand the transactions, other events, and conditions that have occurred.

Where offsetting is allowed

If a public sector entity incurs an expense, related to a provision that is reimbursed under a contractual arrangement with a third party (for instance, a supplier's warranty agreement), this may be offset against the related reimbursement.

Gains and losses on the disposal of non-current-assets are reported by deducting from the proceeds on disposal the carrying amount of the asset and the related selling expenses.

It should be noted that, for example, making doubtful debts allowances on receivables or the reduction of property, plant, and equipment by depreciation, reduces the value of the asset, but is not an act of offsetting.

Comparative Information

IPSAS 1 requires that comparative information is disclosed in respect of the previous period for all amounts reported in the financial statements, except when an IPSAS permits or requires differently. Comparative information shall be included for narrative and descriptive information when it is relevant to an understanding of the current period's financial statements (IPSAS 1.53).

For entities adopting IPSAS for the first time there is a transition relief on comparative information. IPSAS 1 stipulates that comparative information is not required in respect of the financial statements for which accrual accounting is first adopted in accordance with IPSAS (IPSAS 1.51). Example 5.2 illustrates what a statement of financial position may look like for a first-time adopter and Chapter 20 is devoted to first-time adoption of IPSAS.

STRUCTURE, FREQUENCY, AND CONTENT OF FINANCIAL STATEMENTS

The purpose of financial statements is to provide information about financial position, financial performance, and cash flows. The objective of IPSAS 1 is to set out the basis for the presentation of financial statements and to ensure comparability with previous periods and with other entities. IPSAS 1 identifies the minimum content that should be included in a set of financial statements as well as guidelines as to how the statements should be structured. IPSAS 1 applies to all general purpose financial statements prepared in accordance with IPSAS (IPSAS 1.2).

It is required under IPSAS 1 (IPSAS 1.66) that the financial statements are issued at least annually. See Example 5.6 for the requirements of a change in year-end taking place. IPSAS further stipulates that the usefulness of financial statements is impaired if they are not made available to users within a reasonable period after the reporting date, and therefore the standard lays down that an entity should be in a position to issue its financial statements within six months of the reporting date. IPSAS 1 states that continuing factors relating to the complexity of an entity's operations are not sufficient reason for failing to report on a timely basis (IPSAS 1.69).

Example 5.6   Change in year-end

If an entity changes its year-end and, as a result, the financial statements report a shorter or longer period, the entity is required to explain why such a change has been made. In addition, where a shorter or longer period is reported, comparative information will not be entirely comparable and it is critical that the entity provides information on this.

Under IPSAS 1 a complete set of financial statements consists of:

- A statement of financial position;
- A statement of financial performance;
- A statement of changes in net assets/equity;
- A cash flow statement;
- Notes, comprising a summary of significant accounting policies and other explanatory information;
- A comparison of budgeted and actual amounts either as a separate additional statement or as a budget column in the financial statements (this requirement only applies for those public sector entities that make their approved budget publicly available).

In addition to prescribing what makes up a complete set of financial statements, IPSAS 1 describes items that, as a minimum, must be presented on the face of each statement.

The financial statements may be included as part of a wider document. IPSAS 1 therefore requires that they should be clearly identified and distinguished from other information presented (IPSAS 1.61). IPSAS 1 also states that each component of the financial statements should be clearly identified (IPSAS 1.63).

Additional information is recognized by IPSAS 1 as being important to support the correct interpretation of information presented. Such information includes, for example, the name of the reporting entity, whether the financial statements are for an individual entity or a group, the period to which the financial statements relate, the currency used to present the financial statements, and the level of rounding used (for examples in thousands or millions).

Statement of Financial Position

The statement of financial position is one of the key financial statements. It is the public sector entity's presentation of its assets, liabilities, and equity. It should be noted that at the end of IPSAS 1, the standard provides illustrative examples of the presentation of the statement of financial position (as well as the statement of financial performance and the statement of changes in net asset/equity).

Financial Reporting in Practice 5.1 is an illustrative example of an IPSAS-compliant statement of financial position, as issued by UNESCO (2013 Financial Statements).[8] Note that this example (and all the other examples throughout this book), are for illustration purposes only. Public sector entities that adopt IPSAS can use their own terminology and can show more detail if necessary. The requirements of the specific standard dealing with the line items respectively should also be taken into account in deciding what should be disclosed as a minimum on the face of the statement of financial position. Note that in IPSAS Financial Reporting in Practice 5.1 one can observe the IPSAS requirement of showing separately receivables and payables from exchange and from non-exchange transactions.

IPSAS Financial Reporting in Practice 5.1 UNESCO, Statement of Financial Position, 2013[9]

I. STATEMENT OF FINANCIAL POSITION AS AT 31 DECEMBER 2013

Expressed in '000 US Dollars	Note	31/12/2013	31/12/2012
ASSETS			
Current Assets			
Cash and cash equivalents	6	146 035	89 289
Short-term investments	7	577 139	556 690
Accounts receivable (non-exchange transactions)	8	19 515	29 367
Receivables for exchange transactions	9	1 724	1 921
Inventories	10	1 203	1 482
Advance payments	11	40 667	34 160
Other current assets	12	4 727	3 053
Total current assets		**791 010**	**715 962**

---

[8] The UNESCO materials can be accessed at en.unesco.org/ (last accessed 15 January 2015).

[9] UNESCO's 2013 financial statements are their fourth set of annual financial statements prepared in accordance with IPSAS.

Non-current assets			
Accounts receivable (non-exchange transactions)	8	1 364	1 485
Long-term investments	7	2 676	2 269
Property, plant and equipment	13	595 287	608 301
Intangible assets	14	280	490
Total non-current assets		**599 607**	**612 545**
TOTAL ASSETS		**1 390 617**	**1 328 507**
LIABILITIES			
Current liabilities			
Accounts payable (exchange transactions)	15	19 700	21 602
Employee benefits	16	23 102	8 930
Transfers payable	17	20 173	23 792
Conditions on voluntary contributions	18	39 619	35 913
Advance receipts	19	148 716	93 772
Current portion of borrowings	20	8 283	7 924
Other current liabilities	21	11 287	13 671
Total current liabilities		**270 880**	**205 604**
Non-current liabilities			
Employee benefits	16	882 518	825 027
Conditions on voluntary contributions	18	2 868	5 203
Long-term loans	20	39 991	43 559
Other non-current liabilities	21	9 884	5 661
Total non-current liabilities		**935 261**	**879 450**
TOTAL LIABILITIES		**1 206 141**	**1 085 054**
NET ASSETS		**184 476**	**243 453**
NET ASSETS/EQUITY			
Reserves and fund balances	22	184 479	243 453
NET ASSETS/EQUITY		**184 476**	**243 453**

Making the distinction between current and non-current

IPSAS 1 stipulates that assets and liabilities are classified as current and non-current assets and liabilities on the face of the statement of financial position (IPSAS 1.70). It should however be noted that it is also allowed to present assets and liabilities in order of liquidity if this provides information that is reliable and more relevant (cf. IPSAS 1.70 and 1.73).

Definition. Current Asset and Current Liabilities

Current Assets	Current Liabilities
An asset that is classified as current must satisfy **one** of the following criteria (IPSAS 1.76). • It is expected to be realized in, or be intended for sale or consumption in, the entity's normal operating cycle; • It is held primarily for trading purposes; • It is expected to be realized within 12 months of the reporting date; or • It is cash or cash equivalent (see IPSAS 2 for a definition on cash and cash equivalents).	A liability that is classified as current must satisfy **one** of the following criteria (IPSAS 1.80): • It is expected to be settled in the entity's normal operating cycle; • It is held primarily for trading purposes; • It is due to be settled within 12 months of the reporting date; • The entity does not have an unconditional right to defer settlement of the liability for at least 12 months after the reporting period.
All other assets are classified as non-current.	All other liabilities are classified as non-current.

The definitions of current assets and current liabilities both refer to an entity's "operating cycle." The operating cycle of an entity is often known as the time between the acquisition of assets for processing and their realization in cash or cash equivalents. For a public sector entity, there is a twist to this that is reflected in IPSAS 1, in that it states that the operating cycle is the time taken to convert inputs or resources into outputs (IPSAS 1.78).

Under each section of current assets or current liabilities, entities will provide sub-classifications. As an example, the illustrative statement of financial position (IPSAS Financial Reporting on Practice 5.1) shows that UNESCO has four sub-classifications of its non-current assets, namely: accounts receivable, long-term investments, property, plant and equipment,[10] and intangible assets.

In preparing an IPSAS-compliant statement of financial position, a public sector entity shall, following paragraph 1.80, include the line items below that present the following amounts at the face of the statement:

(a) Property, plant, and equipment;
(b) Investment property;
(c) Intangible assets;
(d) Financial assets (excluding amounts shown under (e), (g), (h) and (i));
(e) Investments accounted for using the equity method;
(f) Inventories;
(g) Recoverables from non-exchange transactions (taxes and transfers);
(h) Receivables from exchange transactions;
(i) Cash and cash equivalents;

[10] IPSAS 17 on Property, Plant and Equipment will provide guidance on disaggregation of PP&E.

(j) Taxes and transfers payable;
(k) Payables under exchange transactions;
(l) Provisions;
(m) Financial liabilities (excluding amounts shown under (j), (k), and (l));
(n) Minority interest, presented within net assets/equity; and
(o) Net assets/equity attributable to owners of the controlling entity.

Additional headings, sub-classifications, and subtotals can be used either on the face of the statement of financial position or in the notes if it aids the users' understanding of the entity's financial position (IPSAS 1.89 and 1.93) or to meet the requirements of other standards.

The following additional information must be given about each class of share capital (IPSAS 1.98):

- Number of shares authorized, issued and fully paid up, and issued but not fully paid up;
- Par value per share;
- A reconciliation of number of shares outstanding at the start and end of the period;
- Rights, preferences, and restrictions if appropriate;
- Shares held by the entity in itself or held by its subsidiaries or associates;
- Shares reserved for issue under options.

In addition, a full reconciliation of the movement during the year in the number of shares outstanding is required, specifying any rights, preferences, and restrictions attaching to the shares. Disclosure should also be made of any shares in the entity, held by the entity or by its subsidiaries or associates, and any shares reserved for issue under options and contracts for the sale of shares.

Many public sector entities will not have share capital and in such cases IPSAS 1 requires net assets/equity to be disclosed either on the face of the statement of financial position or in the notes, showing separately (IPSAS 1.95):

- Contributed capital;
- Accumulated surpluses or deficits;
- Reserves;
- Minority interest.

First-time adoption and the statement of financial position

As highlighted earlier, comparative information is not compulsory in respect of the financial statements for which accrual accounting is first adopted in accordance with IPSAS (IPSAS 1.151). IPSAS Financial Reporting in Practice 5.2 illustrates what the statement of financial position can look like if the public sector entity opts to include three columns, to show (1) the audited closing balances of 2011 (non-IPSAS compliant); (2) the restated IPSAS-compliant opening balances of 2012 and (3) the balances as at 31 December 2012. UNAIDS (2013) describe in the introduction to their financial statements that the application of IPSAS entailed some modification to the presentation and structure of the financial statements. UNAIDS note that the adoption of the new accounting policies has resulted in changes to the assets and liabilities recognized in the statement of financial position. Therefore, the audited statement of financial position, dated 31 December 2011, was restated and the resulting changes are reported in the Statement of Changes in Net Assets/Equity and under note 3 on first-time implementation of IPSAS (the chapter on first-time adoption of IPSAS will explore these matters in more detail).

IPSAS Financial Reporting in Practice 5.2 provides an illustration of the statement of financial performance for the first-time IPSAS financial statements of UNAIDS.

IPSAS Financial Reporting in Practice 5.2. First-time adoption, UNAID Statement of financial position. All sources of funds as at 31 December 2012 (in US dollars)

	Note	31 December 2012	1 January 2012 (opening balance restated)	31 December 2011 (as audited)
ASSETS				
Current assets				
Cash and cash equivalents held by WHO	4.1	204 672 570	240 468 956	240 599 111
Accounts receivable – current	4.2	77 358 261	81 996 207	81 996 207
Advances to UNDP		–	–	9301705
Staff receivables	4.3	1 682960	1 982 795	–
Other receivables	4.4	–	144 670	871 597
Prepayments	4.5	20 475 470	10 504 961	1 203 256
Total current assets		**304 189 261**	**335 097 589**	**333 971 876**
Non-current assets				
Accounts receivable – non-current	4.2	7 560 611	5 398 050	5 398 050
Property, plant and equipment	4.5	23 367 086	23 478 989	25 613 444
Total non-current assets		30 927 697	28 877 039	31 011 494
TOTAL ASSETS		**335 116 958**	**363 974 628**	**364 983 370**
LIABILITIES				
Current liabilities				
Deferred revenue – current	4.7	18 811 463	27 242 365	27 242 365
Accounts payable	4.8	2 403 108	1 659 863	1 715 092

Staff payable	4.9	419 033	55 229	–
Employee benefits	4.10	10 044 304	11 339 025	–
Other liabilities	4.12	235 612	891 616	891 616
Total current liabilities		31 913 520	41 188 098	29 849 073
Non-current liabilities				
Employee benefits	4.10	52 083 403	47 125 287	13 243 279
Deferred revenue – non-current	4.7	7 560 611	5 398 050	5 398 050
Long-term borrowings	4.11	21 172 074	22 036 297	21 058 670
Total non-current liabilities		80 816 088	74 559 634	39 699 999
TOTAL LIABILITIES		**112 729 608**	**115 747 732**	**69 549 072**
NET ASSETS/EQUITY				
Net assets/reserves	4.15			
Operating reserve fund	4.16	35 000 000	35 000 000	35 000 000
Equity in capital assets		4 010 562	3 480 643	4 458 270
Depreciation reserve		(2 634 076)	(2 134 455)	–
Non-restricted	4.17	164 887 579	211 570 482	211 700 637
Restricted		46 244 636	44 275 391	44 275 391
Building renovation fund		2 600 000	–	–
Staff benefits		(31 667 752)	(49 556 503)	–
Non-payroll entitlements fund		3 946 401	5 591 338	–
TOTAL NET ASSETS/EQUITY		**222 387 350**	**248 226 896**	**295 434 298**
TOTAL LIABILITIES AND NET ASSETS/EQUITY		**335 116 958**	**363 974 628**	**364 983 370**

Statement of Financial Performance

The statement of financial performance shows the reader of the financial statements the entity's performance during the financial year. It includes revenue and expenses and the net total of these provides the surplus or deficit for the period.

IPSAS 1 requires that the statement of financial performance includes only the items which are required to be recognized in surplus or deficit. This means that the items below need to be presented on the face of the statement of financial performance:

- Revenue;
- Finance costs;
- Share of the surplus or deficit of associates and joint ventures accounted for using the equity method;

- Pre-tax gain or loss recognized on the disposal of assets or settlement of liabilities attributable to the discounted operations; and
- Surplus deficit for the financial period.

There is a requirement to include additional information on the face of the statement (or in the notes) relating to other events that result in changes in the components of net assets/equity such as the amounts of transactions with owners acting in their capacity as owners, showing separately distributions as owners (IPSAS 1.119–1.125).

Where the nature and amount of items of revenue and expenses are material they are disclosed separately. For example, IPSAS Financial Reporting in Practice 5.3 illustrates that UNESCO, in their 2013 financial statements, categorized their revenue into six material line items and a line item for other/miscellaneous revenue.

IPSAS Financial Reporting in Practice 5.3. UNESCO 2013 Statement of Financial Performance based on a Presentation of Expenses by Nature

II. STATEMENT OF FINANCIAL POSITION FOR THE YEAR ENDED 31 DECEMBER 2013

Expressed in '000 US Dollars	Note	31/12/2013	31/12/2012
			Restated
REVENUE			
Assessed contributions		358 616	352 970
Voluntary contributions		369 196	391 278
Other revenue producing activities		19 470	17 801
Other/miscellaneous revenue		17 368	17 828
Foreign exchange gains		2 976	602
Finance revenue		11 502	11 960
Total revenue	23	**779 128**	**792 439**
EXPENSES			
Employee expenses		402 061	383 234
Consultants, external experts and mission costs		49 882	42 282
External training, grants and other transfers		55 890	61 221
Supplies, consumables and other running costs		58 696	61 988
Contracted services		130 844	132 911
Depreciation and amortization		18 734	19 024
Allowance for assessed contributions		83 058	79 267
Other expenses		2 220	5 243
Finance costs		9 428	7 211
Total expenses	23	**810 813**	**792 381**
SURPLUS/(DEFICIT) FOR THE PERIOD		**−31 685**	**58**

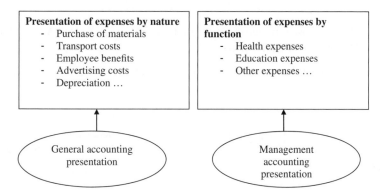

Figure 5.1   The two methods of presentation of the statement of financial performance

An entity should choose its expenses classification method based on which one would provide the most relevant and reliable information (see Figure 5.1 below). If an entity chooses to present expenses by function, it must still provide separate disclosure of depreciation, amortization, and employee benefit expense (IPSAS 1.115).

Example 5.7   Expense classification

If a public sector entity chooses this format they may define and use their own functional headings, but it is important to note that it is not permitted to "mix up" costs by function and nature on the face of the performance statement.

Example 5.8   Disclosure of significant estimates and judgments made by management

Health expenses	XXXX
Education expenses	XXXX
Social protection	XXXX
Other expenses	XXXX
Finance costs	XXXX
Total expenses	XXXX

Example 5.9   Expenses by nature and function. United Kingdom Ministry of Defence, 2013 Financial Statements[11]

Statements of Comprehensive Net Expenditure (SoCNE) for the year ended 31 March 2013

	Note	Core Department £000	2012–13 Departmental Group £000	Core Department £000	2011–12 Departmental Group £000
Administration costs					
Staff costs	6.2	2 100 182	2 100 182	2 505 314	2 505 314
Other administration costs	7.1	44 548	44 548	18 316	18 316
Total administration costs		**2 144 730**	**2 144 730**	**2 523 630**	**2 523 630**
Programme costs					
Staff costs	6.2	9 836 452	9 923 254	10 334 868	10 423 509
Other programme costs	7.2	26 723 578	26 697 617	26 979 082	26 961 894
Gross programme costs		**36 560 030**	**36 620 871**	**37 313 950**	**37 385 403**
Operating income	8	(1 380 212)	(1 494 429)	(1 345 504)	(1 405 930)
Net programme cost before interest		**35 179 818**	**35 126 442**	**35 968 446**	**35 979 473**
Net interest payable/ (receivable)	9	433 433	433 075	479 466	479 294
Net programme cost		**35 613 251**	**35 559 517**	**36 447 912**	**36 458 767**
Net operating cost	3.1	**37 757 981**	**37 704 247**	**38 971 542**	**38 982 397**

Example 5.9 is drawn from the UK's Ministry of Defence for the year ended 31 March 2013. It should be highlighted that following IPSAS one does *not* prepare a statement of comprehensive net expenditure. Example 5.8 is included to illustrate

[11] This example was highlighted to us by IASeminars (www.iaseminars.co.uk).

how expenses can be presented when combining expenses by nature and function. The UK public sector has adopted a financial reporting framework based upon IFRS as adapted by the UK to the public sector context and informed by IPSAS. The format in their statement of comprehensive net expenditure separates elements of expense by broad function, e.g., administration and program costs and then within the functional analysis separates the main elements of cost by nature, which are staff costs, from other elements. While IPSAS says that costs by function and nature should not be "mixed up," the presentation adopted here clearly shows the costs by nature within their appropriate costs by function and that would be an acceptable presentation under IPSAS, if adopted within a statement of financial performance. This example thus illustrates a combination of expense by cost and nature, rather than "mixing" them up.

IPSAS Financial Reporting in Practice 5.4. First-time Adoption UNAID Statement of Financial Performance, all sources of funds as at 31 December 2012 (in US dollars)

STATEMENT II STATEMENT OF FINANCIAL PERFORMANCE ALL SOURCES OF FUNDS FOR THE YEAR ENDED 31 DECEMBER 2012

(in US Dollars)	Notes	31 December 2013
REVENUE		
Voluntary contributions	5.2	
Governments		234 695 113
Cosponsoring organizations		4 211 767
Others		8 966 635
Financial revenue	5.3	5 670 510
Total revenue		**253 544 025**
EXPENSES		
Salary and other personnel costs		129 932 894
Transfers and grants to counterparts		94 942 607
Contractual services		28 302 720
General operating expenses		14 015 173
Travel		7 477 129
Equipment, vehicles and furniture		1 385 764
Depreciation		499 621
Finance costs		3 357 583
Total expenses		**279 913 491**
SURPLUS/(DEFICIT) FOR THE PERIOD		**(26 369 466)**

The Statement of Changes in Net Assets/Equity

The statement of changes in net assets/equity explains the fluctuations in the net wealth of the entity during the financial year. The overall change in the net assets represents:

1. Total surplus or deficit for the period;
2. Revenue or expenses directly recognized as a change in net assets; and
3. Contributions by and distribution to owners in their capacity as owners.

The following is an illustrative example of what should be shown, as a minimum, on the face of the statement of changes in net assets.

Example 5.10   Statement of changes in net assets

		R
20x0		
Balance as at 31 March 20x0		**XXX**
Correction of error	x	XX
Changed in accounting policy	x	(XX)
Restated balance at 31 March 20x0		**XXX**
Surplus for the period		XX
20x1		
Balance as at 31 March 20x1		**XXX**
Deficit for the period		(XX)
Balance as at 31 March 20x1		**XXX**

IPSAS Financial Reporting in Practice 5.5 provides an example of how UNESCO drew up their statement of changes in net assets/equity.

IPSAS Financial Reporting in Practice 5.5 UNESCO 2013 Statement of Changes in Net Assets/Equity

III. STATEMENT OF CHANGES IN NET ASSETS/EQUITY FOR THE YEAR ENDED 31 DECEMBER 2013

Expressed in '000 US Dollars	Note	31/12/2013	31/12/2012 Restated
NET ASSETS/EQUITY AT THE BEGINNING OF THE PERIOD		243 453	250 321

Exchange differences on certain foreign currency transactions	22	−11 495	−9 612
Increase in Working Capital Fund	22	138	992
Actuarial gain/(loss)	22	1 866	23 734
Other adjustments	22	−14 446	−8 016
Return of funds to donors	22	−3 355	−14 024
Total of item recognized directly in Net Assets/Equity		**−27 292**	**−6 926**
Surplus/(Deficit) for the period	22	−31 685	58
Total recognized revenue and expense for the period		**−58 977**	**−6 868**
NET ASSETS/EQUITY AT THE END OF THE PERIOD		**184 476**	**243 453**

IPSAS 1 provides further guidance and example illustrations on the presentation of the above statements to support consideration of the relevant issues.

Notes to the Financial Statements

The notes are an integral part of the financial statements and provide additional relevant information to ensure that users can fully understand the financial statements of an entity. Notes can be in a number of forms, for example: narrative disclosures, disaggregation of information presented on the face of the component statements, or additional information which has not been recognized in the balance sheet but is relevant to the understanding of the financial statements (IPSAS 1.128).

Notes to the financial statements can be divided into two sections:

- Notes that support the line items in the statement of financial position, statement of financial performance, statement of change in net assets, and the cash flow statement. This could for example be notes on property, plant, and equipment and cash and cash equivalents, and so forth.
- Notes that do not necessarily relate to line items in the financial statements. Examples include the accounting policies, contingent liabilities, unrecognized contractual commitments, and non-financial disclosures such as an entity's financial risk management policy and procedures, and so forth.

Following IPSAS 1, the notes will include the following (see IPSAS 1.127, 1.132, 1.140, 1.149, and 1.150):

- Present information about the basis of preparation of the financial statements and significant accounting policies including details of the measurement basis used in preparing the financial statements and details of other accounting policies relevant to an understanding of the financial statements;
- Disclose key sources of estimation uncertainty (e.g., key assumptions);

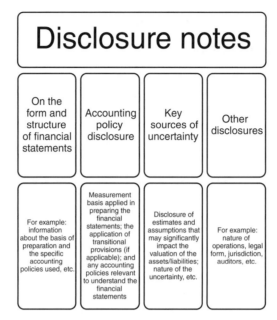

Figure 5.2   Key categories of notes

- Disclose information required by IFRS that is not presented on the face of any of the primary statements;
- Provide additional relevant information;
- Be presented in a systematic manner;
- Disclose information to enable evaluation of the entity's policies and processes for managing capital;
- Disclose dividends proposed or declared but not recognized and the related amount per share;
- Disclose the domicile and legal form of the entity, its country of incorporation, and address of its registered office;
- Disclose a description of the entity's operations and principal activities;
- Disclose the name of the entity's parent and ultimate parent.
  The listed requirements can be divided into four key themes (see Figure 5.2).

Specific disclosure requirements can either be found in the IPSAS dealing with specific disclosure matters (such as IPSAS 22 on the Disclosure of Financial Information about the General Government Sector) or they can be located in together with requirements in other IPSAS (for example IPSAS 31 Intangible Assets).

Estimation of Uncertainty – Key Sources

Using accounting estimates and the exercise of judgment are an essential part of the preparation of financial statements. Determining the carrying amount of some assets and liabilities requires estimation of the effect of uncertain future events on the assets and liabilities at the reporting date. The estimates can involve specific assumptions, such as, for example: what discount rate to use, future cash flows, or what risk rate should be used to adjust future cash flows and future changes in prices.

The key sources of estimation uncertainty that could cause a material adjustment to the carrying amount of assets and liabilities in the next period should be disclosed. These assumptions and uncertainties need to be disclosed in such a way that the users of the financial statements understand the judgments made by management.

Examples of estimations

Estimation of the amount of inventory to be written off due to obsolescence;

The fair value of accounts receivable and payable;

The useful lives and residual values.

Examples of judgments

Whether assets are investment properties;

Whether some sales of goods constitute financing arrangements in substance and therefore do not give rise to revenue;

When substantially all the significant risks and rewards of ownership of financial assets and lease assets are transferred to other entities.

As described in the above section on disclosure notes, it is required to disclose information on key estimation uncertainty and judgments made. It should be highlighted that the entity should not only disclose the nature of these, but also the reasons why there is uncertainty and the impact this has on the amounts presented in the financial statements to which it relates. IPSAS Financial Reporting in Practice 5.6. illustrates the disclosure of significant estimates and judgments made by management.

IPSAS Financial Reporting in Practice 5.6. UNAIDS Note on Use of Estimates, Financial Statements, 2013

Note. 2.19 Use of estimates

The financial statements necessarily include amounts based on estimates and assumptions by management. Estimates include, but are not limited to: defined benefit medical insurance and other post-employment benefit obligations (the value of which is calculated by an independent actuary), financial risk on accounts receivable accrued charges, and the degree of impairment of fixed assets. Actual results could differ from these estimates. Changes in estimates are reflected in the period in which they become known.

If we then, for example, look at employee benefits and the use of estimates (p. 42, UNAIDS 2013 Financial Statements), we will find that:

Staff Health Insurance rule 470 A stipulates that a reserve is maintained in the Trust Fund, equal to:

- an amount corresponding to one-third of the previous year's reimbursements, for settlement of outstanding claims should the Insurance have to be liquidated; plus

- an amount which the Headquarters Surveillance Committee **estimates** to be required based on actuarial projections to cover the projected costs of benefits to current retirees (former staff insured under paragraphs 60 and 90.3), to the extent that **such estimated costs** will not be met by contributions received in respect of such persons.
- an amount which the Headquarters Surveillance Committee estimates to be required based on actuarial projections to cover the projected costs of benefits to future retirees (staff members insured under paragraphs 30 and 50), to the extent that such **estimated costs** will not be met by contributions received in respect of such persons.

Cash Flow Statement

IPSAS 1 Presentation of Financial Statements sets out the content of an entity's financial statements and includes the requirement for a statement of cash flows to be presented. IPSAS 2 Statement of Cash Flows is to provide information about the historical changes in cash and cash equivalents of an entity.[12] As such the cash flow statement provides information regarding the entity's ability to use and/or generate cash and cash equivalents. All public sector entities that prepare their accounts under IPSAS must prepare a cash flow statement and present it as an integral part of the financial statements (IPSAS 2.1, 2.3).

Cash is defined as cash-in-hand and demand deposits (IPSAS 2.8). Cash equivalents are short-term, highly liquid investments that are readily convertible into known amounts of cash and which are subject to an insignificant risk of changes in value (IPSAS 2.8).

Example 5.11   Cash equivalents

Cash equivalents are held for the purpose of meeting short-term cash commitments. To meet the definition of a cash equivalent, the item should be "readily convertible" which suggests that it has a short maturity of, say, three months or less from the date of acquisition. Cash equivalents may therefore include:

- Short-term deposits and government securities;
- Short-term loan notes;
- Bank deposit accounts.

Equity investments are normally excluded as they are subject to a significant risk of changes in value. This differs from government securities that are not exposed to the risk of significant change in value.

---

[12] Cash is a fundamental part of entities operating cycles. It is possible for an entity reporting profit or surplus to have liquidity problems if it does not effectively manage the flow of cash. Cash denotes the liquidity of an entity and hence cash flows provide an apprehension of the change in that liquidity.

Bank borrowings can be a part of an entity's financing activities. A bank overdraft however, is often used as a key element of an entity's daily cash management. In such circumstances the overdraft should be included as a component of cash and cash equivalents.

IPSAS Financial Reporting in Practice 5.7. UNESCO Note on Cash and Cash Equivalents, 2013 Financial Statements

Expressed in '000 US dollars	31/12/2013	31/12/2012
Cash with banks	145 984	89 242
Cash in hand	48	47
Total cash and cash equivalents	**146 035**	**89 289**

Cash is principally held in UNESCO Headquarters interest bearing euro and US dollar bank accounts including cashable investments that amounted to K$133,086 and generated an average return of 0.25% in USD and 0.56% in EUR. A limited amount of cash balances are also held on the Headquarters interest bearing convertible currency accounts, field offices and Institutes US dollar and local currency accounts.

Cash and cash equivalents include K$73,762 available under proprietary funds. The remaining balance of K$72,273 is held by UNESCO in a fiduciary capacity (see Note 5 Segment Information).

Restricted cash

IPSAS 2 (para. 61) stipulates that additional information can be useful to readers of the financial statement in understanding the financial position and liquidity of an entity. Disclosure of this information, together with a description in the notes to the financial statements, is therefore encouraged, and can include:

(a) The amount of undrawn borrowing facilities that may be obtainable for future operating activities and to settle capital commitments, indicating any restrictions on the use of these facilities;
(b) The aggregate amounts of the cash flows from each of operating, investing, and financing activities related to interests in joint ventures reported using proportionate consolidation; and
(c) The amount and nature of restricted cash balances.

Restricted cash (and cash equivalents) is reported as a non-current asset. Restricted cash and cash equivalents are resources that are available only for specific purposes. Therefore these resources are not available for immediate and/or general use (see for example Wang, 2014). Restrictions can, for example, include legally restricted deposits held as compensating balances against short-term borrowing arrangements, contracts entered into with others, or company statements of intention with regard to particular deposits; however, time deposits and short-term certificates of deposit are not generally included in legally restricted deposits (EY, 2014). As can be seen in IPSAS Financial Reporting Practice 5.8, UNESCO (2013) highlight that their cash and cash equivalents held in a fiduciary capacity are considered restricted.

IPSAS Financial Reporting in Practice 5.8 UNESCO Accounting Policy Note on Cash and Cash Equivalents, Financial Statements, 2013 (p. 39)

2.5 CASH AND CASH EQUIVALENTS

Cash and cash equivalents includes cash in hand, deposits held at call with banks and other short-term highly liquid investments that are readily convertible to cash and subject to an insignificant risk of changes in value. Cash and cash equivalents held in a fiduciary capacity (Programme Fiduciary Funds and Staff Fiduciary Funds) that can only be used for a specific purpose are considered as restricted.

Question and Answer: Restricted and unrestricted cash and cash equivalents

Question:

Is restricted cash part of cash and cash equivalent?

Answer:

IPSAS 1.76 states:
"An asset shall be classified as current when it satisfies any of the following criteria:

(a) It is expected to be realized in, or is held for sale or consumption in, the entity's normal operating cycle;
(b) It is held primarily for the purpose of being traded;
(c) It is expected to be realized within twelve months after the reporting date; or
(d) It is cash or a cash equivalent (as defined in IPSAS 2), unless it is restricted from being exchanged or used to settle a liability for at least twelve months after the reporting date."

It does mean that, from a practical point of view, cash which is restricted from being exchanged or used to settle a liability for at least 12 months after the reporting date cannot be classified as current asset. It does not answer the question. From the above criteria, nothing prevents an entity from presenting restricted cash in cash and cash equivalent.

IPSAS 2.57 specifies: "In view of the variety of cash management practices and banking arrangements around the world, and in order to comply with IPSAS 1, an entity discloses the policy that it adopts in determining the composition of cash and cash equivalents." It does mean that the entity may well choose to classify restricted cash in cash and cash equivalent, or else may choose not to do so. In any case, the entity is to disclose the adopted policy concerning restricted cash presentation as long as it is material.

The entity is encouraged to disclose the amount and nature of restricted cash balances as stated in IPSAS 2.61, in the notes to the financial statements because this additional information may be relevant to users in understanding the financial position and liquidity of an entity.

As a conclusion, restricted cash may or may not be part of cash and cash equivalent, depending on the policy chosen by the entity.

Another illustrative example is the financial statements of the OECD (2013) that show to the reader in the disclosure note on cash and cash equivalents the breakdown between non-restricted and restricted cash. The note also explains to the reader how the restricted cash is constituted.

IPSAS Financial Reporting in Practice 5.9. OECD disclosure on restricted cash (2013, p. 17)

Note 5: Cash and cash equivalents

	31 December 2013 '000	31 December 2012 '000
Cash on hand	6	5
Deposits with banks unrestricted – euros	126 556	129 698
Deposits with banks unrestricted – other currencies	1 213	2 325
Total unrestricted cash	**127 775**	**132 028**
Deposits with banks restricted	34 285	31 158
Deposits with banks and cash equivalents – PBRF	18 998	18 144
Total restricted cash	**53 283**	**49 302**
Total cash and cash equivalents	**181 058**	**181 330**

OECD extended explanation on restricted cash (Disclosure note 5).
Restricted cash and cash equivalents (53.3 M at 31 December 2013) are deposits earmarked for specific purposes. Appropriations are to reserves; the breakdown and movements in the reserves are described in Note 18 to the Financial Statements.

- Funds allocated to the Capital Investment Budget Reserve Fund (CIBRF), initially sourced from proceeds received from the sale in 2004 of offices at Chardon Lagache, amounted to 15.4 M at 31 December 2013 (13.7 M at 31 December 2012).
- Funds allocated to the Post Employment Healthcare Liability (PEHL) Reserve, which were initially sourced from the Medical Plan reserve and the equalisation provision of the insurance contract, amounted to 18.9 M at 31 December 2013 (17.5 M at 31 December 2012).
- Funds from the Pension Budget and Reserve Fund (PBRF). PBRF assets, including cash deposits, are restricted to the payment of pension benefits and Fund administration expenses as defined by the Fund's Statutes. As at 31 December 2013, these cash holdings and bank deposits accounted for 4.3% of the PBRF's total assets, versus 4.8% at 31 December 2012. At 31 December, these corresponded to the estimated amount of cash and cash equivalents that, along with contributions receipts, are needed for benefit disbursements.

The Organisation has no confirmed credit lines but does maintain limited and informal overdraft arrangements with its banks. These arrangements may be withdrawn by the banks at any time. No borrowing was done on overdraft facilities in 2013 or in 2012.

Foreign currency cash

Accounting for foreign currency transactions is dealt with in IPSAS 4 accounting for the effects of changes in foreign exchange rates. The translation of foreign currency cash flows should be consistent with the application of IPSAS 4.26.

Although changes in foreign exchange rates are not cash flows, the effect of exchange rate changes on cash or cash equivalents held or due in a foreign currency are reported in the cash flow statement in order to reconcile cash and cash equivalents at the beginning and the end of the period. These amounts are to be presented separately from cash flows from operating, investing, and financing activities, and include the differences, if any, if those cash flows had been reported at end-of-period exchange rates.

Where an entity has a foreign controlled entity, its cash flows should be translated to the functional currency at the exchange rates on the dates that the cash flows occurred (IPSAS 2.37).

Non-cash transactions

Non-cash transactions, such as investing and financing transactions that do not impact cash (for example purchasing a building in exchange for equity), should not be included in the statement of cash flows. However, IPSAS 2 stipulates that such transactions, and their impact, have to be disclosed elsewhere in the financial statements as appropriate (IPSAS 2.54).

Presentation and structure of cash flow statement

The statement of cash flows classifies cash flows under the following headings (IPSAS 2.18) as shown in Table 5.1:

Table 5.1   Classification of cash flows

Headings	Definitions and explanation
Operating activities	The activities of the entity that are not investing or financing activities (IPSAS 2.8).
Investing activities	The acquisition and disposal of long-term assets and other investments not included in cash equivalents (IPSAS 2.8).
Financing activities	Activities that result in changes in the size and composition of the contributed capital and borrowings of the entity (IPSAS 2.8).

Tables 5.2–5.4 below illustrate examples of cash in and cash out for the three sections of the cash flow statement:

Table 5.2   Examples of cash flows arising from operating activities

Statement of financial position element	Cash in	Cash out
Tax receivables	Cash receipts from taxes	
Inventories	Cash receipts from charges for goods and services provided by the entity	Cash payments to suppliers for goods
Suppliers		Cash payments to suppliers for services
Prepayment	Cash received in advance	
Interest	Interest received	Interest paid
Employees		Cash payments to and on behalf of employees
Provisions		Cash payments in relation to litigation settlements
Tax payables	Cash payments of local property taxes or income taxes (where appropriate) in relation to operating activities	

Table 5.3　Examples of cash flows arising from investing activities

Statement of financial position element	Cash in	Cash out
Property, plant, and equipment	Cash receipts from sales of property, plant, and equipment	Cash payments to acquire property, plant, and equipment. These payments include those relating to capitalized development costs and self-constructed property, plant, and equipment.
Equity or debt instruments of other entities and interests in joint ventures	Cash receipts from sales of equity or debt instruments of other entities and interests in joint ventures (other than receipts for those instruments considered to be cash equivalents and those held for dealing or trading purposes)	Cash payments to acquire equity or debt instruments of other entities and interests in joint ventures (other than payments for those instruments considered to be cash equivalents or those held for dealing or trading purposes)
Cash advances and loans made to other parties	Cash receipts from the repayment of advances and loans made to other parties (other than advances and loans of a public financial institution)	Cash advances and loans made to other parties (other than advances and loans made by a public financial institution)

Table 5.4　Examples of cash flows arising from financing activities

Statement of financial position element	Cash in	Cash out
Debentures, loans, notes, bonds, mortgages	Cash proceeds from issuing debentures, loans, notes, bonds, mortgages	Cash repayments of amounts borrowed
Liability relating to a finance lease		Cash payments by a lessee for the reduction of the outstanding liability relating to a finance lease

---

IPSAS Financial Reporting in Practice 5.10. Illustrative example of cash flow statement of UNESCO (2013)

IV. CASH FLOW STATEMENT FOR THE YEAR ENDED 31 DECEMBER 2013

Expressed in '000 US Dollars	Note	31/12/2013	31/12/2012 Restated
Cash flows from operating activities			
Surplus/(Deficit) for the period		−31 685	58
Depreciation and amortization		18 734	19 024
(Increase)/Decrease in accounts receivable		10 120	−5 418
Decrease in inventories		300	3 007
(Increase)/Decrease in advance payments		−6 987	9 242

(Increase)/Decrease in other current assets	−10 596	1 167
(Decrease) in accounts payable	−1 328	−7 855
Increase in employee benefits	59 552	42 886
(Decrease) in transfers payable	−1 958	−14 024
Increase in borrowings due to revaluations	1 768	1 342
(Decrease) in investments due to revaluations	–	−10
Increase in conditions on voluntary contributions	4 347	4 216
Increase/(Decrease) in advance receipts	53 939	−24 425
Increase/(Decrease) in other liabilities	7 739	−8 894
Loss/Gain on disposal of property, plant and equipment	−103	361
Net cash flows from operating activities	**103 842**	**20 677**
Cash flows from investing activities		
Purchase of property, plant and equipment	−5 510	−3 536
Purchase of intangible assets	−44	−378
Sale of property, plant and equipment	468	–
(Increase) in short-term investments	−33 212	−34 118
(Increase) in long-term investments	−407	−722
Net cash flows from investing activities	**−38 705**	**−38 754**
Cash flows from financing activities		
Repayment of loans	−8 077	−7 829
Increase in working capital contributions	138	992
Net cash flows from financing activities	**−7 939**	**−6 837**
NET INCREASE/(DECREASE) IN CASH AND CASH EQUIVALENTS	**57 198**	**−24 914**

In reviewing IPSAS Financial Reporting in Practice 5.10 it should be noted that interest paid can be part of operating activities in the cash flow statement if it is part of the surplus or deficit reported by the entity in its statement of financial performance. Interest received can be shown as part of the investing activities or as part of the operating or financing activities (IPSAS 2.40).

IPSAS 2 however also permits interest paid to be reported as part of the entity's financing or investing activities (IPSAS 2.40). It can be deduced from the cash flow statement of UNESCO above that interest paid is included in financing activities, in "repayment of loans."

If an entity has any dividends received this can be shown as part of the investing activities or can be reported as part of the operating or financing activities (IPSAS 2.40).

It is important to note that cash flows and dividends or similar distributions received or paid are classified on a consistent basis and are separately disclosed under the activity appropriate to their nature.

In terms of the structure of the cash flow statement it should be noted that the separate line items set out under the required cash flow headings should represent the major classes of gross cash receipts and payments arising for each of the activities (IPSAS 2.31) of the entity. This is of course not obvious for operating activities presented under the indirect method, which is the case for the cash flow statement of UNESCO.

In some specific cases cash flows from operating, investing, or financing activities may be reported on a net basis under the relevant cash flow heading. Transactions that may be shown net may include, for example, the collection of taxes by one level of government for another level of government. Cash flows may also be presented on a net basis where the related inflow and outflow takes place within a short time frame, where the cash flows are large, and the maturity dates are within three months. Examples are the purchase and sale of the same investment, or advances made for and the repayment of short-term borrowings that have a maturity period of three months or less (IPSAS 2.32).

Cash flows from operating activities

The cash flows from an entity's operating activities can be prepared using one of two permitted methods (IPSAS 2.27), as shown in Table 5.5:

Table 5.5 Methods for preparation of cash flows from operating activities

Method	The direct method	The indirect method
Description	The direct method discloses the major classes of gross cash receipts and payments	In using the indirect method, the entity starts with the net surplus or deficit for the period and then adjusts it for non-cash transactions, deferrals or accruals of past or future operating cash receipts or payments, and items of revenue or expense that will form part of the entity's investing and financing cash flows.
Examples	The direct method shows the actual cash flows that are part of the operating activities of the entity. Such cash flows should therefore include, for example: • payments to suppliers • receipts from clients/other entities • payments to employees • other payments and receipts made or received as part of the entity's operating activities. Where this approach is adopted, the information will generally be obtained from the entity's accounting records directly.	The indirect method of calculating the cash flows from an entity's operating activities makes adjustments to the net surplus or deficit for the period. The adjustments are for non-cash transactions, deferrals, or accruals of income and expenditure and for items that will form part of the investing and financing activities of the entity (IPAS 2.27).

Regardless of the method applied, i.e., the direct or the indirect method of calculating net cash flow from operating activities, the same end result will be achieved.

According to IPSAS 2.45, entities reporting cash flows from operating activities using the direct method are also encouraged to report a reconciliation of the surplus/deficit from ordinary activities with the net cash flow from operating activities, as part of the cash flow statement or in the notes to the financial statements.

Cash flows arising from taxes on net surplus must be separately disclosed and classified as cash flows from operating activities, unless they can be specifically identified with financing and investing activities (IPSAS 2.44). Although public sector entities are generally exempt from taxes on net surpluses, some public sector entities may operate under tax-equivalent regimes, where taxes are levied in the same way as they are on private sector entities. For these entities, while tax expense may be readily identifiable with investing or financing activities, the related tax cash flows are often impracticable to identify, and may arise in a different period from the cash flows of the underlying transaction. Therefore, IPSAS 2.46 states that taxes paid are usually classified as cash flows from operating activities. This is actually what most private sector entities using IFRS do.

Example 5.12   Treatment of taxes in the cash flow statement

Although net surplus-based taxes may relate to items throughout the statement of cash flows, it may not be practicable to identify separately the elements of tax which relate to each of the three components of the statement of cash flows. As a result, tax will normally be reported as part of an entity's operating activities, although it may be split between the relevant headings where it is practicable to do so (IPSAS 2.44) (see IPSAS Financial Reporting in Practice 5.11).

The cash flow in relation to tax should be separately identified in the statement of cash flows and, where it has been allocated between the different headings, a total should be disclosed (IPSAS 2.46).

IPSAS Financial Reporting in Practice 5.11 below illustrates property taxes and taxation paid as components of operating activities.

IPSAS Financial Reporting in Practice 5.11. EY IPSAS model financial statements

	Notes	2013 €000	2012 €000
Cash flows from operating activities			
Receipts			
Property taxes		5 387 898	4 589 492

Public contributions and donations	63 661	79 920
Fines, penalties and levies	1 781 670	1 677 436
Licenses and permits	41 471	37 645
Government grants and subsidies	4 314 907	2 635 544
Rendering of services	1 442 398	1 745 995
Sale of goods	9 257 191	8 201 772
Finance income	454 183	408 496
Other income, rentals and agency fees	315 281	290 668
	23 058 660	**19 666 768**
Payments		
Compensation of employees	10 914 327	9 301 878
Goods and services	5 934 897	5 686 507
Finance cost	663 394	710 888
Rent paid	23 789	21 164
Taxation paid	4 663	9 981
Other payments	156 293	139 449
Grants and subsidies paid	103 502	93 393
	17 800 865	**15 963 260**

Net cash flows from operating activities	45	**5 257 795**	**3 703 508**
Cash flows from investing activities			
Purchase of property, plant, equipment and intangible assets		(4 253 098)	(2 895 348)
Proceeds from sale of property, plant and equipment		46 066	63 544
Decrease in non-current receivables		15 633	1 819
Increase in investments		(736 806)	(1 962 720)
Net cash flows used in investing activities		**(4 928 205)**	**(4 792 705)**
Cash flows from financing activities			
Proceeds from borrowings		431	335
Repayments of borrowings		(199 363)	(262 568)
Increase in deposits		46 746	2 102
Net cash flows used in financing activities		**(152 186)**	**(260 131)**
Net increase/(decrease) in cash and cash equivalents		177 404	(1 349 328)
Cash and cash equivalents at 1 January	26	3 304 129	4 653 456
Cash and cash equivalents at 31 December	26	**3 481 533**	**3 304 128**

Cash flows from investing activities

Cash flows from investing activities are acquisitions and disposals of long-term assets or other investments that do not qualify as cash equivalents. Examples of cash flows arising from investing activities include:

- Cash paid to purchase, or a receipt from the sale of, an item of property, plant, or equipment;
- Cash paid to purchase, or a receipt from the sale of, a separate entity;
- Cash given as an advance or loan to another entity, or the repayment of such items.

It should be noted that cash inflows or outflows arising from the sale or acquisition of an entity should be shown as a net figure and identified separately in the statement of cash flows (IPSAS 2.49).

In addition it should be highlighted that when a long-term asset is sold, there will be a cash inflow from the proceeds of the sale, and the entity will make a surplus or deficit on the sale transaction. The cash proceeds received from such sale transactions are reported in the statement of cash flows.

Special requirements are stipulated for cash flows that occur as a result of making an acquisition of, or disposing of, a controlled entity.[13] Information on such transactions need to be separated out so that the reader of the financial statements is able to make a sound assessment regarding cash flows that are likely to be ongoing and those that are not (IPSAS 2.49–2.53[14]).

Cash flows from financing activities

Financing activities are activities that result in changes in the size and composition of an entity's contributed capital and borrowings. Examples of financing activities are:

- Cash paid to repay debt instruments;
- Cash proceeds received from issuing debt instruments;
- The capital element in finance lease payments made during the financial period.

Dividends paid by an entity can be included in an entity's financing activities depending on the analysis chosen (IPSAS 2.43).

---

[13] Or other operating unit that has a direct impact on the entity's cash flows reported in the period and its likely future cash flows.

[14] IPSAS 2.50 stipulates that specific disclosures are required for transactions on purchasing or selling controlled entities: (a) the total purchase or disposal consideration, separately identifying the proportion that is discharged by cash and cash equivalents; (b) the amount of cash and cash equivalents that is included in the entity being purchased or sold; and (c) a summary of the assets and liabilities, other than cash and cash equivalents, of the entity acquired or disposed of.

Question and Answer

Question:

In the cash flow statement, cash receipts from taxes during the period amount to 2 970, including 90 of prepayment.

The opening balance of tax receivables is 1 080 and the balance of this account decreases by 720 at the end of the period.

Determine the amount which should be recognized in revenue in the statement of financial performance during the period.

Answer:

The amount recognized in revenue in the statement of financial performance during the period is 2 160.

Tax receivables have been impacted as follows during the period:

Opening balance	1 080
Revenue	+ X
Cash settlements	(2 970-90)
Closing balance	1 080 - 720

Revenue = 1 080 – 720 – 1 080 + 2 970 – 90 = 2 160.

The amount recognized in revenue in the statement of financial performance during the period differs from cash receipts from taxes during the period. It is therefore necessary to analyze these amounts separately because the amount recognized as revenue during the period does not give any indication of the amount of cash received during the period.

This is why it is so important to understand the meaning of financial statements under the accrual basis of accounting. The take-away lesson: revenue is not cash.

Disclosures

In sum IPSAS 2 requires the following key disclosures:

- The components of cash and cash equivalents and a reconciliation between this and the corresponding items in the statement of financial position has to be disclosed (IPSAS 2.56);
- The policy adopted in determining the composition of cash and cash equivalents (IPSAS 2.57);
- The effect of any change in the policy for determining components of cash and cash equivalents (IPSAS 2.58);
- Significant cash and cash equivalent balances that are restricted should also be disclosed and the nature of the restrictions explained (IPSAS 2.59). A commentary should be also disclosed in the notes to the financial statements.

Other disclosures are required where such additional information is relevant to users in their understanding of an entity's financial statements. Additional disclosures can include, for example:

- The amount of an entity's undrawn borrowings that may be available for future operating activities and to settle capital commitments (IPSAS 2.61);
- The aggregate amounts of the cash flows from each of operating, investing, and financing activities related to interests in joint ventures reported using proportionate consolidation (IPSAS 2.61);
- The amount and nature of restricted cash balances (IPSAS 2.61);
- Where appropriations or budget authorizations are prepared on a cash basis, the cash flow statement may assist users in understanding the relationship between the entity's activities or programs and the government's budgetary information (IPSAS 2.62).

SEGMENT REPORTING

A segment is a distinguishable activity, or group of activities, of an entity for which it is appropriate to separately report financial information. Public sector entities often operate in a number of different areas. These areas could be distinguished by either different types of services or types of products or geographical locations. These areas of activities can be described and classified into segments.

The objective of IPSAS 18 Segment Reporting is to prescribe the principles for reporting financial information of an entity by segment to help users understand and appraise both the nature and financial effect of its activities. IPSAS 18 Segment Reporting provides a link between the entity's activities and the chief components of the financial statements, by requiring information to be disaggregated into each major segment. Segment reporting supports the reader of the financial statements to better understand and to subsequently better assess the performance of each area of operation of the entity.

IPSAS 18 applies equally to the preparation of separate or individual financial statements as well as consolidated financial statements. If both consolidated financial statements of a government and the separate financial statements of the parent entity are presented together, segment information is only compulsory in the consolidated financial statements.

Identifying Segments

IPSAS 18 stipulates that operating segments are to be identified based on the components of the activities that are considered to be significant for internal management reporting purposes. IPSAS 18 specifies: "A segment is a distinguishable activity or group of activities of an entity for which it is appropriate to separately report financial information for the purpose of (a) evaluating the entity's past performance in achieving its objectives, and (b) making decisions about the future allocation of resources" (IPSAS 18.9).

IPSAS 18 does not define segments on the basis of volume or size. Instead it highlights that the segments reported should generally be based on those which are reported to the governing body and senior staff/management,[15] which themselves should be based on the expectations of stakeholders, qualitative characteristics such as relevance, and reporting lines suitable to the objectives of the entity. Therefore segments will typically be either:

Service segments	**Geographical segments**
Identifiable parts of an entity that is operating to provide related outputs or achieving particular operating or policy objectives.	Identifiable parts of an entity that is operating to provide outputs or achieving particular operating objectives within a particular geographical area.
Example: A safety department is organized to reflect public safety, road safety, and military actions.	Example: The safety department is structured on a regional basis.

The decision on which segments should be reported will be based on a number of factors such as lines of management and reporting, primary operating objectives of the entity, nature of services provided or activities undertaken, nature of service delivery, relationship with the different regions, and similarities or differences between operations in different regions.

An entity may report on the basis of more than one segment structure, for example by both service and geographical segments, if this is determined to provide useful information.

It is suggested that other methods of segment reporting, for example by nature of expenditure (wages, rent, supplies, capital acquisitions) or by type of entity, for example budget-dependent entities and trading entities, would not in principle meet the objectives of the standard.

Example 5.13   Whole-of-government accounts

At the whole-of-government level segments might be based on economic classifications of activities undertaken by general government, such as health, education, defence, and welfare, and major trading activities such as state power stations, banks, and insurance entities.

IPSAS 18 stipulates a requirement for the disclosure of general information, such as the type of goods and services from which each segment generates its revenue or which are provided by it; the composition of geographical segments or the nature of

---

[15] Management comprises those persons responsible for planning, directing, and controlling the activities of the entity, including those charged with the governance of the entity in accordance with legislation, in instances where they are required to perform such functions.

other segments; and their activities along with the key aspects that have been used by management to identify segments.

IPSAS Financial Reporting in Practice 5.12 below illustrates the relation between fund accounting and segment reporting as applied at the IAEA. The IAEA presents segment reporting according to the IAEA major programmes, which form the structure for budget appropriations, that is to say, reporting information as it is reported internally to the top management of the IAEA, presenting four programmes as four segments and joining programmes 5 and 6 in a single segment.

IPSAS Financial Reporting in Practice 5.12. IAEA Fund Accounting and Segment Reporting (IAEA, 2013, Financial Statement)

Fund accounting and segment reporting

A fund is a self-balancing accounting entity established to account for the transactions of a specified purpose or objective. Funds are segregated for the purpose of conducting specific activities or attaining certain objectives in accordance with special regulations, restrictions or limitations. The financial statements are prepared on a fund accounting basis, showing at the end of the period the consolidated position of all funds. Fund balances represent the accumulated residual of revenue and expenses.

Segment reporting information is presented on the basis of the Agency's activities on **both a major programme basis and a source of funding (fund groups) basis.**

Major Programmes

The Agency's six major programmes form the structure for Regular Budget appropriations.

The six major programmes are:

1. Nuclear Power, Fuel Cycle and Nuclear Science
2. Nuclear Techniques for Development and Environmental Protection
3. Nuclear Safety and Security
4. Nuclear Verification
5. Policy, Management and Administration Services
6. Management of Technical Cooperation for Development.

For purposes of segmental disclosure, Major Programme 5 and Major Programme 6 are shown as a single segment – Policy, Management and Administration.

Fund Groups

Agency activities across these six major programmes are financed through six fund groups. The funds are established on the basis of resolutions passed by the General Conference and are administered in accordance with the Financial Regulations adopted by the Board of Governors, and Financial Rules issued by the Director General. Each fund group has differing parameters relating to how the revenue may be utilized. The groups of funds are described below. […]

Discontinued Operations[16]

A discontinued operation is a component[17] of an entity that either has been disposed of or is classified as held for sale. The component should represent a separate major activity or geographical area of the entity's operations. The effective closure of the component should be part of a single plan. IPSAS 18 does not stipulate any specific requirements in terms of discontinued operations.[18] Nevertheless, it makes reference to IPSAS 1 as follows: "IPSAS 1 requires that when items of revenue or expense are material, their nature and amount of such items are disclosed separately. IPSAS 1 identifies a number of examples of such items, including [...] discontinued operations [...]" (IPSAS 18. 57).

Example 5.14   Accounting policy on segment reporting, including note on discontinued operations (UNOPS, 2014: 10)

IPSAS 18. Segment reporting

In general, IPSAS prescribe principles for reporting financial information by segment to help users of financial statements gain a better understanding of the performance of each part of the operations, leading to a better understanding about the entity as a whole. UNOPS will therefore undertake segment reporting based on its principal activities undertaken across its core operating segments.

These segments will be determined based on UNOPS' components that are considered to be important for the purpose of internal management reporting.

UNOPS will disclose:

- A disaggregation of the financial statements (using the same underlying accounting policies) in the format of a reconciliation relating the reported segment information back to corresponding items in UNOPS' financial statements;
- Details on segment revenue and expenses, assets and liabilities.

UNOPS will also provide information on:

- The type of products and services relating to each segment;
- The factors used by management to identify its segments;
- Additional disclosures which are also required for discontinued operations.

Public sector entities reporting under IPSAS can, as illustrated in Example 5.14, include discontinued operations in their accounting policies. The objective of

---

[16] See IFRS 5 Non-current Assets Held for Sale and Discontinued Operations, for detailed guidance on discontinued operations.
[17] A component of an entity comprises operations and cash flows that can be clearly distinguished, operationally and for financial reporting purposes, from the rest of the entity.
[18] There is no IPSAS dealing with discontinued operations. Other IPSAS refer users to the relevant international or national standard dealing with discontinued operations, and users of IPSAS will therefore follow the requirements of IFRS 5.

Table 5.6   Required and recommended disclosures

Required disclosures	• Revenue and expenses. Revenue should be split between budget appropriations or allocations, external sources and internal sources.
	• Total carrying amount of segment assets and liabilities for each segment.
	• Total cost incurred during the period on assets to be used during more than one period, which would be primarily property, plant, and equipment.
	• Aggregate of net surplus/deficit, and aggregate of investment in associates, joint ventures, and other investments accounted for under the equity method, if substantially all their operations are within a single segment
	• Reconciliation of external revenues, expenses, assets, and liabilities disclosed for segments and total amounts disclosed in the financial statements.
	• The basis of pricing inter-segment transfers.
	• Changes in accounting policies with a material effect on segment information, including nature of and reasons for change, with restatements or reasons why these cannot be made.
Recommended disclosures	• Significant individual amounts of segment income or expenses.
	• Segment cash flows.
	• Segment depreciation expense and other significant non-cash expenses or revenue.
	• Additional information about service or geographical segments if the main segments are chosen on the other basis.
	• Broad operating objectives for each segment.

disclosures on discontinued operations is to provide readers of the financial statements with adequate information to enable their analysis and evaluation of the financial effect of such discontinued operations.

Disclosure

IPSAS 18 stipulates certain required disclosures and recommended disclosures (see Table 5.6). The information required by IPSAS 18 is prepared by disaggregating the entity's financial statements into segments. The accounting policies underlying the disaggregated segment information are the same as those underlying the financial statements.

Where there have been changes in the internal structure of an entity that have led to corresponding changes in the reportable segments, comparative segment information should be restated to reflect this change where it is practicable to do so.

If changes to the internal structure lead to a change in the identification of segments and the comparative segments have not been restated because it is not practicable to do so, then the old and new segment bases should both be reported for the year in which the change takes place. This is to ensure that useful comparisons can still take place.

IPSAS Financial Reporting in Practice 5.13. IAEA 2013 Segment Reporting

STATEMENT VI: STATEMENT OF SEGMENT REPORTING BY MAJOR PROGAMME
For the year ended 31 December 2013
(expressed in euro '000s)

Expenses	Nuclear Power, Fuel Cycle and Nuclear Science	Nuclear Techniques for Development and Environmental Protection	Nuclear Safety and Security	Nuclear Verification	Policy, Management and Administration Services a/	Shared Services and Expenses not Directly Charged to Major Programmes b/	Eliminations c/	Total
Staff costs	24 167	25 313	34 317	90 909	65 618	11 997	–	252 321
Consultants, experts	4 028	4 683	6 986	328	1 812	1 763	–	19 600
Travel	8 790	13 530	18 931	7 798	1 668	109	–	50 826
Transfers to development counterparts	4 825	28 101	5 155	–	188	6	–	38 275
Buildings management and security services	11	16	41	1 200	21 308	1 788	–	24 364
Training	1 538	9 439	6 927	1 149	1 853	106	–	21 012
Depreciation and amortization	318	850	580	8 649	2 827	1 120	–	14 344
Other operating expenses	3 522	9 842	7 113	21 298	12 615	7 535	(25 741)	36 184
Total expenses	**47 199**	**91 774**	**80 050**	**131 331**	**107 889**	**24 424**	**(25 741)**	**456 926**

94

Assets

Property, plant & equipment, and intangibles	1 378	3 059	2 172	81 766	19 791	6 293	–	114 459

Asset additions

Property, plant & equipment, and intangibles	779	1 492	1 037	30 178	4 605	2 336	–	40 427

a/ Includes project management and technical assistance for the Technical Cooperation Programme.

b/ Expenses not directly charged to Major Programmes primarily include expenses tracked centrally pertaining to shared services, reimbursable work for others, doubtful debt expenses, etc.

c/ Major Programme expenses are shown inclusive of allocated shared services costs and programme support costs. Eliminations column includes elimination of programme support costs and other transactions occurring between Major Programmes to reconcile to total expenses in the statement of financial performance.

The accompanying Notes are an integral part of these Statements

STATEMENT VIIa: STATEMENT OF SEGMENT REPORTING BY FUND – FINANCIAL POSITION
As at 31 December 2013
(expressed in euro '000s)

	Regular Budget Fund and Working Capital Fund	Technical Cooperation Fund	Extrabudgetary Programme Fund	Low Enriched Uranium Bank	Technical Cooperation Extrabudgetary Fund	Trust Funds, Reserve Funds and Special Funds	Total
Assets							
Cash and cash equivalents	66 121	590	6 310	9 809	6 558	1 933	91 321
Investments	12 000	64 363	176 835	98 299	23 274	–	374 771
Accounts receivable	40 245	1 104	8 692	59	5 451	–	55 551

Advances and prepayments	38 195	937	127	–	2 294	5	41 558
Inventory	561	4 487	1 684	–	542	39	7 313
Property, plant & equipment	36 547	9	52 473	5	–	759	89 793
Intangible assets	24 038	8	541	–	–	79	24 666
Investment in common service entities	4 400	–	–	–	–	–	4 400
Total assets	**222 107**	**71 498**	**246 662**	**108 172**	**38 119**	**2 815**	**689 373**
Liabilities							
Accounts payable	5 346	2 092	1 435	5	389	–	9 267
Deferred revenue	32 150	3 952	44 059	20 116	8 663	–	108 940
Employee benefit liabilities	203 398	15	3 517	91	–	–	207 021
Other financial liabilities	295	1	402	–	–	–	698
Provisions	41	–	3 067	–	–	–	3 108
Total liabilities	**241 230**	**6 060**	**52 480**	**20 212**	**9 052**	**–**	**329 034**
Net assets	**(19 123)**	**65 438**	**194 182**	**87 960**	**29 067**	**2 815**	**360 339**
Equity							
Fund balances	(51 399)	38 560	178 546	87 887	22 039	2 698	278 331
Reserves	32 276	26 878	15 636	73	7 028	117	82 008
Total equity	**(19 123)**	**65 438**	**194 182**	**87 960**	**29 067**	**2 815**	**360 339**

The accompanying Notes are an integral part of these Statements

IPSAS Financial Reporting in Practice 5.14. UNESCO 2013 Segment Reporting

STATEMENT OF FINANCIAL POSITION BY SEGMENT AS AT 31 DECEMBER 2013

Expressed in '000 US dollars	GEF	OPF	PFF	SFF	Inter-fund balances	TOTAL UNESCO
ASSETS						
Current Assets						
Cash and cash equivalents	61 250	12 512	61 003	11 270	–	146 035
Short-term investments	4 262	42 516	510 846	19 515	–	577 139
Accounts receivable (non-exchange transactions)	14 394	–	5 121	–	–	19 515
Receivables from exchange transactions	59	568	535	640	–78	1 724
Inventories	–	603	44	556	–	1 203
Advance payments	18 121	377	21 783	1 028	–642	40 667
Other current assets	11 324	5 055	2 721	362	–14 735	4 727
Total current assets	**109 410**	**61 631**	**602 053**	**33 371**	**–15 455**	**791 010**
Non-current assets						
Accounts receivable (non-exchange transactions)	1 364	–	–	–	–	1 364
Long-term investments	–	–	2 676	–	–	2 676
Property, plant and equipment	583 790	754	10 597	146	–	595 287
Intangible assets	114	–	166	–	–	280
Total non-current assets	**585 268**	**754**	**13 439**	**146**	**–**	**599 607**
TOTAL ASSETS	**694 678**	**62 385**	**615 492**	**33 517**	**–15 455**	**1 390 617**

LIABILITIES
Current liabilities

Accounts payable (exchange transactions)	5 365	1 015	12 370	1 028	−78	19 700
Employee benefits	17 084	840	4354	824	−	23 102
Transfers payable	306	−	19 867	−	−	20 173
Conditions on voluntary contributions	1 113	−	38 506	−	−	39 619
Advance receipts	34 563	378	113 663	112	−	148 716
Current portion of borrowings	8 283	−	−	34	−34	8 283
Other current liabilities	1 547	2 012	15 511	7 560	−15 343	11 287
Total current liabilities	**68 261**	**4 245**	**204 271**	**9 558**	**−15 455**	**270 880**

Non-current liabilities

Employee benefits	853 549	2 940	26 029	−	−	882 518
Conditions on voluntary contributions	2 868	−	−	−	−	2 868
Long-term loans	39 991	−	−	−	−	39 991
Other non-current liabilities	4 010	5 108	766	−	−	9 884
Total non-current liabilities	**900 418**	**8 048**	**26 795**	**−**	**−**	**935 261**

TOTAL LIABILITIES	**968 679**	**12 293**	**231 066**	**9 558**	**−15 455**	**1 206 141**

NET ASSETS	**−274 001**	**50 092**	**384 426**	**23 959**	**−**	**184 476**

NET ASSETS/ EQUITY						
Reserves and fund balances	−274 001	50 092	384 426	23 959	–	184 479

NET ASSETS/ EQUITY	**−274 001**	**50 092**	**384 426**	**23 959**	**–**	**184 476**

STATEMENT OF FINANCIAL PERFORMANCE BY SEGMENT FOR THE YEAR ENDED 31 DECEMBER 2013

Expressed in '000 US dollars	**GEF**	**OPF**	**PFF**	**SFF**	**Inter-fund transactions**	**TOTAL UNESCO**
REVENUE						
Assessed contributions	354 902	–	3 714	–	–	358 616
Voluntary contributions	15 080	637	354 290	–	−811	369 196
Other revenue producing activities	77	12 689	2 683	8 070	−4 049	19 470
Other/ miscellaneous revenue	1 364	2 191	1 058	26 229	−13 474	17 368
Foreign exchange gains	2 786	1	–	858	−669	2 976
Finance revenue	281	3 451	7 377	303	–	11 502
Inter-segment transfers	106	18 681	10 733	–	29 520	–
Operating revenue	**374 596**	**37 740**	**379 855**	**35 460**	**−48 523**	**779 128**
EXPENSES						
Employee benefit expenses	261 103	23 167	103 629	27 771	−13 609	402 061
Consultants, external experts and mission costs	11 205	2 962	37 847	–	2 132	49 882
External training, grants and other transfers	22 455	142	43 845	1	−10 553	55 890

Supplies, consumables and other running costs	27 936	4 439	27 812	2 777	−4 268	58 696
Contracted services	15 381	3 941	110 981	608	−67	130 844
Depreciation and amortization	15 540	419	2 694	81	−	18 734
Allowance for assessed contributions	83 058	−	−	−		83 058
Other expenses	719	206	1 141	154	−	2 220
Foreign exchange losses	−	−	846	−	−846	−
Finance costs	1 647	26	7 747	8	−	9 428
Inter-segment transfers	−	162	16 886	−	−17 048	−
Operating expenses	**439 044**	**35 464**	**353 428**	**31 400**	**−48 523**	**810 813**
SURPLUS (DEFICIT) FOR THE PERIOD	**−64 448**	**2 276**	**26 427**	**4 060**	**−**	**−31 685**

ACCOUNTING POLICIES, CHANGES IN ACCOUNTING ESTIMATES, AND ERRORS

IPSAS 3 Accounting Policies, Changes in Accounting Estimates and Errors, stipulate the requirements for accounting policies and their changes. The objective of IPSAS 3 is to enhance the relevance, reliability, and comparability of financial statements and it should be applied by an entity to select and apply its accounting policies. IPSAS 3 specifies that accounting policies are the specific principles, bases, conventions, rules, and practices applied by an entity in preparing and presenting its financial statements (IPSAS 3.7). Accounting policies shall be applied consistently for similar transactions (IPSAS 3.16). In the absence of specific guidance in IPSAS, management should use its judgment in developing and applying an accounting policy that results in information that is relevant to the economic decision-making needs of users and that is reliable (IPSAS 3.12).

Changes in Accounting Policy

Changes in accounting policies are allowed where required by new IPSAS or where making such a change would provide reliable and more relevant information to users of financial statements (IPSAS 3.17). Accounting policies are to be developed based on the recognition and measurement requirements laid down in IPSAS. Some IPSAS provide explicit or implicit choices which provide management with a certain degree of flexibility, using judgment, estimates, and assumptions in establishing accounting policies. A change of an existing accounting policy to another policy of equal relevance is not permitted on the grounds that, in these circumstances, comparability should take precedence.

Changes in accounting policies are required to be accounted for retrospectively except where it is not practicable to determine the effect in prior periods (IPSAS 3.27, 3.28). Retrospective application is where the financial statements of the current period and each prior period presented are adjusted so that it appears as if the new policy had always been followed. This is achieved by restating the surpluses or deficits in each period presented and adjusting the opening position by restating accumulated surpluses or deficits held in the balance sheet as part of assets/equity (IPSAS 3.7).

Example 5.15   Retrospective application

An entity was established on 1 January 2012, and adopted the accounting policy allowed by IPSAS 5 Borrowing Costs of recognizing all interest costs in surplus or deficit (IPSAS 5.17).

In each year, borrowing costs attributable to qualifying assets have been recognized in surplus or deficit. Property, plant, and equipment are depreciated on a straight-line basis over their useful life.

The entity is to be consolidated in a group of entities applying the other policy allowed by IPSAS 5, that is to say borrowing costs that are directly attributable to the acquisition, construction, or production of a qualifying asset shall be capitalized as part of the cost of that asset (IPSAS 5.18). In order to comply with the group accounting policies, the entity has chosen to change its accounting policy for borrowing costs.

This change in accounting policy should be applied retrospectively. The new treatment should be applied consistently to all borrowing costs that are directly attributable to the acquisition, construction, or production of all qualifying assets of the entity.

Where it is not practicable to determine either the specific effect in a particular period or the cumulative effect of applying a new policy to past periods, the new policy should be applied from the earliest date that it is practicable to do so (IPSAS 3.29).

It should be highlighted that the reasons for, and effects of, a change in accounting policy should be disclosed (IPSAS 3.33, 3.34). Where a new standard has been issued but an entity is not yet required to implement it and the entity has not implemented it early, it should disclose this fact. The information provided should quantify the effect on future periods if this can be reasonably estimated. This provides useful information to users of the financial statements about an entity's future reported performance (IPSAS 3.35).

IPSAS Financial Reporting in Practice 5.15. IAEA, Change in Accounting Policy, 2013 (p. 48)

During 2013, the Agency **changed its accounting policy** with respect to refunds of voluntary contributions for which revenue was recognized in prior years. Beginning in 2013, all such refunds are recorded as direct adjustments to equity, rather than as reductions in revenue. As a result of this change in accounting policy, 2012 amounts have been restated with a resulting increase in revenue from voluntary contributions and a direct adjustment to equity of €1.584 million.

IPSAS Financial Reporting in Practice 5.16. BIPM, Change in Accounting Policy, 2012 (p. 100)[19]

In 2012, a change in accounting policies was implemented in regard to buildings. The change was applied retrospectively, because this change results in the financial statements providing improved and more relevant information about the effects of transactions, other events, and conditions on the BIPM's financial position and financial performance (IPSAS 3.17 and 3.27).

The BIPM has implemented this change in accounting policy, based on its experience of the use of its buildings. These buildings, initially recognized using the reproduction cost approach, are now evaluated using the depreciated replacement cost approach.

Changes in Accounting Estimates

The preparation of financial statements requires many estimates to be made on the basis of the latest available, reliable information. Key areas in which estimates are made include, for example, the recoverability of amounts owed by customers, the obsolescence of inventories, and the useful lives of non-current assets (IPSAS 3.37). As more up-to-date information becomes available estimates should be revisited to reflect this new information. These are changes in estimates and are not changes in accounting policies or the correction of errors (IPSAS 3.7).

Example 5.16   Change in estimate

A government is considering the recoverability of its tax receivables on corporate income tax, consistent with its accounting policy to recognize assets at no more than their recoverable amount.

---

[19] http://www.bipm.org/utils/common/pdf/rapport-annuel/Rapport-annuel-BIPM-2012.pdf

> It decides that, as the economy is entering a period of recession, it should raise its provision from 2% of the total to 5%, considering that it is likely that more companies will go bankrupt and that the State will not be able to recover income tax receivables.
>
> This is not a change in accounting policy. What has changed is the level of the receivables that are recoverable. This is a change in estimate which is to be recorded prospectively.

By its very nature the revision of an estimate to take account of more up-to-date information does not relate to prior periods. Instead such a revision is based on the latest information available and therefore should be recognized in the period in which that change arises. The effect of a change in an accounting estimate should therefore be recognized prospectively, i.e., by recognizing the change in the current and future periods affected by the change (IPSAS 3.7, 3.41).

Example 5.17   Change in estimate

A piece of equipment with an original cost of CU100 000, has an originally estimated useful life of 10 years and residual value of nil. The annual straight-line depreciation charge will be CU10 000 per annum and the carrying amount after three years will be CU70 000.

If in the fourth year it is decided that, as a result of changes in conditions, the remaining useful life is only two years (i.e., a total of five years), then the depreciation charge in that year (and in the next year) will be the carrying amount brought forward divided by the revised remaining useful life, CU70 000/2 = CU35 000. There should be no change to the depreciation charged for the past three years.

The effect of the change (in this case an increase in the annual depreciation charge from CU10 000 to CU35 000) in the current year, and the next year, should be disclosed (if material).

IPSAS Financial Reporting in Practice 5.17. BIPM, Change in Estimate, 2012 (p. 100)[20]

The following changes in accounting estimates were implemented, recognized prospectively (i.e., the change is recorded in the 2012 BIPM financial statements and onwards):

- Amortization of the KCDB, JCRB, and JCTLM databases, which were considered to have an indefinite useful life. Some triggering events occurred in 2012

---

[20] See BIPM (2012) Annual Report, available at http://www.bipm.org/utils/common/pdf/rapport-annuel/Rapport-annuel-BIPM-2012.pdf, last accessed 1 March 2015.

> (the decision to revamp the BIPM website, the KCDB, as well as the predicted upgrade of the software supporting the JCTLM database) have indicated an expected end of their useful life, respectively in four years, four years, and nine years.
> - De-recognition of some elements of the watt balance, scientific equipment which was previously recognized as scientific equipment under development and is no longer useful for the new watt balance prototype. These elements amount to 2004 thousand euros. This new watt balance prototype remains recognized as scientific equipment under development for 768 thousand euros.
> - De-recognition of the superconducting watt balance which was previously recognized as scientific equipment under development for 110 thousand euros, since the superconducting watt balance is a completed project which will not be used in the future.

Errors

Financial statements do not comply with IPSAS if they contain errors made intentionally to achieve a particular presentation in the financial statements. A prior period error is where an error has occurred even though reliable information was available when those financial statements were authorized for issue and could reasonably be expected to have been taken into account at that time.

Examples of such errors are: mathematical errors; errors in applying an accounting policy; oversights or misinterpretation of facts and fraud.

As such errors can relate to a number of past periods reported, IPSAS 3 stipulates that it is required that these errors are adjusted in those past periods in which the error arose rather than in the current period. Adjustment in the current period would lead to a distorted result in the period in which the error was identified (IPSAS 3.47).

If it is impracticable to determine the effect of an error on an individual period then the adjustment should be made to the opening balance of the earliest period in which it is possible to identify such information (IPSAS 3.48, 3.49, 3.50).

It is important to distinguish between prior period errors and changes in accounting estimates. Accounting estimates are best described as approximations, being the result of considering what is likely to happen in the future (e.g., how many customers will pay their outstanding invoices and the period over which non-current assets can be used productively within the business). By their very nature, estimates result from judgments made on the basis of information available at the time they are made, so they may need to be adjusted in the future in the light of additional information becoming available.

Prior period errors, on the other hand, result from discoveries which undermine the reliability of the previously published financial statements (e.g., unrecorded income and expenditure, fictitious inventory, or the incorrect application of accounting policies such as classifying maintenance expenses as part of the cost of non-current assets). Prior period errors should be rare.

Disclosure

Key disclosures include disclosure of information pertaining to the nature, the reason, and the impact of changes in accounting policies and prior period errors. IPSAS 3 also requires that the nature and amount of a change in accounting estimate are disclosed.

EVENTS AFTER THE REPORTING DATE

Sometimes key events arise after the cut-off date for which financial statements are prepared. Such events may have important implications for the financial position and performance in the year just ended. The end of the financial reporting period is a cut-off date; transactions and events that occur after this point in time are commonly not recognized in the financial statements of the period just ended. Nevertheless, if an entity gets information on events or transactions after the end of the reporting period that can provide additional information about events that actually occurred before the end of the reporting period then it is appropriate to take it into account. It should be highlighted that financial statements reflect the most up-to-date facts about events that took place at the end of the reporting period. It can however be difficult to establish whether an event occuring after the end of the reporting period is new information about an existing event or a new event.

IPSAS 14 Events after the Reporting Date provide guidance on to how to deal with events that occur after the end of the reporting period but before the date on which the financial statements are authorized for issue. These are described as events after the end of the reporting period. IPSAS 14 describes events after the reporting date as those events, both favourable and unfavourable, that take place between the reporting date and the date when the financial statements are authorized for issue.

The treatment of such events is dependent upon whether they are considered to be adjusting or non-adjusting events.

Authorizing Financial Statements for Issue

IPSAS 14 outlines how the date of authorization may be determined for the accounts of public sector bodies (IPSAS 14.6–14.8). The process will often be determined in the context of the particular process of approval, sector, and jurisdiction. IPSAS distinguish between events that occur during this period which should be adjusted for in the financial statements and those that should instead only be disclosed.

As illustrated in Example 5.16 below, the authorization date for the Ministry of Defence in the United Kingdom will be the date on which the financial statements are authorized for issue by the Accounting Officer.

Example 5.18   United Kingdom, Ministry of Defence (2013: 151)

Events After the Reporting Date. These accounts have been authorized for issue by the Accounting Officer on the same date as the C&AG's Audit Certificate.

Adjusting versus Non-adjusting Events

Events that occur after the end of the reporting period can be considered either adjusting or non-adjusting events (IPSAS 14.10–14.14) – see Table 5.7.

Dividends

If dividends on shares have been proposed or declared after the end of the reporting period they do not meet the definition of a liability and therefore cannot be recognized as a liability at the end of the reporting period (IPSAS 14.14). Dividends may arise in the public sector when, for example: a public sector entity controls and consolidates the financial statements of an entity that has outside ownership interests to whom it pays dividends.

To be recognized as a liability, the entity should have an obligation at the end of the reporting period. The obligation to pay the dividend only arises when it has been declared, so it is at the declaration date that a liability should be recognized. Where dividends have been proposed or declared after the end of the reporting period, this should be disclosed in the notes to the financial statements.

Going Concern

Financial statements are usually prepared on what is described as the "going concern" basis (see also Conceptual Framework). This assumes that the entity will continue to operate for the foreseeable future. Where the going concern assessment changes after the end of the reporting period, this will need to be disclosed and will normally affect other aspects of the presentation of the financial statements (IPSAS 14.18). It should be highlighted that IPSAS 14 (17–24) provides public sector specific guidance.

In order to assess whether the going concern assumption is appropriate for an individual entity within government, those responsible for the preparation of the financial statements, and/or the governing body, need to consider a number of factors. Those factors will include the current and expected performance of the entity, any announced and potential restructuring of entity units, the likelihood of continued government funding and so forth. In the case of entities whose operations are substantially budget-funded, going concern issues generally only arise if the government announces its intention to cease funding the entity. IPSAS 14 highlights that the influence of any given change will depend on factors such as whether the operations are to be transferred or discontinued, and that judgment will be necessary to decide whether a change in the value of assets and liabilities is required.

Disclosure

IPSAS 14 requires that public sector entities disclose when the financial statements were authorized for issue and who (it could be a person or a body) gave authorization. An illustration is provided in IPSAS Financial Reporting in Practice 5.18 below. For non-adjusting events after the reporting date that are deemed material there is a requirement to disclose both the nature of the event and the estimate of its financial effects.

Table 5.7 Adjusting versus non-adjusting events

	Adjusting	**Non-adjusting events**
Description	Events that provide evidence of conditions that existed at the end of the reporting period (IPSAS 14.5).	Events that are indicative of conditions that arose after the end of the reporting period (IPSAS 14.5).
Accounting implications	If a transaction or event meets the definition of an adjusting event, then the entity shall adjust the amounts recognized in the financial statements to reflect such events/ transactions (IPSAS 14.10).	If a transaction is deemed non-adjusting, following the description provided in IPSAS 14 (IPSAS 14.5) the entity should not adjust amounts recognized in the financial statements (IPSAS 14.12). However, non-adjusting events should instead be disclosed where the outcome of such events would influence the economic decisions made by users of the financial statements. Where the disclosure of such an event is required, the entity should provide details of the nature of the event and an estimate of its financial effect, or state that such an estimate cannot be made.
Example	• The discovery of fraud or errors which show that amounts recognized or information disclosed at the end of the reporting period were incorrect; • The settlement after the reporting date of a case that confirms that the entity had a present obligation at the reporting date, provision which should be adjusted according to the new information made available after the end of the reporting period. • The sale of an inventory after the reporting date which gives evidence about its net realizable value at the reporting date being lower than its net book value. The receipt of this information after the reporting date indicates that this inventory was impaired at the reporting date, and that an impairment loss is to be recorded.	• The announcement of major government re-organization; • The destruction of assets caused by a fire occurring after the end of the reporting period; • An unusually large decline in the value of property carried at fair value, where that decline is unrelated to the condition of the property at reporting date, but is due to circumstances that have arisen since the reporting date; • Abnormally large changes after the reporting date in asset prices or foreign exchange rates (either with a positive or a negative impact); • Issuing significant guarantees after the reporting date.

IPSAS Financial Reporting in Practice 5.18. IAEA 2013 Financial Statements (p. 97)

NOTE 42: Events after the reporting date

The Agency's reporting date is 31 December 2013. The financial statements were authorized for issuance by the Director General on 21 March 2014, the date at which they were submitted to the External Auditor.

There were no significant events impacting the financial statements, favourable or unfavourable, between the reporting date and the financial statements issuance date.

In addition it should be noted that if certain information arises after the end of the reporting period about conditions that existed at the end of the reporting period, the original disclosures should be updated to reflect this new information (IPSAS 14.28).

6 DISCLOSURE STANDARDS

This chapter presents two disclosure standards: one which is mandatory, namely IPSAS 20 on Related Party Disclosures and one that is voluntary, namely IPSAS 22 on the Disclosure of Financial Information about the General Government Sector.

RELATED PARTY DISCLOSURES

The objective of IPSAS 20 is to require the disclosure of the existence of related party relationships where control exists. IPSAS 20 related party disclosures therefore ensure that an entity's financial statements contain the disclosures necessary to draw attention to the possibility that its financial position, and financial performance, may have been affected by the existence of related parties and by related party transactions. Knowledge of related party transactions, any outstanding balances with a related party, and the nature of related party relationships may affect the assessment of an entity's operations by users of the financial statements. Not only does IPSAS 20 require disclosure on transactions with key management personnel, for example the directors or board members, but it also stipulates that key information about the rewards and incentives available to them are clearly set out in the financial statements. Such assessments are likely to include the risks and opportunities facing an entity.

IPSAS 20 does not contain any recognition or measurement requirements; they merely require disclosure in the financial statements of the nature of related party relationships and of certain of the transactions between such parties.

IPSAS 20 does not require the disclosure of information about transactions which are consistent with normal operating relationships between public sector entities and are undertaken on normal terms and conditions for such transactions in these circumstances (IPSAS 20.29).

Disclosure of related party transactions between members of an economic entity is not necessary in consolidated financial statements, because consolidated financial statements present information about the controlling entity and controlled entities as a single reporting entity (IPSAS 20.33). Therefore related party transactions and outstanding balances arising from transactions with other entities in a group are eliminated on consolidation in the financial statements of the group. However transactions with associated entities accounted for under the equity method are not eliminated, and therefore require separate disclosure as related party transactions in the financial statements of the group.

Definition of a Related Party

A related party transaction is defined as a transfer of resources, services, or obligations between a reporting entity and a related party, regardless of whether a price is charged (IPSAS 20.4). This means that it takes into account any transaction between two related parties even if the transaction takes place at a full arm's length price. However, IPSAS 20 requires disclosure only of those transactions which are not on normal terms and conditions, except for those requirements related to key management personnel (IPSAS 20.29).

A party is related to an entity if it:

- Is directly or indirectly controls, is controlled by, or is under common control with, the entity;
- Has significant influence over the entity;
- Has joint control over the entity;
- Is a close member of the family of any individual who controls, or has significant influence or joint control over, the entity;
- Is an associate of the entity;
- Is a joint venture in which the entity is a venturer;
- Is a member of the key management personnel of the entity or its parent/controlled entity;
- Is a close member of the family of any of the aforementioned key management personnel;
- Is an entity that is controlled, jointly controlled, or significantly influenced by, or for which significant voting power in such entity resides with, any of the key management personnel or their close family members.

A close family member, under IPSAS 20, specifically includes:

- Any relative living in a common household (for example if an elected member has an aunt or uncle living with them);
- A grandparent or parent;
- A brother or sister;
- A parent-in-law or a sibling-in-law.

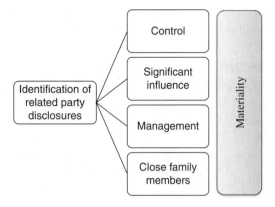

Figure 6.1 Identifying related parties

Identifying Related Parties

A party may be related to an entity in a number of different ways (see Figure 6.1). Some related party relationships are easier to identify than others. For example, a joint venture undertaking of an entity is related to that entity, as are the key management personnel of an entity or its controlling entity.

Control and significant influence

Control is the ability to obtain benefits by governing the financial and operating policies of an entity. An entity has control over another entity when it has certain decision-making capabilities over another and it benefits from the activities of that entity.

Joint control is the sharing of control through a contractual arrangement and significant influence is the ability to participate in, rather than control, the financial and operating policy decisions (IPSAS 20.4).

Example 6.1   Related parties in the South Africa government (GRAP 20 Guideline, 2014)

In the South African context, the government is divided into three spheres, namely the national, provincial, and local spheres of government. Although provinces and municipalities are responsible for executing its assigned functions in line with the overall policies and objectives set by the relevant national department, the autonomy of the different spheres is guaranteed in terms of the Constitution of South Africa and provinces and municipalities can therefore decide how it will achieve those objectives. The national government does not control provinces or municipalities for accounting purposes, although funding may be received from the national government.

The following figure illustrates the related parties in the South African government context (note that the different spheres of government are not related to each other):

National sphere of government	• All departments and public entities in the national sphere of government are related parties.
Provincial sphere of government	• All departments and public entities in each province are related parties.
Local sphere of government	• Each municipality and its own municipal entities are related parties. A municipalitys is not 'related' to another municipality as they are not under common control.

Related parties within the relevant spheres of government

National sphere:

For example: Telkom, the Post Office, Transnet, the National Departments of Public Works and Trade and Industry, the Competition Commission, and the Market Theatre will all be related parties, as they fall within the national sphere of government.

Provincial sphere:

For example: The Gauteng Department of Health, Gauteng Economic Development Agency, Gauteng Gambling Board, and the Gauteng Tourism Authority will all be related parties, as they fall within the same province. Note that these entities will be unrelated to any departments or public entities from another province.

Local sphere:

For example: The City of Johannesburg and its municipal entities are related parties. The City of Tshwane and the City of Johannesburg are not related parties as they are not under common control.

Note that the above example is based on South African GRAP (Generally Recognised Accounting Practice). GRAP, which is being developed in South Africa is based on the IPSAS.

Management

The term "key management personnel" includes the directors or board members but goes much wider to include any person who has authority or responsibility for running the entity. Because such personnel are key to the successful operation of the entity, the definition of a related party extends to the close members of their family and any entity that is controlled, jointly controlled, or significantly influenced by either the key management personnel or a close member of their family (IPSAS 20.4).

Close members of family

Close members of the family of an individual are family members who may be expected to influence, or be influenced by, that individual in their dealings with the entity. Examples of close family members include the individual's domestic partner and any dependants of the individual or of his or her partner (IPSAS 20.4).

Example 6.2   Transaction with an entity under the control of a close family member of a member of management

The daughter of the Chief Executive Officer of Public Entity A is the sole shareholder of Company ABC, which has been awarded a contract for the provision of cleaning services to Public Entity A. The contract was established following proper supply chain management procedures.

As Company ABC is under the control of a close family member of a key member of management, Company ABC and Public Entity A will be related parties. The nature of the relationship, all transactions with Company ABC, and any other relevant information should be disclosed in the financial statements of Public Entity A.

Substance over form

In identifying a related party relationship, attention should be directed to the substance of the relationship rather than focusing on its legal form.

Example 6.3   Substance over form

Two entities have a member of management in common; it is therefore required to consider the possibility, and to assess the likelihood, that this person would be able to affect the policies of both entities in their mutual dealings. However, the mere fact that two entities have a shared member of management does not necessarily create a related party relationship.

Disclosures

IPSAS 20 is based on the principle that it is the identification of the related party relationship that triggers the disclosure requirements.

Table 6.1 Related party disclosures

Related party relationship where control exists, regardless of whether there have been transactions between the related parties. Thus disclose the nature of relationships between parent or controlling entity and subsidiary or controlled entity, even if there were no transactions between those related parties (IPSAS 20.25).

The name of the entity's parent or controlling entity and, if different, the ultimate controlling entity (IPSAS 20.26).

Compensation or remuneration of key management personnel (IPSAS 20.34). See IPSAS Financial Reporting in Practice 6.1 below for an example from UNDPs disclosure note on related parties that illustrated the compensation of key management and close family members of key management.

Detail of loans to key management personnel and their close family members, including advances, repayments, and closing balances.

If there have been transactions between related parties: (a) the nature of the relationship (but there is no requirement to identify the related parties by name); (b) the amount of the transactions during the period. Under IPSAS 20 only those transactions not on normal terms and conditions; and (c) any balance outstanding at the period end.

Disclosures are made separately for each of the following categories: Note that IPSAS 20 requires disclosure of the nature of the relationship, a description of the transactions, and the broad terms and conditions:
* The parent or controlling entity;
* Entities with joint control or significant influence over the entity;
* Subsidiaries or controlled entities;
* Associates;
* Joint ventures in which the entity is a venturer;
* Key management personnel; and
* Other related parties.

IPSAS 20 requires a number of related party disclosures, which are detailed in Table 6.1:

IPSAS Financial Reporting in Practice 6.1. UNDP (2012) Related Party Disclosure Note 32 (p. 97)

Note 32

Related parties

Key management personnel

The leadership structure of UNDP consists of an Executive Group of 12 members. The Executive Group is responsible for the strategic direction and operational management of UNDP and is entrusted with significant authority to execute the UNDP mandate. Collectively this Executive Group comprises four tiers: an Under-Secretary-General and Administrator (Administrator); an Under-Secretary-General (Associate

Administrator); nine Assistant Secretaries-General (Assistant Administrators); and a Chief of Staff and Director (Chief of Staff and Director, Office of the Administrator (ex officio)).

Remuneration

(Thousands of United States *dollars*)

Tier	Number of positions	Salary and post adjustment	Other entitlements	Total remuneration	After-service health insurance, repatriation, death benefit and annual leave liability
Key management personnel	12	2 746	781	3 527	4 221
Close family members of key management personnel	1	66	4	70	6
Total	**13**	**2 812**	**785**	**3 597**	**4 227**

The remuneration paid to key management personnel includes salary, post adjustment and other entitlements as applicable in accordance with the Staff Regulations of the United Nations and Staff Rules.

Loans

Staff advances are available to UNDP staff, including key management personnel, for specific purposes as provided for in the Staff Regulations of the United Nations and Staff Rules. As at 31 December 2012, there were no advances issued to key management personnel and their close family members that were not available to all UNDP staff.

United Nations system

UNDP is engaged in United Nations system initiatives such as joint funding arrangements (Multi-Donor Trust Funds and joint programmes) and common services arrangements. Within joint funding mechanisms, United Nations entities work together to implement activities and achieve results. Each of the participating United Nations entities assumes its share of responsibilities related to planning, implementing, monitoring and evaluating these activities.

UNDP is a cosponsoring organization of the Joint United National Programme on HIV/AIDS (UNAIDS), an innovative joint effort of the United Nations family to respond in a coordinated manner on the issue of HIV/AIDS. UNDP participates in setting the financial and operating policies of the Programme Coordinating Board of UNAIDS, which is headquartered in Geneva.

IPSAS Financial Reporting in Practice 6.2. WHO (2013) Related Party Disclosure Note 10 (p. 70)

10. Related party and other senior management disclosures

Staff members considered to be "key management personnel" are the Director-General, regional directors and all other upgraded staff.

The table below details the number of key management personnel who held these positions over the course of the year as well as their aggregate remuneration.

Key Management personnel

Number of individuals	16
Compensation and post adjustment	3 882 929
Entitlements	281 552
Pension and health plans	974 903
Total remuneration	**5 139 384**
Outstanding advances against entitlements	**128 541**
Outstanding loans (in addition to normal entitlements, if any)	**–**

The aggregate remuneration of key management personnel includes: net salaries, post adjustment, entitlements such as representation allowance and other allowances, assignment and other grants, rental subsidy, personal effect shipment costs, and employer pension and current health insurance contributions.

Key management personnel are also qualified for post-employment benefits at the same level as other employees. These benefits cannot be reliably quantified. Key management personnel are ordinary members of the United Nations Joint Staff Pension Fund.

The Regional Director for the Americas is included among the key management personnel. However, as the Regional Director is receiving all entitlements and benefits from PAHO, the entitlements and benefits concerned are disclosed in PAHO's financial statements and not in WHO's financial statements.

During the year, no loans were granted to key management personnel beyond those widely available to staff outside this grouping.

In the intergovernmental organizations, such as the WHO (IPSAS Financial Reporting in Practice 6.2), related party disclosure relates mainly to key management personnel information, as well as relations with other intergovernmental organizations. The focus is on providing information that is important and relevant to ensure transparency towards their stakeholders.

DISCLOSURE ABOUT THE GENERAL GOVERNMENT SECTOR

IPSAS 22 considers circumstances where governments may carry out additional analysis of their financial statements in line with aggregation approaches used in

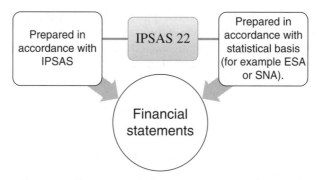

Figure 6.2   The role of IPSAS 22 (cf. Scumesch, 2012: 78)

statistical reporting and subsequently stipulates the disclosures for governments who **elect** to present information about the General Government Sector (GGS) in their consolidated financial statements. This means that IPSAS 22 only applies on a voluntary basis for government's consolidated financial statements. If, however, a government opts to apply IPSAS 22, the government is required to disclose information about the GGS in a manner that is consistent with the accounting policies adopted in the consolidated financial statements.

Objective

IPSAS 22 stipulates that its objective is to prescribe disclosure requirements for governments which elect to present information about the GGS in their consolidated financial statements. The disclosure of appropriate information about the GGS of a government can enhance the transparency of financial reports, and provide for a better understanding of the relationship between the market and non-market activities of the government and between financial statements and statistical bases of financial reporting (IPSAS 22.1).

The Link to Government Statistical Reporting

National governments of many countries produce significant bodies of information in the form of statistical reporting based on surveys and other information-gathering techniques, and these may include financial statements which are prepared in accordance with statistical bases. Figure 6.2 illustrates IPSAS 22 as a means of reconciling the two forms of reporting.

Government statistics may be used to inform policy development and to provide accountability to citizens and to external funding providers. Some countries maintain their accounting records and align their financial reporting with the requirements of statistical bases, while many maintain separate systems. Accounting and financial reporting requirements under most statistical bases differ in important respects from accounting and financial reporting in accordance with, for example, IPSAS. Statistical reporting will include consideration of the General Government

Sector (GGS), which is defined as those parts of government which operate on a non-market basis and excludes those which operate on a market or commercial basis, whether financial (such as state banks) or operational (such as utilities or railways). Thus the GGS includes central, state, and local government units, social security funds, and other non-market non-profit institutions controlled by government units.

By contrast governments reporting under IPSAS are required to consolidate the financial statements of all entities which they control.

The Nature of the General Government Sector (GGS)

This section provides only a high-level introduction to the nature of the GGS. For more information readers should consult the literature relating to Government Financial Statistics (GFS) (see for example, IMF, 2014; IPSASB, 2005).

In line with definitions in statistical reporting frameworks, the GGS comprises all organizational entities of the general government, or more specifically all resident central, state, and local government units, social security funds at each level of government, and non-market non-profit institutions controlled by government units. The GGS thus encompasses the central operations of government and typically includes all those resident non-market non-profit entities that have their operations funded primarily by the government and government entities. The financing of these entities is typically sourced from appropriation or allocation of the government's taxes, dividends from government corporations, other revenues, and borrowings. The GGS typically includes entities such as government departments, law courts, public educational institutions, public health care units, and other agencies (IPSAS 22.18). Typically the GGS includes those entities of government which are essential to the operation of government, but excludes those market or commercial operations which in some jurisdictions might be carried out by non-government agencies or the private sector.

The GGS does not include:

1. Public Financial Corporations (PFCs) and similar institutions which mainly engage in financial intermediation and the provision of financial services to the market. This could, for example, be government-controlled banks, including central banks, and other government financial institutions which operate on a market basis (IPSAS 22.18 and 22.19); or
2. Public Non-Financial Corporations (PNFCs) that produce goods or non-financial services for the market, such as publicly-owned entities and other entities that trade in goods and services (IPSAS 22.18 and 22.20). This might for example be state-owned railways or airlines.

Accounting Policies

General IPSAS 22 requires that financial information about the GGS is disclosed in a manner consistent with the accounting policies adopted for preparing and presenting the consolidated financial statements of the government, except that investments in PFCs and PNFCs are separately disclosed rather than consolidated (IPSAS 22.23–22.25).

At times the application of IPSAS-compliant accounting policies to the GGS aggregates will result in assets and liabilities being measured on a different basis than that under statistical bases of financial reporting. There are no requirements for a reconciliation of the financial information about the GGS, as presented under the requirements of IPSAS and as presented under the requirements of statistical bases of financial reporting.

Investments in Other Sectors

IPSAS 22 requires the separate presentation of financial information about the GGS, and the financial information which does not relate to that sector is restated in simplified form, as net amounts rather than the line items used for consolidation. IPSAS 22 requires that investments in PFCs and PNFCs shall be treated as assets (or liabilities) measured at the carrying amount of net assets of their investees, i.e., at the book value of the individual corporations. Changes in such carrying amounts/book values will be recognized as a single line item of income or expenditure.

Disclosure Requirements

IPSAS 22 requires disclosures showing those amounts which reflect the operations of the GGS. In other words it requires the disaggregation (or removal) of figures relating to market-based operations from the totals given in the consolidated financial statements. IPSAS 22 requires disclosures of disaggregated information for at least the following:

(a) Assets by major class, showing separately the investment in other sectors;
(b) Liabilities by major class;
(c) Net assets/equity;
(d) Total revaluation increments and decrements and other items of revenue and expense recognized directly in net assets/equity;
(e) Revenue by major class;
(f) Surplus or deficit;
(g) Cash flows from operating activities by major class;
(h) Cash flows from investing activities; and
(i) Cash flows from financing activities (IPSAS 22.35).

The disclosures correspond to the main disclosures required by IPSAS 1 Presentation of Financial Information and IPSAS 2 Cash Flow Statements. IPSAS 22 does not however prescribe how the GGS information should be presented and suggests that it be disclosed in notes or in additional columns in the primary financial statements or in any other way deemed appropriate for that jurisdiction (IPSAS 22.37). IPSAS

22 includes an example that shows how the GGS results combine with other sector results to build up to total whole of government results, using a columnar format as follows:

General Government Sector		Public Financial Corporations and Public Non-Financial Corporations		Eliminations (which sum to zero overall)		Total whole of government	
20X1	20X2	20X1	20X2	20X1	20X2	20X1	20X2
A	B	C	D	E	F	A+C+E	B+D+F

In addition to this information the standard requires that the GGS disclosures shall be reconciled to the consolidated financial statements of the government showing separately the amount of the adjustment to each equivalent item in those financial statements (IPSAS 22.43). This requirement provides an additional reason for giving such information in columnar form as described above and as shown in the examples in the standard.

In addition to the disclosures described IPSAS 22 requires that "[e]ntities presenting GGS disclosures shall disclose the significant controlled entities that are included in the GGS and any changes in those entities from the prior period, together with an explanation of the reasons why any such entity that was previously included in the GGS is no longer included" (IPSAS 22.40). This requirement is in addition to the requirement in IPSAS 6 Consolidated and Separate Financial Statements to disclose a list of the significant controlled entities included in the consolidated financial statements. This information will enable readers better to understand the relationship between the GGS and other public sector entities within government.

The first set of accounts in New Zealand applying Public Benefit Entity (PBE)[1] IPSAS 22 will be for the year ending June 2015.[2] As shown in the IPSAS Financial Reporting in Practice 6.3 the New Zealand Accounting Standards Board (NZASB) has modified the disclosure requirements in IPSAS 22 Disclosure of Financial Information about the General Government Sector for the various tiers of financial reporting that have been established in New Zealand. Figure 6.3 provides an overview of the four reporting tiers in New Zealand.

---

[1] Public benefit entities are defined in each standard as "reporting entities whose primary objective is to provide goods or services for community or social benefit and where any equity has been provided with a view to supporting that primary objective rather than for a financial return to equity holders" (see for example EY http://www.ey.com/NZ/en/Issues/IFRS/EY_IFRS_Public-Benefit-Entity-Accounting-Standards, last accessed 22 January 2015).
[2] We thank Professor Rachel Baskerville for highlighting the developments in New Zealand in regard to the adoption of IPSAS and the basis of conclusion accompanying PBE IPSAS 22.

IPSAS Financial Reporting in Practice 6.3. Public Benefit Entity International Public Sector Accounting Standard 22 Disclosure of Financial Information about the General Government Sector

This Basis for Conclusions accompanies, but is not part of, PBE IPSAS 22.

1. BC1. The New Zealand Accounting Standards Board (NZASB) has modified the disclosure requirements in IPSAS 22 *Disclosure of Financial Information about the General Government Sector* for application by Tier 1 public sector entities to accommodate the presentation of a statement of comprehensive revenue and expense. No disclosure concessions have been identified for Tier 2 entities as no Tier 2 entity will apply the Standard.

2. BC2. The NZASB noted that PBE IPSAS 22 will apply only in the event that the New Zealand Government elects to present information on the general government sector in its consolidated financial statements. At the time that PBE IPSAS 22 was issued, the New Zealand Government made information on the general government sector available in a variety of ways, but that information was not included in the consolidated financial statements of the New Zealand Government. The NZASB agreed that if the New Zealand Government were to do so, the requirements of PBE IPSAS 22 would be appropriate.

3. BC3. The NZASB considered whether it was appropriate to issue a standard which would have such limited application. The NZASB noted that developing PBE IPSAS 22 would be consistent with the intention of the External Reporting Board to move towards full adoption of IPSASs.

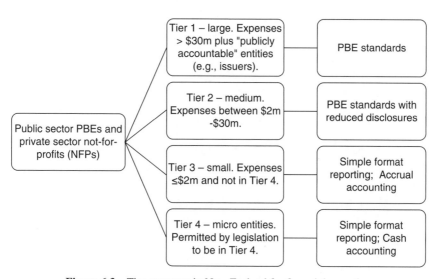

Figure 6.3 Tier structure in New Zealand for financial reporting

In New Zealand the following accounting and financial reporting tiers have been established (Figure 6.3). The New Zealand PBE IPSAS will be revised for not-for-profit entities and are expected to be effective from 1 April 2015 (i.e., the 2015/16 financial year) for Tier 1 and Tier 2 registered charities and other private sector not-for-profit entities. It should be noted that a suite of 39 standards will apply to large and medium-sized public sector PBEs (Tiers 1 and 2). These standards are primarily based on IPSAS, with some modifications for application in New Zealand (see EY, 2013; see also New Zealand Treasury webpage[3]).

---

[3] See http://www.treasury.govt.nz/ (last accessed 22 January 2015).

7 LONG-TERM (NON-CURRENT) ASSETS

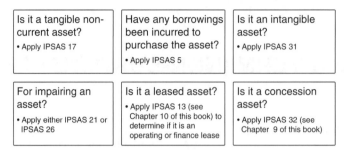

Figure 7.1 Key questions to determine asset and asset related transactions

This chapter covers the IPSAS that detail the requirements for accounting for, and reporting on, long-term assets and related transactions. The chapter thus includes: IPSAS 17 Property, Plant and Equipment; IPSAS 5 Borrowing Costs; IPSAS 31 Intangible Assets; IPSAS 16 Investment Property; IPSAS 21 Impairment of Non-Cash-Generating Assets; and IPSAS 26 Impairment of Cash-Generating Assets. It should also be noted that, where relevant, the requirements, in terms of first-time adoption of the standards pertaining to long-term assets, stipulated in IPSAS 33 on First-time Adoption of Accrual Basis International Public Sector Accounting Standards (IPSAS), will be highlighted. As shown in Table 1.1 in Chapter 1, it becomes mandatory to comply with IPSAS 33, as of 1 January 2017.

In terms of accounting and reporting on assets, following IPSAS, there are items and issues that are specific to the public sector. Examples include heritage assets and infrastructure assets. In addition, the concept of non-cash-generating assets does not exist in private sector accounting (see also for example Bandy, 2014; Jones and Pendlebury, 2010).

Figure 7.1 provides an overview of some key, important questions with answers in terms of which IPSAS to use for which asset and asset-related transactions.

PROPERTY, PLANT AND EQUIPMENT (PP&E) (IPSAS 17)

Accounting and reporting principles for tangible assets are stipulated in IPSAS 17 Property, Plant and Equipment. Property, plant, and equipment (PP&E) are, basically, tangible non-current assets. Examples include land and buildings, machinery, office equipment, motor vehicles, and so forth. More specifically, IPSAS 17 (IPSAS 17.13) defines PP&E as tangible items that (a) are held for use in the production or supply of goods or services, for rental to others, or for administrative purposes; and (b) are expected to be used during more than one reporting period.

Public sector entities typically have ownership of substantial items of PP&E in their statement of financial position. PP&E within the public sector is often held for use in the production or supply of goods and services or for use in the delivery of services.

Objectives and Scope

The principal accounting issues addressed in IPSAS 17 are the recognition of assets, the measurement of assets, and thus the determination of their carrying amounts and the charging of depreciation. In addition, IPSAS 17 embraces assets specific to the public sector. Examples include specialist military equipment and infrastructure assets (cf. IPSAS 17.5). More specifically IPSAS 17 prescribes that PP&E can be separated into different classes, for example (see IPSAS 17.52):

Land
Operational buildings
Machinery
Motor vehicles
Furniture and fixtures
Office equipment
Aircraft
Ships.

It should be noted that the following types of asset are outside the scope of these standards: biological assets and mineral rights (IPSAS 17.6).

In IPSAS 17, some assets are described as heritage assets because of their cultural, environmental, or historical significance (IPSAS 17.9). IPSAS 17 neither requires nor prohibits the recognition of heritage assets. However, a public sector entity that recognizes heritage assets is required to comply with the disclosure requirements of IPSAS 17, including the measurement basis used (IPSAS 17.12).

IPSAS Financial Reporting in Practice 7.1. IAEA PP&E Classes

As an example, the IAEA (2013) Financial Statements provides the following classes of PP&E (see disclosure note 12):

- Buildings and Leasehold Improvements[1]
- Furniture and Fixtures
- Communications and Information Technology Equipment
- Inspection Equipment
- Laboratory Equipment
- Vehicles
- Other Equipment
- Assets under Construction.

---

[1]This chapter includes a mini-case study on the Organization for Security and Co-operation in Europe (OSCE) and questions regarding the right to use assets and leasehold improvements.

The IAEA includes leasehold improvements and buildings as a class of PP&E.[2] In reading IPSAS 17, the standard does not refer to leasehold improvements,[3] although this may be a material class of assets in certain public sector entities. If one turns to the IPSASB Study 14 (2011), it states that "[l]easehold improvements are to be depreciated either over the unexpired period of the lease or the useful lives of the improvements, whichever is the shorter" (p. 181).

Definition

Property, plant, and equipment are defined as tangible items (i.e., they have physical substance) that (IPSAS 17.13):

- Are held for use in the production or supply of goods or services, for rental to others, or for administrative purposes; and
- Are expected to be used during more than one period.

The key issue in terms of whether an asset should be classified as PP&E is the use to which an asset is being put. Many items may be either non-current or current assets (i.e., utilized in more than one period or in only one period) depending on how they are used. For example, aircraft are classified as inventory for aircraft manufacturers (a current asset), whereas aircraft held for use by the Army are PP&E (a non-current asset).

The cost of an item of PP&E is recognized as an asset, if the cost can be measured reliably and it is probable that the asset will generate future economic benefits or service potential for the entity. It is important to note that legal ownership of the item of PP&E is not required for recognition by the entity (IPSAS 17.14).

IPSAS 17 does not prescribe "the unit of measurement" for an item of PP&E, which is thus left to the discretion of management of the public sector entity. It may be appropriate to aggregate individually insignificant items, such as for instance tables and chairs in a school class, to apply the criteria to the aggregate value.

Use and Control of PP&E

To meet the criteria for capitalization and depreciation, assets should be controlled by the public sector entity in question, as a result of past events through purchase, construction, or donation. Future economic benefits or service potential should be expected to flow to the entity as a result (cf. IPSAS 1).

The terms "use" and "control" are critical when applying IPSAS 17. These terms are fundamental in determining whether an asset should be recognized and capitalized or not. When an asset is capitalized, the total cost of the asset is expensed over several accounting periods instead of expensed upon purchase. Public sector entities may need to develop an internal accounting policy to assist the determination of "use" and "control" of PP&E in order to ensure proper and consistent application of these criteria and avoid individual interpretations. Below is an example of how this was done at UNDP.

---

[2] Please see also the case study on leasehold improvements included further down in this chapter.
[3] Neither does IPSAS 13 on Leases.

IPSAS Financial Reporting in Practice 7.2. UNDP Property, Plant and Equipment (PP&E)

UNDP defines the following in its administrative manual, in regards to PP&E:

The term "Property Plant and Equipment" refers to a tangible or physically verifiable item that meets ALL the following five criteria:

- Provides future economic or service benefits to UNDP – i.e., the PP&E item is held for use in the implementation of UNDP Programmes or for administrative purposes;
- Is expected to be used during more than one reporting period, which, in UNDP, is 12 months;
- Has a value of USD1,500 (USD 2,500 for UNCDF) or more;
- Is used and controlled by UNDP; and
- Has a cost that can be reliably determined.

UNDP stipulates that it has control of an asset when it can use or otherwise benefit from the asset in pursuit of its objectives and can exclude or otherwise regulate the access of others to that benefit. In general, an asset will meet the "use and control" criteria where it is physically located on UNDP premises (whether owned or leased).

It is recognized that UNDP operates under various implementation modalities. These implementation modalities are also a useful indicator of whether UNDP uses and controls an asset.

All assets bought from the biennium support budget or institutional budget qualify for capitalization if they meet all the five criteria listed above. In addition, assets acquired for projects implemented through Country Office Support […] may qualify for capitalization, provided the assets are under the "use and control" of UNDP. Such assets are referred to in this policy as development project assets.

If a project under which UNDP has "use and control" over the assets is expected to last exactly one year or less and the assets are under UNDP's use and control before the project is closed, Offices should record and capitalize such assets instead of expensing, as the process to transfer assets takes time and such assets will end up having been used and controlled by UNDP for more than 12 months.

In addition to location as a means of determining control, additional criteria that may be used to determine whether UNDP has control over PP&E are, as follows:

- Was the act of purchasing the PP&E item carried out (or resulted from) instructions given by UNDP?
- Is Legal title in the name of UNDP?
- Is the PP&E item physically located on premises or locations used by UNDP?
- Is the PP&E item physically used by staff employed by UNDP or by personnel working under UNDP's instructions?
- Can UNDP decide on an alternative use of the PP&E item?

- Is it UNDP that decides to sell, or dispose of, the PP&E item?
- If the PP&E item were to be removed or destroyed, would UNDP take the decision to replace it?
- Does a UNDP representative regularly inspect the PP&E to determine its current working condition?

In determining whether or not an asset should be recorded in UNDP's books the substance of the transaction needs to be considered. For example, If UNDP hands over a vehicle to an implementing partner that has total "use and control" over the asset but nevertheless retains the vehicle title in UNDP's name, then the vehicle should not be recorded in UNDP's books as UNDP does not manage this vehicle on a daily basis nor does it have control over how it is used. It is recommended that in all cases, apart from the case of NGO implementation, handing over of a vehicle is accompanied by transfer of title as well.

Source: See UNDP, https://info.undp.org/global/popp/asm/pages/property-plant-and-equipment.aspx

The mini-case study on the Organization for Security and Co-operation in Europe (OSCE), which is located in Vienna, Austria, is presented later in this chapter and will provide an interesting analysis of the OSCE's approach to determining use and control of an asset.

Initial Recognition and Elements of Cost

PP&E should initially be recognized in an entity's statement of financial position at cost (IPSAS 17.26). Cost is the amount of cash and cash equivalents paid to acquire the asset at the time of its acquisition or construction, plus the fair value of any other consideration given (IPSAS 17.13).

Cost can include (IPSAS 17.30):

- Purchase price;
- Any costs directly attributable to bringing the asset to its current location and condition; and
- The initial estimate of dismantling and removing the item and restoring the site where it is located if the entity is obliged to do so.

Costs that are not directly attributable to the item cannot be recognized as part of PP&E. Such costs are expensed as they are incurred, unless it is appropriate to recognize them under another accounting standard. Examples of costs that should normally be expensed as they are incurred include the cost of opening a new facility, introducing new service, staff training in order to be able to use the new asset, administration, and general overheads.

Question and Answer

Question:

A difficult point for public sector entities adopting IPSAS can be to identify when a purchase of new good is a **spare part** and when it is just **consumable**; when does it give added or renovated value, and when would the residual value not be increased?

Answer:

Spare parts are usually inventory and are expensed when consumed (IPSAS 12.12). However, some spare parts are not classified as inventory but as property, plant, and equipment. This is the case for major spare parts which are expected to be used during more than one period. The same applies to spare parts that can be used only in connection with a specific PP&E (IPSAS 17.17).

In practice, it has to be sufficiently material not to be considered as inventory.

In order to prevent an individual interpretation of spare parts qualified as PP&E, public sector entities may consider a limited list of spare parts qualifying as PP&E (major and strategic spare parts with a material impact on the financial statements) and decide that other spare parts are pieces of inventory.

Entities may adopt the same materiality approach for purchased goods giving added or renovated value, limiting capitalization to material items only. These criteria can be explained in their internal accounting manual, and a summary of these main assumptions disclosed in the notes to the financial statements.

Recognition of an Asset Acquired through Non-Exchange Transaction

An asset acquired through a non-exchange transaction[4] is initially measured at its fair value as at the date of acquisition (IPSAS 17.27). Note that non-exchange revenue and assets arising from such transactions are described in detailed in Chapter 11 of this book.

In case of exchange of unlike assets or asset trade-in, the cost is measured at the fair value of the asset received, equivalent to the fair value of the asset relinquished adjusted by the amount of any cash transferred.

IPSAS Financial Reporting in Practice 7.3. Goods-in-kind at IAEA, 2013 Financial Statements

Goods that are donated to the Agency are recognized as revenue if the item value is worth €3 000 or more, with a corresponding increase in the appropriate asset, when such

---

[4] This would be when an asset is acquired at no cost (gifted, contributed, or donated) or for a nominal cost.

> donations are received by the Agency. Revenue is recognized at fair value, measured as of the date the donated goods are recognized. Fair value is generally measured by reference to the price of the same or similar goods in an active market. (p. 43)

In the above example, IAEA discloses how goods-in-kind are recognized. IAEA has decided to apply a threshold limiting the recognition as PPE of items whose value is €3 000 or more. This is an application of the materiality concept, meaning that items below this threshold have been considered as insignificant. It does mean that the fact of not recognizing them as assets in the statement of financial position with a corresponding revenue in the statement of financial performance has been judged as having no impact for the reader of the financial statements.

Capitalization Threshold

A capitalization threshold settles the cut-off point at which expenditure that provides future economic benefits greater than 12 months (i.e., non-current) is capitalized as an asset (cf. Edgerton, 2013). Expenditure below the determined threshold is expensed and is referred to as either operational expenditure or maintenance.

As described by Edgerton (2013) the rules around capitalization can become quite complex, depending upon the type and nature of the asset and the relative size of the organization. In addition it may also depend upon whether the asset is part of a network that, in combination, provides the future economic benefit, such as a reticulated water network.

It is appropriate to establish a capitalization threshold for each asset class based on an assessment of materiality, cost, and benefit. This is also illustrated in IPSAS Financial Reporting in Practice 7.2, UNDP Property, Plant and Equipment (PP&E) where you can see the set threshold for UNDP.

Accounting for infrastructure assets is complex. It is appropriate that the development of the asset management framework would include determination of what intervention activities represent capital treatments, with the lower cost being referred to as maintenance activities (cf. Edgerton, 2013).

Costing of a Self-Constructed Asset

The cost of a self-constructed asset is determined using the same principles as for an acquired asset. It is thus not appropriate to include, as part of the cost of constructing the asset, an allocation for internal profit. Any abnormal costs incurred by the entity, for example those arising from design errors, wastage, or industrial disputes, should be expensed as they are incurred and do not form part of the capitalized cost of the PP&E asset.

Under IPSAS it is permitted, but not required, to capitalize borrowing costs (IPSAS 5) that are directly attributable to the acquisition, construction, or production of a qualifying asset in accordance with IPSAS 5 Borrowing Costs (IPSAS 17.36).

The recognition of costs as part of a PP&E asset should stop when the item is able to function/operate in the manner intended by management. For self-constructed assets, this would be when the asset has been fully constructed and tested and is installed in the location intended, even if the asset has not yet been put into use. Any operating losses that are incurred during the early part of an asset's life while demand is being built up, should not be recognized as part of the asset.

Cost is measured as the cash price at the time of recognition of the asset. If payment is deferred beyond normal credit terms, the cost recognized is discounted to take account of the time value of money. The difference is recognized as interest (IPSAS 17.37).

If the entity exchanges one of its assets instead of paying cash to acquire an asset, the new asset should be recognized at "fair value." Fair value is defined as "the amount for which an asset could be exchanged between knowledgeable, willing parties in an arm's length transaction." This treatment assumes that the exchange transaction has commercial substance and fair value is reliably measurable (IPSAS 17.38–17.40). Otherwise, its cost is measured at the carrying amount of the asset relinquished.

Heritage Assets

IPSAS 17 stipulates that "some assets are described as heritage assets because of their cultural, environmental or historical significance," providing specific examples and characteristics. IPSAS 17 does not require an entity to recognize heritage assets that would otherwise meet the definition of, and recognition criteria for, PP&E. However, if an entity does recognize heritage assets, it is required to apply the disclosure requirements stipulated in IPSAS 17 and may, but is not required to, apply the measurement requirements of IPSAS 17.

IPSAS Financial Reporting in Practice 7.4. Heritage Assets, UNESCO 2013 Financial Statements

Heritage assets are not recognized in the financial statements, but appropriate disclosure is made in the notes to the accounts. (p. 40)

Heritage assets

UNESCO also has a significant number of "Works of Art" (also referred to as heritage assets), including paintings, statues and various other objects, which have been mainly donated by governments, artists and other partners. An internal fund has been set-up to cover accidental damage to these works, which have a considerable intrinsic value. The value of these works is not recognized in the financial statements of UNESCO in compliance with IPSAS 17. (p. 50)

Aversano and Ferrone (2012) highlight some peculiarities of cultural heritage assets, which cause implications for accounting for such assets. More specifically they point out that (p. 574):

- It is very difficult to identify a book value based on market prices that fully reflects the value of cultural, environmental, educational, or historical assets;
- There are legal or statutory restrictions that prohibit or limit the sale;
- Are often irreplaceable and their value may increase over time, even if their physical condition deteriorates;
- Can be difficult to estimate the useful life, which in some cases, may also be indefinite.

Infrastructure Assets

Infrastructure is composed of those assets required to meet the public need for access to major economic and social facilities and services. IPSAS 17 states that, while there is no universally accepted definition of infrastructure assets, these assets usually display some or all of the following (see IPSAS 17.21):

(a) They are part of a system or network;
(b) They are specialized in nature and do not have alternative uses;
(c) They are immovable; and
(d) They may be subject to constraints on disposal.

Infrastructure assets represent a significant economic resource managed by public sector entities (usually governments) on behalf of the citizens they represent. Examples of infrastructure assets include road networks, sewer systems, water and power supply systems, and communication networks.

Infrastructure assets accounting requires significant enhancements to public sector entities' (usually governments') asset management systems and is extremely complex.

It is necessary to establish formal guidelines about defining and reporting asset physical condition, in order to adequately maintain and/or replace critical infrastructure assets, and therefore determine their useful life. It creates the implicit need for regular updates of the financial and physical condition of these assets; otherwise, governments would have no means of planning for or predicting when infrastructure asset replacement is necessary.

Commonly, infrastructure or specialized public sector assets are valued applying the cost approach, with the replacement cost used to determine fair value based on the cost of replacing the service potential delivered by the existing asset (Edgerton, 2013).

For instance, Australian local governments are responsible for providing basic infrastructure services to their communities. These services include roads, drainage, recreation facilities, and public buildings and in some states water supply and sewerage. Social services are mainly the responsibility of the state governments together with education, police, fire services, and public housing. And the community is demanding more and better quality services at a lower cost. Local government is a highly capital-intensive industry requiring management effort to ensure that the community receives maximum value for its investment in infrastructure and that services can be provided at the lowest life-cycle cost. In 1993, Australian Accounting Standard 27 (AAS27) was applied to local governments. The standard, issued by the Australian Accounting Research Foundation, specifies the nature and form of local governments' general purpose financial reports. The major impact for engineers was that local governments were required to report on the current value and rate of consumption of their infrastructure assets. The value of investment in infrastructure by Australian local governments is approximately $135 billion. These infrastructure assets provide services essential for the community; the assets are being consumed at a rate of $2.6 billion per year ($300 000 per hour). AAS27 gave engineers the tools to report annually on asset condition and consumption to councilors, management, and the community (Howard, 2001).

As described in Chapter 3, the IPSASB recognizes that further work is required to better define the accounting for infrastructure assets.

Subsequent Expenditure

Subsequent expenses are major renovations and improvements to property, plant, and equipment. They are considered to increase the future economic benefits or service potential of the asset. Subsequent expenses should improve the condition of the asset, measured over its estimated useful life, beyond its most recently assessed standard of performance. Where subsequent expenditure enhances the value of the asset to the extent that additional economic benefits will flow to the entity, the additional expenditure should be recognized as part of the asset's cost.

Typically, in practice, to capitalize subsequent expenses: (a) the relevant property, plant, and equipment must have a remaining estimated useful life of more than one year after the completion of the expense; and (b) the cost of subsequent expense must exceed the cost threshold applicable to the class of assets.

It should be highlighted that subsequent expenses differ from routine repairs and maintenance and servicing costs which should normally be recognized in surplus or deficit when the costs are incurred (IPSAS 17.23).

In cases where an asset is made up of many distinct parts, these should be separately identified. Therefore, where part of an asset is replaced at regular intervals, the additional cost will replace the cost of the original part of the asset (IPSAS 17.24). This is, for instance, the case of buildings, which can be split into the structure, roof, doors/windows, and fittings. The structure will not need to be replaced, while the roof will need to be replaced from time to time, but less often than the fittings.

IPSAS 17 stipulates that where major overhauls take place, the cost of such overhauls should be recognized as part of the carrying amount of the item of PP&E, assuming that the overhaul meets the recognition criteria. An example is where an aircraft is required to undergo a major overhaul after a certain number of flying hours. Without the overhaul the aircraft would not be permitted to continue flying (IPSAS 17.25). This is also the case for nuclear power plants.

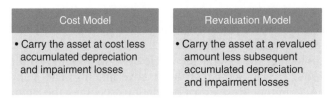

Figure 7.2   Cost vs. revaluation model

Impairment loss

If an asset's carrying amount on the balance sheet exceeds its recoverable amount, its carrying amount should be reduced to reflect this (IPSAS 17.13). Impairment and impairment losses are covered by IPSAS 26 Impairment of Cash Generating Assets and IPSAS 21 Impairment of Non-Cash Generating Assets. Impairment is described in detail in section 7.5 of this chapter.

The Cost Model and Depreciation

Depreciation is defined as the systematic allocation of the cost of an asset, less any residual value, over its useful life. This is a way of charging part of the net cost of an asset in each period, so that at the end of the asset's useful life to the entity, the whole of its net cost has been recognized in surplus or deficit. In each period, the carrying amount of the asset in the statement of financial position is reduced by the depreciation charged (see Figure 7.2).

The residual value of an asset is the estimated amount that an entity would currently obtain from the disposal of the asset, after deducting costs of disposal, if the asset were already of the age and condition expected at the end of its useful life (IPSAS 17.13). Depreciable amount is the cost of an asset less its residual value (IPSAS 17.13). An asset's useful life is the period over which an asset is expected to be available for use by an entity (IPSAS 17.13).

Depreciation does not relate to the value of an asset, because it is a way of writing off its cost over its useful life. Therefore an increase in the current value of an asset does not itself justify not depreciating the asset.

A variety of depreciation methods can be used to allocate the depreciable amount of an asset over its systematic life. The most common method is the straight-line method (IPSAS 17.78).

Example 7.1   Depreciation

An entity buys a car for a total cost of CU20 000. It is estimated that the car has a useful life of four years, at the end of which its residual value is CU4 000 and it can be sold for this amount as a second-hand car. The entity adopts the straight-line method of depreciation.

The depreciable amount is CU20 000 less CU4 000 = CU16 000.

The depreciable amount is allocated systematically over the useful life of the asset. On the straight-line basis, an equal cost is taken to surplus or deficit each year. This can be calculated as follows:

Annual depreciation charge = Depreciable amount/Useful life

Annual depreciation charge = CU16000/4 years = CU4 000 per annum

Each year the carrying amount of the asset decreases by CU4 000 and there is a depreciation expense of CU4 000 in surplus or deficit.

The straight-line method results in a constant depreciation charge over the asset's useful life.

Other common methods of depreciation are the diminishing balance method and the units of production method (IPSAS 17.78). Under the diminishing balance method, the depreciation charge decreases over the life of the asset. The units of production method results in a charge based on the expected use or output. An entity should select a depreciation method that most closely reflects the expected pattern of the consumption of the future economic benefits embodied in the asset (IPSAS 17.76). The depreciation method should be reviewed at least annually and changed if appropriate (IPSAS 77).

IPSAS Financial Reporting in Practice 7.5. Depreciation at IAEA, 2013 Financial Statements

Depreciation method and useful life

35. Depreciation is charged so as to allocate the cost of assets over their estimated useful lives using the straight-line method. The estimated useful lives for the different PP&E classes are as follows, and are subject to annual review:

Asset Class	Useful Life (Years)
Communications and IT equipment	4
Vehicles	5
Furniture and Fixtures	12
Buildings	5 years (for prefabricated and containerized structures) and 15 to 100 years for others
Leasehold Buildings and Improvements	Shorter of lease term or useful life
Inspection Equipment	5
Laboratory Equipment	5
Other Equipment	5

IAEA uses only the straight-line method, which is, in most cases, the method used by entities, unless they find a more appropriate one. IAEA uses a wide range of useful lives for its buildings, from five years for prefabricated and containerized structures up to 100 years for other buildings.

Significant parts of PP&E and depreciation

In accordance with IPSAS, each significant part of an item of PP&E should be depreciated separately. For example, within a road system, pavements, formation, curbs and channels, footpaths, bridges, and lighting will be depreciated separately, when they have different useful lives (IPSAS 17.60).

Land and buildings are separable assets and should therefore be accounted for separately even if they were acquired together. Land usually has an infinite life, with some exceptions such as quarries and landfill sites, whereas buildings do not and should therefore be depreciated (IPSAS 17.74).

The Revaluation Model

An entity can, following IPSAS 17, choose to revalue its assets to their fair value (see Figure 7.2). For land and buildings this is normally determined based on their market values as determined by an appraisal undertaken by professionally qualified valuers (IPSAS 17.44, 17.45).

However, for some specialized property, such as heritage assets used as offices, there is no ready market because such items are rarely sold, except as part of a continuing business. In these circumstances, the standard sets out that the fair value should be estimated using an income, or a depreciated replacement cost approach. A depreciated replacement cost approach looks at what the replacement cost of an asset would be and then depreciates that value for the current age of the asset held (IPSAS 17.48).

Example 7.2   Depreciated replacement cost approach

Here is an example of where the depreciated replacement cost approach would be appropriate.

An entity acquires a specialized scientific equipment for CU2 000 000. Due to the specialized nature of the equipment, there is no active resale market for it.

The entity revalues its equipment. The equipment is currently half way through its life and therefore its carrying amount would have been CU1 000 000 using a cost model and assuming a straight-line method of depreciation with no residual value. To replace the asset new would cost CU2 600 000.

The estimated depreciated replacement cost would, therefore, be 50% of the CU2 600 000, i.e., CU1 300 000.

If the revaluation model is used, regular revaluations are required (IPSAS 17.49).

If the revaluation model is applied to one asset, it must also be applied to all other assets in the same class of property, plant, and equipment. In other words, if you apply the revaluation model to one building, you must apply it to all buildings (IPSAS 17.51).

Note that when the revaluation model is used, PP&E must still be depreciated. The revalued amount is depreciated over the asset's remaining useful life.

Example 7.3   Classes of PP&E and their valuation, New Zealand Government

The following table shows examples of classes of PP&E valued either at amortized cost or at fair value by the New Zealand Government, and the method chosen to determine fair value for each class of assets.

Class of PP&E	Accounting policy
Land and buildings	Land and buildings are recorded at fair value less impairment losses and, for buildings, less depreciation accumulated since the assets were last revalued.
	Valuations undertaken in accordance with standards issued by the Property Institute of New Zealand are used where available.
	Otherwise, valuations conducted in accordance with the Rating Valuation Act 1998 may be used if they have been confirmed as appropriate by an independent valuer.
	When revaluing buildings, there must be componentization to the level required to ensure adequate representation of the material components of the buildings. At a minimum, this requires componentization to three levels – structure, building services, and fit-out.
Specialist military equipment	Specialist military equipment is recorded at fair value (which is determined using depreciated replacement cost) less depreciation and impairment losses accumulated since the assets were last revalued.
	Valuations are obtained through specialist assessment by New Zealand Defence Force advisers, and the bases of these valuations are confirmed as appropriate by an independent valuer.
State highways	State highways are recorded at fair value (which is determined using depreciated replacement cost) less depreciation and impairment losses accumulated since the assets were last revalued. Land associated with the state highways is valued using an opportunity cost based on adjacent use, as an approximation to fair value.
Aircraft	Aircraft (excluding Specialized Military Equipment) are recorded at fair value less depreciation and impairment losses accumulated since the assets were last revalued.
Electricity distribution	Electricity distribution network assets are recorded at cost, less accumulated depreciation and accumulated impairment losses.
Electricity generation	Electricity generation assets are recorded at fair value less depreciation and impairment losses accumulated since the assets were last revalued.
Other PP&E	Other property, plant, and equipment, which include motor vehicles and office equipment, are recorded at cost less accumulated depreciation and accumulated impairment losses.
Specified cultural and heritage assets	Specified cultural and heritage assets comprise national parks, conservation areas, and related recreational facilities, as well as National Archives holdings and the collections of the National Library, Parliamentary Library, and Te Papa. Such physical assets are recorded at fair value less subsequent impairment losses and, for non-land assets, less subsequent accumulated depreciation.

Most of the above classes of PP&E are valued at fair value, except electricity distribution network assets, motor vehicles, and office equipment, and some other PP&E. It shows that the New Zealand Government has clearly chosen to revalue its PP&E to fair value on a regular basis (not specified here) in order to give a more accurate and up-to-date value of its assets.

De-recognition

Property, plant, and equipment are to be de-recognized (i.e., removed from the statement of financial position) either on disposal or when no future economic benefits (or service potential) are expected from their use or disposal (IPSAS 17.82).

The gain or loss arising from de-recognition is included in surplus or deficit. This gain or loss is calculated by comparing the sale proceeds to the asset's carrying amount. The gain or loss is calculated in the same way, regardless of whether the asset is revalued or not (IPSAS 17.83 and 17.86).

If, on disposal of a revalued asset, there remains a balance on the revaluation surplus relating to the asset, this balance should be transferred to surplus or deficit. This transfer is shown as a movement between reserves and does not form part of any surplus or deficit on disposal of the item.

Example 7.4   Asset de-recognition

An entity has an item of equipment with a carrying amount of CU2 000. It is sold for CU5 000. How is this accounted for?

In this case the entity has made a gain on disposal of CU5 000 - CU2 000 = CU3 000.

This gain would be recognized in surplus or deficit.

The asset would be removed from the statement of financial position, i.e., de-recognized.

Let's imagine that an entity has equipment with a carrying amount of CU2 000. It decides to replace this item by a new one and therefore no future economic benefits (nor service potential) are expected from its use or disposal.

In this case the entity has made a loss on disposal of CU2 000. This loss would be recognized in surplus or deficit.The asset would also be de-recognized from the statement of financial position at the date of its disposal.

Professional Judgment

Under IPSAS there is a requirement to disclose areas where significant judgment has been exercised (IPSAS 1.137). In terms of PP&E there are a number of aspects in which professional judgment is required. A few examples will be highlighted here. Judgment is for example necessary when estimating the useful lives of PP&E. It is often the case that manufacturers of assets will provide the entity with an expected lifetime for the asset. This may however be influenced by a range of factors.

Example 7.5   Useful lives for vehicles

A public sector entity operates in a country with differing weather and road conditions. This entity has a large number of vehicles which are thus of material value to the entity. Some vehicles are based in city areas while others are based in rural, desert areas. Based on analysis of the vehicle fleet, the entity observed that the vehicles (of the same brand and type) in city areas last approximately three years longer than those in the rural, desert areas.

This means that vehicles of the same type have different useful lives: shorter ones in rural, desert areas than in city areas since climatic and road conditions make them last less time in the rural, desert areas.

The determination of cost of an asset, or part of an asset, may require the exercise of judgment. For example, the capitalization of the appropriate amount of interest relating to qualifying assets where borrowing costs are not related directly requires judgment (IPSAS 5 Borrowing Costs is covered later in this chapter).

MINI CASE STUDY: Right to use buildings and leasehold improvements –The case of OSCE Headquarters in Vienna, Austria[5]

Background

The Headquarters of the Organization for Security and Co-operation in Europe (OSCE) are located in Vienna, Austria, more specifically in the former Palais Palffi in the Wallnerstrasse. During the Ministerial Council Decision MC(10).DEC/9 taken at the Porto MC on 7 December 2002, the OSCE welcomed the offer of the Austrian Government to endow the Organization with a new representative office premises in Vienna. Prior to Wallnerstrasse, the OSCE was also located in the city center, but within a commercial building which was largely devoted to a shopping mall.

The total estimated costs of the partial reconstruction, refurbishing, and building adjustment of the former Palais Palffi in the Wallnerstrasse were initially estimated at €30 million. Of this amount the Austrian Government agreed to pay 90% and the OSCE was called upon to allocate funds for the remaining amount along with the costs of security arrangements.

Is this building an OSCE asset?

The user agreement concluded between the Republic of Austria (RoA) and the OSCE on November 2007 was analyzed for the purpose of determining if there was any indication that a substantial transfer of the risks and rewards incidental to the use of the building would transfer to the OSCE, which would constitute a basis for the capitalization of the building.

---

[5]Contributing author Melissa Dias Buerbaumer, Ph.D., CPA, Chief of Accounts at the OSCE.

IPSAS 13 Leases provides guidance regarding the circumstances which would lead to a lease being qualified as a finance lease (capitalized in the Statement of Financial Position of the lessee). These include:

   (i) Ownership being transferred by the end of the lease term to the lessee;

  (ii) Lease containing a bargain purchase option;

 (iii) Lease term is for the majority of the asset's economic life if without transfer of title;

 (iv) Specialized nature of the asset, so that only the lessee can use it without major modifications.

In this case, the OSCE has been offered the right to use the premises at Wallnerstrasse, so the agreement as such is not of a commercial nature. However the above criteria for capitalization of leases can be used as authoritative comparative guidance for the analysis of the case which lead us to recommend the policy of not capitalizing the building premises based on the "user agreement":

   (i) *Is there transfer of ownership of the building at the end of the agreement to the OSCE?* No. The RoA is the legally registered owner of the property. On the termination of the use relationship the premises together with all fixtures and fittings shall be returned to the RoA in good condition, apart from the normal wear and tear or damage through force majeure.

  (ii) *Does the agreement contain a bargain purchase option?* No. See also the above answer.

 (iii) *Is the agreement for the majority of the asset's economic life?* No. While the agreement specifies that the property is provided free of charge to the OSCE for use as the permanent HQ of the Organization, the palace dates back from the beginning of the 19th century[6] whereas the OSCE has only been using it as an office building since 2007.

 (iv) *Is the asset specialized in nature?* No. While improvements were undertaken prior to hosting OSCE's HQ in the palace, these were generic in nature. So should the OSCE hand the premises back to the RoA, the building could be further utilized by other companies, organizations, or institutions.

In addition to the above, further analysis of risks and rewards of the usage of the building revealed that:

- The property may be used only as offices of the permanent HQ of the OSCE in Vienna and may in no way be transferred to third parties without the written agreement of the RoA.

---

[6] In 1811 Count Johann Palffy commissioned a three-storey Empire-style palais to be built on the site. In 1922 the architect Leopold Bauer planned renovation of the palais for the Anglo-Austrian Bank. In 2001 the Burghauptmannschaft Austria took charge of the project and a new location for the OSCE was planned.

- The RoA covers the insurance against the risks of fire, storm, water damage, and third party liability for the property. While the OSCE just covers the insurance against breakage of glass, and contents insurance.
- The property is classified as a *protected historical building*. Therefore it remains the responsibility of the RoA to carry out and bear the costs of maintainance of the fabric of the premises, such as all foundations, pillars, beams, roofs, walls, facades, stairs, exterior paint work and glass, etc. Also the RoA carries out and bears the costs of material maintenance and building service equipment.
- The OSCE must inform the RoA in advance in case of any alterations to the premises.
- Any fixtures, improvements, or additions remain the sole property of the RoA.

Based on the above analysis, we concluded that the risks and rewards associated with the use of the Wallnerstrasse premises (a protected historical building) were not fully transferred to the OSCE but remained with the Republic of Austria.

Leasehold improvements

Pursuant to PC.DEC 709 of 15 December 2005, the Wallnerstrasse fund was established, with the purpose of financing OSCE's share of the costs related to the renovation and refurbishment of the designated premises, as well as those related to the required adjustments to the building and security arrangements. An amount of €3.96 million was allocated to the Wallnerstrasse fund from the cash surplus of 2004 for this purpose.

Following PC.DEC 774 from 21 December 2006, the fund was further increased by an amount of €1.1 million from the cash surplus of 2005.

The additional funding was allocated to financing OSCE's costs related to removal expenditure from Kaertner Ring to the Wallnerstrasse premises, the reinstatement of the former premises, and the costs of new fixtures and fittings at the Wallnerstrasse.

Costs incurred under the Wallnerstrasse fund were analyzed to determine which would meet the criteria for capitalization as leasehold improvements.

From the total EUR 5 million allocated to the Wallnerstrasse fund, €4.1 million or 82% qualify as leasehold improvements. These refer to building adjustments (including elevator); technical infrastructure (electricity, heating, and cooling system); and the communication infrastructure, security, and IT (LAN and cabling, optic cabling, optic fibre installation, etc.).

Since these building components have different useful lives, they were aggregated accordingly in three different categories.

The impact of this capitalization is reflected as an increase in Net Assets/Equity (IPSAS reserve) equivalent to the current net book value of the improvements.

Leasehold improvements are reported as a separate class in the Notes to the Financial Statements.

Costs also charged against the above-mentioned fund but that do not qualify for capitalization refer to: the office move from former premises in Kaernter Ring, new furniture and equipment, supplies, software, printing costs, etc.

Transitional Provisions

In order to cater for situations where it may be difficult to compile information on assets for the first-time application of IPSAS 17, IPSAS 17.95 offers some flexibility allowing entities a five-year period to bring PP&E onto the balance sheet.

IPSAS 17 stipulates that the cost of an infrastructure asset, acquired at no or nominal cost, is its fair value at the date of acquisition. Where the cost of acquisition is not known, cost may be estimated by reference to fair value at the date of acquisition (IPSAS 17.98).

Note on Upcoming Change 7.1. IPSAS 33 on First-time Adoption of Accrual Basis International Public Sector Accounting Standards (IPSASs)

It should be noted that a first-time adopter of IPSAS shall apply IPSAS 33 if its first IPSAS financial statements are for a period beginning on or after January 1, 2017. Earlier application is allowed. IPSAS 33 stipulates that a three-year relief for recognition and/or measurement of assets and changing the accounting policy to measure assets is permitted. This means that IPSAS 33 reduces the transition provision from five years to three years.

Disclosures

IPSAS 17 requires a number of disclosures (see IPSAS 17.88–17.94).

A reconciliation of the carrying amount at the beginning and end of each period is disclosed in relation to the movement in PP&E. The reconciliation should show all movements during the period, including additions, assets classified as held for sale and other disposals, impairment losses, revaluations, depreciation, and acquisitions made as part of a business combination. The most practical way to meet these disclosure requirements is to present the information in the form of a table. The reconciliation should be set out for each class of assets (IPSAS 17.88).

In addition to a full reconciliation, the entity should disclose its depreciation policy and rates (or length of the useful lives). Where the entity adopts a policy of revaluation, this should be explained along with information on when the last valuation exercise was carried out, whether the valuation was carried out by an independent valuer, the major assumptions used in the valuation, and on what basis the fair value was determined, for example by reference to an active market. In addition, the carrying amount of the revalued asset based on cost should be set out, along with the amount of the revaluation surplus, with any movements during the period highlighted (IPSAS 17.92).

Information is also required to be disclosed on a number of ancillary items which involve PP&E. These disclosures include the existence and amount of any restrictions on the title of PP&E (where PP&E has been pledged as security over some of the entity's liabilities), the amount of any expenditure recognized in respect of assets in the course of construction, the amount of any contractual commitments for the future acquisition of items of PP&E, and the amount of any compensation received in respect of impaired or lost assets (IPSAS 17.89).

IPSAS Financial Reporting in Practice 7.6. Property, Plant and Equipment, UNESCO, 2013

Financial Statements

NOTE 13 – PROPERTY, PLANT AND EQUIPMENT (PP&E)

Expressed in '000 US dollars	Land	Buildings	Comms & IT Equipment	Vehicles	Furniture and Fixtures	Other equipment	Total
As at January 1, 2013							
Cost or fair value	254 713	383 314	28 242	6 427	2 887	14 979	690 562
Accumulated depreciation	–	−41 275	−23 608	−5 111	−2 438	−9 829	−82 261
Carrying amount	254 713	342 039	4 634	1 316	449	5 150	608 301
Movements period to 31/12/2013							
Additions	–	234	3 101	706	199	1 270	5 510
Disposals	–	–	−1 492	−336	−16	−2 039	−3 883
Disposals depreciation	–	–	1 479	336	16	1 687	3 518
Impairment	–	–	–	–	–	–	–
Depreciation	–	−13 766	−2 525	−645	−210	−1 334	−18 480
Exchange adjustments depn	–	−19	−272	−6	−31	−183	−511
Exchange adjustments cost	–	109	347	6	38	332	832
Total movements 12 months to 31 December 2013	–	**−13 442**	**638**	**61**	**−4**	**−267**	**−13 014**

As at December 31, 2013

Cost or fair value	254 713	383 657	30 198	6 803	3 108	14 542	693 021
Accumulated depreciation	–	−55 060	−24 926	−5 426	−2 663	−9 659	−97 734
Carrying amount	**254 713**	**328 597**	**5 272**	**1 377**	**445**	**4 883**	**595 287**

As at December 31, 2013, UNESCO holds fully depreciated PP&E which is still in use for a gross value of K$17,041.

The carrying value of UNESCO buildings is detailed in the following table:

Description Expressed in '000 US dollars	Opening carry value 31/12/2012	Depreciation for period	Additions for period	Exchange adjustment	Closing carry value 31/12/2013
7 Place Fontenoy	186 739	−7 616	–	–	179 123
1 Rue Miollis	138 458	−5 649	–	–	132 809
Apartment, place Vauban	5 476	−117	–	–	5 359
IBE building, Geneva	7 818	−271	–	–	7 547
Ocampo Villa, Buenos Aires	1 410	−28	–	–	1 382
IHE building renovation, Delft	2 138	−85	234	90	2 377
Total	**342 039**	**−13 766**	**234**	**90**	**328 597**

The above note shows the presentation of PP&E disclosures in the UNESCO financial statements for 2013. UNESCO focuses on significant information on PP&E, which are the carrying values of UNESCO buildings, which are recognized as finance leases (see Chapter 10), as well as on the gross value of PP&E which are fully depreciated but still in use.

BORROWING COSTS (IPSAS 5)

Public sector entities may finance the construction of major capital projects, such as roads or other infrastructure assets through borrowings, on which the entity incurs finance costs. IPSAS 5 on Borrowing Costs stipulates the accounting treatment of such costs.

IPSAS 5 is only applicable for what is termed "qualifying assets" (IPSAS 5.13). Examples of qualifying assets include the construction of office buildings, hospitals, and infrastructure assets (IPSAS 5.13) and the construction of manufacturing plants and power-generating facilities (see Figure 7.3).

IPSAS 5 Borrowing Costs allows both the expensing of all borrowing costs in the period in which they were incurred and the alternative treatment of capitalizing borrowing costs that are directly attributable to the acquisition, construction, or production of a qualifying asset.

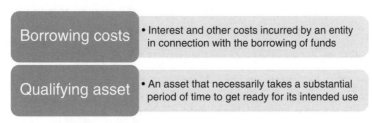

Figure 7.3   Borrowing costs and qualifying assets

Capitalization of Borrowing Costs

If funds are borrowed specifically for the purpose of obtaining a qualifying asset, the amounts capitalized should be those actually incurred during the period less any investment income on the temporary investment of those borrowings (IPSAS 5.23).

Example 7.6   Borrowing costs

An entity is in the process of constructing a building, corresponding to the definition of a qualifying asset. On the same day as the planning of the project is started, the entity borrows funds for CU10 000 000 specifically for this purpose and incurs borrowing costs of CU80 000 during the construction period. It earns CU10 000 of interest by investing these funds prior to spending them on the qualifying asset.

The amount of interest that can be added to the cost of the asset is CU80 000 less CU10 000 = CU70 000. Only borrowing costs can be added to the cost of the qualifying asset; borrowing funds cannot.

There may be periods when the development of an asset is temporarily suspended. During such inactive periods the capitalization of borrowing costs should be discontinued, and instead, finance costs incurred during this period should be expensed (IPSAS 5.34).

It is possible that a temporary delay is part of the production or construction process and, during such periods, borrowing costs should continue to be capitalized. Examples include where the maturity of an asset is an essential part of the production process or where there is expected non-activity due to geological features (such as periods of very high tides).

In some instances the construction of assets is completed in stages. If each part is capable of being used separately while other parts continue to be constructed, the termination of capitalizing borrowing costs should be assessed on the substantial completion of each part (IPSAS 5.38). This could for example be the construction and completion of one hospital wing out of three.

Example 7.7　Timing of capitalization of borrowing costs

The following events take place for the construction of a hospital:

- The entity buys some land on 1 November;
- Planning permission is obtained on 15 January;
- Payment for the land is deferred until 1 February;
- The entity takes out a loan to cover the cost of the land and the construction of the hospital on 1 February; and
- Due to adverse weather conditions, there is a delay in starting the building work for six weeks and work does not commence until 15 April.

When should capitalization of borrowing costs commence?

The key dates to take into consideration are as follows:

- Expenditure on the acquisition is incurred on 1 February when construction of the hospital commences;
- Borrowing costs start to be incurred from 1 February;
- Although work was being undertaken on planning permission during November, December, and January, no borrowing costs were incurred during this period;
- During the ten-week inactive period, capitalization of borrowing costs is not permitted.

Therefore capitalization of borrowing costs should commence from 15 April.

Disclosures

IPSAS 5 requires disclosure of:

- The amount of borrowing costs capitalized during the period;
- The capitalization rate used to determine the amount of borrowing costs eligible for capitalization (IPSAS 5.40); and
- The accounting policy adopted for borrowing costs (IPSAS 5.40).

INTANGIBLES (IPSAS 31)

An intangible asset is an identifiable non-monetary asset that has no physical substance (IPSAS 31.16). Examples of intangible assets include patents, trademarks, goodwill, computer software, and brands. This means that the key difference between property, plant, and equipment, and intangible assets is that while the former have physical substance, the latter do not.

Public sector entities can face different considerations when trying to identify intangible assets. Computer software, patents, and licenses are relatively straightforward, but there is an ongoing debate as to whether the power to raise taxes and the power to grant rights are intangible assets.

Objectives and Scope

The objective of IPSAS 31 Intangible Assets is to prescribe the accounting treatment for intangible assets. IPSAS 31 requires a public sector entity to recognize an intangible asset if certain criteria are met. It also stipulates how to measure the carrying amount of intangible assets and the nature of the disclosures required.

It should be noted that certain assets are outside the scope of IPSAS 31. These include (IPSAS 31.3):

- Goodwill which is accounted for under IFRS 3 Business Combinations or an equivalent national accounting standard (see IPSAS 31.3);
- Financial assets as defined in IPSAS 28 Financial Instruments: Presentation; and
- Exploration and evaluation assets.

In addition, IPSAS 31.3 excludes from the scope of the standard powers and rights conferred by legislation, a constitution, or by equivalent means. There are differing views on whether these powers and rights meet the definition of an intangible asset and, if so, whether they would meet the recognition criteria. This issue is addressed in the Conceptual Framework, but not yet in IPSAS 31, which still excludes them from the scope of the standard.

IPSAS 31 specifically applies to expenditure incurred on activities such as advertising, training, start-up activities, and research and development, and IPSAS 31 states whether they should be expensed or capitalized. The standard also applies to rights under licensing agreements for items such as motion pictures, video recordings, plays, manuscripts, patents, and copyrights.

An identifiable intangible asset

The definition of an intangible asset, as illustrated above, includes the requirement for the asset to be identifiable (see Figure 7.4). The definition therefore distinguishes intangible assets from goodwill. Goodwill arises on the acquisition of a controlled

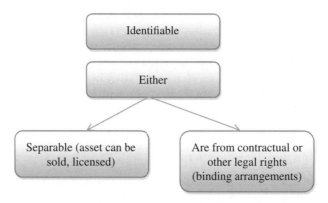

Figure 7.4 An identifiable intangible asset

entity. Goodwill is measured as the excess of the consideration transferred plus the amount of any non-controlling interest in the acquiree over the identifiable assets and liabilities recognized. Goodwill is not identifiable itself since it represents future economic benefits arising from assets not capable of individual identification and separate recognition. Goodwill is typically not a significant feature of public sector financial reporting.

An intangible asset, like other assets, has to be controlled by the entity. This means that the entity should have the power to obtain future economic benefits or service potential from the asset. Control also means that the entity can restrict these benefits from third parties. Control can often be evidenced by legal rights that are enforceable in a court of law; it is however important to note that this is not necessary for control to be evident.

Example 7.8   Control of intangible assets

Staff are a common example of an asset that is not controlled by the entity, since they can usually leave at short notice, and do not therefore meet the definition of an intangible asset. An entity cannot, therefore, recognize its workforce as an intangible asset. This is also the reason why training of staff cannot be capitalized. Training adds value and qualification to staff, but, since staff cannot be controlled, training cannot be capitalized and is to be expensed.

Without the protection of a legal right, public sector entities typically have insufficient control over the expected future economic benefits or service potential from customer relationships to meet the definition of an intangible asset. Nevertheless, under some circumstances and in some jurisdictions, an entity may be allowed to sell, for example, a part of a customer list, as a separate item. In that case, the ability to sell a customer relationship list is evidence that the entity has control over the future economic benefits or service potential flowing from that relationship, and therefore meets the definition of an intangible asset. In some jurisdictions it is forbidden to sell a customer list. In that case, entities have insufficient control over the expected future economic benefits or service potential from customer relationships for the customer list to meet the definition of an intangible asset.

Future economic benefits or service potential flowing from an intangible asset may result in increased revenue, but may also result in the reduction of costs as a result of, for example, a legal right to use a new technology, or may result in improved service delivery.

Initial Recognition and Measurement

An intangible asset should be initially measured at cost (IPSAS 31.31). It is important to note that when an intangible asset is acquired through a non-exchange transaction, its cost is measured at its fair value at the acquisition date (IPSAS 31.31).

Before an intangible asset can be recognized in the statement of financial position, not only does it need to meet the definition discussed above but it also needs to meet certain recognition criteria.

The recognition criteria are that (IPSAS 31.28):

- It is probable that future economic benefits or service potential from the asset will flow to the entity; and
- The cost or fair value of the asset can be measured reliably.

IPSAS 31 gives guidance on how different items should be accounted for:

Items which must be expensed as incurred are as follows:

- Separately purchased intangible assets; and
- Exchanges of assets.

IPSAS 31 also gives guidance on:

- Intangible assets acquired through a non-exchange transaction;
- Intangible heritage assets; and
- Items which must be expensed as incurred.

IPSAS 31 gives examples of where expenditure is incurred to provide future economic benefits or service potential to the entity, but where no intangible asset should be recognized. Such expenditure should instead be recognized in surplus or deficit. Examples include expenditure on start-up activities, staff training costs (even where this is directly related to a new asset), advertising and promotional activities, and expenditure on relocating an activity.

Separately Purchased Intangible Assets

Most separately acquired intangible assets meet the above recognition criteria. For such intangible assets they are initially recognized at cost. Cost includes the net amount paid for the asset after taxes, trade discounts, and other directly attributable costs. Other directly attributable costs might include, for example, professional fees, or costs incurred to test the functionality of the asset.

The requirements for the recognition and timing of costs capitalized as part of the cost of the intangible asset are comparable to those set out in IPSAS 17. Capitalization of costs should stop when the asset is ready for use even if the asset has not yet been put into use, or is operating at below expected levels.

Exchanges of Assets

If one non-monetary asset is exchanged for another, then the intangible asset acquired is typically measured at its fair value. Where it is not possible to give a fair value to the asset acquired, for example, where the fair value is not reliably measurable, it should be recognized at the carrying amount of the intangible asset relinquished.

Intangible Assets Acquired through a Non-Exchange Transaction

The cost of an intangible asset acquired through a non-exchange transaction should be measured at its fair value as at the date of acquisition (IPSAS 31.31).

Quoted market prices in an active market provide the best estimate of the fair value of an intangible asset. If no active market exists, its fair value is the amount the entity would have paid for the asset in an arm's length transaction. This may be estimated using a variety of techniques.

Intangible Heritage Assets

In a similar vein to IPSAS 17 on Heritage Assets, IPSAS 31 also does not require an entity to recognize intangible heritage assets, even if they otherwise meet the definition of an intangible asset, and satisfy the recognition criteria. However, if an entity chooses to recognize such assets, it must provide the disclosures required by IPSAS 31, and may (but is not required to) apply the measurement requirements of that standard (IPSAS 31.11).

Intangible heritage assets are those that have cultural, environmental, or historical significance. Examples include national archives and the right to use the likeness of a significant public person on stamps and coins (IPSAS 31.12).

Such assets are rarely held for their ability to generate cash flows. Where they have future economic benefits or service potential, they may be recognized and measured on the same basis as other cash-generating intangible assets. An example of this type of asset would be a historical recording that continues to earn royalties.

Internally Generated Intangible Assets

The key difficulties in determining whether an internally generated asset should be recognized are those of identifying accurately when it comes into existence and measuring its costs reliably. It is typically difficult to distinguish the costs of generating an intangible asset from those of maintaining or enhancing the day-to-day operations of the entity.

In order to support the defininition of an internally generated asset, its development is considered in terms of a research phase and a development phase. These phases relate to all intangible assets and are not limited to the area of research and development expenditure.

It is important to emphasize that internally generated goodwill should not be recognized as an asset (IPSAS 31.46).

Research phase

All expenditure identified as arising during the research phase should be recognized as an expense as it is incurred. An intangible asset should not be generated during the research phase (IPSAS 31.52).

During this phase, the probability that future economic benefits or service potential will be generated for the entity is too low. Examples of activities within the research phase include:

- Activities aimed at obtaining new knowledge;

- The search for alternative materials, devices, products, processes, systems, or services;
  and
- The formulation, design, evaluation, and final selection of possible alternatives for new or improved materials, devices, products, processes, systems, or services.

Development phase

During the development phase it may be possible to identify an intangible asset which should be recognized. The development phase of a project is further advanced than the research phase; it is the next stage and therefore the probability of determining whether economic benefits will be generated is greater. The development phase will typically see the design and development of a new product, tool, process, operation, or system.

To be recognized as an intangible asset arising from development, or the development phase, a number of stringent conditions should be satisfied. IPSAS 31 explicitly states that internally generated brands, mastheads, publishing titles, customer lists, and similar items should not be recognized as intangible assets. Such items cannot be identified separately from the cost of developing the business as a whole (IPSAS 31.61, 31.62).

The characteristics that should be demonstrated if an intangible asset is to be recognized are (IPSAS 31.55), as shown in Figure 7.5:

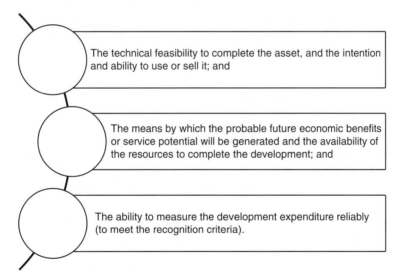

The technical feasibility to complete the asset, and the intention and ability to use or sell it; and

The means by which the probable future economic benefits or service potential will be generated and the availability of the resources to complete the development; and

The ability to measure the development expenditure reliably (to meet the recognition criteria).

Figure 7.5 Characteristics which an intangible asset must possess in order to be recognized

All three characteristics described in Figure 7.5 should be present. The second of these criteria specifically requires that the entity be able to demonstrate the existence of a market for the output of the intangible asset or, if it is to be used internally, the usefulness of the intangible asset.

If an internally generated intangible asset is recognized, it should be measured at cost. This is the directly attributable cost necessary to create, produce, and prepare the asset for its intended use. Such costs include, among other things:

- Materials and services consumed;
- Employment costs of those directly engaged in generating the asset; and
- Legal, patent, or license registration fees.

It is important to note that it is only expenditure incurred after the project has entered its development phase that can be included as part of the cost. It is not possible at the time of recognition to go back and recognize expenditure which occurred during the research phase.

A website has many of the characteristics of both tangible and intangible assets.

Example 7.9   Websites

Appendix A Application Guidance as part of IPSAS 31 provides guidance on consistent treatment of website costs. (For further reading on this topic see SIC 32 Intangible Assets Web Site Costs.)

Appendix A of IPSAS 31 provides the link between the standard and the specific characteristics of the development of a website. The application guidance in IPSAS 31 stipulates that a website that has been developed for the purposes of promoting and advertising an entity's products and services does not meet the requirement in IPSAS 31 to generate probable future benefits or service potential and therefore costs incurred in its development should be expensed as incurred.

Measurement after Initial Recognition

Measurement of intangible assets, following initial recognition, is similar to IPSAS 17. An entity can choose to follow a cost model or to use a revaluation model. The revaluation model may, however, only be used if fair value can be determined by reference to an active market.

Intangible assets may have finite or indefinite useful economic lives.

Finite economic useful life	**Indefinite economic useful life**
An economic useful life is finite, when it is not indefinite.	Based on an analysis of all of the relevant factors, there is no foreseeable limit to the period over which the asset is expected to generate net cash inflows for, or provide service potential to, the entity (IPSAS 31.87).
	The term "indefinite" does not mean "infinite" (IPSAS 31.90).

Cost model

Intangible assets are held at their cost less amortization and impairment.

Revaluation model

Intangible assets are carried at a revalued amount. Where an intangible asset is revalued, subsequent amortization is based on the revalued amount.

IPSAS 31 sets out a number of factors that should be considered in determining what the useful life of an intangible asset is. These factors include:

- Expected usage of the asset by the entity, typical product life cycles for similar assets, and dependence on other assets of the entity;
- The stability of the industry in which the asset operates, and the expected actions of competitors; and
- The speed of technological change and expected obsolescence.

Amortization should normally be recognized in the surplus or deficit. An entity should review its amortization periods and methods, and the residual value of intangible assets in each reporting period.

Disposal of Intangible Assets

Intangible assets should be removed from the statement of financial position when they are sold, or when no future economic benefits or service potential are expected from them. When the intangible asset is removed from the statement of financial position, a gain or loss should be calculated based on any proceeds received and the current carrying amount of the asset. This gain or loss should be recognized directly in surplus or deficit (IPSAS 31.111–31.112).

Disclosures

A number of detailed disclosures are required for each class of intangible assets to enable users to determine the mechanisms and factors affecting intangible asset values. If the entity has recognized internally generated intangible assets, then the disclosure information should be shown separately for these assets (IPSAS 31.117).

A public sector entity shall disclose:

- The amortization rates for intangible assets and the methods used;
- The identification of the line item in the statement of comprehensive income/statement of financial performance where amortization has been charged, and separate disclosure of any impairment losses incurred (with any reversals);
- A full reconciliation of movements in the carrying amount of intangible assets, for example additions, amortization, impairment, and disposals;
- Net exchange differences that arose on translation; and
- The aggregate amount of research and development expenditure recognized as an expense during the period.

In addition to these disclosures, if an intangible asset has been assessed as having an indefinite life, its carrying amount and the reasons supporting the indefinite life assessment should be disclosed.

If an individual intangible asset is considered to be material to the entity's financial statements, a description of the asset should be provided, along with its carrying amount and, in the case of an asset with a finite useful life, the remaining amortization period should be set out.

Disclosure is required where the title of an intangible asset is restricted in some way, or the asset is pledged as security for the entity's liabilities. If the entity is contractually committed at the period-end to acquiring intangible assets, the amount of this commitment should be disclosed.

For intangible assets that have been revalued, information should be disclosed about the effective date of the last valuation, the methods and assumptions used in calculating fair value, the current carrying amount for the class of intangibles, and what the carrying amount would have been had the entity continued to use the cost method. A reconciliation of the revaluation reserve should be set out to the extent that it contains balances in relation to revalued intangible assets.

Where intangible assets were acquired through a non-exchange transaction, IPSAS 31 also requires the disclosure of their fair value at initial recognition, their carrying amount, and whether they are measured (after recognition) using the cost model or the revaluation model (IPSAS 31.121).

Impairment of intangible assets is recognized following IPSAS 21 Impairment of Non-Cash-Generating Assets or IPSAS 26 Impairment of Cash-Generating Assets as appropriate.

Transitional Provisions

The transitional provisions of IPSAS 31 stipulate that an entity that has previously recognized intangible assets shall apply IPSAS 31 retrospectively in accordance with IPSAS 3. In addition entities that have not previously recognized intangible assets and use the accrual basis of accounting shall apply IPSAS 31 prospectively. Nevertheless, retrospective application is permitted.

It is thus clear that the application of IPSAS 31 will be dependent on the former (pre-IPSAS) accounting policy of the first-time adopter entity.

An entity that had not recognized intangible assets under the former accounting standards may apply IPSAS 31 prospectively. In that case, no former missing intangible asset is to be recorded in the opening balance sheet. But it is only an option. The entity also has the right to apply IPSAS 31 retrospectively. In that case, the entity will reconstitute the cost of intangible assets.

And for entities which used to recognized intangible assets under the former accounting policy, there is no option. They have to apply IPSAS 31 retrospectively and reconstitute the cost of intangible assets. Actually the cost could be either the original cost, or the revalued amount in presence of an active market (which should be rare).

According to IPSAS 31.130, "an entity may elect to measure an intangible asset on the date of transition, at its fair value and use that fair value as its deemed cost at that date," which means that the entity does not need to reconstitute the original cost of intangible assets according to IPSAS 31 criteria, and can instead use the fair value of the intangible assets at the date of the opening balance sheet.

Applied to the example, the transitional provisions may lead to reconstitution of the cost of the ERP (Enterprise Resource Planning) system or use of the fair value of the ERP at the date of the opening balance sheet. The revaluation model cannot be used since there is no active market for customized ERPs (see IPSAS 31.74 "For the purpose of revaluations under this Standard, fair value shall be determined by reference to an active market").

In the first case, the cost of the internally generated intangible asset, here the ERP, is the sum of expenditure incurred from the date when the intangible asset first meets the recognition criteria (IPSAS 31.63). However, identified inefficiencies and initial operating deficits incurred before the asset achieves planned performance are not components of the cost of an internally generated intangible asset (IPSAS 31.65). Therefore, it is necessary to determine whether the costs incurred during the first stage (Foundation) are to be capitalized or else considered as expenses since the original design for the Foundation stage was not detailed enough. The answer may not be straightforward, some costs being capitalized and others expensed. Apart from that specific topic, all costs incurred in order to develop the ERP should be capitalized since they comply with the development cost criteria:

> An intangible asset arising from development (or from the development phase of an internal project) shall be recognized if, and only if, an entity can demonstrate all of the following:
>
> (a) The technical feasibility of completing the intangible asset so that it will be available for use or sale;
> (b) Its intention to complete the intangible asset and use or sell it;
> (c) Its ability to use or sell the intangible asset;
> (d) How the intangible asset will generate probable future economic benefits or service potential. Among other things, the entity can demonstrate the existence of a market for the output of the intangible asset or the intangible asset itself or, if it is to be used internally, the usefulness of the intangible asset;
> (e) The availability of adequate technical, financial and other resources to complete the development and to use or sell the intangible asset; and
> (f) Its ability to measure reliably the expenditure attributable to the intangible asset during its development. (IPSAS 31.55)

In the second case, the entity may choose to use the fair value as the deemed cost of the ERP at the date of the opening balance sheet. In that case, the Foundation stage may be worth less than its cost since some part of the development may be useless and may need replacement in the Foundation Enhancement phase. It is very unlikely that the fair value of the ERP is much higher that its development cost, at least for the Extension 1 and Foundation Enhancement phases. For the Foundation stage, the fair value is likely to be less than its development cost.

In both cases, the entity will also have to apply the requirements of IPSAS 21 relating to testing intangible assets under development during the reporting period, which should normally lead to the same value of the ERP:

> Irrespective of whether there is any indication of impairment, an entity shall also test an intangible asset with an indefinite useful life or an intangible asset not yet available for use for impairment annually by comparing its carrying amount with its recoverable service amount. This impairment test may be performed at any time during the reporting period, provided it is performed at the same time every year. Different intangible assets may be tested for impairment at different times. However, if such an intangible asset was initially recognized during the current reporting period, that intangible asset shall be tested for impairment before the end of the current reporting period. (IPSAS 21.26A)

IPSAS Financial Reporting in Practice 7.7. UNESCO (2013) Intangible Assets

2.10 INTANGIBLE ASSETS

Intangible assets are carried at cost less accumulated amortization and impairment. Intangible assets are capitalized in the financial statements if they have a cost exceeding $50,000.

Software acquisition and development

Acquired computer software licenses are capitalized based on costs incurred to acquire and bring to use the specific software. Costs that are directly associated with the development of software for use by UNESCO are capitalized as an intangible asset. Direct costs include the software development employee costs and an appropriate portion of relevant overheads.

Amortization

Amortization is provided on a straight-line basis on all intangible assets of finite life, at rates that will write off the cost or value of the assets over their useful lives. The useful lives of major classes of intangible assets have been estimated as follows:

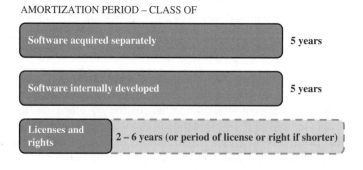

AMORTIZATION PERIOD – CLASS OF

Software acquired separately — 5 years

Software internally developed — 5 years

Licenses and rights — 2 – 6 years (or period of license or right if shorter)

The above example shows the way UNESCO has disclosed information relating to intangible assets in its financial statements for 2013. UNESCO has selected a threshold of USD 50 000 to capitalize intangible assets, meaning that items qualifying for the definition of an intangible asset which are below this threshold are not capitalized. UNESCO intangible assets relate mainly to software, either acquired or internally developed, and licenses and rights, which are amortized over their useful lives, of five years for software and two to six years for licenses or rights (or less when the period of the license is shorter).

INVESTMENT PROPERTY (IPSAS 16)

An investment property is land or buildings, or both, held by an entity to earn rentals and/or for its capital appreciation potential (IPSAS 16.7). Investment property does not include property held to provide a social service and which also generates cash inflows, for example social housing. Such property is not considered an "investment property" and would be accounted for in accordance with IPSAS 17 (IPSAS 16.13(f)).

In summary, an investment property generates cash flows largely independent of the other assets held by an entity. This distinguishes investment property from owner-occupied property, which is held by the owner for the delivery of services, for use in the production or supply of goods or services, for administrative purposes, or for sale in the ordinary course of operations. The definition of an investment property includes a building that is currently vacant but is held with a view to its being let out and an existing investment property that is being redeveloped with a view to its continued use as an investment property.

It should be noted that a property interest held by a lessee under an operating lease may be classified by the lessor as an investment property if certain conditions are met (IPSAS 16.8).

Recognition and Measurement

An investment property should be recognized when the normal conditions for asset recognition are satisfied. These are when (cf. IPSAS 16.20):

- It is probable that the future economic benefits associated with the investment property will flow to the entity; and
- The cost of the investment property (or fair value (IPSAS 16) if the investment property is acquired through a non-exchange transaction) can be measured reliably. An investment property should initially be measured at cost, except where it is acquired through a non-exchange transaction in which case it should be recognized at fair value.

Initial cost includes transaction costs. These are expenses that are directly attributable to the investment property.

IPSAS 16 requires self-constructed investment properties to be held at cost under IPSAS 17 Property, Plant and Equipment. On completion, the property is recognized as an investment property (see IPSAS 16.29).

Where a property held under a lease is classified as an investment property, IPSAS 13 Leases requires the property both to be recognized at the lower of fair value and at the present value of the minimum lease payments under the lease (IPSAS 16.34).

Changes in Use

A change in the use of a property may lead to its no longer being recognized as an investment property. The following illustration sets out where there might be evidence that a change in use has occurred and how the property should be treated following such a change in use (IPSAS 16.66).

Occupation of the property by the entity itself

- The property is now owner-occupied and should therefore be recognized as a property in use by the entity in accordance with IPSAS 17, Property, Plant and Equipment.
- Where the investment property was measured at fair value, its fair value at the date of change of use should be deemed cost for future accounting (IPSAS 16.71).
- Development of the property commences with the intention that it will be sold by the entity.
- The property is being held for sale in the normal course of business and should therefore be reclassified as inventory and accounted for in accordance with IPSAS 12 Inventories.
- Where the investment property was measured at fair value, its fair value at the date of change of use should be treated as the deemed cost (IPSAS 16.71).
- Development of the property commences with the intention that it will continue to be let after completion of the development works.
- The property should continue to be held as an investment property under IPSAS 16.
- A building that was occupied by the entity is vacated so that it can be let to third parties.
- The property is no longer owner-occupied and therefore should be transferred to investment properties and accounted for under IPSAS 16.
- Where investment properties are measured at fair value, the property should be revalued at the date of change of use and any difference should be recognized as a revaluation under IPSAS 17 (IPSAS 16.72).

A property that was originally held as inventory has now been let to a third party

- The property is no longer held for resale and is instead held to generate future rental income and therefore should be transferred to investment properties in accordance with IPSAS 16.
- Where investment properties are measured at fair value, the property should be revalued at the date of change of use and any difference should be recognized immediately in surplus or deficit (IPSAS 16.74).

Disposal of Investment Properties

An investment property should be eliminated from the balance sheet when it is disposed of, either through sale or by entering into a finance lease. An investment property which is permanently withdrawn from use and will not generate any future economic benefits, even on its ultimate disposal, should be eliminated from the statement of financial position (IPSAS 16.77).

When an investment property is disposed of or permanently withdrawn from use, and no future benefit will accrue to the entity, a gain or loss should be calculated and recognized directly in surplus or deficit in the period in which the disposal or "retirement" takes place.

The gain or loss should normally be determined as the difference between the net disposal proceeds and the carrying amount of the asset (IPSAS 16.80).

Disclosure

The disclosures required in relation to investment properties are in three broad groups:

- Those applicable to both the fair value model and the cost model;
- An entity should disclose which measurement basis it uses for its investment properties, so whether it uses the cost model or fair value model. When it has been particularly difficult to establish whether the property is an investment property or an owner-occupied property, the entity should set out the criteria that it considered in making its decision (IPSAS 16.86);
- An entity should separately identify the amount of rental income recognized in the period, along with any related operating expenses attributable to the rentals.

If restrictions exist on the realization of income, either through rentals or sale proceeds, or if the entity has a contractual obligation to purchase or construct an investment property, these facts should be disclosed.

Applicability only to the fair value model

Where an entity applies the fair value model, it should present a detailed reconciliation, showing all movements between the carrying amount of investment property at the beginning and the end of the period (IPSAS 16.87).

An entity should disclose the methods and significant assumptions made, including whether there was market evidence or not, in determining the fair value of investment property and whether the valuation was carried out by an independent qualified valuer (IPSAS 16.86). Equipment such as elevators or air-conditioning is often an integral part of a building and is generally included in the fair value of the investment property, rather than recognized separately, in order to avoid the double counting of such items (IPSAS 16.59 and 16.88).

The same applies to offices leased on a furnished basis. In that case, the fair value of the office generally includes the fair value of the furniture, because the rental revenue relates to the furnished office. When furniture is included in the fair value of investment property, an entity does not recognize that furniture as a separate asset (IPSAS 16.59 and 16.88).

Applicability only to the cost model

An entity that applies the cost model should disclose the depreciation methods and rates, or useful life, used. A detailed reconciliation should be presented for the gross cost of investment properties and the related accumulated depreciation showing all movements during the year. The carrying amount (i.e., the cost less the accumulated depreciation) should be clearly disclosed for both the beginning and end of the period.

In addition, an entity is required to disclose the fair value of investment properties where possible. If it is not possible, this fact should be explained and a range of estimates should be provided instead (IPSAS 16.90).

IMPAIRMENT (IPSAS 21 AND IPSAS 26)

This section deals with impairment. Impairment is a loss in the value of an asset, i.e., its carrying amount recognized in the statement of financial position is greater than its recoverable amount.

There are two IPSAS dealing with impairment of assets, which are IPSAS 21 Impairment of Non-Cash Generating Assets and IPSAS 26 Impairment of Cash-Generating Assets. The key distinction recognized by these standards, which has driven the decision to issue two standards, is the distinction between cash-generating assets and non-cash-generating assets. Non-cash-generating assets is a public sector-only accounting concept.

Impairment usually arises where a substantial change has come about which adversely affects the way in which an asset is being used by the entity. A simple example is where there have been technological advances that limit the planned use of an asset. It should be emphasized that judgment is required by management to establish when an asset's value is impaired, and how to measure the impairment.

IPSAS 26 and IPSAS 21 apply to all assets apart from those specifically excluded from these standards. They most commonly apply to assets such as:

- Property, plant, and equipment accounted for in accordance with IPSAS 17 Property, Plant and Equipment; and
- Intangible assets accounted for in accordance with IPSAS 31 Intangible Assets (note that IPSAS 26 excludes intangible assets that are regularly revalued to fair value).

The standards also apply to some financial assets, namely investments in subsidiaries, associates, and joint ventures. Impairments of all other financial assets are accounted for in accordance with IPSAS 29 Financial Instruments: Recognition and Measurement.

An entity is required to assess at each reporting date whether there is an indication of impairment. If such an indication is identified, the asset's recoverable amount should be calculated and compared to its carrying amount.

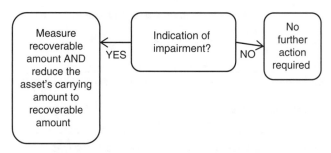

Figure 7.6 Action if indication of impairment

In addition, regardless of whether there have been any indicators of impairment during the period, IPSAS 26 includes specific situations where the recoverable amount of the asset should be assessed for impairment annually. IPSAS 21 only requires an estimate of the recoverable amount to be made where an indication of impairment exists (IPSAS 21.25).

The scenarios included in IPSAS 26 are:[7]

- Where the entity has intangible assets that have been identified as having indefinite lives (IPSAS 26.23);
- Where the entity has an intangible asset that is not yet ready for use, (IPSAS 26.23); and
- The impairment test in these circumstances may be carried out at any time during the period, provided that it is carried out at the same time each period.

Stages in the Impairment Process

The stages in the process of identifying and accounting for an impairment loss are as follows (see Figures 7.6 and 7.7):

1. Assess whether there is an indication that an asset may be impaired. Note that if there is no such indication, then normally no further action is required. There are some exceptions to this rule. Annual impairment testing is needed under IPSAS 26 where:
   - Intangible assets have been identified as having indefinite lives;
   - Intangible assets are not yet ready for use; and/or
   - Goodwill has been recorded as a result of a business combination.
2. If there is an indication of impairment, then measure the asset's recoverable amount.
3. Reduce the asset's carrying amount to its recoverable amount, usually by treating the loss as a separately disclosed expense.

If the carrying amount of an asset is greater than its recoverable amount, then impairment has taken place. There has been a loss in the value of the asset.

---

[7] If goodwill has been recorded as a result of a business combination then one can turn to IFRS 3 in the absence of any IPSAS on the topic.

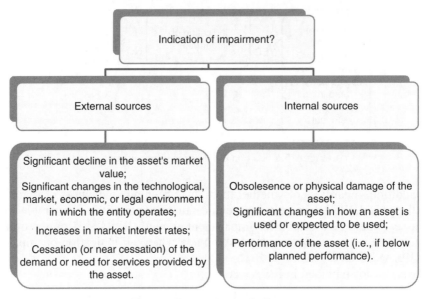

Figure 7.7 Impairment indicators

How do we measure recoverable amount (see Figure 7.8)?

Fair value less costs to sell

Fair value is the amount obtainable from a sale in an arm's length transaction between a willing buyer and seller, less the costs of disposal (IPSAS 26.38).

Value in use: cash-generating assets

The "value in use" calculation is a measure of the future cash flows expected to be derived from an individual asset or a cash-generating unit.

Since cash flows are likely to be over several periods, they should be discounted to take account of the time value of money, i.e., based on their present value.

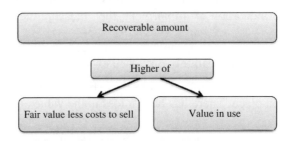

Figure 7.8 Measure recoverable amount

Recognizing an Impairment Loss

If the recoverable amount of an asset is less than its carrying amount, the asset should be reduced to its recoverable amount. The difference is an impairment loss (IPSAS 21.52 and IPSAS 26.72). IPSAS 21 and IPSAS 26 do not apply to assets carried at revalued amounts.

Example 7.10   Impairment testing

A hospital entity has a building that was originally acquired for CU1 000 000. The entity measures PP&E using the cost model.

The following approach would be followed under IPSAS 26 and IPSAS 21 for impairment testing.

The current carrying amount for the building is CU650 000. Due to a fall in the local property market, the entity has undertaken an impairment review.

The fair value less costs to sell the building is now estimated to be CU400 000 and the value in use of the property is calculated as being CU500 000. The recoverable amount of the property is therefore the higher of the two: CU500 000.

An impairment of CU150 000 has occurred, being the difference between the current carrying amount of CU650 000 and the recoverable amount of CU500 000. It should be recognized immediately in surplus or deficit.

Following the recognition of an impairment loss, any depreciation charged in respect of the asset in future periods will be based on the revised carrying amount, less any residual value expected, over the remaining useful life of the asset as per IPSAS 17.

Reversing an Impairment Loss

If the recoverable amount subsequently increases then in certain circumstances the impairment is reversed. A reversal of an impairment loss reflects an increase in the estimated future economic benefits or service potential of an asset or group of assets. The increased future economic benefits or service potential may be through use or sale.

The increased carrying amount, other than goodwill, attributable to a reversal of an impairment loss should not exceed the carrying amount that would have been determined (net of amortization and depreciation) had no impairment loss been recognized for the asset in prior years. Any increase above this amount other than goodwill is a revaluation.

The reversal of any impairment is recognized consistently with the original recognition of the impairment loss. The reversal will therefore normally be recognized in surplus or deficit (IPSAS 26.106, 26.108; IPSAS 21.68, 21.69).

Revalued assets are not impaired under IPSAS 21 or IPSAS 26. However, a revaluation gain will have the same result.

If the reversal of the impairment is in relation to a cash-generating unit, then the reversal is recognized on a pro-rata basis with the carrying amount of the assets, excluding goodwill[8] (IPSAS 26.110).

However one should note that goodwill is less likely to arise in the public sector.

Disclosures

The following information should be disclosed for each class of assets:

- The amount of any impairment loss recognized or reversed in surplus or deficit, identifying the line item in the statement of financial performance where it has been included (IPSAS 26.115; 21.73);
- If the entity applies IPSAS 18 Segment Reporting, the reportable segment(s) to which the recognition or reversal relates.

If an impairment loss recognized or reversed for an individual asset, including goodwill, or a cash-generating unit, is significant to the financial statements as a whole, additional information should be disclosed, including (IPSAS 26.120):

- The events which led to the recognition/reversal;
- The amount;
- The nature of the asset and the reportable segment to which the asset belongs if appropriate; and
- Whether the recoverable amount is fair value less costs to sell or value in use, with information about the basis of any fair value calculation or the discount rate applied (approach used for non-cash-generating assets) in the value in use calculation.
- In addition, IPSAS 26 requires the following disclosures for cash-generating units:
- A description of the cash-generating unit;
- The amount of the impairment loss recognized or reversed by class of asset; and/or
- If the aggregation of assets for identifying the cash-generating unit has changed since the previous estimate of the cash-generating unit's recoverable amount (if any), a description of the current and former way of aggregating assets and the reasons for changing the way the cash-generating unit is identified.

It should be noted that additional information is required for each cash-generating unit where the carrying amount of the indefinite life intangibles is significant compared with the entity's total goodwill or indefinite life intangibles (IPSAS 26.123).

---

[8] In accordance with the private sector IFRS, an impairment loss recognized in respect to goodwill should not subsequently be reversed. This is due to the fact that it is probable that any increase in the recoverable amount of goodwill in future periods will arise as a result of increases in internally generated goodwill rather than the reversal of an impairment. The same could be applied in IPSAS.

The following also needs to be disclosed if fair value less costs to sell is determined using cash flow projections:

- The period over which management has projected cash flows;
- The growth rate used to extrapolate cash flow projections; and/or
- The discount rate(s) applied to the cash flow projections (IPSAS 26.123).

Information should also be provided where the carrying amount of indefinite life intangibles is allocated to a number of cash-generating units and this amount is not significant compared with the total carrying amount of indefinite life intangibles (IPSAS 26.124).

IPSAS Financial Reporting in Practice 7.8. Impairment at UNESCO, 2013 Financial Statements (pp. 38, 49, 50)

Impairment

The carrying values of fixed assets are reviewed for impairment if events or changes in circumstances indicate that the book value of the asset may not be recoverable. If such an indication exists, the recoverable amount of the asset is estimated in order to determine the extent of impairment loss if any. Any provision for impairment is included in the Statement of Financial Performance.

The "measurement after recognition" method used for property, plant and equipment is the "cost model" described in IPSAS 17, paragraph 43, which provides that "after recognition as an asset, an item of property, plant, and equipment shall be carried at its cost, less any accumulated depreciation and any accumulated impairment losses."

NOTE 13 – PROPERTY, PLANT AND EQUIPMENT (PP&E)

Expressed in '000 US dollars	Land	Buildings	Comms & IT Equipment	Vehicles	Furniture and fixtures	Other Equipment	Total
As at January 1, 2013							
Cost or fair value	254 713	383 314	28 242	6 427	2 887	14 979	690 562
Accumulated depreciation	–	–41 275	–23 608	–5 111	–2 438	–9 829	–82 261
Carrying amount	**254 713**	**342 039**	**4 634**	**1 316**	**449**	**5 150**	**608 301**
Movements period to 31/12/2013							
Additions	–	234	3 101	706	199	1 270	5 510
Disposals	–	–	–1 492	–336	–16	–2 039	–3 883
Disposals depreciation	–	–	1 479	336	16	1 687	3 518
Impairment	–	–	–	–	–	–	–
Depreciation	–	–13 766	–2 525	–645	–210	–1 334	–18 480
Exchange adjustments depreciation	–	–19	–272	–6	–31	–183	–511
Exchange adjustments cost	–	109	347	6	38	332	832
Total movements 12 months to 31 December 2013	**–**	**–13 442**	**638**	**61**	**–4**	**–267**	**–13 014**

As at December 31, 2013

Cost or fair value	254 713	383 657	30 198	6 803	3 108	14 542	693 021
Accumulated depreciation	–	−55 060	−24 926	−5 426	−2 663	−9 659	−97 734
Carrying amount	**254 713**	**328 597**	**5 272**	**1 377**	**445**	**4 883**	**595 287**

NOTE 14 – INTANGIBLE ASSETS

As at January 1, 2013

Cost or fair value	19 532	701	20 233
Accumulated amortization	−19 378	−365	−19 743
Carrying amount	**154**	**336**	**490**

Movements 12 months to 31 December 2013

Additions	–	44	44
Disposals	–		
Disposals amortization	–		
Impairment	–		
Amortization	−154	100	−254
Total movements 12 months to 31 December 2013	−154	−56	−210

As at 31 December 2013

Cost or fair value	19 532	745	20 277
Accumulated depreciation	−19 532	−465	−19 997
Carrying amount	**–**	**280**	**280**

UNESCO currently only recognizes software as intangible assets, as it is not considered probable that significant future economic benefits from copyrights and intellectual property will flow to UNESCO.

In the above example, UNESCO states its policy relating to the impairment of PP&E. As disclosed in the notes relating to intangible assets and PP&E, no impairment has been recognized in 2013.

8 CURRENT ASSETS

Current assets are key in assessing the liquidity of a public sector entity. Current assets will provide an indication of the efficiency of working capital management within the entity. IPSAS 1 stipulates that when an entity supplies goods or services within a clearly identifiable operating cycle, separate classification of current and non-current assets and liabilities on the face of the statement of financial position provides useful information by distinguishing the net assets that are continuously circulating as working capital from those used in the entity's long-term operations. It also highlights assets that are expected to be realized within the current operating cycle, and liabilities that are due for settlement within the same period (IPSAS 1.72).

Current assets include two types of asset:

- Assets (such as taxes receivable, user charges receivable, fines and regulatory fees receivable, inventories, and accrued investment revenue) that are either realized, consumed, or sold, as part of the normal operating cycle even when they are not expected to be realized within 12 months of the reporting date; and
- Assets held primarily for the purpose of trading (examples include some financial assets classified as held for trading in accordance with IPSAS 29, Financial Instruments: Recognition and Measurement) and the current portion of non-current financial assets (IPSAS 1.79).

The key current assets of any entity include inventories, receivables, and bank and cash balances as well as pre-payments and potential short-term investments.

Accounting for most current assets arises from the application of the underpinning accruals concept, and as such is rather straightforward. The accounting for, for example, accounts receivable is related to when revenue is recognized (covered in Chapter 15 of this book). Cash balances, in particular restricted cash, was discussed in Chapter 6, under the section on the cash flow statement.

This chapter focuses on the inventory element of current assets.

INVENTORIES VERSUS PROPERTY, PLANT, AND EQUIPMENT

The table below describes the key differences between inventories and PP&E.

Inventory	PP&E
Current asset	Non-current asset
Used, distributed, consumed, or sold within an entity's operating cycle.	Expected to be used during more than one reporting period.
Assets: • Held for sale or distribution within the ordinary course of activities of the entity; or • In the process of production for distribution or sale; or • In the form of materials or supplies to be consumed in the production process or to be consumed/distributed in the rendering of services.	Assets held for: • Use in the production or supply of goods or services; or • Administrative purposes; or • Rental to third parties.

INVENTORY (IPSAS 12)

Inventories include goods purchased and held for resale, work-in-progress, and finished goods. Inventory can be of major significance to some public sector entities. The level and hence importance of inventories depends not only on the type of industry and market within which an entity operates, but also on the manner in which they are managed.

Additional measurement issues arise in the public sector, where inventories are often held for distribution or for use in the provision of services at no or nominal consideration, and where inventories may be acquired for no or nominal consideration.

The determination of the cost attributable to specific inventory items and its subsequent recognition as an expense will have an effect on the surplus or deficit reported for the period and is therefore an important consideration. Consequently, the measurement, presentation, and disclosures required by IPSAS 12 Inventories provide significant information to users of the financial statements.

IPSAS 12 stipulates the accounting treatment for inventories. The main issue in accounting for inventories is that of determining what amount of cost should be carried forward as an asset until related revenues are recognized or until the asset is distributed or used to provide services. IPSAS 12 also provides guidance on the determination of this cost and subsequent measurement, including write-downs to net realizable value where appropriate.

IPSAS 12 applies to all types of entity, but not to types of inventory covered by other standards, such as:

- Work-in-progress under construction contracts (see IPSAS 11);
- Financial instruments (IPSAS 28 Financial Instruments: Presentation and IPSAS 29 Financial Instruments: Recognition and Measurement); and
- Biological assets at the point of harvest (IPSAS 27 Agriculture).

IPSAS 12 also excludes from its scope work-in-progress of services to be provided for no or nominal consideration directly in return from the recipients, as this area raises complex public sector-specific accounting issues that are still being developed.

Inventories are assets that are (IPSAS 12.9):

- Held for sale or distribution in the ordinary course of business;
- In the process of production for such sale;
- In the form of materials or supplies to be consumed in the production process or in the rendering of services; or
- In the form of materials or supplies to be distributed in the rendering of services.

Inventories can include (IPSAS 12.11):

- Merchandise purchased by a retailer and held for resale;
- Land, property, and other assets held for resale;
- Finished goods produced;
- Work-in-progress – i.e., partially completed goods; and
- Materials and supplies awaiting use in the production process.

For service providers, inventory includes the cost of a service for which the entity has not recognized related revenues (the cost of work undertaken but not yet billed).

IPSAS 12.12 lists additional items of inventory that occur specifically in the public sector, including:

- Ammunition;
- Strategic stockpiles (for example, energy reserves);
- Stocks of unissued currency; and
- Postal service supplies held for sale (for example, stamps).

Example 8.1   Distinguish between inventory and PP&E

A public sector entity, a medical institute, maintains spare parts that can be used to replace a medical equipment part. These spare parts can also be used in the entity's daily operations and can be sold as well. The lifespan of the spare parts is at least three years.

This type of spare part should be recognized as inventory. It is recognized as property, plant, and equipment, once it is used to replace a part of the medical equipment. The remaining spare parts should be recognized as inventory even though it may take two years to realize.

Initial Recognition

Under IPSAS, an entity is to recognize inventory on the day when the risks and rewards of ownership of the inventory have been transferred to the entity. This is typically the date on which the inventory is delivered. It should nevertheless be noted that there are exceptions. For example when inventory is shipped free on board (FOB),

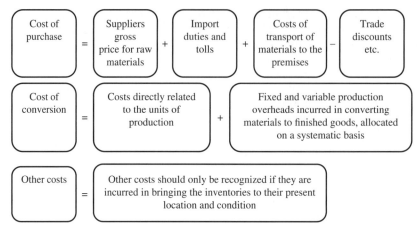

Figure 8.1   Defining costs

in which case the risks and rewards are transferred to the buyer when the goods are loaded onto the ship, resulting in the buyer recognizing inventory on the FOB date.

Measurement

Inventories shall be measured at the lower of cost and net realizable value (NRV) (IPSAS 12.15); however IPSAS 12 also provides that where:

- They are acquired through a non-exchange transaction, their cost shall be measured at their fair value as at the date of acquisition (IPSAS 12.16); and
  They are held for distribution, or consumption in the production process of goods to be distributed at no charge or for a nominal charge, they are measured at the lower of cost and current replacement cost (IPSAS 12.17).

Cost

The cost of inventories shall comprise all costs of purchase, costs of conversion, and other costs incurred in bringing the inventories to their present location and condition (IPSAS 12.18). Figure 8.1 illustrates what is meant by these types of cost.

Net realizable value

The net realizable value is the estimated selling price in the ordinary course of operations less estimated costs of completion and the estimated costs necessary to make the sale, exchange, or distribution (IPSAS 12.9).

Valuing inventory at the lower of cost and NRV ensures that any profit to be earned on their sale is not recognized before the sale takes place although any loss is recognized as soon as it is identified. In most businesses, inventories will be sold at a profit so they will be measured at cost (since this is lower than NRV).

In the retail industry it is common practice to value inventory at selling price less the normal gross profit margin. This practice is permitted because it is often impracticable to use other valuation methods due to the large volume of rapidly changing items and it generally results in a valuation which is very close to actual cost.

Fixed production overheads

Fixed production overheads are those indirect costs of production that remain relatively constant regardless of the volume of production (e.g., the cost of factory management, rent of the processing factory, and administration).

The standard emphasizes that fixed production overheads must be allocated to items of inventory on the basis of the normal capacity of the production facilities (IPSAS 12.20).

Variable production overheads

Variable production overheads are costs incurred in the processing of raw materials that vary directly, or nearly directly, with the volume of production (e.g., indirect materials, labour, and power) (IPSAS 12.20).

Where inventories contain items which are not interchangeable and/or are produced for a specific project (e.g., a special order for a customer), their costs shall be built up through specific identification of their individual costs (IPSAS 12.32).

In all other cases, such as where there are thousands of a particular type of nail in a particular storage bin, cost shall be assigned using the first-in, first-out (FIFO) or weighted average cost formula (IPSAS 12.35).

Expensing Inventory

When inventories are sold, the carrying amount is recognized as an expense in the period in which the related revenue is recognized (IPSAS 12.44). If there is no related revenue, the expense is recognized when the goods are distributed or the related service is rendered.

Any write-down of inventories to NRV and all losses of inventories are recognized.

Any reversal of any write-down of inventories, arising from an increase in NRV, is recognized.

For example, an international organization produces specific items of inventory on demand for its Member States. These items are sold to the requesting Member States at the production cost. No margin is made on the production and sale of these items. However, in order to produce these items, the organization needs to buy very expensive raw material. The cost of the final product is charged to the requesting Member State. Nevertheless, some raw materials remain as inventory at the end of the year, and among these raw materials, some "scrap" from the production process. Since this raw material is extremely expensive, it is kept as inventory, valued at the purchase price.

Deciding that this "scrap" material is of no use to the organization, it decides to sell some of it back to the supplier and, in return, to receive some new raw material. Since the scrap value is lower than the normal initial raw material value, the organization can determine the net realizable value of its scrap inventory using the price offered by the supplier to buy back scrap.

For scrap material remaining as inventory at the end of the year, its book value is to be impaired from its initial purchase price to its resale price. At the end of the following year, the value of scrap material is to be revised to take into account the new resale opportunity available. Therefore it may lead to an additional write-down of inventory or to a (total or partial) reversal of the former write-down.

Disclosure

The financial statements should disclose (IPSAS 12.47):

- Accounting policies adopted in measuring inventories;
- Total carrying amount of inventories classified in a manner appropriate to the entity;
- Carrying amount of inventories at NRV;
- The amount of inventories recognized as an expense during the period;
- The amount of any write-down that is recognized as an expense during the period;
- The amount and circumstances of any reversal of a write-down that is recognized during the period;
- Carrying amount of inventories pledged as security for liabilities.

IPSAS Financial Reporting in Practice 8.1. Inventories of the IAEA (Financial Statements, 2013). Inventories

20. Inventories are stated at the lower of cost and either current replacement cost or net realizable value.

21. Current replacement cost, which is used for inventories to be distributed to beneficiaries at no or nominal charge, is the cost the Agency would incur to acquire the asset on the reporting date.

22. Net realizable value, which is used for inventories to be sold at broadly commercial terms or used by the Agency, is the estimated selling price in the ordinary course of business, less the costs of completion and selling expenses.

23. Cost is determined using a weighted average cost formula unless the inventory items are unique in nature, in which case the specific identification method is used.

24. These policies apply to the Agency's major inventory categories as follows:

Inventory item	Valuation method	Cost formula
Project inventories in transit to counterparts	Lower of cost or current replacement cost	Specific identification method
Safeguards spare parts and maintenance materials	Lower of cost or net realizable value	Weighted average cost
Printing supplies	Lower of cost or net realizable value	Weighted average cost

25. The Agency manages its Safeguards spare parts and maintenance materials inventory primarily in a centralized fashion. Inventories managed in central locations with a cost of €0.100 million or greater are capitalized. Currently, such inventories are comprised of batteries and cables. Other minor inventory items centrally managed or held in decentralized locations are not capitalized due to the immateriality of such balances.

26. A charge for impairment is recorded in the Statement of Financial Performance in the year in which the inventory is determined to be impaired due to obsolescence or excess quantities relative to demand.

27. The Agency also produces and holds publications and reference materials. The inventories of publications and reference materials are not recognized as assets in these financial statements. Amounts spent on the acquisition and/or production of publications and reference material inventories are expensed when incurred.

The above example describes the IAEA note on accounting policy for inventories. The first paragraphs (20–23) refer to the IPSAS 12 requirements. Paragraph 23 specifies that cost of inventories is determined using a weighted average cost formula, which is useful information since IPSAS 12 allows one to choose between this method and FIFO (first-in first-out) for inventories which are not unique in nature.

Paragraph 24 presents the three major inventory categories and the cost formula applied in each case.

It is interesting to note that publications and reference materials are not recognized as assets. IAEA has decided to spend them on acquisition and/or production. Moreover, IAEA discloses the threshold used to capitalized inventory items (para. 25). This information is useful to the reader in order to understand the materiality threshold applied by the Agency.

9 SERVICE CONCESSION ARRANGEMENTS: GRANTOR

A service concession arrangement is an arrangement (usually contractual) whereby a private sector entity provides assets and related services that give the public access to major economic and social facilities. Examples include roads, schools, and telecommunication networks. Within such arrangements there are two parties – a concession operator (normally a private sector entity) and a grantor (a public sector entity), who is the party that grants the service arrangement. The operator is compensated for its services over the period of the arrangement and in return has the obligation to provide public services. At the end of the arrangement the residual interest in any assets constructed or transferred as part of the arrangement (e.g., the motorways, bridges, or telecommunication networks) is controlled by the grantor, not the operator.

The outsourcing of an entity's internal services is not a service concession, for example building maintenance and employee restaurant facilities, as these do not involve the construction or transfer of assets. Service concession arrangements have many of the characteristics of a finance lease contract (such as the transfer of a non-current asset) but also include a service arrangement. A service concession arrangement is a typical feature of public–private partnerships (PPP) (see also Alla, 2014).

Service concession arrangements are arrangements in which:

- The operator uses the service concession asset to provide a public service on behalf of the grantor for a specified period of time; and
- The operator is compensated for its services over the period of the service concession arrangement.

A grantor (the government) is the entity that grants the right to use the service concession asset to the operator. An operator (the company) is the entity that uses the service concession asset to provide public services subject to the government's control of the asset.

IPSAS 32[1] on Service Concession Arrangements prescribes the accounting treatment for service concession arrangements for the grantor, including the disclosure requirements. Below is an example of the recommendations made in an IMF country report on Iceland in terms of considering the application of IPSAS 32.

Example 9.1   IPSAS implementation in Iceland and service concession arrangements

In a 2014 IMF country report on IPSAS implementation in Iceland, the following was identified in terms of service concession arrangements:

The Government of Iceland currently does not include in its financial statements any service concession arrangements. IPSAS, however, requires recognition of the service concession asset and related liability if certain conditions are met. These conditions relate to control over the asset, both during and at the end of the arrangement. The recognition of service concession assets and related liabilities in accordance with IPSAS is likely to have only a limited impact on the statement of financial position (balance sheet) of the Government of Iceland at this stage.

However, this situation may change if more such contracts are entered into in the future as is currently being contemplated by the Ministry of Finance. The mission therefore recommends the adoption of IPSAS 32 *Service Concession Arrangements: Grantor*, and:

- Analyze existing and future service concession arrangements;
- Recognize service concession assets if required by the standard;
- Recognize liabilities under the financial liability model or grant of a right to the operator model, as appropriate; and
- Account for arrangements that are not within the scope of IPSAS 32 using other IPSASs, as appropriate to their specific terms and conditions.

Source: Khan et.al (2014).

SERVICE CONCESSION ARRANGEMENTS: GRANTOR

For arrangements that are within the scope of IPSAS 32 Figure 9.1 applies:

The operator will, in addition, disclose obligations to acquire or build items of property, plant, and equipment, while the grantor will disclose how the arrangement has been classified, and give details of any assets recognized as infrastructure/service concession assets during the period. Both operators and grantors are

---

[1] IPSAS 32 applies the same tests as IFRIC 12 in determining which party to the service concession arrangement should recognize property, plant, and equipment on its balance sheet, and provides guidance on the grantor's accounting requirements that is complementary to the guidance on the operator's accounting requirements in IFRIC 12. The disclosure requirements in IPSAS 32 are based on SIC 29.

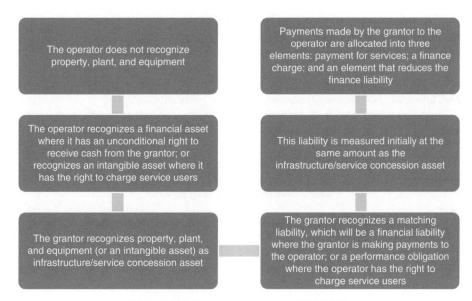

Figure 9.1   Illustration of scope of IPSAS 32

required to provide the relevant disclosures required by other standards, for example: property, plant, and equipment under IPSAS 17 (Property, Plant and Equipment) or financial instruments under IPSAS 29 (Financial Instruments: Recognition and Measurement).

A common service concession arrangement that falls within the scope of IPSAS 32 is a "build-operate-transfer" arrangement. Within this type of arrangement, an operator constructs the infrastructure to be used to deliver a public service, and it operates and maintains that infrastructure for a specified period of time. The operator is paid for its services over the period of the arrangement. A contract sets out performance standards, pricing mechanisms, and arrangements for arbitrating disputes. The operator may, in some cases, upgrade the existing infrastructure and maintain and operate the upgraded infrastructure. This second type of arrangement is sometimes referred to as a "rehabilitate-operate-transfer" arrangement (see Khan et al., 2014). Outsourcing the operation of an entity's internal services (for example employee restaurant, building maintenance, or IT functions) does not constitute a service concession arrangement.

Example 9.2   Construction of a bridge and a concession

An entity wins a call for tender and is chosen to construct and operate a new bridge on behalf of the State. The construction cost of CU30 million is payable at the end of Year 1 when the construction of the bridge will be complete. The operating term of the bridge is 15 years and will commence at the start of Year 2. The annual operating costs are CU4 million, payable at the end of each of Years 2 to 16.

The entity will generate revenue from tolls charged to users of the bridge. The entity estimates that the annual revenue will be CU7 million per annum.

The cost of constructing the bridge is recognized as a non-current asset, but as an intangible asset (the right to collect tolls) rather than property, plant and equipment (the bridge itself is State property and will return to the State when the concession expires). This intangible is then amortized over its 15-year useful life.

Assuming revenue is as estimated the financial statements will contain the following:

Year 1 Statement of financial position

Intangible asset	CU30 million

Year 2 Statement of financial position

Intangible asset	CU28 million (CU30 less 1/15)

Year 2 Statement of comprehensive income/Statement of financial performance

Revenue	CU7 million
Operating costs	CU4 million
Amortization	CU2 million

Some typical features of service concession arrangements are (see also Alla, 2014; Khan et al., 2014):

- The grantor is a public sector entity.
- The operator is responsible for at least some of the management of the service concession asset and related services and does not only act as an agent on behalf of the government.
- The arrangement sets the initial prices to be levied by the operator and regulates price revisions over the period of the service concession arrangement.
- The operator is obliged to hand over the service concession asset to the government in a specified condition at the end of the period of the arrangement, for little or no incremental consideration, irrespective of which party initially financed it.
- The arrangement is governed by a binding agreement that sets out performance standards, mechanisms for adjusting prices, and arrangements for arbitrating disputes.

Question and answer

Question:

What measurement rules apply to a service concession asset?

Answer:

Usually a service concession asset is measured at its fair value, except when it was already owned before the service concession was granted. Where an existing asset

> of the grantor meets the conditions to be recognized as a service concession asset, the grantor reclassifies the existing asset as a service concession asset. The reclassified service concession asset is accounted for following IPSAS 17, or where it is an intangible asset, following IPSAS 31.

Grantor Accounting: Treatment of the Asset

IPSAS 32 requires the government to recognize an asset as a service concession asset if the following conditions are met:

- The government controls or regulates what services the operator must provide with the asset, to whom it must provide them, and at what price; and
- The government controls (through ownership, beneficial entitlement. or otherwise) any significant residual interest in the asset at the end of the term of the arrangement.

For a "whole-of-life" asset, that is to say an asset used during its entire useful life, only the conditions in the first of the above points (i.e., the government controls or regulates what services the operator must provide with the asset, to whom it must provide them, and at what price) need to be met. Only assets provided by the operator (existing asset of the operator, constructed or developed, purchased or an upgrade to an existing asset of the government) are recognized. Existing assets of the government (other than upgrades thereto) used in a service concession arrangement are reclassified as service concession assets, no additional asset and related liability are recognized in such cases.

It should be emphasized that IPSAS 32 does not create new principles for timing of recognition of the service concession asset, or its measurement. Rather, IPSAS 32 refers to the IPSAS standards where those principles are set out, and provides relevant application guidance. One area on which guidance was provided related to assets that were constructed or developed by the operator to illustrate how the service concession assets are be recognized in accordance with IPSAS 17 Property, Plant, and Equipment or IPSAS 31 Intangible Assets.

Under IPSAS 32, the government must recognize the service concession asset and related liability if the conditions for asset recognition in IPSAS 17 or IPSAS 31 are also met.

Grantor Accounting: Treatment of the Liability

If the grantor has recognized the infrastructure/service concession asset as its property, plant, and equipment (or as its intangible asset), IPSAS 32 requires the grantor to also recognize a liability. This liability is initially measured at the same amount as the infrastructure/service concession asset.

The nature of the liability, and the accounting treatment after initial recognition, depend on how the operator is compensated for providing the infrastructure/service concession asset and the related services. There are two models: the financial liability model and the grant of a right to the operator model (see Table 9.1).

Table 9.1 The financial liability model vs. grant of a right to the operator model

Key characteristics of each model	Financial liability model	Grant of a right to the operator model
Presentation of each model	**The grantor makes payments to the operator**	**The grantor gives the operator the right to charge service users**
	The transaction meets the definition of a financial liability and is accounted for in accordance with IPSAS 28, Financial Instruments: Presentation, the de-recognition requirements in IPSAS 29, Financial Instruments: Recognition and Measurement, and IPSAS 30, Financial Instruments: Disclosures, except as required by IPSAS 32.	The transaction is an exchange transaction involving dissimilar assets (a service concession asset for the government and an intangible asset for the operator) that gives rise to revenue for the government.
		However, as the service concession arrangement covers a period of time, the government does not recognize the revenue immediately.
		The government recognizes a liability for any portion of the revenue that is not yet earned.
Nature of liability	The grantor recognizes a financial liability, reflecting its obligation to make payments to the operator.	The grantor recognizes a performance obligation, reflecting its obligation to make the infrastructure/service concession asset available to the operator.
Accounting treatment after initial recognition	Payments made to the operator are allocated into three elements: payment for services; a finance charge; and an element that reduces the finance liability.	The performance obligation is reduced as access to the infrastructure/service concession asset is provided. The grantor recognizes the reduction in the performance obligation as revenue.
Treatment of revenues and expenses	Payments to the operator are allocated and accounted for according to their substance as a reduction in the liability, a finance charge, and charges for services provided by the operator.	The government earns the benefit associated with the assets received in the service concession arrangement in exchange for the right granted to the operator over the period of the arrangement.
	If the asset and service components of a service concession arrangement are separately identifiable, the amount allocated to each component is determined by reference to their relative fair values.	A liability is recognized for any portion of the revenue that is not yet earned. Revenue related to the recognition of the service concession asset is recognized according to the economic substance of the service concession arrangement, and the liability is reduced as revenue is recognized.
	If they are not, the components are determined using estimation techniques.	
	The finance charge and charges for services provided by the operator are accounted for as expenses.	

Where the grantor makes payments to the operator, and also gives the operator the right to charge service users, the grantor will recognize both a financial liability and a performance obligation, and will account for these liabilities separately.

Example 9.3   Mixed concessions

For some motorways in France, where traffic is not expected to be high, and therefore tolls charged to drivers are not expected to be sufficient to cover the operating costs of the motorway concession, the State gives the operator the right to charge tolls to drivers (a maximum toll level is granted) and also agrees to make payments to the operator to be compensated for the expected low level of traffic. These motorways, which are not supposed to generate enough revenue to cover operating costs, have been decided by the State in order to divert some traffic from high traffic motorways and to help some isolated territories in their development.

Grantor accounting – main points to consider

The principles that underlie the accounting for service concession arrangements are relatively straightforward, as we have seen. However, service concession arrangements are often complex, and are normally in place for long periods of time. These factors introduce complexity into the accounting arrangements (see Table 9.2).

Table 9.2   Overview of grantor accounting for service concession arrangements

Replacement of assets or components	Because service concession arrangements are normally in place for long time periods, it is not uncommon for assets, or components of assets, to be replaced by the operator periodically through the arrangement. Where the asset (or component) is to be replaced at set dates, the operator has an obligation that meets the definition of a liability. This is recognized and measured in accordance with IPSAS 19 Provisions, Contingent Liabilities and Contingent Assets. The grantor will recognize the new infrastructure/service concession asset when it is brought into use, in accordance with ED 43. When the grantor recognizes the new infrastructure/service concession asset, it also recognizes a new or increased liability.
	Both the operator and the grantor will need to exercise judgment in the more complicated scenario where the operator is required to provide an asset to a specified standard throughout the life of the arrangement, but can achieve this either by replacing the asset or by increased maintenance throughout the arrangement.

(continued)

Table 9.2 *(Continued)*

Guarantees	The grantor may provide guarantees to the operator. Guarantees can take two forms: financial guarantees (where the grantor guarantees the loan debt of the operator) and performance guarantees (where the grantor guarantees a minimum return or a minimum level of income). The grantor will recognize and measure financial guarantees in accordance with IPSAS 29 Financial Instruments: Recognition and Measurement. Performance guarantees are recognized and measured in accordance with IPSAS 19 Provisions, Contingent Liabilities and Contingent Assets.
Long-term nature of service concession arrangements	Because service concession arrangements are normally in place for long time periods, the time value of money will normally be significant. Both operators and grantors will need to adjust their accounting treatments accordingly. Examples include increasing the amount of any annual payments (normally by reference to an index); the operator discounting the liability in relation to an obligation to replace an asset; and the grantor discounting financial guarantees.
Existing assets of the grantor	Existing assets of the grantor may form part of a service concession arrangement. There are two scenarios. In the first, the asset is used by the operator to deliver services under the arrangement. In this scenario, the grantor will normally continue to control the asset under IPSAS 32 and will therefore reclassify the asset as infrastructure/service concession asset. The operator will not control the asset and therefore does not account for it. In the second scenario, the grantor gives the operator access to an asset not used in the arrangement, and the operator uses this asset to generate income. Where the asset is transferred to the operator, the operator will account for these assets as their property, plant, and equipment. The grantor would derecognize the asset, and recognize a performance obligation. As the performance obligation is reduced, the grantor will recognize the reduction as revenue.

Question and Answer

Question:

Do concession assets have to be the "infrastructure" type of assets or can they also be vehicles, helicopters, etc.?

Answer:

The IPSASB agreed not to use the term "infrastructure" to refer to the asset used in a service concession arrangement, even though IFRIC 12 uses the term. The IPSASB noted that the term is used in IPSAS in ways that may not be fully compatible with IPSAS 32. Further, the term has a prescribed meaning in some jurisdictions that differs from that used in IFRIC 12. To ensure that it is clear that the asset referred to is the one recognized on the basis of the conditions for recognition in IPSAS 32.9–32.10), the asset in IPSAS 32 is referred to as the "service concession asset" (IPSAS 32.BC 9).

Let's go back to the definition of a service concession asset:

"A service concession asset is an asset used to provide public services in a service concession arrangement that:

(a) Is provided by the operator which:
   (i) The operator constructs, develops, or acquires from a third party; or
   (ii) Is an existing asset of the operator; or
(b) Is provided by the grantor which:
   (i) Is an existing asset of the grantor; or
   (ii) Is an upgrade to an existing asset of the grantor."

The conditions of recognition of the asset by the grantor are as follows:

"The grantor shall recognize an asset provided by the operator and an upgrade to an existing asset of the grantor as a service concession asset if:

(a) The grantor controls or regulates what services the operator must provide with the asset, to whom it must provide them, and at what price; and
(b) The grantor controls – through ownership, beneficial entitlement or otherwise – any significant residual interest in the asset at the end of the term of the arrangement." (IPSAS 32.9)

Of course, there is no question of recognition under (b)(i) of IPSAS 32.8, because the asset is an existing asset of the grantor and is already recognized in the grantor's financial statements!

And IPSAS 32.10 specifies that it "applies to an asset used in a service concession arrangement for its entire useful life (a "whole-of-life" asset) if the conditions in paragraph 9(a) are met."

The main underlying question is not as to the "type" of asset, but rather the use of the asset. Is this asset used to provide public services during its entire useful life?

When the asset is provided by the operator, the grantor has to control and regulate the service operated by the operator and also control any significant residual interest in the asset at the end of the term of the concession arrangement.

For "infrastructure" assets, the answer is usually yes. The asset is to provide a public service through a concession arrangement, and may continue to provide a public service later through some other concession arrangements with some other operators.

For other assets, such as vehicles or helicopters, the grantor is to control any significant interest in those assets at the end of the term of the arrangement.

Imagine that a municipality signs a concession arrangement for five years with an operator to run the fire brigade of the town. The municipality owns the fire station which is provided by the concession arrangement as well as fire engines. If the concession arrangement states that the fire station, the fire engines originally provided by the municipality, as well as new fire engines acquired by the operator during the concession arrangement will return to the municipality at the end of the term of the arrangement, all these assets are service concession assets.

> If new fire engines acquired by the operator during the concession arrangement will not return to the municipality at the end of the term of the arrangement, these assets are not service concession assets.
>
> This example shows that assets are classified as service concession assets according to their intended use, not according to their nature.

Disclosures

The disclosure requirements of IPSAS 32 apply only to grantors following IPSAS. The following key disclosures are required:

- A description of the service concession arrangement;
- Details of significant terms of the arrangement that may affect the amount, timing, and certainty of future cash flows;
- The nature and extent of:
  - Rights to use assets;
  - Obligations to provide or rights to expect provision of services;
  - Obligations to deliver or rights to receive specified assets at the end of the concession period;
  - Renewal and termination options; and
  - Other rights and obligations.
- Changes in the arrangement during the accounting period.

The operator will also disclose obligations to acquire or build items of property, plant, and equipment, while the grantor will disclose how the arrangement has been classified, and give details of any assets recognized as infrastructure/service concession assets during the period.

Both operators and grantors will also need to provide the relevant disclosures required by other standards, for example:

- Property, plant, and equipment under IPSAS 17 Property, Plant and Equipment;
- Intangible assets under IPSAS 31 Intangible Assets;
- Financial instruments under IPSAS 29 Financial Instruments: Recognition and Measurement.

IPSAS Financial Reporting in Practice 9.1. Public Private Partnerships, Financial Statements of the Government of New Zealand for the Year Ended 30 June 2014, Note 1: Summary of Accounting Policies

A public–private partnership (also known as a service concession arrangement) is an arrangement between the Government and a private sector partner in which the private sector partner uses specified assets to supply a public service on behalf of the Government for a specified period of time and is compensated for its services over the period of the arrangement. The costs of the specified assets are financed by the private sector partner, except where existing assets of the Government (generally land) are allocated to the arrangement. Payments made by the Government to a private sector partner over the period of a service concession arrangement cover the costs of the provision of services, interest expenses and repayment of the liability incurred to acquire the specified assets.

The assets in a public private partnership are recognised as assets of the Government. If the assets are progressively constructed, the Government progressively recognises work-in-progress at cost and a financial liability of the same value is also recognised. When the assets are fully constructed, the total asset cost and the matching financial liability reflect the value of the future compensation to be provided to the private-sector partner for the assets.

Subsequent to initial recognition:

- The assets are accounted for in accordance with Government accounting policy applicable to the classes of property, plant and equipment that the specified assets comprise, and
- The financial liabilities are measured at amortised cost.

The financial statements of the Government of New Zealand have not been prepared according to IPSAS. However, these financial statements have been prepared in accordance with the Public Finance Act 1989 and with New Zealand Generally Accepted Accounting Practice (NZ GAAP) as defined in the Financial Reporting Act 2013. They have been prepared in accordance with New Zealand equivalents to International Financial Reporting Standards (NZ IFRS) as appropriate for public benefit entities, meaning that they are almost IPSAS-compliant. On the concession arrangement topic, they may be considered IPSAS-compliant.

In the above example, the Government of New Zealand accounts for concession arrangements according to the grant of a right to the operator model.

10 LEASES AND LEASING ARRANGEMENTS

Public sector entities may obtain financing from a number of different sources. While simple borrowing arrangements are easy to understand, financing can also be obtained as part of purchasing arrangements such as leasing and hire. These arrangements may vary significantly in nature, and may include complex sale and leaseback transactions.

Leases can be a major source of finance and it is therefore important that the financial statements provide sufficient information for users to be able to understand fully the substance of such transactions.

IPSAS 13 on leases sets out the treatment for reporting lease transactions and provides a framework for users of the financial statements to understand how an entity may access financing in the form of leases.

> A "lease" is a transaction between two parties, a lessor and a lessee, whereby the right to use an asset is transferred to the lessee in return for a defined series of payments to the lessor (IPSAS 13.8).

Lease accounting generally applies even if under the terms of the lease the lessor provides substantial services in connection with the operation or maintenance of the asset. An example of such a service would be the provision of building facilities management for the asset (IPSAS 13.4).

Nevertheless, public sector bodies enter into a variety of arrangements which may combine the use of an asset and the provision of goods and services, some of which are not accounted for using lease guidance.

Determining whether an arrangement is, or contains a lease
Determining whether an arrangement is, or contains, a lease is based on the substance of the arrangement and requires an assessment of whether: • Fulfilment of the arrangement is dependent on the use of a specific asset or assets • The arrangement conveys a right to use the asset.

Fulfilment is dependent on the use of a specific asset	**Arrangement conveys right to use the asset**
• Although a specific asset may be explicitly identified in an arrangement, it is not the subject of a lease if fulfillment of the arrangement is not dependent on the use of the specified asset, e.g., if the supplier is obliged to deliver a specified quantity of goods or services and has the right and ability to provide those goods or services using other assets not specified in the arrangement, then fulfilment of the arrangement is not dependent on the specified asset and the arrangement does not contain a lease. • A warranty obligation that permits or requires the substitution of the same or similar assets when the specified asset is not operating properly does not preclude lease treatment • A contractual provision (contingent or otherwise) permitting or requiring the supplier to substitute other assets for any reason on or after a specified date does not preclude lease treatment before the date of substitution.	An arrangement conveys the right to use the asset if the arrangement conveys to the purchaser (lessee) the right to control the use of the underlying asset. The right to control the use of the underlying asset is conveyed if any one of the following conditions is met: • The purchaser has the ability or right to operate the asset or direct others to operate the asset in a manner it determines while obtaining or controlling more than an insignificant amount of the output or other utility of the asset. • The purchaser has the ability or right to control physical access to the underlying asset while obtaining or controlling more than an insignificant amount of the output or other utility of the asset. • Facts and circumstances indicate that the likelihood is remote that one or more parties other than the purchaser will take more than an insignificant amount of the output or other utility that will be produced or generated by the asset during the term of the arrangement, and the price that the purchaser will pay for the output is neither contractually fixed per unit of output nor equal to the current market price per unit of output as of the time of delivery of the output.

Figure 10.1   Determining whether an arrangement is or contains a lease

DOES AN ARRANGEMENT CONTAIN A LEASE?

The determination of whether an arrangement contains a lease should be based on the substance of the arrangement, rather than its legal form, which in turn requires an assessment of whether two conditions are met. Figure 10.1 illustrates the assessment of these two conditions.

IPSAS 13.25 states that a contract may consist solely of an agreement to lease an asset. However, a lease may also be one element in a broader set of agreements with private sector entities to construct, own, operate, and/or transfer assets. Public sector entities often enter into such agreements, particularly in relation to long-lived physical assets and infrastructure assets. Other agreements may involve a public sector entity leasing infrastructure from the private sector.

The entity determines whether the arrangement is a service concession arrangement, as defined in IPSAS 32, Service Concession Arrangements: Grantor.

Example 10.1   Right to use an asset

Entity B requires substantial power to operate its administrative building heating system. Entity B therefore enters into an arrangement with Entity E to erect a power station next to Entity B's building.

Under the terms of the arrangement, Entity B will be the sole user of the power station for the next 20 years and will pay Entity E for the electricity consumed.

Assume that the expected economic life of the power station is 25 years.

Entity B and E will have to determine whether or not the arrangement is or contains a lease.

Condition 1:

Does the fulfilment depend on the use of a specified asset?

    Yes, the power station.

Condition 2:

Does the arrangement convey the right to control the use of the asset?

    Yes, Entity B will obtain more than an insignificant amount of the output as it is using the power station exclusively for the major part of its economic life, i.e., 20 out of the 25 years.

    Therefore both conditions have been met and the arrangement contains a lease.

Re-assessment of Whether Arrangements Contain a Lease

The assessment of whether an arrangement contains a lease is made at the inception of the arrangement, being the earlier of the date of the arrangement and the date of commitment by the parties to the principal terms of the arrangement, on the basis of all of the facts and circumstances.

If at any time the lessee and the lessor agree to change the provisions of the lease, other than by renewing the lease, in a manner that would have resulted in a different classification of the lease if the changed terms had been in effect at the inception of the lease, the revised agreement is regarded as a new agreement over its term.

A reassessment of whether the arrangement contains a lease after the inception of the arrangement is made only if any one of the following conditions is met:

- There is a change in the contractual terms, unless the change only renews or extends the arrangement;

- A renewal option is exercised or an extension is agreed to by the parties to the arrangement, unless the term of the renewal or extension had initially been included in the lease term;
- There is a change in the determination of whether fulfilment is dependent on a specified asset;
- There is a substantial change to the asset, for example a substantial physical change to PP&E.

A reassessment of an arrangement is based on the facts and circumstances as of the date of reassessment, including the remaining term of the arrangement. Changes in estimates (for example, changes in estimates of the economic life or the residual value of the leased property) or changes in circumstances (for example, default by the lessee) do not trigger a reassessment. If an arrangement is reassessed and is determined to contain a lease (or not to contain a lease), lease accounting is applied (or ceases to apply) (IPSAS 13.18).

Classification of Leases

The classification of a lease is based on the extent to which risks and rewards associated with ownership are transferred from the lessor to the lessee. If a lease transfers substantially all the risks and rewards normally associated with the ownership of an asset it should be classified as a finance lease; otherwise, it should be classified as an operating lease (IPSAS 13.13). The classification of the lease is made at inception of the lease and is not changed, except if both parties agree to change the provisions of the initial lease (other than by renewing it), and these changes would have resulted in a different classification of the lease at its inception (see the table below on commencement date versus inception date). The amended lease is considered a new lease agreement.

Commencement date	**Inception date**
The commencement date is the date from which the lessee is entitled to exercise its right to use the asset and therefore when the lease will be initially recognized in the accounting records and when depreciation commences.	The inception date is the earlier of the date of the lease agreement and the date of commitment by the parties to the principal provisions of the lease. This is also when the lease should be classified as either a finance lease or an operating lease.
Therefore, the commencement date of the lease is typically when the lessee takes possession of the leased asset.	Furthermore this is when the amounts to be recognized at commencement of a finance lease are determined.
	The inception date is thus commonly the date on which the lease agreement is signed by both parties and becomes legally binding.

IPSAS 13.9 specifies that recognition takes place at the commencement of the lease term ("the date from which the lessee is entitled to exercise its right to use the leased asset") based on values measured at the inception of the lease ("the earlier of the date of the lease agreement and the date of commitment by the parties to the principal provisions of the lease"). If the lease is adjusted for changes in the lessor's

costs between the inception of the lease and the commencement of the lease term, the effect of any such changes is deemed to have taken place at the inception.

Under IPSAS 13, the classification of a lease does not depend on where the legal ownership of the leased asset lies, but is instead based on the extent to which the risks and rewards incidental to ownership of the asset have been transferred from the lessor to the lessee. If substantially all of the risks and rewards have been transferred to the lessee, it is a finance lease; otherwise it is an operating lease.

Examples of the key risks and rewards that arise from the ownership of an asset include those shown in Figure 10.2:

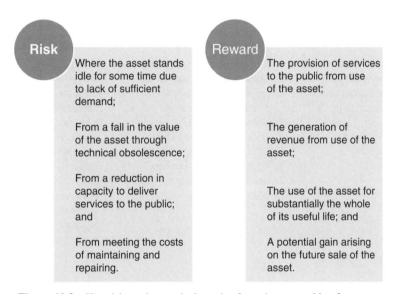

Figure 10.2   Key risks and rewards that arise from the ownership of an asset

IPSAS 13 also sets out specific situations that, individually or collectively, would normally lead to a lease being classified as a finance lease.

Such situations include the following:

- Ownership of the asset transfers to the lessee by the end of the lease term;
- While ownership of the asset does not automatically pass to the lessee at the end of the agreement, the lessee has an option to purchase the asset. The price at which the option is set is such that it is reasonably certain that the option will be exercised. This means that the price is set significantly below the fair value (see table below) expected of the asset at the date the option becomes exercisable (i.e., a "bargain purchase option");
- Though ownership of the asset is not transferred at the end of the lease term, the term of the lease is for the majority of the economic life of the asset. At the end of the lease, therefore, the asset will have practically no further ability to generate future economic benefits;

- The asset is so specialized that only the lessee can use it without major modifications;
- The present value of the minimum lease payments payable by the lessee under the lease is equal to substantially all of the fair value of the asset. Where this is the case, the lessee has effectively paid for the asset in full and therefore should treat the asset as if it had acquired it through a financing arrangement; and
- The leased asset is not easily replaceable by another asset.

The table below provides the explanations for three key terms used in elaborating on the indicators for classifying leases.

Fair value	Economic life	Minimum lease payments
Is the amount "for which an asset could be exchanged, or a liability settled, between knowledgeable, willing parties in an arm's length transaction." (IPSAS 13.8)	The period over which the asset either generates income or provides service potential. IPSAS 13 broadens the definition to make it clear that both the narrower IAS view of economic benefits and the wider concept of service potential are relevant. (IPSAS 13.8)	The minimum amounts that are payable by the lessee to the lessor under a lease agreement. This comprises all amounts payable under the contract, including any amounts guaranteed to the lessor by the lessee or any party related to it. In addition, in the context of a lessee, where there is an option to purchase the asset at the end of the contract and it is expected to be exercised because it has been set at a "bargain price," then this amount should also form part of the minimum lease payments. (IPSAS 13.8)

IPSAS 13 provide three additional situations that may lead to classification as a finance lease:

- Losses associated with any cancellation of the lease are borne by the lessee;
- Fluctuations in the fair value at the end of the lease term fall to the lessee; and
- The lessee has the option to extend the lease for a secondary period at a rate that is substantially below market rate (this is often known as a "peppercorn rent").

To identify the characteristics of a lease over land and buildings, the two elements should be separated. Land is generally considered to have an indefinite life and therefore an associated lease will normally be classified as an operating lease, unless there are other characteristics, such as title of the land transferring to the lessee, that suggest otherwise (IPSAS 13.19).

SUBSTANCE OVER FORM

The IPSASB Conceptual Framework 3.10 states that "[t]o be useful in financial reporting, information must be a faithful representation of the economic and other phenomena that it purports to represent. Faithful representation is attained when the depiction of the phenomenon is complete, neutral, and free from material error. Information that faithfully represents an economic or other phenomenon depicts the substance of the underlying transaction, other event, activity or circumstance—which is not necessarily always the same as its legal form."

Therefore substance over form is a key quality that information must possess, and it has a direct application in determining the classification of leases.

Example 10.2   Substance over form and lease classification (1)

An entity may sell a building to a third party, and therefore transfer the ownership of the asset to the third party. The entity signs a rental agreement with this third party. In this contract, it is specified that the third party can either rent or sell the building to the entity. The third party has a put option to sell the building back to the entity any time after two years at a defined price and this entity cannot refuse to buy back the building.

In that case, the entity keeps substantially all the risks and rewards from the building. Therefore recording this transaction as a sale would not give a true and fair view of the substance of the transaction.

Whether a lease is a finance lease or an operating lease depends on the substance of the transaction rather than the form of the contract (IPSAS 13.15). It is necessary to understand the substance of the transaction to perform this analysis. Accountants cannot usually analyze complex situations by themselves because they do not have access to enough information to define the transaction in substance. In order to implement the accounting for leases under IPSAS, it is necessary to structure the inflow of information from different actors in the entity (managers, lawyers, internal auditors …) to understand and record the transaction according to its substance.

Example 10.3 will help to show how the substance of a finance lease may differ from its legal form.

Example 10.3   Substance over form and lease classification (2)

A university needs to buy a new item of video conference equipment which would cost CU10 000 if bought for cash and which has a useful life of five years. The university has no funding available from revenues or grant and has identified the following two financing options:

Option 1

- Borrow CU10 000.
- This loan is repayable in five annual instalments of CU2 400 each (each instalment including interest of CU400).

Option 2

- Lease the asset from the reseller or a bank leasing division for five years, in return for annual lease instalments of CU2 400 each.

Let's look at the accounting for both options, assuming IPSAS 13 are not applied. The transaction will be accounted for by recording:

- An asset for the purchase of the new item of PPE at CU10 000;
- A liability of CU10 000;
- As each annual instalment is paid, a reduction in cash of CU2 400, a reduction in the liability of CU2 000, and interest of CU400 recognized in profit or loss; and
- Depreciation of CU2 000 per annum recognized as expense.

Without IPSAS 13 the transaction would involve recording in surplus or deficit the annual rental instalments of CU2 400 as they become payable.

The two accounting treatments are different and have a significant impact on the "picture" presented by the financial statements. In option 2 no asset or debt is recognized in the statement of financial position and hence there is no finance cost or depreciation recognized.

The substance of these two options is, however, the same, since the university:

- Has possession and use of the asset for the whole of its five-year useful life; and
- Is paying a total of CU12 000 for the use of the asset – CU2 000 more than its cash price, so CU2 000 is interest.

In substance, the university has "bought" the asset under both options, and the lender or lessor has provided the finance.

The only real difference is that under option 2 the entity never gets legal title. Option 2 would allow the university to avoid showing borrowing in the statement of financial position and take advantage of a form of financing that is not recognized in the financial statements.

IPSAS 13 ensures that the substance of the transaction is recorded. Therefore both option 1 and option 2 would be accounted for as if the university had bought the asset.

ACCOUNTING TREATMENT BY LESSEES

Table 10.1 provides a basic overview of the recognition requirements for the two types of lease.

Table 10.1   Recognition requirements for operating and finance leases

Operating lease recognition	Finance lease recognition
Statement of financial position	**Statement of financial position**
No asset or liability recognized unless payments are in advance or arrears	Recognize a non-current asset.
	Recognize a liability for the total amount of the lease obligation (i.e., the total payments outstanding including repayment instalments and finance charges accrued to date).
Statement of financial performance	**Statement of financial performance**
Recognize the lease instalment charge for the year.	Recognize a charge for the depreciation of the non-current asset.
	Recognize a finance charge for the year.

As already described, the classification of a lease as finance or operating is made at the inception of the lease and should only be revisited if changes to the lease conditions are made which, if made at the outset, would have resulted in a different classification.

Accounting for Finance Leases

Initial recognition at the commencement of the lease term:

Asset	Liability
The lessee has, in substance, bought the leased asset so it should appear in its statement of financial position.	The total amount of the lease obligation that the lessee owes to the lessor in relation to this asset.

The amounts should be recorded at the fair value of the asset or, if lower, the present value of the minimum lease payments, determined at the inception of the lease (IPSAS 13.28).

The present value of the minimum lease payments is calculated by establishing the minimum lease payments due under the lease and discounting them to take account of the time value of money (IPSAS 13.28).

If the minimum lease payments under the lease (including any unguaranteed residual value, i.e., the amount that the asset could be sold for at the end of the lease term that is not guaranteed by the lessee) are discounted at the "interest rate implicit in the lease," the result should equal the fair value of the leased asset. Any initial indirect costs incurred by the lessee are added to the asset's cost (IPSAS 13.8).

Initial indirect costs are incremental costs that are directly attributable to "negotiating and arranging a lease" (IPSAS 13.8).

Question and Answer

Question:

The public sector entity, Berty's school, entered, as lessee, the following lease agreements:

1. Asset One is rent of €5 000/year over a minimum period of three years. Asset One has a useful life of three years and can be bought for €12 000.
2. Asset Two is rent of €500/month. Asset Two has a useful life of 10 years and can be bought for €40 000. The contract is cancellable by the lessee at any time at no cost.

Determine whether these contracts are finance leases or operating leases.
Please use a 10% discount rate.

Answer:

1. The present value of the minimum lease payments is:
   $$5\ 000\ /\ 1.1 + 5\ 000\ /\ 1.1^2 + 5\ 000\ /1.1^3 = 12\ 434\ €$$
   The present value of the minimum lease payments exceeds the fair value of Asset One.
   Moreover the lease term is for the entire economic life of the leased asset. The contract is a finance lease contract.
2. The present value of the minimum lease payments is: 0.
   The contract is cancellable by the lessee any time. The lessor's losses associated with the cancellation are not borne by the lessee.
   It is not specified that Asset Two is of a specialized nature such that only the lessee can use it without major modifications. The contract is an operating lease.

Question and Answer

Question:

On 1 January 2015 an entity enters into a lease for a servor with a fair value of CU4 000. The lease term is for three years, with no option to extend, and the servor will be returned to the lessor at the end of the three years. This represents the majority of the asset's life. The present value of the minimum lease payments is CU3 800. At what amount would the asset, and corresponding liability, be initially recorded? CU4 000 or CU3 800?

Answer:

CU3 800 because it should be the fair value of the asset (CU4 000) or, if lower, the present value of the minimum lease payments, determined at the inception of the lease (CU3 800) (IPSAS 13.28).

Under a finance lease a non-current asset is recognized in the lessee's statement of financial position; IPSAS 13 also requires the asset to be depreciated in accordance with IPSAS 17 Property, Plant and Equipment.

The asset should be depreciated over its useful life or, if there is no reasonable certainty that the lessee will obtain ownership of the asset at the end of the lease term, the period of the lease if that is shorter. The depreciation policy for leased assets should be consistent with those of legally owned assets (IPSAS 13.37) because there is no difference in substance between an asset bought and an asset rented under a lease agreement

Each instalment made under a finance lease consists of a mixture of a finance charge and the reduction of the outstanding liability (IPSAS 13.34).

The total interest cost should be recognized over the accounting periods for which the lease liability exists, i.e., from the start of the lease until the last repayment is made.

The period over which the lease liability exists is not necessarily the same as the term of the lease. For example, if lease rentals are paid annually in advance, the lease finance will be paid off when the final payment is made at the start of the last year, but the lease term will include the last year, even though no liability will remain.

IPSAS 13 requires the total finance charge to be allocated over accounting periods so as to produce a constant periodic rate of interest on the outstanding lease obligation (IPSAS 13.34). This is done using the actuarial method.

The actuarial method charges interest at a constant percentage on the outstanding liability and therefore matches the interest to the "loan" balance. This is the most accurate method, but to apply it, the rate of interest implicit in the lease is required. The interest charge for each period is the interest rate multiplied by the balance remaining immediately after a rental payment has been made.

Question and Answer

Question:

The public sector entity HospitalEquipment enters into a leasing agreement with the company Alpha on 1 January N for a machine with an economic life of eight years. HospitalEquipment agrees to pay €1 000 per year for five years and has the option to purchase the machine for €129 after five years.

The discount rate to be used is 8% and the market value of the machine is €4 400 on 1 January N.

Determine the journal entries on 1 January N and 31 December N.

For the purpose of the exercise, let's assume that there is no VAT and that HospitalEquipment ends its period on 31 December.

Answer:

The initial value of the asset and liability is to be determined at the lower of the fair value of the asset and the present value of the minimum lease payments (discounted at the interest rate implicit in the lease, if practicable to determine, otherwise the entity's incremental borrowing rate should be used) (IPSAS 13.28).

The fair value of the machine is usually its market value, that is to say €4 400 when there is an active market for this item.

The present value of the minimum lease payments is $1\,000 \times (1-1.08^{-5})/0.08 \times 1.08 + 129 \times 1.08^{-5} = 4\,400$ euros

The machine is depreciated over eight years: $4400/8 = €550/year$

Lease payments are apportioned between the finance charge and repayment of principal by using the implicit rate of interest. The finance charge is to be allocated so as to produce a constant periodic rate of interest on the remaining balance of the liability (IPSAS 13.34).

Date	Outstanding liability	Finance charge	Repayment of principal	Lease payment
1 January N	4 400		1 000	1 000
1 January N+1	3 400	272	728	1 000
1 January N+2	2 672	214	786	1 000
1 January N+3	1 886	151	850	1 000
1 January N+4	1 036	83	917	1 000
31 December N+5	119	10	119	129
		730	4 400	5 129

The journal entries are as follows:

On 1 January N

Property, plant and equipment	4 400	
Non current liability		3 400
Current liability		1 000

On 1 January N

Current liability	1 000	
Bank		1 000

On 31 December N

Finance charge	272	
Current liability		272
Non-current liability	728	
Current liability		728
Depreciation expense	550	
Depreciation		550

In case there is an uncertainty whether HospitalEquipment is to exercise the option at the end of the lease term, it is still a finance lease because, at the inception of the lease, the present value of the minimum lease payments amounts to at least substantially all of the fair value of the leased asset. In that situation, the initial amount (4 400) minus the residual amount of the outstanding liability (119) would be depreciated over five years (the length of the contract).

The annual depreciation expense would be: $(4\,400 - 119) / 5 = €856$

Example 10.4   Five-year operating lease

An entity moves into new offices. It enters into a five-year operating lease. As an incentive they are offered a one-year rent free period with annual rentals thereafter reverting to CU250 000 per annum.

The total rentals of CU1 000 000 should be recognized on a straight-line basis over the life of the lease. The annual expense would therefore be CU200 000.

An entity should disclose the outstanding payments under non-cancellable operating leases allocated between the following periods (IPSAS 13.44):

- Within one year;
- Within two to five years; and
- After more than five years.

Where an entity expects to receive sublease rentals under an operating lease arrangement the total minimum sublease payments expected to be received under non-cancelable subleases should be disclosed at the end of the reporting period (IPSAS 13.40). The total amount recognized in profit or loss for amounts under operating leases, including subleases, should be disclosed identifying amounts representing the minimum lease payments, contingent rents, and sub lease amounts (IPSAS 13.44).

A description of an entity's significant leasing arrangements should be presented. Such information will normally include the basis on which any contingent rents are payable, the existence and terms of any options to extend the lease term, any escalation clauses or purchase options, and any restrictions that are imposed on the lease arrangements (IPSAS 13.44).

IPSAS Financial Reporting in Practice 10.1. IAEA Finance Lease Disclosures, 2013 Financial Statements

The Agency (i.e., IAEA) entered into a "Headquarters Agreement" with the Austrian Government in 1979 for a 99-year lease for its share of the VIC premises for a nominal rent of 1 Austrian schilling per year. As part of the agreement, the Agency must operate its headquarters seat from Austria, otherwise it must return its share of the VIC premises to the Austrian Government. Since the Headquarters Agreement is essentially in the nature of a finance lease, the Agency was required to capitalize its share of the VIC buildings on the basis of the BMS cost-sharing ratio. However, the Agency has availed itself of transitional provisions under IPSAS 17 Property, Plant and Equipment for the VIC buildings, and accordingly has not recognized its share of the VIC buildings as an asset in the statement of financial position. An external valuation of the depreciated replacement cost as at 1 January 2011 for the VIC buildings resulted in an amount of €311.686 million (the IAEA's share is €167.899 million based on the 2012 BMS cost-sharing ratio) and the fair rental value of the VIC land was €1.393 million per annum (the IAEA's share for the year is €0.750 million).

> Since the initial adoption of IPSAS, the IAEA has spent amounts on improvements and additions to the VIC premises. The IAEA has availed of the transitional provisions under IPSAS 17 for these amounts as the improvements and additions are integral to the VIC. Therefore, all such amounts have been expensed as incurred. Upon capitalization of the VIC buildings, these amounts will also be capitalized.

In the above note from its 2013 financial statements, IAEA explains that its headquarters buildings can be considered as leased under a finance lease from the Austrian Government, even though they have to be returned to Austria after the term of the lease. In substance, IAEA acts as the owner of these buildings even though the legal title remains with Austria.

UNESCO faces the same type of situation for its headquarters described below:

IPSAS Financial Reporting in Practice 10.2. UNESCO Critical accounting estimates and judgments, 2013 Financial Statements (note 3)

UNESCO leases the land for its headquarters sites at Place de Fontenoy and Rue Miollis from the host government. Under the lease agreements, the lease terms are for 99 years, and can be renewed for unlimited subsequent periods of 99 years. UNESCO pays a nominal amount in rent for the use of the land. Given that the agreements effectively grant UNESCO the right to use the land at the two sites in perpetuity for a nominal rent, it is considered appropriate to recognize the land as an asset in the UNESCO financial statements – see Note 13 Property, Plant & Equipment.

UNESCO discloses this important information in the note relating to critical accounting estimates and judgments in order to point out the fact that these buildings are recorded as non-current assets in its statement of financial position even though UNESCO is not the legal owner of these assets.

ACCOUNTING TREATMENT BY LESSORS

Just as a lessee accounts for the substance, not the form, of a finance lease, so should a lessor. See Table 10.2.

The net investment in the lease is defined as being the "gross investment in the lease discounted at the interest rate implicit in the lease." This gross investment is calculated as the lessee's minimum lease payments (which includes any residual value guaranteed by the lessee) plus any unguaranteed amount accruing to the lessor (IPSAS 13.8). The interest rate implicit in the lease is the same as that explained in relation to the lessee. The way it is calculated automatically includes any initial direct costs incurred by the lessor in the amounts receivable from the lessee, so they should not be added separately.

Table 10.2   Finance vs. operating lease

Finance lease	Operating lease
Under a finance lease the lessor is entitled to a stream of leasing receipts, so it should recognize the amounts receivable as an asset, rather than the leased item as a non-current asset.	A lessor should recognize assets that are leased under operating leases in its statement of financial position according to the nature of the asset.
The receivable should be measured so that it is equal to the net investment in the lease, at an amount equal to the net investment in the lease (IPSAS 13.48).	The lessor will recognize depreciation on depreciable non-current assets under operating lease arrangements in accordance with IPSAS 17 (IPSAS 13.66).
The income receivable under a finance lease arrangement should be recognized based on "a pattern reflecting a constant period rate of return on the lessor's net investment in the finance lease" (IPSAS 13.51).	Initial direct costs, as described above, should be added to the carrying amount of the asset and will therefore be recognized as an expense over the period of the useful life of the asset as it is depreciated (IPSAS 13.65).
	The income received under an operating lease should be recognized by the lessor based on a straight-line basis over the lease term. A different systematic basis of recognition should be used where it represents more fairly the timing of the benefits derived from the asset as the lessee uses it (IPSAS 13.63).

IPSAS 13 requires the following for a lessor, in terms of finance versus operating leases (see Table 10.3).

SALE AND LEASEBACK TRANSACTIONS

An entity may enter into a financing arrangement to improve its liquidity through what is commonly referred to as a sale and leaseback transaction. In such circumstances, the entity sells the asset to a third party, receives proceeds for the sale, and then leases the asset back and pays rental for its use.

A sale and leaseback transaction involves the sale of an asset and the leasing back of the same asset. The lease payment and the sale price are usually interdependent, because they are negotiated as a package. A sale and leaseback transaction can result in a finance or an operating lease, depending on the substance of the transaction. The accounting treatment of a sale and leaseback transaction depends upon the type of lease involved:

If a sale and leaseback transaction results in a finance lease, any excess of sales proceeds over the carrying amount shall not be immediately recognized as revenue by a seller-lessee. Instead, it shall be deferred and amortized over the lease term (IPSAS 13.71).

If a sale and leaseback transaction results in an operating lease, and it is clear that the transaction is established at fair value, any gain or loss shall be recognized immediately. If the sale price is below fair value, any gain or loss shall be recognized

Table 10.3   Key disclosures for finance leases vs. operating leases

Finance leases	Operating leases
• A lessor should provide a general description of its significant leasing arrangements (IPSAS 13.60).	• Disclosures should include a general description of the entity's leasing arrangements and the amount of contingent rents received in the period (IPSAS 13.69).
• A lessor should present a reconciliation of the gross investment in finance leases to the present value of the future minimum lease receipts due under them at the end of the reporting period.	• A lessor should disclose the future minimum receipts under non-cancellable operating leases allocated between the following periods: (IPSAS 13.69)
• The gross investment in the lease and the present value of the minimum lease payments for each of the following periods should also be disclosed: (IPSAS 13.60)	
• Within one year;	• Within one year;
• Within two to five years; and	• Within two to five years; and
• After more than five years.	• After more than five years.
• In addition, a lessor should disclose any unearned finance revenue, any unguaranteed residual values that accrue to the lessor (the amount that the asset will be worth at the end of its useful life), and contingent rents received during the period (IPSAS 13.60).	
• A lessor should also identify any allowance that has been made for uncollectable lease payments receivable (IPSAS 13.60).	

immediately except that, if the loss is compensated by future lease payments at below market price, it shall be deferred and amortized in proportion to the lease payments over the period for which the asset is expected to be used. If the sale price is above fair value, the excess over fair value shall be deferred and amortized over the period for which the asset is expected to be used (IPSAS 13.73).

DISCLOSURES

The disclosures for leases are divided into two sections, one attending to the disclosure requirements for finance leases and a second attending to operating leases.

Disclosures for Finance Leases

Lessee disclosure for finance leases

Lessees shall disclose the following for finance leases:

- For each class of asset, the net carrying amount at the reporting date;
- A reconciliation between the total of future minimum lease payments at the reporting date, and their present value;

- The total of future minimum lease payments at the reporting date, and their present value, for each of the following periods:
  - Not later than one year;
  - Later than one year and not later than five years; and
  - Later than five years;
- Contingent rents recognized as an expense in the period;
- The total of future minimum sublease payments expected to be received under non-cancelable subleases at the reporting date; and
- A general description of the lessee's material leasing arrangements including, but not limited to, the following:
  - The basis on which contingent rent payable is determined;
  - The existence and terms of renewal or purchase options and escalation clauses; and
  - Restrictions imposed by lease arrangements, such as those concerning return of surplus, return of capital contributions, dividends or similar distributions, additional debt, and further leasing (IPSAS 13.40).

Lessor disclosure for finance leases

Lessors shall disclose the following for finance leases:

- A reconciliation between the total gross investment in the lease at the reporting date, and the present value of minimum lease payments receivable at the reporting date;
- The gross investment in the lease and the present value of minimum lease payments receivable at the reporting date, for each of the following periods:
  - Not later than one year;
  - Later than one year and not later than five years; and
  - Later than five years;
- Unearned finance revenue;
- The unguaranteed residual values accruing to the benefit of the lessor;
- The accumulated allowance for uncollectible minimum lease payments receivable;
- Contingent rents recognized in the statement of financial performance; and
- A general description of the lessor's material leasing arrangements (IPSAS 13.60).

Disclosures for Operating Leases

Lessee disclosure for operating leases

Lessees shall disclose the following for operating leases:

- The total of future minimum lease payments under noncancelable operating leases for each of the following periods:
  - Not later than one year;
  - Later than one year and not later than five years; and
  - Later than five years;

- The total of future minimum sublease payments expected to be received under non-cancelable subleases at the reporting date;
- Lease and sublease payments recognized as an expense in the period, with separate amounts for minimum lease payments, contingent rents, and sublease payments; and
- A general description of the lessee's significant leasing arrangements including, but not limited to, the following:
  - The basis on which contingent rent payments are determined;
  - The existence and terms of renewal or purchase options and escalation clauses; and
  - Restrictions imposed by lease arrangements, such as those concerning return of surplus, return of capital contributions, dividends or similar distributions, additional debt, and further leasing (IPSAS 13.44).

Lessor disclosure for operating leases

Lessors shall disclose the following for operating leases:

- The future minimum lease payments under non-cancelable operating leases in the aggregate and for each of the following periods:
  - Not later than one year;
  - Later than one year and not later than five years; and
  - Later than five years;
- Total contingent rents recognized in the statement of financial performance in the period; and
- A general description of the lessor's leasing arrangements (IPSAS 13.69).

Disclosure requirements for lessees and lessors apply equally to sale and leaseback transactions (IPSAS 13.77).

IPSAS Financial Reporting in Practice 10.3. UNESCO Operating Lease Commitments Disclosures 2013 Financial Statements

25.2 OPERATING LEASE COMMITMENTS

UNESCO enters into operating lease arrangements for the use of field offices and institute premises, and for the use of photocopying and printing equipment. Future minimum lease rental payments for the following periods are:

Expressed in '000 US dollars	31/12/2013	31/12/2012
Within one year	2 358	2 995
Later than one and not later than five years	3 121	3 914
Later than five years	-	-
Total operating lease commitments	**5 479**	**6 909**

Operating lease arrangements for field office premises can generally be cancelled by providing notice of up to 90 days. Individual operating lease agreements for photocopiers at headquarters generally made under the auspices of overall long-term supply agreements.

Due to construction damages at the façade of IHE building caused by the construction activities in front of the building, the lease is extended at 1 year Euribor (including credit margin) and for the remaining value of K€4,162.

In the above note from its 2013 financial statements, UNESCO shows its operating lease commitments, i.e., the total of its future minimum lease payments under non-cancelable operating leases for the periods requested by IPSAS 13 (not later than one year; later than one year and not later than five years; and later than five years). UNESCO also discloses its significant leasing arrangements.

11 REVENUES AND EXPENSES

This chapter will consider revenue and expense recognition under IPSAS. Public sector entities can derive revenue from exchange and non-exchange transactions (see Figure 11.1). IPSAS 9 Revenue from Exchange Transactions is the current standard to be applied when determining how and when revenue should be recognized for exchange transactions. IPSAS 9 sets the principles for the recognition of revenue arising from the sale of goods and the rendering of services. IPSAS 23 Revenue from Non-Exchange Transactions (taxes and transfers) prescribes the requirements

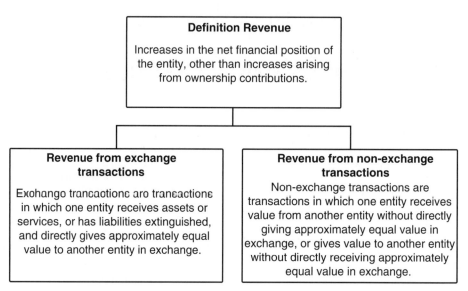

Figure 11.1   An overview of revenue definitions

for accounting and reporting for revenue arising from non-exchange transactions. Common sources of non-exchange revenue in the public sector include taxes and transfers. The difference between exchange and non-exchange transactions is the substance rather than the form of the transaction. It should also be noted that within the public sector, revenue transactions can include both exchange and non-exchange components. IPSAS 11 on Construction Contracts sets out the principles for the recognition of revenue arising from long-term construction contracts. In order to cover the accounting for revenue-generating transactions, this chapter will include IPSAS 23, IPSAS 9, and IPSAS 11. The IPSASB Conceptual Framework and IPSAS 1 provide the definition of revenue[1] (see Figure 11.1) and expenses.

Revenue is further defined in IPSAS 1 Presentation of Financial Statements as follows: "The gross inflow of economic benefits or service potential during the reporting period when those inflows result in an increase in net/assets equity, other than increases relating to contributions from owners" (IPSAS 1.7).

The Conceptual Framework highlights the volume and significance of non-exchange transactions within the public sector.

Expenses are defined as: "Decreases in the net financial position of the entity, other than decreases arising from ownership distributions" (Conceptual Framework 5.30). Prior to proceeding with the specific IPSAS on revenue, Example 11.1 will illustrate the difference in practice between exchange and non-exchange revenue.

---

[1] In IPSAS 1 revenue is also defined. Paragraph 7 defines revenue as the "the gross inflow of economic benefits or service potential during the reporting period when those inflows result in an increase in net assets/equity, other than increases relating to contributions from owners."

Example 11.1   Difference in practice between exchange and non-exchange revenue

Exchange transaction: Public sector Entity A provides dental services to a customer to the value of €1 000, which was paid by the customer. This is an exchange transaction as the entity will receive €1 000 from the customer in return.

Non-exchange transaction: Public sector Entity A received €2 000 from a customer for property taxes. The customer does not receive any direct goods or services in exchange for the €2 000. This is a non-exchange transaction as the entity does not provide any services directly to the customer.

This chapter will, in addition to explaining the requirements of the IPSAS on revenue, address transactions that contain both exchange and non-exchange components. Accounting for principal–agent transactions is also covered.

NON-EXCHANGE REVENUE (IPSAS 23)

What is typical for public sector entities is that:

1. A major part of their revenue is received as taxation or other mandatory payments by citizens or companies, rather than being paid in exchange for goods and services; many public sector bodies also receive donations or grants; and
2. A major part of their expenditure involves making payments or providing services for no cost, a nominal amount, or an amount which will not recover costs. These may include payments to relieve poverty, debt forgiveness, and other social expenditures.

These are deemed "non-exchange transactions," as the entities involved do not make exchanges of approximately equal value. This is a key characteristic of public sector financial reporting.[2] Sound reporting of the financial consequences of government revenue-raising, current expenditure, and future commitments is crucial if the financial statements of governments and other public sector reporting entities are to be transparent and both to support informed assessments of financial condition and to discharge accountability obligations.

IPSAS 23 Revenue from Non-Exchange Transactions stipulates the requirements for the financial reporting of non-exchange revenue. The standard defines non-exchange revenue as shown in Figure 11.2:

---

[2] Non-exchange transactions are rare in the private sector and subsequently there is no IFRS covering non-exchange transactions.

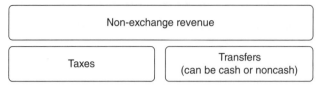

Figure 11.2 Types of non-exchange revenues

In addition to taxes and transfers, IPSAS 23 stipulates special requirements for recognizing non-exchange revenue that is not classified as taxes or transfers, by considering potential stipulations on transferred assets (see Figure 11.2).

The Conceptual Framework elaborates on taxes by stating:

> Taxation is a legally mandated, compulsory non-exchange transaction between individuals or entities and the government. Tax-raising powers can vary considerably, dependent upon the relationship between the powers of the national government and those of sub-national governments and other public sector entities. Governments and other public sector entities are accountable to resource providers, particularly to those that provide resources through taxes and other compulsory transactions. International public sector entities are largely funded by transfers from national, regional and state governments. Such funding may be governed by treaties and conventions or may be on a voluntary basis. (para. 6, p. 7)

Transfers on the other hand include debt forgiveness, fines, grants, gifts, donations, goods and services in-kind, bequests, and concessionary loans.

In certain cases of non-exchange transactions the recipient obtains assets for nil consideration and does not make any payment. Certain transactions can also be at subsidized prices – these also constitute non-exchange transactions.

Example 11.2   Grants received – exchange or non-exchange transaction?

Determining whether a grant is exchange or non-exchange in nature requires judgment about the substance of the transaction between the grantor and the recipient. At one end of the spectrum, if the grantor expects nothing in exchange for the grant provided (i.e., a donation), the recipient's revenue is clearly from a non-exchange transaction.

At the other end of the spectrum, if the grantor expects to receive specified services or goods in exchange for the grant, and directly gives approximately equal value in exchange for those services or goods, the recipient's revenue would meet the definition of an exchange transaction.

In between the two ends of the spectrum, there may be a variety of arrangements and contracts with different exchange and non-exchange components.

Deciding whether a grant is exchange or non-exchange is particularly important when the grant is received in advance of the services or goods being provided, to determine whether a liability should be recognized.

Source: New Zealand Treasury[3]

Recognizing Non-Exchange Revenue

IPSAS 23 draws on a transactional approach (cf. Schumesch, 2013) which means that the first step is to determine whether an asset should be recognized in regard to the inflow of resources from the non-exchange transaction. If an asset can be recognized, the revenue is recognized, except to the extent that a liability is recognized in respect of the same inflow.

Recognizing an asset

The principle underlying the recognition of revenue from non-exchange transactions is that if an entity receives an asset in a non-exchange transaction it recognizes revenue in the same amount, provided that the asset can be measured reliably. An asset is defined as: "A resource presently controlled by the entity as a result of a past event" (see Conceptual Framework 5.6). Revenue is recognized when: it is probable that future economic benefits or service potential will flow to the entity; and the amount of revenue can be measured reliably.

Within the public sector assets arising from non-exchange transactions can take a number of forms such as:

- Cash and cash receivable;
- Other assets or receivables which provide economic benefit;
- Assets or assets receivable which have service potential.

Revenue is recognized when the public sector entity exercises control over these resources or has reliable information on enforceable claims on these resources. Control of an asset arises when the entity can use or otherwise benefit from the asset in pursuit of its objectives and can exclude or otherwise regulate the access of others to that benefit.

Example 11.3   Control of transferred funds

Control of transferred funds is obtained when:

- Resources have been transferred; *or*
- Entity has an enforceable claim against the transferor; *and*
- Entity expects to receive benefit/service potential.

---

[3] http://www.treasury.govt.nz/publications/guidance/reporting/ipsas/comparison-nzifrs/pdfs/tsy-pbe-ipsas-23.pdf.

| Contributions from owners, which are disclosed separately and are not part of revenue. These occur when a "contributing" entity provides and designates funding or other assets as being a permanent contribution, establishing a financial interest in the net assets/equity of the receiving entity (IPSAS 23.37–23.38). | Advance receipts. An entity may receive an asset, generally cash, in advance of the period for which it was intended. Such advance receipts relate generally to taxes but IPSAS 23 also gives an example of annual contributions received in the preceding year. In line with standard accruals principles, these advance receipts are treated as a liability until the taxable or other event triggering recognition occurs, and only at that point is revenue recognized (IPSAS 23.66). | Assets with linked obligations. The receipt of assets can give rise to a present obligation, in the form of a duty to act or perform in a certain way. In certain cases this will indicate that the asset has been exchanged for acceptance of an obligation, and normal accounting for exchange transactions should be followed. In other cases it is more helpful to treat the asset as being received as a non-exchange transaction, and to recognize a balancing liability in respect of the obligation (IPSAS 23.50–23.53). |

Figure 11.3   Assets received are not reflected as non-exchange revenue

Revenue should only be recognized when control has passed to the receiving entity, on the basis of information which is sufficiently reliable. Pledges, promises, or announcements of intention to pay are not generally regarded as sufficient to ensure an enforceable claim and thus control of an asset. It should be noted that revenue collected on behalf of third parties is not classified as part of the entity's revenue.

It is important to note that there are three significant situations where assets received are not reflected as non-exchange revenue (see Figure 11.3).

An example of an asset with a linked obligation would be that of funding provided by a donor agency to improve and maintain a school. If such a condition is set, the recipient has an obligation to spend the money in this way and therefore a liability to incur such expenditure, or to return the money received.

Stipulations on transferred assets

IPSAS 23 presents three important definitions in terms of recognition of non-exchange revenue that does not classify as transfers or taxes, namely (Figure 11.4).

Stipulations are enforceable through legal or administrative processes. If a term in laws or regulations or other binding arrangements is unenforceable then it is not a stipulation. This means that stipulations cannot be imposed by an entity on itself.

Following IPSAS 23, stipulations can either be in the form of conditions or in the form of restrictions. For both conditions and restrictions, a recipient may be required to use the transferred asset for a particular purpose. The key difference between a restriction and a condition is that a condition has an additional requirement which states that the asset or its future economic benefits or service potential should be returned to the transferor should the recipient not use the asset for the particular purpose stipulated.

> **Stipulations on transferred assets:**
>
> Terms in laws or regulations, or a binding arrangement, imposed upon the use of a transferred asset by entities external to the reporting entity (IPSAS 23.7).

> **Conditions on transferred assets:**
>
> Stipulations that specify that the future economic benefits or service potential embodied in the asset is required to be consumed by the recipient as specified or future economic benefits or service potential must be returned to the transferor (IPSAS 23.7).

> **Restrictions on transferred assets:**
>
> Stipulations that limit or direct the purposes for which a transferred asset may be used, but do not specify that future economic benefits or service potential is required to be returned to the transferor if not deployed as specified (IPSAS 23.7).

Figure 11.4   Stipulations on transferred assets

Conditions

When applying IPSAS 23, public sector entities typically need to review all agreements with, for example, donors and other parties, and analyze any and all stipulations attached to an inflow of resources, to determine whether those stipulations impose conditions or restrictions. Stipulations can be either conditions or restrictions on the transferred assets.

Stipulations on transferred assets are terms in the agreement, imposed upon the use of a transferred asset by entities external to the reporting entity. Conditions on transferred assets are stipulations that specify that the future economic benefits or service potential embodied in the asset is required to be consumed by the recipient as specified or future economic benefits or service potential must be returned to the transferor.

Example 11.4   Transfer with stipulations that do not satisfy the definition of a condition

The central government makes a cash transfer of €100 million to the national agency of social housing, specifying that it:

1. Increases the stock of social housing by an additional 1 000 housing units over and above any other planned increases; and/or
2. Uses the cash transfer in renovating 1 000 old housing units. No less than 1 000 housing units have to be either constructed or renovated, which is the objective of the agency.

If neither of these stipulations is satisfied, the recipient entity must return the cash to the central government. The national agency of social housing recognizes an increase in an asset (cash) and revenue in the amount of €100 million.

The stipulation is stated broadly enough so as not to impose on the recipient a performance obligation – the performance obligation is imposed by the operating mandate of the entity, not by the terms of the transfer.

Example 11.5.   Grant to another sphere of government with conditions (see paragraphs 15 to 16)

The transferor, the national government, grants CU100 million to a reporting entity, a national railways public operator to be used to improve and maintain mass transit systems. Specifically, the money is required to be used as follows: 40% for existing suburban railway modernisation, 40% for new suburban railway lines, and 20% for rolling stock purchases and improvements. Under the terms of the grant, the money can only be used as stipulated. The agreement requires the grant to be spent as specified in the current year or be returned to the national government. The national railways public operator is required to include a note in its audited financial statements detailing how the grant money was spent.

The national railways public operator recognizes the grant money as an asset. It also recognizes a liability in respect of the condition attached to the grant. As it satisfies the condition, that is, as it makes authorized expenditures, it reduces the liability and recognizes revenue in the statement of financial performance of the reporting period during which the liability is discharged.

Restrictions

Restrictions on transferred assets are stipulations that limit or direct the purposes for which a transferred asset may be used, but do not specify that future economic benefits or service potential are required to be returned to the transferor if not deployed as specified.

Example 11.6   Transfer to a hospital with restrictions

The transferor, the government, transfers 20 hectares of land in a major city to a reporting entity, a hospital, for the establishment of new hospital buildings for cancer treatment. The transfer agreement specifies that the land is to be used for a hospital dealing with cancer treatment, but does not specify that the land is to be returned if not used for as stated.

The hospital recognizes the land as an asset in the statement of financial position of the reporting period in which it obtains control of that land. The land should be recognized at its fair value in accordance with IPSAS 17 on Property, Plant and Equipment.

The restriction does not meet the definition of a liability or satisfy the criteria for recognition as a liability. Therefore, the hospital recognizes revenue in respect of the land in the statement of financial performance of the reporting period in which the land is recognized as an asset.

Recognizing a liability

A present obligation that arises from a non-exchange transaction that meets the definition of a liability is recognized as a liability when, and only when:

- It is probable that an outflow of resources embodying future economic benefits or service potential will be required to settle the obligation; and
- A reliable estimate can be made of the amount of the obligation.

See Figure 11.3. for a description of assets with linked obligations.

The amount recognized as a liability is the best estimate of the amount required to settle the present obligation at the reporting date. The estimate takes account of the risks and uncertainties that are encompassed in the events causing the liability to be recognized. Where the time value of money is material, the liability will be measured at the present value of the amount expected to be required to settle the obligation.

MEASUREMENT

As described above, IPSAS 23 recognizes revenue when an asset is received and controlled by the entity and when it can be measured reliably.

Under IPSAS 23, assets acquired through non-exchange transactions are measured at their fair value at the date of acquisition. Revenue is valued at the amount of the increase in assets, less any associated liability attached to the asset. Many such assets are in the form of cash received immediately or within a short period, and establishment of fair values will be straightforward. As with all receivables, questions of collectability due to disputes and delays in payment may need to be addressed (IPSAS 23.42 and 23.48).

Liabilities relating to present obligations also need to be valued. Where non-performance of the obligation would, in principle, require the asset to be returned, these are generally valued at an amount equal to the asset value. The liability will be reduced when the event or events occur to discharge the obligation and these will also trigger revenue recognition.

IPSAS 23 applies to taxes from whatever source, including property taxes, and other transfers such as grants, fines, bequests, gifts, donations, and services in-kind.

Tax Revenue

IPSAS 23 requires a public sector entity to recognize an asset in respect of taxes when the taxable event occurs and the asset recognition criteria (including control, expectation of future economic benefits or service potential, and reliable measurement) are met (IPSAS 23.59).

Taxes are a major source of revenue for many governments and public sector entities. Taxes are defined as economic benefits compulsorily payable to public sector entities, in accordance with laws or regulations established to provide revenue to the government.

Table 11.1   Taxable events according to type of tax levied

Types of taxes	Taxable events
Income tax	The earning of assessable income during the taxation period by the taxpayer.
Value added tax (VAT)	The undertaking of taxable activity during the taxation period by the taxpayer.
Goods and services tax	The purchase or sale of taxable goods or services during the taxation period.
Customs duty	The movement of dutiable goods or services across the customs boundary.
Death duty	The death of a person owning taxable assets.
Property tax	The passing of the date on which the tax is levied or the period for which the tax is levied, if the tax is levied on a periodic basis.

Taxes vary significantly from jurisdiction to jurisdiction, but have many common characteristics. Laws and regulations establish a government's right to collect tax and identify the basis on which tax is calculated. They also typically require taxpayers to provide evidence of the level of activity subject to tax, which forms the basis on which the amount of tax is calculated. Tax laws are usually rigorously enforced and often impose penalties on individuals or other entities breaching the law.

The taxable event will vary following the type of tax levied; IPSAS 23 (65) provides a list of frequently seen cases (see Table 11.1).

IPSAS (23.68) describes key features of taxation issues in many jurisdictions which may serve to delay settlement of tax and make the level of settlement uncertain, and may require the development of statistical models or other estimation approaches. These include the long periods allowed for filing of returns, failures to file returns by the due date, complexities in tax law, and inherent problems in gathering relevant information.

Because of the need for governments to maintain cash flows from tax receipts it is normal for tax authorities to require payments in advance, particularly from self-employed persons and businesses. IPSAS 23 makes it very clear that the very significant volume of advance tax receipts encountered in many jurisdictions should not be recognized as revenue until the tax is properly due. Governments applying accruals accounting should recognize tax revenue in line with the taxable events, applying tax rates to taxable income or assets.

The tax area is one where many (perhaps most) governments face significant practical difficulties in producing reliable estimates of total tax due and the likely level of bad debts. In many jurisdictions government will not be able to estimate these *even after collection processes have been completed*; they may only be able to objectively and reliably measure the net amount of taxes collected.

Furthermore, governments will often face additional constraints from limitations in the systems used to collect and account for tax receipts (whether their own or systems used by other entities collecting tax on behalf of government), which may not provide sufficient information on the period to which tax receipts relate.

For the reasons set out above, many governments either do not account for tax revenue on an accruals basis, or provide accruals information which is limited due to difficulties in producing reliable estimates. IPSAS 23 recognizes the difficulties and requires disclosure of information on "missing" tax revenue.

Example 11.7   Calculation of tax revenue

Situation

A central government imposes a 25% tax on personal income earned within the country. Employers are required to withhold taxes from payroll and remit withholdings on a monthly basis. Individuals with significant non-salary (for example investment) income are required to make estimated tax payments on a quarterly basis. In addition, individuals must file a tax return with the taxation department by 15 April of the year following the tax year (calendar year) and must pay the remaining tax owed or claim a refund at that time. The government's reporting period ends on 30 June N.

Suggested method of calculating/estimating tax revenue

The annual tax revenue might be calculated as follows:

1. Withholding taxes received during the year, adjusted to remove taxes received in respect of the previous year and to include taxes received in the following year (principally in July N) which relate to the reporting period.
2. Quarterly estimated tax payments received for non-salary income during the reporting year plus similar adjustments for payments relating to the previous year or received in the following year.
3. Adjustments to 2 above, based on tax returns received and assessed incorporating:
   - An additional estimated amount for the 6 months not covered by the returns; reduced by
   - The amount of the similar estimate included in the previous year's financial statements.
4. Additions or deductions for late returns based on prior years' experience and known problem cases.

Application to Other Types of Non-Exchange Revenue

IPSAS 23 applies the same recognition principles to other non-exchange revenue. That is, a public sector entity recognizes an asset when the asset recognition criteria (including control, expectation of future economic benefits or service potential, and reliable measurement) are met. Revenue is only recognized to the extent that a gain from the asset value is not reduced by an associated liability.

Although grants are not defined in IPSAS 23, they represent a significant type of revenue from non-exchange transactions. Grants are frequently provided from one level of government to another or from donor agencies to governments. Several of the examples in the Implementation Guidance relate to grants.

Grants are often provided with limitations on how money should be spent or assets utilized. The standard separates such "stipulations" into:

- Conditions, where the money must be spent as specified or returned to the donor (in other words a performance obligation); and
- Restrictions, where there is a more general requirement to spend the money in a specified area but not to return it if this is not achieved.

This distinction may not always be clear cut and it is necessary to consider the substance of the stipulation and not merely its form. This might take into account the likelihood of enforcement, prior experience with the donor, the extent of specification of detailed requirements, and the degree of monitoring by the donor (IPSAS 23.14–23.19).

Where the recipient entity considers that the donor has imposed conditions, they will set up a liability for the obligation generally to the value of the money received, which will be reduced as the conditions are satisfied (by spending the money or through other actions) in accordance with the agreement. There is no such requirement for grants with restrictions and revenue is therefore recognized immediately.

Other Types of Non-Exchange Revenue

Fines

Fines are levies on individuals or entities for breaches of the law. Fines are recognized in the period in which the fine is imposed (IPSAS 23.88, 23.89).

Bequests

Bequests are instructions in a deceased person's will to transfer cash or other assets to an entity. Bequests are recognized when the nature of the bequest is known and it has been established that the estate is sufficient to meet all claims. As with grants, bequests may contain stipulations as to how the money or assets are to be spent or utilized (IPSAS 23.90–23.92).

Gifts and donations

Gifts and donations are voluntary transfers of cash or other assets to an entity. Gifts and donations are generally recognized on receipt of the cash or other asset. Pledges to give in the future are not generally recognized as they are not controlled by the entity, but may warrant disclosure as a contingent asset. As with grants and bequests, gifts and donations may be subject to stipulations as to how the money or assets are to be spent or utilized (IPSAS 23.93–23.97).

Debt forgiveness

Lenders may waive their right to collect a debt owed by a public sector entity, thus effectively cancelling the debt. In such a case the entity has an increase in net assets/equity and treats the amount forgiven as revenue from a non-exchange transaction (IPSAS 23.84–23.87).

Services in-kind

Services in-kind are voluntary services provided to an entity by an individual or individuals. Such services may include free technical assistance from other governments or international organizations, voluntary work in schools and hospitals, or community services performed by convicted offenders. The standard provides that entities may, but are not required to, recognize services in-kind as revenue and expenditure where the amount can be measured, is material, and its inclusion enhances the presentation of the financial statements. Disclosure of the nature of significant in-kind services in all cases is encouraged (IPSAS 23.98–23.103).

IPSAS Financial Reporting in Practice 11.1. Interest-free Loans, In-kind Contributions at UNESCO, 2013 Financial Statements

2.12 BORROWINGS

Borrowings are initially recognized at fair value, net of transaction costs incurred. Borrowings are currently stated at amortized cost; any difference between the proceeds and the redemption value is recognized in the Statement of Financial Performance over the period of the borrowings using the effective interest method.

Borrowings are classified as current liabilities unless UNESCO has an unconditional right to defer settlement of the liability for at least 12 months after the reporting date. Where UNESCO holds interest-free loans or does not pay interest on loans, the benefit to UNESCO of the arrangement is treated as an in-kind contribution.

UNESCO (2013) Financial Statements (p. 41)

UNESCO recognizes interest-free loans as in-kind contributions, considering the fact of not paying interests on loans benefits UNESCO and is therefore a service in-kind.

Question and Answer

Question:

IPSAS 23 sets out the considerations for the recognition of grants as revenue or for the establishment of corresponding liabilities. Which of the following are likely to result in the establishment of a corresponding liability?

1. Restrictions
2. Conditions
3. Stipulations
4. Advance receipts.

Answer:

1. No. Restrictions indicate where the grant money should be spent but not in sufficient detail to constitute a performance obligation.
2. Yes. Conditions impose a performance obligation for which a liability needs to be established.
3. Yes. Stipulations is a general term covering requirements of grant or other agreements, and these are likely to result in establishing a corresponding liability.
4. Yes. Advance receipts do not constitute revenue until the event occurs which triggers recognition of the revenue; until then they are recognized as a liability which balances the cash asset.

Non-Exchange Revenue: Principal–Agent

Amounts collected as an agent of the government or another government organization or other third parties will not give rise to an increase in net assets or revenue of a public sector entity. This is due to the fact that the public sector entity, in this case, cannot control the use of, or otherwise benefit from, the collected assets in the pursuit of its objectives.

Example 11.8   Grants received as an agent

The Government of one of the Member States of the European Union provided a €100 000 financial assistance to three EU Member States through the European Commission. The financial assistance will be divided equally between the three countries and is expected to be used in sending at least four delegates from each country to attend a European Commission hosted meeting.

The recipient countries could also choose to use the funds to only partially fund individuals in order to support a higher number of attendees if they wish. Amounts collected as an agent of the government or another government organization or other third parties will not give rise to an increase in net assets or revenue of European Commission.

This is because the agent entity cannot control the use of, or otherwise benefit from, the collected assets in the pursuit of its objectives. Therefore, the receipt of the grant shall be accounted for as an asset and a liability and a corresponding reversal shall be made at the time of disbursement as illustrated below:

Receipt of grant:

Cash Euro 100 000
Liability Euro 100 000

Distribution to the recipient countries:

Liability Euro 100 000
Cash Euro 100 000

Transitional Provisions

IPSAS 23 (23.116–23.123) stipulates the transitional provisions which exist in the standard. IPSAS 23 provides that: (1) Entities are not required to change their accounting policies in respect of the recognition and measurement of taxation revenue for reporting periods beginning on a date within five years following the date of first adoption of IPSAS 23; and (2) Entities are not required to change their accounting policies in respect of the recognition and measurement of revenue from non-exchange transactions, other than taxation revenue, for reporting periods beginning on a date within three years following the date of first adoption of IPSAS 23.

The transitional provisions are providing for entities to apply the transition period to develop reliable models for measuring revenue from non-exchange transactions during the transitional period. Entities may adopt accounting policies for the recognition of revenue from non-exchange transactions that do not comply with the provisions of IPSAS 23 during the transitional period. Considering the difficulty of implementing IPSAS 23, the transitional provisions allow entities to apply IPSAS 23 incrementally to different classes of revenue from non-exchange transactions. It should be emphasized that when an entity applies the transitional provisions in paragraphs 116 or 117, that fact shall be disclosed in order to alert the user of the financial statements to the fact that IPSAS 23 is not yet fully implemented. The entity shall also disclose (a) which classes of revenue from non-exchange transactions are recognized in accordance with IPSAS 23; (b) those that have been recognized under an accounting policy that is not consistent with the requirements of this Standard; and (c) the entity's progress towards implementation of accounting policies that are consistent with IPSAS 23. The entity shall disclose its plan for implementing accounting policies that are consistent with IPSAS 23 (IPSAS 23.119).

In addition, when an entity takes advantage of the transitional provisions for a second or subsequent reporting period, details of the classes of revenue from non-exchange transactions previously recognized on another basis, but which are now recognized in accordance with IPSAS 23, shall be disclosed (IPSAS 23.120).

Note on upcoming changes. IPSAS 33 on First-time Adoption of Accrual Basis International Public Sector Accounting Standards (IPSASs)

It should be noted that a first-time adopter of IPSAS shall apply IPSAS 33 if its first IPSAS financial statements are for a period beginning on or after 1 January 2017. Earlier application is allowed. Under IPSAS 33, a first-time adopter is not required to change its accounting policy in respect of the recognition and measurement of non-exchange revenue for reporting periods beginning on a date within three years following the date of adoption of IPSASs. A first-time adopter may change its accounting policy in respect of revenue from non-exchange transactions on a class-by-class basis.

The transitional provision in paragraph 42 (IPSAS 33.42) is intended to allow a first-time adopter a period to develop reliable models for recognizing and measuring revenue from non-exchange transactions in accordance with IPSAS 23, *Revenue from Non-Exchange Transactions (Taxes and Transfers)* during the period of transition. The first-time adopter may apply accounting policies for the recognition and/or measurement of revenue from non-exchange transactions that do not comply with the provisions of IPSAS 23. The transitional provision in paragraph 42 allows a first-time adopter to apply IPSAS 23 incrementally to different classes of revenue from non-exchange transactions. For example, a first-time adopter may be able to recognize and measure property taxes and some other classes of transfers in accordance with IPSAS 23 from the date of adoption of IPSASs, but may require three years to fully develop a reliable model for recognizing and measuring income tax revenue.

The existing transitional provisions in IPSAS 23 allow a first-time adopter to not change its accounting policy in respect of the recognition and measurement of taxation revenue for a period of five years. IPSAS 23 also allows a first-time adopter to not change its accounting policy in respect of recognition and measurement of revenue from non-exchange transactions, other than taxation revenue, for a period of three years. It also requires that changes in accounting policies should only be made to better conform to IPSAS 23.

In establishing IPSAS 33, the IPSASB concluded that it will be challenging for many public sector entities to implement IPSAS 23 as new systems may be required and/or existing systems may need to be upgraded. Due to these practical challenges, the IPSASB agreed that a transitional relief period should be provided. The IPSASB, nevertheless, acknowledged that a first-time adopter should build up models to assist with the transition to accrual accounting prior to the adoption of the accrual basis. In line with the relief period of three years provided for the recognition of assets and/or liabilities in other IPSASs, and in line with the existing three year transitional relief period provided for other non-exchange revenue in IPSAS 23, it was agreed that a first-time adopter should be granted a relief period of three years to develop reliable models for recognizing and measuring revenue from non-exchange transactions. The IPSASB agreed that a transitional period of three years is manageable, and reduces the period over which an entity will not be able to assert compliance with accrual basis IPSASs, from five years to three years as a maximum. During the period of transition, a first-time adopter will be allowed to apply accounting policies for the recognition of non-exchange revenue transactions that do not comply with the provisions in IPSAS 23.

Disclosure Requirements for Non-Exchange Revenue

IPSAS 23 requires disclosure of the following (IPSAS 23.106–23.107):

- The accounting policies for the recognition of revenue from non-exchange transactions including, for major classes, the basis of assessing fair value;
- Information about the nature of taxes which cannot be measured reliably and are therefore not recognized;
- The nature and types of major classes of bequests, gifts and, donations;
- The amount of revenue from taxation, split by major classes;
- The amount of other revenue/transfers from non-exchange transactions, split by major classes;
- The amount of receivables in respect of revenue from non-exchange transactions;

- The amount of liabilities from amounts received with conditions, and from advance payments, as well as liabilities forgiven;
- The amount of assets subject to restrictions.

The disclosure of information about services in-kind is encouraged (IPSAS 23.108).

IPSAS Financial Reporting in Practice 11.2. Non-Exchange Revenue UNESCO, 2013 Financial Statements

Non-Exchange Revenue

Revenue from non-exchange transactions is measured based on the increase in net assets recognized. Where the full criteria for recognition of an asset under a non-exchange agreement are not fulfilled, a contingent asset may be disclosed.

Assessed contributions are assessed and approved for a two-year budget period. The amount of these contributions is then apportioned between the two years for invoicing and payment. Assessed contributions are recognized as revenue at the beginning of the apportioned year in the relevant two year budget period.

Voluntary contributions and other transfers which are supported by enforceable agreements are recognized as revenue at the time the agreement becomes binding and when control over the underlying asset is obtained, unless the agreement establishes a condition on transferred assets that requires recognition of a liability. In such cases, revenue is recognized as the condition liability is discharged. Voluntary contributions such as pledges and other promised donations which are not supported by binding agreements are recognized as revenue when received.

In-kind contributions of goods that directly support approved operations and activities and can be reliably measured, are recognized and valued at fair value. These contributions include the use of premises and utilities. In-kind contributions of services, such as the services of volunteers, are not currently recognized.

NOTE 8 – ACCOUNTS RECEIVABLE (NON-EXCHANGE TRANSACTIONS)

Expressed in '000 US dollars	31/12/2013	31/12/2012
Assessed contributions (current)	260 933	183 762
Assessed contributions (non-current)	4 137	3 895
Gross assessed contributions	**265 070**	**187 657**
Allowance for assessed contributions (current)	−245 826	−163 131
Allowance for assessed contributions (non-current)	−2 773	−2 410
Net assessed contributions	**16 471**	**22 116**
Voluntary contributions (current)	4 408	8 736
Voluntary contributions (non-current)	–	–
Total accounts receivable (non-exchange transactions)	**20 879**	**30 852**
Current portion	19 515	29 367
Non-current portion	1 364	1 485
Net accounts receivable (non-exchange transactions)	**20 879**	**30 852**

Assessed contributions receivable represent uncollected revenues committed to UNESCO by Member States and Associated Members for completion of the programme of work. Non-current assessed contributions are those contributions which are due more than 12 months after the reporting date. This relates to payment plans agreed.

The allowance for assessed contributions is calculated by providing against the entire balance of arrears up to the 2010–2011 biennium which are not under payment plans. Outstanding assessed contributions from the 2012–2013 biennium and amounts under payment plans are discounted to their present value based on the year in which they are expected to be received:

Expressed in '000 US dollars	31/12/2013	31/12/2012
Arrears not under payment plans:		
1988–2003	3 103	3 103
2004–2005	22	29
2006–2007	25	46
2008–2009	32	57
2010–2011	79 199	83 488
	82 381	**86 723**
Other current assessed contributions	178 552	97 039
Gross assessed contributions (current)	**260 933**	**183 762**
Allowance for arrears	−245 795	−162 977
Discount other current assessed contributions	−31	−154
Net assessed contributions (current)	**15 107**	**20 631**
Gross assessed contributions (non-current)	4 137	3 895
Discount for non-current assessed contributions	−2 773	−2 410
Net assessed contributions (non-current)	**1 364**	**1 485**
Total net assessed contributions	**16 471**	**22 116**

Specific allowance for an amount of K$241,921 has been made against contributions due from two Member States who have suspended their contributions to the Organization.

UNESCO (2013) Financial Statements (pp. 42, 47)

UNESCO discloses the accounting policies for the recognition of revenue from non-exchange transactions. UNESCO does not recognize other in-kind contributions such as the services of volunteers. However, the nature of this significant in-kind contribution is discloses in the note relating to non-exchange revenue. UNESCO specifically discloses the amount of receivables in respect of revenue from non-exchange transactions, which relate mainly to assessed contributions from Member States and Associated Members.

REVENUE FROM EXCHANGE TRANSACTIONS (IPSAS 9)

Public sector entities receive revenue in payment for goods or services under normal contractual arrangements similar to those undertaken by private sector businesses ("exchange transactions"). Examples of services provided by public sector entities for which "equal value" revenue is typically received include the provision of housing and toll roads. Goods sold may include goods produced by the entity for the purpose of sale, such as publications, and goods purchased for resale. Revenue may also be received where others use entity assets in the form of interest, royalties, charges for the use of patents, trademarks, copyrights and computer software, and dividends. Effective and sound accounting for revenue is imperative to disclose the substance of what can be complex transactions.

IPSAS 9 apply to revenue from the following transactions and events:

- The sale of goods
- The rendering of services
- Interest, royalties and dividends.

These standards do not deal with revenue arising from actitivies which are the subject of other standards, and therefore exclude:

- Lease agreements
- Dividends arising from investments accounted for under the equity method
- Insurance contracts in insurance enterprises
- Changes in the fair value of financial assets and financial liabilities
- Changes in the fair value of other assets
- Biological assets, agricultural produce, or the extraction of mineral ores
- Non-exchange revenue transactions, such as taxes and grants.

The primary issue in accounting for revenue is determining when to recognize revenue. Exchange revenue is recognized when:

- It is probable that future economic benefits will flow to the entity
- The amount of revenue can be measured reliably.

All costs associated with the revenue should be accounted for in the same period as the revenue is recognized. This is commonly referred to as the matching of revenue and expenses.

Measurement

Revenue should be measured at the fair value of the consideration received or receivable. It should be highlighted that consideration is not limited to payments in cash (IPSAS 9.14).

The amount of the payment will normally be expressed in the agreement between the buyer and the seller. Revenue is recognized after taking into account trade discounts or volume rebates that are given.

In most cases consideration is in the form of cash and this will be paid on receipt of the goods or services or shortly afterwards. Here the amount of revenue recognized is the amount of cash received or receivable.

In some cases the payment may be deferred for a longer period providing the buyer with an interest-free credit period. In such cases the amount of revenue recognized should be determined by discounting all future receipts to present value.

Example 11.9   An example of accounting for deferred payments

A public sector entity sells a car to a purchaser for CU17 000 on 1 July N. Although delivery will take place as soon as possible, the entity has given the purchaser an interest-free credit period of 12 months. The entity has a 31 December year end.

The fair value of the consideration receivable is CU16 700, meaning that if the entity sells this car for cash it would expect to immediately receive CU16 700 rather than CU17 000.

The balance of CU300 represents implicit interest revenue (= CU17 000 – CU16 700).

Therefore the entity should split CU17 000 between revenue and interest:

Revenue of CU16 700 should be recognized immediately on 1 July N, with the balance of CU300 being recognized as interest revenue over the 12-month credit period. The entity should recognize CU300 × 5/12 = CU125 as interest revenue for N and CU300 × 7/12 = CU175 as interest revenue for N+1.

Question and Answer

Question:

An entity sells goods to a customer for CU100 000 less a trade discount of CU15 000. Due to the volume of trade with this customer a further discount of CU2 000 is given. Payment will be made in cash. Credit terms are 30 days. What revenue will be recognized?

Answer:

The amount of revenue recognized is the amount of cash receivable after taking into account trade discounts. There is no need to discount the amount receivable to present value. As the payment terms are short, the impact is not material. The answer is: CU100 000 – CU15 000 – CU2 000 = CU83 000.

Question:

An entity sells goods to a customer for CU100 000 less a trade discount of CU15 000 on one year's interest-free credit. Assuming that the applicable discount rate is 2%, what revenue should be recognized immediately?

Answer:

The revenue recognized immediately should be the present value of future receipts. After taking into account the trade discount, the entity expects to receive CU85 000 in one year's time. Applying the discount rate of 2%, the net present value is of CU83 333 (CU85 000/1.02). The remaining revenue of CU1 667 will be recognized as interest income over the life of the credit agreement.

For all forms of exchange revenue the two general conditions for revenue recognition have to be met, i.e., that (1) it is probable that future economic benefits (or service potential) will flow to the entity; and (2) the amount of revenue can be measured reliably.

The Sale of Goods

The conditions below apply to the sale of goods (IPSAS 9.28):

- It is probable that the future economic benefits (or service potential) will flow into the entity;
- The amount of revenue can be measured reliably;
- The seller must have transferred to the buyer all of the significant risks and rewards of ownership;
- The seller no longer has management involvement or effective control of the goods;
- The costs incurred in relation to the transaction can be reliably measured.

All five of these above-listed conditions must be met before revenue on the sale of goods can be recognized.

The transfer of the significant risks and rewards of ownership to the buyer can sometimes be challenging to determine. Nevertheless, in most instances, the transfer of significant risks and rewards of ownership coincides with the transfer of legal title or the passing of possession to the buyer. This is the case for most sales of goods. In other cases, the risks and rewards of ownership may pass at a different time to the transfer of legal title or the passing of possession to the buyer.

Examples of where the risks and rewards of ownership would not pass to the buyer and where no sale or revenue would be recognized include:

- When the seller retains an obligation for unsatisfactory performance not covered by a normal warranty arrangement;
- When goods are sold on a sale or return basis;
- When the buyer has the right to rescind the purchase and the enterprise is uncertain about the probability of return.

In each of these cases no revenue would be recognized.

Example 11.10   Exchange revenue recognition

The Ministry of Education sells interactive whiteboards to primary schools in order to familiarize children with new technology. It sells an interactive whiteboard to a primary school for CU15 000 on 1 April N, and includes a two-year warranty. A deferred payment option is being offered by the Ministry to pay in 12 months' time (when a new budget line is available for capital investment). The Ministry has a 31 December year end.

The following steps are needed to account for the sale.

- Split the CU15 000 payment between the cash sale price and the effective interest.
- Recognize the cash sale price as revenue on 1 April
- Recognize interest income for the 9 months' credit given in N (the accounting period in which the sale is recognized).
- Recognize the remaining 3 months' interest in N+1 (the following period).
- Product cost will be recognized in the same period that the revenue relating to the sale of the software is recognized.
- A warranty provision will be set up in the period in which the revenue relating to the sale of the interactive whiteboard is recognized for expected costs under the warranty provision (in accordance with IPSAS 19 Provisions, Contingent Liabilities and Contingent Assets).
- Costs incurred under the warranty provision will be charged to the warranty provision to the extent that the provision covers the costs. Any excess costs incurred will be recognized in surplus or deficit, and any balance remaining on the provision at the end of the second year will be released to the statement of financial performance.

The Rendering of Services

Additional conditions also apply to the rendering of services (IPSAS 9.19):

- The stage of completion can be measured reliably;
- The costs incurred and the costs to complete in relation to the transaction can be reliably measured.

All of these conditions must be met before revenue can be recognized.

Revenue is recognized by reference to the stage of completion using what is known as the percentage of completion method. The stage of completion can be determined via a number of methods. IPSAS 9 stipulates three possibilities, namely:

- Surveys of work performed;
- Assessing the services performed to date against the total services to be performed under the contract;
- Assessing the costs incurred to date against the total costs to be incurred under the contract.

When the outcome of a transaction involving the rendering of services cannot be estimated reliably, revenue should only be recognized to the extent that costs incurred to date are recoverable from the customer.

Example 11.11   Accounting for the rendering of services under the percentage of completion method

An entity enters into a CU500 000 fixed price contract for the provision of IT services. At the end of N, the first accounting period, the contract is assessed as being 20% complete, and costs incurred to date are CU95 000.

If costs to complete can be estimated reliably at CU300 000, the overall contract is profitable as the total revenue of CU500 000 exceeds total costs of CU395 000.

Revenue to be recognized in the first accounting period will be CU100 000 (= CU500 000 × 20%). Costs of CU95 000 would also be recognized and matched against the related revenue.

If the costs to complete cannot be estimated reliably (but the contract is not supposed to result in loss), then the outcome of the total contract cannot be estimated accurately and revenue is recognized to the extent that the costs incurred are believed to be recoverable from the client, i.e., revenue recognized is limited to CU95 000.

Interest, Royalties, and Dividends

Revenue should be recognized on the following basis (IPSAS 9.34):

- Interest revenue is recognized on a time apportioned basis.
- Royalties are recognized on an accrual basis.
- Dividends are recognized when the shareholders' right to receive the dividend is legally established. This is usually when dividends are declared.

Exchanges of Assets

Special rules apply where goods or services are exchanged.

Similar goods or services

Where the entity receives similar goods or services as payment, this is essentially a "swap" transaction. The company is replacing one asset for another similar asset. In such cases no revenue is generated, with no additional cost reported. Such transactions are quite common in the sale of commodities, for example milk, with suppliers exchanging inventories to fulfill demand in a particular location.

Dissimilar goods or services

When the payment is receivable in the form of dissimilar goods or services, revenue is generated and costs should be recognized. In such cases the transaction is measured based on the fair value of what will be received. If it is not possible to measure the value of the goods or services received reliably, then the revenue should be based on the fair value of the goods or services supplied.

Disclosure Requirements

The following disclosures should be made in terms of exchange revenue:

- The accounting policies adopted for recognizing revenue, including the methods adopted in determining the stage of completion for transactions involving the rendering of services;
- The amount of each significant category of revenue recognized;
- The amount of revenue recognized from exchanges of goods or services.

TRANSACTIONS THAT INCLUDE BOTH AN EXCHANGE AND NON-EXCHANGE COMPONENT

There are instances where a transaction can be a combination of exchange and non-exchange transactions. In these instances the entity needs to determine what portion of the transaction is an exchange transaction and what portion is a non-exchange transaction and then recognize them separately.

Example 11.12   Transaction that combines exchange and non-exchange elements

A public sector entity (named HealthABC), operating as a health clinic, received €50 000 from Government Entity (Hospital X). In return, the health clinic provides Entity X with x-ray equipment. The x-ray equipment is valued at €150 000.

In this example, HealthABC gave more than equal in value to Hospital X, i.e., €100 000 in additional value.

Following IPSAS 23 an asset received for no or nominal consideration should be recognized at its fair value, the difference, i.e., credit entry will be revenue from non-exchange transactions.

In this example, HealthABC did give some compensation to Hospital X for the x-ray equipment, and therefore the difference should be treated as a donation and recognized as revenue from non-exchange transactions.

	Debit	Credit
X-ray equipment (PP&E)	150 000	
Bank		50 000
Donation received (non-exchange)		100 000

For some transactions it can be difficult to distinguish whether or not a transaction is exchange or non-exchange. In order to make the proper classification between exchange and non-exchange, the entity has to consider the substance of the transaction (IPSAS 9.6).

If it is not possible to distinguish between the exchange and non-exchange components, the transaction should be treated as a non-exchange transaction.

PRINCIPAL–AGENT ACCOUNTING

This section considers principal–agent relations and their implications for accounting. Principal–agent relations raise a number of complex accounting questions and it should be emphasized that this section only provides an overview of these issues. A number of arrangements within the public sector, between public sector entities, involve principal–agent relationships. These relationships affect whether or to what extent an entity recognizes revenue, expenditure, assets, and liabilities as its own. An example is whether an entity recognizes the full amount earned on a sales transaction or commission as revenue.[4]

Distinguishing whether an entity acts as a principal or an agent in an arrangement is often subjective. This assessment becomes more complex in the public sector as the lines between agent, principal, transferor, recipient, and service provider are potentially more blurred in transactions between public sector entities. This is due to the different circumstances under which these arrangements are entered into, the structures within government, the motivation for entering into arrangements between entities being to enhance service delivery.

Identification of Principals and Agents

The key issue when dealing with agent–principal scenarios is being able to identify whether an entity is acting as an agent or not. Table 11.2 provides an overview of indicators that can be used in order to distinguish between principal and agent.

Principal–Agent Identification Impact on Accounting Requirements

Assessing whether the entity acts as a principal or an agent has an immediate impact on the recording of elements: recognition of revenue, expenses, assets, and liabilities arising from the arrangement. Figure 11.5 illustrates the impact visually.

Principal–agent relations also impact the elements to be presented on the face of the financial statements and disclosed in the notes to the financial statements.

Question and Answer

Question:

A municipality enters into an agreement with the local department of public works to provide certain professional services related to the construction of a bridge. The local department appoints Company C (a private company) to construct the bridge. The municipality will also manage the flow of funds from the department of public works to Company C. Determine who is the contractor, who is the client, and what is the role played by the municipality.

---

[4] ASB (2012) prepared a comprehensive discussion paper on accounting for the principal–agent activities in the public sector. This section draws at large on this discussion paper.

> *Answer:*
>
> In this case, Company C is the contractor because they are constructing the bridge. The local department of public works is the client. The municipality is an agent because it does not provide services directly related to the construction of the bridge. The municipality should assess whether the services provided as part of the arrangement are within the scope of IPSAS 9 Revenue from Exchange Transactions.

Table 11.2 Indicators to distinguish between principal and agent

No.	PRINCIPAL	AGENT
1	**Indicator: Decision-making ability** The entity has ultimate decision-making discretion, for example the selection of suppliers.	The entity may have some decision-making discretion and authority, although this is limited and often subject to the ultimate approval of another party and can be revoked at the discretion of another party.
2	**Indicator: Inventory risk** The entity has inventory risk. The entity is not explicitly compensated for the risk assumed.	The entity may have inventory risk conveyed to it (accepted by it) contractually. However, the risk is usually limited and the entity is typically compensated accordingly by the principal.
3.	**Indicator: Credit risk** The entity assumes credit risk for the amount receivable from the end customer. Apart from compensation received directly from the customer in the form of interest or collateral, the entity is generally not compensated by a third party (either explicit or implicit) for the credit risk assumed.	The entity may have credit risk conveyed to it. However, the risk is usually limited and the entity is typically compensated accordingly by the principal.
4.	**Indicator: Price determination** The entity has latitude in establishing prices (within the confines of the economic market and prevailing legislation). It has the ability unilaterally to raise or lower prices (to any level).	The entity may have the ability to determine prices, but subject to the parameters stipulated by a third party.
5.	**Indicator: Value added processes** The entity performs part of the service itself or modifies the goods that are being supplied in some way.	The entity does not add any significant value in the process and merely acts as a go-between.
6.	**Indicator: Accountability** The entity has prime accountability in respect of the arrangement (to other external parties). It does not portray itself as an agent.	The entity is primarily accountable to the principal, rather than to any other party directly. It discloses the fact that it is acting as an agent.

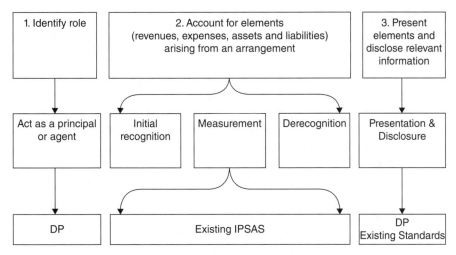

Figure 11.5 Principal–agent relations and accounting impact

IPSAS Financial Reporting in Practice 11.3. Principal–Agent Accounting, UNOPS (2012 Financial Statements)

Implementation of the International Public Sector Accounting Standards

*Background [...]*The adoption of IPSAS introduces new terminology and changes the way in which transactions are treated and presented in the financial statements. Most significantly, UNOPS had for the first time to consider whether it acted as a principal or an agent in projects and disclose revenues and expenditure separately from those in which it acted in the capacity of agent (facilitating third-party transactions such as procurement activities). This presented a significant challenge.[...] (p. 7)

Financial performance

In 2012, total revenue generated by UNOPS amounted to $985.6 million. Under IPSAS rules, $683.2 million is reported in the statement of financial performance, in addition to agency contracts totaling $302.4 million, as explained in the notes to the statements. IPSAS distinguishes between a contract where UNOPS acts as a principal and a contract where UNOPS acts as an agent. For accounting purposes, where UNOPS acts as a principal, the revenue is recognized in full on the statement of financial performance. Where UNOPS operates as an agent on behalf of its partner, only the net revenue is reported on the statement of financial performance. Including agency transactions, total delivery by UNOPS in 2012 was $985.6 million, which, as mentioned, was broadly consistent with the level of activity in 2011. The table provides a summary of revenue and expenses against the three core services of UNOPS: infrastructure, project management and procurement. These are derived from the financial statements, which report the same IPSAS figures against its five project activities (see note 17). (p. 31)

UNOPS explains that it had to consider whether it acted as a principal or an agent in its projects, which happened to be very difficult in practice. UNOPS discloses the differences applying to the methods of recognition and presentation of revenue (either in full as principal or in net as agent).

CONSTRUCTION CONTRACTS (IPSAS 11)

The objective of IPSAS 11 is to prescribe the accounting treatment for revenue and costs relating to construction contracts.

Construction contracts may involve:

- Constructing a single asset such as a bridge, building, or dam;
- Constructing a number of interrelated or interdependent assets such as refineries or other complex pieces of plant or equipment;
- Rendering services directly related to the construction of the asset such as the services of project managers or architects; or
- Destruction or restoration of assets.

The dates on which a construction contract starts and ends usually fall in different accounting periods, so the principal concern is how to allocate revenue and costs to the different accounting periods to reflect the reality of the construction activity as it takes place.

Question and Answer

Question:

The local department of public works (LDPW) is contracted by the Ministry of Transport (MoT) to build a bridge. What is the role of the LDPW and of the MoT respectively?

Answer:

LDPW is the contractor because they are constructing the bridge. LDPW applies IPSAS 11 Construction Contracts in accounting for the relevant costs and, if relevant, revenue.

MoT is the client. MoT will make the required payments to LDPW over the contract period and at the end will receive the bridge. At that stage, MoT will apply IPSAS 17 Property, Plant and Equipment to account for the bridge in its accounting records.

IPSAS Financial Reporting in Practice 11.4. Delivery of Infrastructure Projects, UNOPS (2012 Financial Statements)

Infrastructure projects are projects that construct or refurbish a physical asset. They are a core part of the UNOPS mandate to provide a central resource for the United Nations system in procurement and contracts management, as well as in civil works and physical infrastructure development, including the related capacity-development

> exercises. Construction contracts in which UNOPS was a principal accounted for $239 million of UNOPS expense in 2012, around one third of its total expense. UNOPS was most active in projects in South Sudan ($49 million) and Peru ($39 million) (see table II.3). (p.15)

Construction contracts represent an important part of the activity of UNOPS, around one third of its total expense in 2012. UNOPS discloses the type of contracts of delivery of infrastructure projects they perform, and the list of its most active projects.

There are two distinct types of construction contract, shown in the following table:

Fixed price contracts (IPSAS 11.4)	Cost plus contracts (IPSAS 11.4)
Where the revenue arising is fixed, either for the contract as a whole or on units of output, at the outset of the contract. Under such contracts there is an element of certainty about the revenue accruing, but not about the costs which will arise.	Where costs will be recoverable plus some agreed element of profit. Under such contracts there is a high degree of certainty about the profit arising although there is no certainty about either the revenue or the costs.

The distinction between the two types of contract is particularly important when deciding the stage at which contract revenues and expenses should be recognized.

When a construction contract covers two or more assets, the construction of each asset should be treated separately if (IPSAS 11.13):

(a) Separate proposals were submitted for each asset;
(b) Portions of the contract relating to each asset were negotiated separately;
(c) Costs and revenues of each asset can be identified.

A group of contracts should be accounted for as a single contract when (IPSAS 11.14):

(a) They were negotiated together;
(b) The work is interrelated;
(c) The contracts are performed concurrently or in a continuous sequence.

In case a contract gives the customer an option to order additional assets, construction of each additional asset should be accounted for as a separate contract if (IPSAS 11.15):

(a) The additional asset differs significantly from the original asset(s); or
(b) The price of the additional asset is separately negotiated.

Determination of Contract Revenue and Contract Costs

Contract revenue includes (IPSAS 11.16):

- The amount agreed in the contract initially;
- Contract work variations, claims, and incentive payments.

Contract work variations, claims, and incentive payments are only included to the extent that (a) they are expected to generate revenue; and (b) they can be measured reliably (IPSAS 11.16).

Contract costs concern costs (IPSAS 11.23)

Contract costs include:

- Those directly relating to the specific contract;
- Costs that are attributable to the general activity of the contractor to the extent that they can be systematically and rationally allocated to the contract;
- Other costs that can be specifically charged to the customer under the terms of the contract.

Application of the percentage of completion method

In case the outcome of a construction contract can be estimated reliably, revenue and costs related to the contract should be recognized in proportion to the stage of completion of contract at the reporting date (IPSAS 11.30).

An entity can estimate the outcome of a contract reliably when it is able to make a reliable estimate of total contract revenue, the stage of completion, and the costs to complete the contract (IPSAS 11.31–11.32).

The stage of completion of a contract can be determined in different ways, including the following methods (IPSAS 11.38):

1. The proportion that contract costs incurred for work performed to date bear to the estimated total contract costs;
2. Surveys of work performed;
3. Completion of a physical proportion of the contract work.

Question and Answer

Question:

Entity Bert is contracted to build a viaduct. The contract, which is a fixed-price contract, amounts to CU100 million and is expected to cost CU80 million.

Contractually, the client agreed to accept increases in wage tariffs additional to the contract price.

This contract is a fixed-price contract subject to a cost escalation clause. The revenue receivable by the contractor is fixed at CU100 million, but any wage increases will be added to the amount.

The amount will be recognized based on the stage of completion method.

According to its accounting policy, Entity Bert determines the stage of completion on the basis of the percentage of completion, that is to say the proportion of costs incurred for work performed to date, to the total estimated costs of the contract.

At the end of year 1, Entity Bert has incurred a cost of CU40 million, of which CU1 million results from the increase in wage tariffs. Determine the revenue which should be recognized by Entity Bert.

Then consider the same question if contractually the client had not agreed to accept increases in wage tariffs additional to the contract price.

Answer:

Using the percentage of completion method, the following revenue should be recognized for year 1:

40 million/(80 milllion + 1 million) × (100 million + 1 million) = 49.9 million

1 million resulting from the increase in wage tariffs is added to the original estimated total costs and to the contract price.

If contractually the client had not agreed to accept increases in wage tariffs additional to the contract price, the contract price would not have been adjusted. Only the estimated total cost would have been adjusted:

40 million/(80 milllion + 1 million) × (100 million) = 49.4 million

What if the outcome of the contract cannot be estimated reliably?

In case the outcome cannot be estimated reliably, contract revenue should only be recognized to the extent that contract costs incurred are expected to be recoverable and contract costs should be expensed as incurred (IPSAS 11.40).

Expected deficits on construction contracts should be recognized immediately as an expense as soon as such deficit is probable, but only when it is intended at inception that the contract costs are to be fully recovered (IPSAS 11.44). In case of a non-commercial contract where the contract costs will not be fully recovered from the parties to the contract, when the deficit will be compensated by a government appropriation, general purpose grant, or allocation of government funds to the contractor, the requirement of the recognition of the deficit does not apply (IPSAS 11.46).

Question and Answer

Question:

The local department of public works (LDPW) is contracted by the Ministry of Transport (MoT) to build a bridge. The construction begins on 1 April N and will be finished on 31 November N+1. Then, the bridge will be complete and will be available for use by MoT.

The parties have agreed on a fixed price contract of €350K.

On 31 December N, incurred costs and total expected costs are as follows:

In €K	Year N	Year N+1
Direct construction costs	80	100
Indirect construction costs	30	56
General administrative costs which were specifically included in the contract	10	24
Part of general administrative costs which were not specifically included in the contract	20	40
Total	140	220

Contract revenue and contract costs are determined based on surveys of work performed (work certified to date/contract price).

Which revenue should be recorded for the period ending 31 December N?

Assuming that the result of the construction contract cannot be estimated reliably, which revenue should be recorded for the period ending 31 December N?

Answer:

General administrative costs which were not specifically included in the contract are not included in the cost of the contract (IPSAS 11.28a).

General administrative costs which were specifically included in the contract (such as for instance insurance, costs of design that are not directly related to a specific contract, and construction overheads) are included in the cost of the contract (IPSAS 11.26).

The total expected cost of the contract is: $80 + 30 + 10 + 100 + 56 + 24 = €300K$

On 31 December N, the percentage of completion is: $(80 + 30 + 10)/300 = 40\%$

On 31 December N, LDPW should record the following revenue: $40\% \times 350 = €140K$

If revenue cannot be reliably measured, contract costs should be recognized in surplus or deficit in the period in which they were incurred and contract revenue should be recognized only to the extent that it is probable that the contract costs incurred will be recovered.

Therefore, on 31 December N, LDPW should record the following revenue: $40\% \times 300 = €120K$, which is the amount of the incurred costs up to then.

Disclosures

The following disclosures are required:

- Amount of contract revenue recognized;
- Method used to determine contract revenue;
- Method used to determine stage of completion of the contract.

For contracts in progress at the reporting date:

- Aggregate costs incurred and recognized surpluses (less recognized deficits);
- Amount of advances received;
- Amount of retentions.

EXPENSE RECOGNITION

There is no one specific IPSAS that details all accounting requirements for expenses and expense recognition. Expenses are defined in the Conceptual Framework, and can be considered against the requirements of accrual basis accounting. This results in a "balance sheet" approach to expense recognition, with analysis as to whether an event or transaction has resulted in a decrease in assets or an increase in liabilities. Specific types of expenses are dealt with directly by other standards, for example, IPSAS 17 for depreciation relating to property, plant, and equipment.

Expenses are decreases in economic benefits or service potential during the reporting period in the form of outflows or consumption of assets or increases in liabilities that result in decreases in net assets/equity, other than those relating to distributions to owners.

Expenses such as for example, cost of sales, employee costs, and depreciation result in the consumption of assets such as cash, inventory, and property, plant and equipment, or the increase in a liability such as an accrual or accounts payable. Expenses also result if a liability is recognized for a provision, or when an asset is reduced due to impairment.

Under the accrual basis, expenses are recognized when the transaction or event causing the expense takes place. The recognition of the expense is thus not linked to when cash or its equivalent is received or paid. An expense can result from a transaction that does not have to involve an outflow of cash.

A distinction should be made between the word "expense" and the word "expenditure" from an accounting perspective. It is helpful to restrict the use of the word "expenditure" to cash outlays. Expenditures may be cash outlays for capital assets (capital expenditures) or cash outlays for operating purposes (operating expenditures). A capital expenditure, for example the purchase of a vehicle, generally does not immediately result in an expense, although expenses will follow later as the asset is consumed and depreciation or amortization expenses are accrued. An operating expenditure may follow an expense.

Table 11.3 provides examples of expense amounts and recognition points.

Non-Exchange Expenditure

Governments and public sector entities provide a wide range of services and payments to benefit the general public, individuals, and households. Such items are generally known as social benefits and are, for the most part, either provided free or for a small consideration, and therefore constitute non-exchange transactions. The overall aim of social benefits is to seek to provide all citizens with acceptable minimum standards in such areas as for example education, health, and security.

No standard covering non-exchange expenditure has yet been issued (see Chapter 18 which highlights that this topic is on the future work agenda of the IPSASB). Accounting for non-exchange goods and services is generally considered straightforward. Accounting for cash transfers raises difficult questions about when a liability should be recognized. This is a challenging and politically sensitive area. Expense recognition is discussed in more detail at the end of this chapter.

Table 11.3 Overview of expenses with corresponding recognition points

Type of Item	Expense Amount	Examples	Recognition Point
Purchase of an item that is not capitalized	The cost of the item	Office supplies Utilities Plant and equipment below the capitalization threshold	Delivery of the item
Inventory	The cost of the item	Restaurant stock that meets the definition of inventory	Inventory is sold, distributed, and control passes from the public sector entity in question
Depreciation of property, plant, and equipment	Depreciation expense as determined by IPSAS 17 – a part of the cost of the asset	Computers, vehicles, buildings	As the asset is used (over its useful life)
Impairment	Depends on the estimated decrease in the value of the asset below its previous book value	Impairment affects a variety of different assets, including property, plant, and equipment	An event (such as damage or obsolescence other than normal usage) to cause a drop in asset value
Salary and consulting expenses	Gross salaries or amounts agreed in a contract for consulting services	Salary	Services are provided with the result that the public sector entity in question is obliged to remunerate the staff member or consultant
Provisions	The amount of the provision or increase in the provision as determined by IPSAS 19	Provision for litigation	An obligation that is probable and can be reliably measured exists as a result of a past event

Types of non-exchange expenditure

The IPSASB distinguishes between these main types of social benefits as follows:

- Collective goods, individual goods, and services;
- Cash transfers to individuals and households.

In essence, these are services provided to all members of the public or to all those within a particular area. They include such major activities as:

- National defence;
- International relations;
- Public order and safety (including police services, fire protection services, law courts, and prisons);
- The efficient operation of the social and economic system of a country;

- Certain components of services to individuals such as formulation and administration of government policy; setting and enforcement of standards, regulation, and licensing of personnel and institutions; and applied research and experimental development.

Overall, these services can be seen as seeking to provide a secure environment in which all citizens may live.

Individual goods and services

Most often these are services provided by public sector entities to individuals who have particular need of them. Key examples include education and health services. Governments generally provide schooling for children of the relevant ages. Many governments also provide health services, including consultations with doctors, the supply of medicines, and care in hospitals. Such services may be provided free or at heavily subsidized charges.

Cash transfers to individuals

These include such expenditure as child benefits, invalidity and sickness benefits, unemployment benefits, housing benefits, and old age pensions. A common feature of these benefits is that they are almost always paid in cash, thus leaving the spending priorities to the discretion of the recipients. Otherwise the conditions and eligibility requirements are likely to vary considerably between jurisdictions. In particular, old age benefits (state pensions) may be available to all citizens above a certain age, or only to those who have participated in the workforce or who have paid taxes or contributions for a specified period.

Accounting for non-exchange expenditure and wider views of liability

Accounting for collective goods and services, and for individual goods and services, is generally considered straightforward and expenditure is mostly recognized in the normal way when:

- A liability relating to goods or services is incurred through transactions with an employee or a third-party provider; or
- Assets are depreciated.

When accounting for transactions carried out for nil consideration in particular, there is no significant requirement to recognize expenditure based on a liability to the recipients of goods and services. Whilst a liability to service recipients may be considered to arise, this is normally deemed to closely match the other liabilities so that no separate accounting is needed.

The question of whether, and when, governments should recognize liabilities to recipients of cash transfers is a sensitive matter on which there is considerable debate. Some suggest that the application of private sector reporting approaches means that liabilities do not need to be recognized, or should be recognized very shortly before settlement of the liability through cash transfer. Others suggest that a more general liability might be seen to arise by virtue of taxpayers as a whole providing (or being expected to provide) revenue through taxation which the taxpayers expect to be used for social benefit purposes amongst other things.

Pensions paid to former employees represent an exchange transaction. The pension payment is part of the benefits payable in return for services provided as an employee, which can be interpreted differently from minimum pensions payable to old persons who have not contributed enough to the system and who live below the poverty line. In the latter case, they represent non-exchange transactions.

IPSAS Financial Reporting in Practice 11.5. Non-Exchange Expenditure, UNESCO, 2013 Financial Statements

2.16 EXPENSES

Under accrual accounting, expenses are decreases in economic benefits or service potential during the reporting period in the form of outflows or consumption of assets or incurrences of liabilities that result in decreases in net assets/equity. Expenses are recognized when the transaction or event causing the expense occurs, and the recognition of the expense is therefore not linked to when cash or its equivalent is received or paid.

Non-exchange transactions

Expenses from non-exchange funding agreements are recognized when the funding is legally in force, except where the agreement establishes a condition on transferred assets. In such cases, expenses are recognized as services are performed and the condition on transferred assets fulfilled consistent with the terms of the agreement. Advance payments are amortized based on objective evidence to reflect the risk of non-recovery. Where revenue is recognized from in-kind contributions, a corresponding expense is also recognized in the financial statements.

UNESCO (2013) Financial Statements (pp. 42, 47)

UNESCO discloses its policy relating to non-exchange expenditure, explaining that expenses are recognized when the transaction or event causing the expense to occur (not when cash is received or paid): when funding is legally in force (except when there is a condition on transferred assets), when revenue is recognized from in-kind contributions.

12 EMPLOYEE BENEFITS, SOCIAL BENEFITS, AND OTHER LIABILITIES

The main part of this chapter deals with IPSAS 25 on Employee Benefits, while remaining parts touch on the accounting for other liabilities and social benefits. An issue in public sector financial management during recent years has been that of the funding by entities of their employee pension schemes. Public sector pension schemes represent a significant element of the public finances. These schemes may be administered by separate entities/organizations or within government, but the benefits accruing to members of the schemes are often guaranteed under statute. Pension scheme assets and liabilities therefore often represent assets and liabilities of the government itself. The objective of IPSAS 25 is to prescribe the accounting and disclosure of employee benefits.

In addition to employee benefits, public sector entities can also have liabilities in the form of contributions received (which can be short or long term) and accounts payables (short term) and accrued liabilities (short term).

CONTRIBUTIONS RECEIVED IN ADVANCE, ACCOUNTS PAYABLE, AND ACCRUED LIABILITIES

Liabilities in the form of contributions received (which can be short or long term) and accounts payables (short term) and accrued liabilities (short term) are very common, especially in intergovernmental organizations.

The IPSAS Financial Reporting in Practice 12.1 below shows how the World Health Organization (WHO) described their contributions received in advance, accounts payable, and accrued liabilities.

IPSAS Financial Reporting in Practice 12.1. Contributions Received in Advance, Accounts Payable and Accrued Liabilities, WHO Financial Statements 2012 (p. 29)

Contributions received in advance

Contributions received in advance arise from legally binding agreements between WHO and its contributors – including governments, international organizations and private and public institutions – whereby contributions are received in advance of the amounts concerned falling due to the Organization.

Accounts payable and accrued liabilities

Accounts payable are financial liabilities for goods or services that have been received by WHO but not paid for. Accrued liabilities are financial liabilities for goods or services that have been received by WHO and which have neither been paid for nor invoiced to WHO.

Accounts payable and accrued liabilities are recognized at cost as the effect of discounting is considered immaterial.

Recognition of liabilities in the form of contributions received, accounts payable, and accrued liabilities is one of the major differences from cash accounting. Many stakeholders of intergovernmental organizations keep thinking in terms of cash budgeting – it is important to explain the criteria for recognition of these key elements of the accrual basis of accounting.

EMPLOYEE BENEFITS (IPSAS 25)

Employees generally receive a number of different benefits as part of their complete remuneration package and these are addressed in IPSAS 25.

IPSAS 25 should be applied by all entities in accounting for the provision of all employee benefits.[1] The standard applies regardless of whether the benefits have been provided as part of a formal contract (IPSAS 25.4).

Employee benefits are all forms of consideration given by an employer to employees (or their dependents) in exchange for services rendered.

Accounting issues in terms of employee benefits may arise due to:

- The valuation problems linked to some forms of employee benefits; and
- The timing of benefits, which may not always be provided in the same period as the one in which the employee's services are provided.

---

[1] Please note though that for any share-based transactions IFRS 2 applies.

Table 12.1 Short-term vs. post-employment benefits

Short-term employee benefits	Post-employment benefits
Employee benefits (other than termination benefits) which fall due wholly within 12 months after the end of the period in which employees render the related service.	Employee benefits (other than termination benefits) which are payable after the completion of employment.
Examples include:	Examples include:
• Wages, salaries, and social security contributions; • Paid annual leave and paid sick leave; • Profit-sharing and bonuses (if payable within 12 months of the end of the period); and • Non-monetary benefits, e.g., medical care, housing, cars, free or subsidized goods (IPSAS 25.10, 25.11).	• Pensions; • Other retirement benefits; and • Post-employment life insurance and medical care (IPSAS 25.10, 25.27). • Other long-term employee benefits.

The principle underlying all of the detailed requirements of the standard is that the cost of providing employee benefits should be recognized in the period in which the benefit is earned by the employee, rather than when it is paid or payable.

IPSAS 25 distinguishes between short-term employee benefits, post-employment benefits, and other employee benefits. Table 12.1 highlights the differences.

Other employee benefits (other than post-employment and termination benefits) are benefits which do not fall due wholly within 12 months after the end of the period in which employees render the related service. Examples include:

- Long-term service leave or sabbatical leave;
- Long-term disability benefits;
- Profit-sharing and bonuses (if not payable within 12 months of the end of the period) (IPSAS 25.10, 25.147); and
- Termination benefits.

Termination benefits are employee benefits payable as a result of an entity's decision to terminate an employee's employment before the normal retirement date or on an employee's decision to take voluntary redundancy (IPSAS 25.10, 25.154).

As with IPSAS 25, the principle underlying the standard is that costs should be recognized in the period in which the benefit is earned by the employee, rather than when it is paid or payable.

IPSAS Financial Reporting in Practice 12.2. WHOs Employee Benefits, 2013 Financial Statements (p. 28)

WHO recognizes the following categories of employee benefits:

- Short-term employee benefits that fall due wholly within 12 months following the end of the accounting period in which employees render the related service;
- Post-employment benefits;

- Other long-term employee benefits;
- Termination benefits.

WHO is a member organization participating in the United Nations Joint Staff Pension Fund, which was established by the United Nations General Assembly to provide retirement, death, disability and related benefits to employees. The Pension Fund is a funded, multi-employer defined benefit plan. As specified by Article 3(b) of the Regulations of the Fund, membership in the Fund shall be open to the specialized agencies and to any other international, intergovernmental organization which participates in the common system of salaries, allowances and other conditions of service of the United Nations and the specialized agencies.

The plan exposes participating organizations to actuarial risks associated with the current and former employees of other organizations participating in the Pension Fund, with the result that there is no consistent and reliable basis for allocating the obligation, plan assets, and costs to individual organizations participating in the plan. The Organization and the Pension Fund, in line with the other participating organizations in the Fund, are not in a position to identify the Organization's proportionate share of the defined benefit obligation, the plan assets and the costs associated with the plan with sufficient reliability for accounting purposes. For this reason, WHO has treated this plan as if it were a defined contribution plan in line with the requirements of IPSAS 25. The Organization's contributions to the plan during the financial period are recognized as expenses in the Statement of Financial Performance.

WHO does not recognize any pension provision on the face of its statement of financial position, even if, in essence, its pension system is a defined benefit plan. This is an exception to the principle of recognition of defined benefit obligations. In theory, WHO should recognize post-employment benefits as provisions; however, since WHO participates in the UN common system of salaries and pensions, it is not possible to identify the WHO share of the defined benefit obligation. This is the reason why IPSAS 25 authorizes recognition of the plan as if it were a defined contribution plan. Under a defined contribution plan, contributions to the plan during the financial period are recognized as expenses in the statement of financial performance.

Short-term Employee Benefits

Short-term employee benefits are employee benefits (other than termination benefits) that are due to be settled within 12 months from the end of the period in which the employees provide their services (IPSAS 25.10).

Short-term employee benefits include (IPSAS 25.11):

- Wages, salaries, and social security contributions;
- Paid annual leave and paid sick leave;

- Profit-sharing and bonuses (if payable within 12 months of the end of the period); and
- Non-monetary benefits, e.g., medical care, housing, cars, free or subsidized goods.

The application of the accrual concept in relation to liabilities means that an entity should recognize a liability when it becomes payable rather than when it is actually paid. A short-term benefit should therefore be recognized as an employee provides his or her services to the entity on which the benefits are payable. The benefit will normally be treated as an expense, and a liability should be recognized for any unpaid balance at the end of the reporting period (IPSAS 25.13).

The liability at the end of the reporting period will be reduced by any amounts paid during the period.

Compensated Absences

Compensated absences are periods of absence from work for which the employee receives some form of payment, for example paid annual vacation and paid sick leave. These benefits fall into two categories. The expected cost of such compensated absences should be recognized:

- In the case of accumulating compensated absences, as the employees render service that increases their entitlement. Where an employee has an unused entitlement at the end of the reporting period and the entity expects to provide the benefit, a liability should be created (IPSAS 25.16, 25.17);
- In the case of non-accumulating compensated absences, when the absences occur (IPSAS 25.19).

Accumulating absences

These are benefits, such as paid annual vacation, that accrue over an employee's period of service and can be potentially carried forward and used in future periods.

Non-accumulating absences

These are benefits that an employee is entitled to, but are not normally capable of being carried forward to the following period if they are unused during the period, for example paid sick leave.

Example 12.1   Annual pay leave

An entity has:

- Fifty staff entitled to 37 days of annual paid leave per year, at a rate of CU100 per day;
- Twenty staff entitled to 30 days of annual paid leave per year, at a rate of CU50 per day.

Unused vacation is carried forward to the following year.

All staff work for the entity throughout the year and are therefore entitled to their days of annual paid leave. An expense should be recognized for:

50 staff × 37 days × CU100 + 20 staff × 30 days × CU50 = CU215 000.

Almost all staff use their complete entitlement for the year. Only two members of staff from the first category and one member of staff from the second category have five days, three days, and two days unused, respectively and have permission to carry forward these remaining days to the following period. A liability will be recognized at the end of the reporting period for:

1 staff member × 5 days × CU100 + 1 staff member × 3 days × CU100

+ 1 staff member × 2 days × CU50 = CU900

Profit Sharing and Bonus Payments

An entity should recognize an expense and a corresponding liability for the cost of providing profit-sharing arrangements and bonus payments when (IPSAS 25.20):

- The entity has a present legal or constructive obligation (i.e., payment is part of an employee's employment contract, or the entity has a history of paying bonuses) to make such payments as the result of a past event; and
- A reliable estimate of the obligation can be made.

Post-Employment Benefits: An Overview

Post-employment benefits are employee benefits (other than termination benefits) which are payable after the completion of employment. Such benefits include post-employment benefit plans set up under formal or informal arrangements (IPSAS 25.10):

Post-employment benefits include (IPSAS 25.27):

- Pensions;
- Other retirement benefits; and
- Post-employment life insurance and medical care.

The accounting treatment for a post-employment benefit plan will be determined according to whether the plan is a defined contribution or a defined benefit plan (IPSAS 25.10).

Defined contribution plans

These are post-employment plans under which payments into the plan are fixed. Subsequent payments out of the plan to retired members are based on the size of the "pot." The "pot" represents contributions that have been made into the scheme and investment returns on scheme assets. The risk of the plan not providing adequate payments to retired members lies with the members.

Contributions into a defined contribution plan by an employer are made in return for services provided by an employee during the period. They should recognize contributions payable as an expense in the period in which the employee provides the service by reference to which contributions by the employer become payable. A liability should be recognized where contributions arise in relation to an employee's service, but remain unpaid at the period end IPSAS 25.55).

With a defined contribution plan, an entity makes contributions into a separate entity and carries none of the actuarial or investment risks. An entity recognizes only a liability (or an asset) when these contributions are in arrears (or in advance). This liability (or asset) is not discounted, except where it does not fall due within 12 months. Where contributions are not payable during the period (or within 12 months of the end of the period) in which the employee provides services on which they accrue, the amount recognized should be discounted, to reflect the time value of money[2] (IPSAS 25.56). Where the effect of the time value of money is material, the amount of the liability should be the present value of the expenditures required to settle that obligation.

Where an entity operates a defined contribution plan during the period, it should disclose the amount that has been recognized as an expense during the period in relation to the plan (IPSAS 25.57).

Defined benefit plans

These are defined as all plans other than defined contribution plans.[3] These plans define the amount that retired members will receive from the plans during retirement, by reference to factors such as length of service and salary levels. Contributions are paid into the scheme based on an estimate of what will have to be paid out under it. Typically, an employer retains an obligation to make up any shortfall in a plan, thereby bearing the risk (IPSAS 25.10).

More on the accounting treatment of post-employment benefits is included later in the chapter.

Under defined benefit plans:

- The entity's obligation is to provide the agreed benefits to current and former employees; and
- Actuarial risk (that benefits will cost more than expected) and investment risk fall, in substance, on the entity. If actuarial or investment experience is worse than expected, the entity's obligation may be increased.

---

[2] Time value of money means that CU1 today is worth more than CU1 in one year's time due to the fact that I need less that CU1 today meet an obligation of CU1 in one year's time because this amount of money can be invested today in order to make a return on investment in the future.
[3] In other words a defined benefit plan is any post-employment benefit plan not meeting the definition of a defined contribution plan.

The entity provides employees with the agreed benefits of the plan and carries all the actuarial and investment risks. The entity obligation is measured on a discounted basis because the liability may be settled many years after employees have rendered services.

There are two types of defined benefit plan:

- Funded plans.
- Unfunded plans.

Funded plans

Contributions paid by the employer and employee are paid into a separate fund. The assets held within the fund are effectively ring-fenced for the payment of benefits.

Unfunded plans

In the public sector, these plans are held within the government structure and are managed by government bodies. In some cases, specific assets may be allocated towards the satisfaction of retirement benefit obligations, although these assets are not necessarily ring-fenced for the payment of benefits and remain the assets of the government.

The key feature of a defined benefit plan is that the employer retains an obligation to make up any shortfall in the plan, should there be insufficient funds within it to pay out the promised benefits. It would be inappropriate for the entity to record only the contributions paid as expenses, since in effect it is underwriting some of the risks associated in the plan.

There are many uncertainties in terms of the measurement of an employer's obligation in relation to a defined benefit plan.

An obligation only arises if the investments (where these exist) out of which the payment of benefits will be made are less than the benefits payable. In terms of the investments, the major uncertainties relate to how investments, both those already made and those to be made from future contributions, will perform in terms of investment returns and capital appreciation.

IPSAS 25 is based on the principle that an entity has an obligation under a defined benefit plan when an employee performs services which accrue benefits under the plan.

It is therefore appropriate that an expense is recognized for an employee's services during the period in which they are performed and for which benefits will be payable under the defined benefit plan.

Because of the long-term nature of a defined benefit plan and the level of uncertainty of actual obligations that will fall due under it, the specialist services of an actuary are required. An estimate is made of the level of the obligations payable under the plan and whether the value of any plan assets will be sufficient to meet the estimated liabilities. This is the reason why IPSAS 25 requires the disclosure of actuarial assumptions in order to allow comparisons and full understanding of the parameters of the calculations.

UNESCO discloses the actuarial assumptions and methods used to calculate the liabilities arising from ASHI (After-Service Health Insurance), accrued annual leave, repatriation benefits, and Italian end-of-service benefit in note 16 of its financial statements for 2013. This disclosure is fundamental in order to understand the meaning of the value of the UNESCO staff liabilities (see IPSAS Financial Reporting in Practice 12.3).

IPSAS Financial Reporting in Practice 12.3. Actuarial Valuations, UNESCO 2013 Financial Statements (p. 51)

Liabilities arising from ASHI, accrued annual leave, repatriation benefits and Italian end-of-service benefit are determined by actuaries. Actuarial assumptions are required to be disclosed in the financial statements in accordance with IPSAS 25. The following assumptions and methods have been used to determine the value of post-employment and other long-term benefits for UNESCO as at 31 December 2013:

Actuarial valuations

Discount rate – ASHI	4.00% – the rate used is based on the Mercer Yield Curve as of 31/12/2013 with a maturity around 23.75 years
Discount rate – Repatriation benefits and Accumulated annual leave	4.00% – the rate used is based on the Mercer Yield Curve as of 31/12/2013 with a maturity around 23.75 years.
Salary scale (including inflation)	2.00%
Pension increase rate (including inflation)	2.00%
Medical cost trend rate (including inflation) – Initial	5.00%
Medical cost trend rate (including inflation) – Ultimate	5.00%
Inflation rate	2.00%
ASHI Plan duration (for discount rate justification purposes)	23.75 years
ASHI	It was assumed that 100% of staff eligible to benefit from the ASHI after service actually claim their entitlement.
Repatriation benefits	It was assumed that 75% of staff eligible for repatriation benefits on leaving actually claim their entitlement.
Accumulated annual leave	As the accumulation of annual leave by employee historically remains stable year on year, it is assumed that the total accumulated balance is a long-term employee benefit taken by staff members on separation from UNESCO.

Multi-Employer Plans

The accounting treatment of multi-employer plans depends whether the entity has a legal or constructive obligation to pay future benefits. When these plans are recognized as defined benefit plans, only the entity's proportionate share of the defined benefit obligation is recognized by the entity.

When the entity is not able to identify its share in the underlying financial position and performance of the plan with sufficient reliability, the entity accounts for this plan as if it were a defined contribution plan (see the UNJSPF plan, in the WHO example).

UNESCO explains, in the note to its financial statements 2013, how the United Nations Joint Staff Pension Fund (UNJSPF) works and which part of the pension liability relies on UNESCO.

United Nations Joint Staff Pension Fund (UNJSPF)

The Pension Fund's Regulations state that the Pension Board shall have an actuarial valuation made of the Fund at least once every three years by the Consulting Actuary. The practice of the Pension Board has been to carry out an actuarial valuation every two years using the Open Group Aggregate Method. The primary purpose of the actuarial valuation is to determine whether the current and estimated future assets of the Pension Fund will be sufficient to meet its liabilities.

UNESCO financial obligation to the UNJSPF consists of its mandated contribution, at the rate established by the United Nations General Assembly (currently at 7.9% for participants and 15.8% for member organizations) together with any share of any actuarial deficiency payments under Article 26 of the Regulations of the Pension Fund. Such deficiency payments are only payable if and when the United Nations General Assembly has invoked the provision of Article 26, following determination that there is a requirement for deficiency payments based on an assessment of the actuarial sufficiency of the Pension Fund as of the valuation date. Each member organization shall contribute to this deficiency an amount proportionate to the total contributions which each paid during the three years preceding the valuation date.

The latest actuarial valuation was performed as of 31 December 2011. The valuation revealed an actuarial deficit of 1.87% (0.38% in the 2009 valuation) of pensionable remuneration, implying that the theoretical contribution rate required to achieve balance as of 31 December 2011 was 25.57% of pensionable remuneration, compared to the actual contribution rate of 23.7%. The actuarial valuation using data as of 31 December 2013 is being performed.

At 31 December 2011, the funded ratio of actuarial assets to actuarial liabilities, assuming no future pension adjustments, was 130% (140% in the 2009 valuation). The funded ratio was 86% (91% in the 2009 valuation) when the current system of pension adjustments was taken into account.

After assessing the actuarial sufficiency of the Fund, the Consulting Actuary concluded that there was no requirement, as of 31 December 2011, for deficiency payments under Article 26 of the Regulations of the Fund as the actuarial value of assets exceeded the actuarial value of all accrued liabilities under the Fund. In addition, the market value of assets also exceeded the actuarial value of all accrued liabilities as of the valuation date. At the time of this report, the General Assembly has not invoked the provision of Article 26.

In July 2012, the Pension Board noted in its Report of the fifty-ninth session to the General Assembly that an increase in the normal age of retirement for new participants of the Fund to 65 is expected to significantly reduce the deficit and would potentially cover half of the current deficit of 1.87%. In December 2012 and April 2013, the General Assembly authorized an increase to age 65 in the normal retirement age and in the mandatory age of separation respectively for new participants of the Fund, with effect no later than from 1 January 2014. The related change to the Pension Fund's Regulations was approved by the General Assembly in December 2013. The increase in the normal retirement age will be reflected in the actuarial valuation of the Fund as of 1 January 2014.

During 2013, UNESCO's contributions paid to UNJSPF amounted to K$38,303 (2012 K$33,955). Expected contributions due in 2014 are K$33,545.

The United Nations Board of Auditors carries out an annual audit of the UNJSPF and reports to the UNJSPF Pension Board on the audit every year. The UNJSPF publishes quarterly reports on its investments and these can be viewed by visiting the UNJSPF at www.unjspf.org.

(UNESCO, Financial Statements 2013, note 16 employee benefits, pp. 53–54)

As UNESCO explains in its financial statements, the UNESCO financial obligation to the UNJSPF regarding pensions consists of its mandated contribution, at the rate established by the United Nations General Assembly, together with any share of any actuarial deficiency payments according to the Fund regulations (article 26). These deficiency payments are only payable if and when the United Nations General Assembly has invoked the article 26 provision. If so, each member organization is to contribute to this deficiency an amount proportionate to the total contributions which each paid during the three years preceding the valuation date. This regulation stipulates how the calculation should be performed and how the amount is to be shared among UN member organizations. UNESCO discloses the results of the last actuarial valuation (namely on 31 December 2011) and explains that no requirement was made by the United Nations General Assembly for deficiency payments under article 26 of the regulations of the Fund.

Moreover, in order to be fully transparent, UNESCO explains that changes have been decided in the normal retirement age to 65 years old, which will be reflected in the actuarial valuation of the Fund in the 2014 financial statements.

The above note explains why there is no provision for pensions recognized in the UNESCO financial statements for 2013.

Disclosures

The amount recognized as an expense for defined contribution plans should be disclosed. The key disclosures for defined benefit plans include the following:

- A description of the benefit plans;
- The accounting policy for recognizing actuarial gains and losses;
- Reconciliations of the opening and closing balances of both the present value of the defined benefit obligation and the fair value of plan assets (if such exist);
- A split of the defined benefit obligation into funded and unfunded amounts;

Table 12.2   Social vs. employee benefits (PWC, 2012)

	Employee benefits	**Social benefits**
Scope	Entity's personnel.	Selected individuals, a selected group of individuals, or the wider population.
Counterpart of the benefits	Services rendered by the employee assumed to be approximately equal in value to the benefits provided.	The consideration, if any, received by the entity is not approximately equal in value to the goods or services provided.

- Total expense recognized in the statement of financial performance, split into its separate components;
- Details regarding the principal actuarial assumptions;
- A sensitivity analysis for medical cost trend rates;
- A five-year history of the present value of defined benefit obligation, the fair value of plan assets, and experience-related adjustments in that respect.

Please note that Annex 3 to this book provides an overview of the key principles in IPSAS 25.

SOCIAL BENEFITS

The IPSASB has been working on a project that embraces social benefits since 2004. Two key concepts are social benefits and social risks. Social benefits are defined as benefits payable to individuals and households, in cash or in kind, to mitigate the effect of social risks. Social risks are defined as events or circumstances that may adversely affect the welfare of individuals and households either by imposing additional demands on their resources or by reducing their income.[4]

For the moment, the topic has not been addressed by any IPSAS. However, it is a matter of importance, especially in some Western countries where social benefits represent an important part of the State budget expenses.

IPSAS 19 and Social Benefits

The current IPSAS offer some relevant guidance in IPSAS 19 Provisions, Contingent Liabilities and Contingent Assets. It is important to note that there are some fundamental differences between social benefits and employee benefits. Table 12.2 draws out these differences.

Currently there is no requirement regarding the recognition and measurement for provisions for social benefits. If an entity chooses to recognize such provisions, it discloses the basis on which the provisions have been recognized and measured.

---

[4] For more reading on social benefits see Stanford (2015).

It is important to note that certain liabilities that do not meet the definition of provisions may need to be recognized in respect of social benefits to be paid (i.e., amounts due to entitled beneficiaries under an existing legislation) (cf. PWC, 2012).

In the context of social benefits, it should be highlighted that in 2013 the IPSASB released the Recommended Practice Guideline (RPG) 1, Reporting on the Long-Term Sustainability of an Entity's Finances (see Chapter 18) which embraces social benefits to a limited extent. The current project of the IPSASB on social benefits was described in more detail in Chapter 3 on IPSASB work-in-progress.

13 PROVISIONS AND CONTINGENCIES

Any entity is exposed to a number of uncertainties regarding future events and management and is therefore required to make informed estimates on the outcome of such events. The objective of IPSAS 19 is to ensure that appropriate recognition criteria and measurement bases are applied to provisions, contingent liabilities, and contingent assets and that sufficient information is disclosed in the notes to the financial statements to enable users to understand their nature, timing, and amount.

IPSAS 19 applies when accounting for provisions, contingent liabilities, and contingent assets except for:

- Those relating to financial instruments which are carried at fair value;
- Those resulting from an executory contract. In essence, this is a contract that does not have any loss-making potential, for example both parties to the contract have performed their obligations to an equal extent. An example is a service contract with an employee running for, say, three years. At the end of the first year, the employee has completed one year of service and the employer has paid for one year of services; and
- Those specifically covered by other standards, for example provision for pension liabilities.

The following three definitions in Table 13.1 are key in IPSAS 19 (IPSAS 19.18):

Table 13.1 Key definitions in IPSAS 19

Provision	Contingent liability	Contingent asset
In its simplest form a provision is a liability where there is uncertainty over its timing or the amount at which it will be settled (IPSAS 19.18).	A contingent liability is where there is significant uncertainty about a number of aspects regarding the liability. A contingent liability arises where an event that occurred in the past may lead to the entity having a liability in the future but the financial impact of the event will only be confirmed by the outcome of some future event not wholly within the entity's control. The giving of a guarantee to another entity that is in financial difficulty is likely to be a contingent liability. If the likelihood of making a payment under the guarantee is remote it is not a contingent liability. A liability that does not meet the provision recognition criteria, for example because the amount of the obligation cannot be measured reliably, is a contingent liability (IPSAS 19.18).	A contingent asset is a potential asset that arises from past events but whose existence can only be confirmed by the outcome of future events not wholly within the entity's control (IPSAS 19.18).

HOW TO DISTINGUISH BETWEEN PROVISIONS, ACCRUALS, AND PAYABLES

The difference between provisions and other liabilities is that there is uncertainty about the timing or amount needed to settle the obligation. This is in contrast to:

- Payables, where the goods and services have been invoiced or formally agreed with the supplier; and
- Accruals, where the goods and services have been received but have not been invoiced or formally agreed with the supplier, including amounts due to employees. Although the amount or timing may need to be estimated, there is much less uncertainty involved.

Accruals should be reported as part of trade and other payables, whereas provisions are reported separately in the statement of financial position.

Example 13.1   Classification of leave as an accrual or a provision

The leave liability will be treated as an accrual or a provision depending on the level of uncertainty attached to either the timing or amount; the less uncertainty, the more likely that the liability will be an accrual. Staff regulations of an organization grant an indemnity leave[1] to retiring staff. The amount of the indemnity depends on seniority, as well as the final year salary on the retirement date. At the end of the year, the organization estimates its indemnity leave liability. For staff having already announced that they wish to retire, their indemnity leave is an accrual. For other active staff, since the timing of their retirement is not certain yet, and the amount of their indemnity depends on their final annual salary, which can be estimated but which cannot be known with certainty, their indemnity leave is a provision.

Provisions

IPSAS 19 states that a provision should be recognized when (IPSAS 19.22): the entity has a present legal or constructive obligation as a result of a past event; and it is probable that an outflow of economic benefits (or service potential) will be required to settle the obligation; and a reliable estimate can be recognized of the amount of the obligation. If all conditions are not met, no provision should be recognized.

Past Event

The entity has a present legal or constructive obligation as a result of a past event. This is an event that creates a legal or constructive obligation that results in an entity having no realistic alternative to settling the obligation. Key words in the definition of a past event are *legal* and *constructive* obligations.

Legal obligation

An obligation that derives from a contract, legislation, or other operation of law (IPSAS 19.18).

Constructive obligation

A constructive obligation is where there is an established past practice that has led to an expectation that an entity will discharge those responsibilities in the future. For example a retail store which has a long-established practice of offering a "no quibble" returns policy (IPSAS 19.18).

Example 13.2   Past event vs. ongoing activities

1. An entity incurred penalties and clean-up costs due to unlawful environmental damages.
   - The past event is the environmental damage.
2. An entity is required by law to rehabilitate landfill sites.
   - The entity has a legal obligation to rehabilitate, thus a provision should be raised.

---

[1] Indemnity means that an entity's employees are entitled to termination payments in the event of dismissal or retirement with the amount of payment varying in relation to the employee's compensation, length of service, and manner of termination. For example, it can be observed that often with local labor law, employees are entitled to indemnities for dismissal or retirement, the amount of which varies according to salary, years of service, and whether they are dismissed or retire,

3. An entity is not required by law to rehabilitate landfill sites, but has adopted the policy to rehabilitate landfill sites and has publicly committed itself to rehabilitate landfill sites.

  • The entity has a constructive obligation to rehabilitate, thus a provision should be raised.

4. Because of legal requirements (for example health and safety laws) a government institute needs to incur expenditure to ensure that it will operate within the health and safety laws in the future. To ensure compliance, the government laboratory decides to install sprinklers to protect employees should a fire occur.

  • No obligating event occurred. The institute can avoid this specific expenditure of installing sprinklers by future actions, for example, by changing its operating methods or by incurring a different expense (for instance investing in fire extinguishers), thus it has no present obligation for this future expense and no provision should be raised. In the event that the institute does not comply with the legal requirements, an obligation can possibly be raised for the payment of fines and penalties if the criteria are met. If so, the institute has a legal obligation to pay fines and penalties, thus a provision should be raised, considering the likelihood of having to pay fines and penalties.

In some cases it is not clear whether there is a present obligation or not. In these cases a past event is deemed to give rise to a present obligation when it is more likely than not that a present obligation exists at the end of the reporting period (IPSAS 19.23).

IPSAS 19.25 describes a "past event that leads to a present obligation" as an obligating event. It is the original action causing a liability to arise. As an example, if an entity is required to operate within certain emission levels and these were breached at some point in time, the past event is when the emission levels were breached rather than when the breach was discovered. It is important to realize that an obligating event involves another party, to whom the obligation is owed. In the above example, a penalty may be payable to, say, a regulatory body.

It is probable that an outflow of economic benefits (or service potential) will be required to settle the obligation. An outflow of resources is regarded as probable if the event is more likely than not to occur. Where it is not probable that an outflow will occur, a contingent liability arises (IPSAS 19.31).

Where there are a number of similar obligations (e.g., product warranties) the probability that an outflow is required is determined by looking at the class of obligations as a whole (IPSAS 19.31).

A reliable estimate can be recognized of the amount of the obligation. Except in extremely rare cases, an entity should be able to determine a range of possible outcomes and can therefore make an estimate of the obligation that is sufficiently reliable to use in recognizing a provision (IPSAS 19.33). Where a reliable estimate cannot be made, a contingent liability arises (IPSAS 19.34).

More about Onerous Contracts

When making a best estimate of the provision for an onerous contract the entity should take into account an estimate of any likely income that will be received under the contract. Under IPSAS 19 social benefits provided by a public sector entity, for which it does not receive consideration that is approximately equal to the value of the goods and services provided directly in return from recipients of those benefits, would not be regarded as onerous contracts.

Example 13.3   Annual rent under lease agreement and provisions

An entity entered into a 15-year lease of a warehouse. The annual rent under the lease agreement is CU12 000. The entity has decided to relocate its storage with five years still to run on the original lease. The entity is not allowed to stop its 15-year contract and is committed to pay the 15 years of annual rent.The entity is permitted to sublet the warehouse and estimates that it should be able to sublet the warehouse for three years. The expected rental is CU10 000 per annum.

A provision should be recognized for the excess costs under the lease contract above the expected benefits to be received. The obligating event is the signing of the lease agreement and CU12 000 is required to be paid in each of the remaining five years.

A provision for the following amount should be recognized:

A provision of CU30 000 = [(CU12 000 − CU10 000) × 3 years + CU12 000 × 2 years] should be recognized.

Note: all other costs and the time value of money have been ignored.

More about Restructuring

A provision should only be recognized in respect of restructuring costs, for example closing a division or reducing the number of employees, where specific criteria have been met, as detailed below. A constructive obligation to restructure an entity only arises in these circumstances (IPSAS 19.83).

Let us assume that a detailed formal plan has been made. This should include identifying the area of the activity and location that is going to be restructured, an estimate of the number of employees that will be affected, the likely cost of the restructuring, and the estimated time scales involved.

An announcement about the restructuring plan has been made to those who will be affected. Time scales should be mentioned as part of this announcement, or the entity should have started to carry out the restructuring. Evidence that a restructuring plan has commenced might be the removal or dismantling of assets at the affected location. If an announcement has been made then commencement of the plan should be within a short period of time to reduce the likelihood of significant changes occurring.

A restructuring provision should only include direct expenditure arising from the restructuring. Costs which relate to the future activities of the entity should not be provided for as part of the restructuring, for example relocating or retraining continuing staff (IPSAS 19.93, 19.94).

Contingencies

A contingent liability is:

1. A possible obligation, whose existence will be confirmed only by the occurrence or non-occurrence of one or more uncertain future event(s) not wholly within the control of the entity; or
2. A present obligation that is not recognized because the outflow of economic benefits or service potential is not probable; or
3. A real present obligation, that may not be recognized, either because the "when" (timing) or because the "how much" (measurement) is not known.

An entity should not recognize a contingent liability (IPSAS 19.35). Disclosure may be required depending on the likelihood of settlement being required. Contingent liabilities should be reviewed continuously to determine whether the outflow of resources has become probable. A provision is raised in the financial statements in the period in which the outflow of resources becomes probable.

In the same way that we can have contingent liabilities dependent on some future uncertain event, we can also have contingent assets. A contingent asset is a possible asset that arises from past events, whose existence will be confirmed only by the occurrence or non-occurrence of one or more uncertain future events beyond the control of the entity. An example is a future inflow which could arise from a legal claim being pursued where the outcome is uncertain.

Contingent assets should not be included in the financial statements (IPSAS 19.39). Where the inflow of economic benefits is probable, disclosure should be made in the financial statements (IPSAS 19.105).

Example 13.4   Contingent liability

A governmental institute uses some radioactive sources for ionizing radiation testing. These sources will have to be replaced by some new sources in the future. Staff from the institute are keen to keep their sources as long as they can because they have characterized them and know exactly how they "react" in experiments. The later they have to be replaced the better. However, when they are no longer sufficiently radioactive, they will have to be replaced. A provision for replacement cost cannot be recognized because there is no obligating event. However, it is certain that the institute will have to pay to get rid of radioactive sources. The question is how much and when. It is very unlikely that an accurate estimate can be made because laws can change and constraints (and correlated costs) can be reinforced in this field. Therefore it is very difficult, indeed almost impossible, to estimate the cost of dismantling and cleaning the radioactive sources. The institute cannot recognize a provision, and is to disclose a note in its financial statements explaining the contingent liability.

Example 13.5   Contingent asset

Entity A instituted an action against MK on 31 October 20N for breach of patent. The court case is currently in progress and not yet settled. However, Entity A's lawyers have advised them that it is probable, although not virtually certain, that the court will award an amount of CU1 000 000. MK is a financially sound company and will be able to pay the fine. Entity A's year-end is 31 December 20N.

At the reporting date, the court case is still in progress, therefore nothing is certain. Since IPSAS applies the prudence concept, Entity A can't record an asset which is not certain. However it will disclose a contingent asset in the notes to the financial statements because the amount is significant for its stakeholders. This is a probable asset (the claimed amount) that arose from a past event (breach of patent) and whose existence will only be confirmed by the occurrence or non-occurrence of an uncertain future event (outcome of the court case). When the outcome of the court case is known, this is no longer a contingent asset, but an asset which needs to be recorded. When the outcome of the court case is known before the financial statements are authorized, meaning that it is an event after the end of the reporting period, it is a non-adjusting event; that is to say that the asset cannot be recorded, but the information relating to the outcome of the court case is to be mentioned in the notes to the financial statements.

Difference between Provisions and Contingent Liabilities

Provisions are recognized as liabilities in the statement of financial position (assuming that a reliable estimate can be made), because they are present obligations and it is probable that an outflow of resources embodying economic benefits or service potential will be required to settle the obligations.

Contingent liabilities are not recognized as liabilities because they are either:

- Potential obligations, as it has yet to be confirmed whether the entity has a present obligation that could lead to an outflow of resources embodying economic benefits or service potential; or
- Present obligations that do not meet the recognition criteria of a liability (because either it is not probable that an outflow of resources embodying economic benefits will be required to settle the obligation, or a sufficiently reliable estimate of the amount of the obligation cannot be made).

Measurement

The amount recognized as a provision should be the best estimate of the expenditure required to settle the present obligation at the reporting date (IPSAS 19.44). The best estimate of the expenditure required to settle the present obligation is the amount that an entity would rationally pay to settle the obligation at the reporting date or to transfer it to a third party at that time. It will often be impossible or prohibitively expensive to settle or transfer an obligation at the reporting date. However, the estimate of the amount that an entity would rationally pay to settle or transfer the obligation gives the best estimate of the expenditure required to settle the present obligation at the reporting date (IPSAS 19.45).

The estimates of outcome and financial effect are based on judgments by management and these judgments are supported by experience of similar transactions and, in some cases, reports from independent experts. Any events after reporting date should also be considered and included.

Uncertainties surrounding the amount to be recognized as a provision are dealt with by various means according to the circumstances (IPSAS 19.46–19.48):

- Where there is a continuous range of possible outcomes, and each point in that range is as likely as the other, then the midpoint of the range is used; alternatively;
- Where the provision measured involves a large population of items, the obligation is estimated by weighting all possible outcomes by the associated probabilities. This statistical method of estimation is referred to as the "expected value"; and
- For a single item, the most likely outcome is the best estimate of the liability.

Risks and uncertainties

Provisions are always measured under conditions of uncertainty and risk. Risk describes variability of outcome. The risks and uncertainties that inevitably surround many events and circumstances should be taken into account in reaching the best estimate of a provision (IPSAS 19.50). Caution is needed when making judgments under these conditions, so that revenue and assets are not overstated and expenses or liabilities are not understated. Uncertainty does not justify the creation of excessive provisions or a deliberate overstatement of liabilities. For example, if the projected costs of a particularly adverse outcome are estimated on a prudent basis, that outcome should not then deliberately be treated as more probable than is realistically the case. Uncertainties surrounding the amount of the expenditure should be disclosed.

Present value

Where the effect of time value of money is material, the provision should be measured at the present value of the expenditures expected to be required to settle the obligation (IPSAS 19.53). The discount rate to be used, to determine the present value, should be before tax and should take into consideration the current market assessment of the time value of money as well as risk specifically associated with the liability. The entity should be careful not to adjust the discount rate and the future cash flows for the same risks as this will result in double-counting of risks.

Restructuring

Restructuring is a programme that is planned and controlled by management, and materially changes either: (1) The scope of an entity's activities; or (2) The manner in which those activities are carried out. The following events depicted in Figure 13.1 may fall under the definition of restructuring:

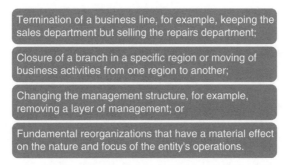

Figure 13.1 Events that may fall under the definition of restructuring

The provision for restructuring cost is only recognized when the general recognition criteria for provisions are met. The definition of a provision requires a past event which gives rise to a legal or a constructive obligation (i.e., present obligation).

A constructive obligation for restructuring arises only when an entity has a detailed plan for the restructuring that identifies at least (see Figure 13.2):

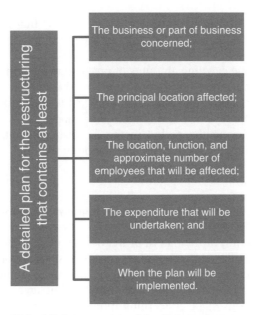

Figure 13.2 Minimum content of detailed plan for restructuring

Should the entity start to implement the plan, announcing its main features to those affected, only after reporting date, the restructuring qualifies as a non-adjusting event after reporting date. In practice, it means that no provision can be recognized at the end of the year, but the information is to be disclosed in the notes to the financial statements.

Additional considerations

Gains from the expected disposals of assets cannot be taken into account in measuring a provision.

Disclosures

The key disclosures for provisions include:

- Provisions as a separate line item on the face of the statement of financial position:
  - A reconciliation of the opening and closing balances of each class of provision in the notes to the financial statements; and
  - The nature of the provision and information on the uncertainty about the amount and/or timing or probability of the outflow of resources.

The reconciliation should show separately the movements relating to the following:

- Additional provisions made in the period, including increases to existing provisions;
- Reductions in the carrying amounts of provisions that result from payments or other outflows of economic benefits or service potential made during the reporting period;
- Reductions in the carrying amounts of provisions resulting from measurement of the estimated future outflow of economic benefits or service potential, or from settlement of the provisions without cost to the entity;
- Unused amounts reversed during the period; and
- The increase during the period in the discounted amount arising from the passage of time and the effect of any change in the discount rate.

Comparative information is not required for the reconciliation to be shown in the notes to the financial statements.

The following should be disclosed for each class of provision (IPSAS 19.98):

- A brief description of the nature of the obligation and the expected timing of any resulting outflows of economic benefits or service potential;
- An indication of the uncertainties as to the amount or timing of those outflows. Where necessary to provide adequate information, an entity shall disclose the major assumptions made concerning future events; and
- The amount of any expected reimbursement, stating the amount of any asset that has been recognized for that expected reimbursement.

It should be noted that this disclosure is not required for other liabilities (for example accruals or other payables).

Where an inflow of economic benefits or service potential is probable, an entity shall disclose a brief description of the nature of the contingent assets at the reporting date, and, where practicable, an estimate of their financial effect.

IPSAS Financial Reporting in Practice 13.1. Provisions Disclosures at IAEA, 2013 Financial Statements

Note 19: Provisions

	(expressed in euro '000s)	
	31/12/2013	**31/12/2012**
Provision for ILOAT cases	41	-
Provision for asset disposal and site restoration	3 067	1 000
Total provisions	**3 108**	**1 000**

148. Provisions for asset disposal and site restoration as on 31 December 2013 included an amount of €1.387 million which represents the present value of the estimated costs expected to be incurred for dismantling/decommissioning of the NML at the end of its useful life. Also included in the provisions are €1.000 million estimated costs to be incurred by the Agency for decontamination and restoration to original condition of the Seibersdorf Analytical Laboratory land in 2015, at the time of expiry of its lease with the Austrian Government, and €0.680 million estimated costs for disposal of glove boxes over the next two years.

149. In February 2014, the Administrative Tribunal of the International Labour Organization (ILOAT) gave a ruling against the Agency in respect of an appeal case filed by a former Agency staff member. Based on this decision, the Agency will be required to make a payment of €0.041 million to the former staff member in 2014. Therefore, a provision for this amount has been recorded in 2013.

In its financial statements for 2013, IAEA has disclosed information relating to two kinds of provisions. The first category relates to provisions for asset disposal and site restoration. The three main items are explained, corresponding to dismantling/decommissioning as well as decontamination and restoration costs at the end of the useful life of some assets or at the time of expiry of a lease contract. The second category relates to a much smaller amount, concerning an ILO (Administrative Tribunal of the International Labour Organization) case. The amount is relatively small, but this type of information is highly sensitive, due to the nature of the case concerning an appeal filed by a former Agency staff member and won by the former staff member after year end. Due to the nature of the case, IAEA has decided to disclose this sensitive information.

IPSAS Financial Reporting in Practice 13.2. Provisions Disclosures at WFP, 2013, Audited Annual Accounts 2013 (pp. 41–42)

Note 2.10: Provisions

	2013	2012
	USD millions	
Provision for refunds to donors	10.7	13.7
Miscellaneous provisions	-	0.6
Total provisions	**10.7**	**14.3**

91. The provision for refunds to donors estimates the level of refunds that are expected to be given back to donors to unspent cash contributions to the project. The provision is based on historical experience.

   92. The change in the provision for refunds to donors during 2013 is as follows:

	2012	Utilization	Increase/ (Decrease)	2013
	USD millions			
Provisions for refunds to donors	**13.7**	**(2.8)**	**(0.2)**	**10.7**

   93. During 2013, refunds made to donors totalled USD 2.8 million. These refunds are recorded as a utilization of the provision for refunds to donors and reported in the Statement of Financial Position. At 31 December 2013, the estimated final provision required is USD 10.7 million. Accordingly, a decrease of USD 0.2 million was recorded as an adjustment to monetary contribution revenue for the period and is reported in the Statement of Financial Performance.

   94. Miscellaneous provisions in 2012 were to meet legal liabilities, advances and payments to be made to the deceased and injured WFP staff who were victims of the 2009 bombing of a WFP country office.

   World Food Programme (WFP) discloses two types of provisions in its financial statements for 2013: provisions for refunds to donors and miscellaneous provisions.

   Provisions for refunds to donors are ongoing provisions, reflecting the estimated level of refunds that are expected to be given back to donors for unspent cash contributions to projects. The estimation is based on judgment and past experience, but, of course, it does not mean that this is the exact amount which will be given back to donors. WFP explains how the provision for refunds to donors varies during 2013.

The other type of provisions, called miscellaneous provisions, in 2012, relate to an exceptional event, namely the 2009 bombing of a WFP country office, and the related legal liabilities, advances, and payments to be made to the deceased and injured WFP staff. Miscellaneous provisions for 2013 are nil.

14 BUDGET REPORTING

In most nation states, resources within the public sector are appropriated to entities by, for example, parliament, the legislatures, or municipal councils through the annual budget process. Budgets therefore provide entities with the authority to incur expenditure to deliver on their mandate.

It is often of significance for users of the financial statements to understand the link between the budget and financial statements and hold entities accountable for their actual activities against what was planned, and how allocated resources were utilized.

In Chapter 2 of this book, the importance of accountability within the public sector was emphasized. Typically entities in all sectors are accountable to their funders and financial supporters and need to demonstrate stewardship of their funds; government and government entities are subject to additional requirements of accountability. An important part of such accountability is achieved through openness in the process of setting financial budgets and reporting actual financial results against such budgets.

Most governments publish their financial budgets. The budget documents are often widely distributed and promoted and reflect the financial characteristics of the government's plans for the forthcoming period. The budget is a key tool for financial management and control and is the central component of the process that provides for government and parliamentary (or similar) oversight of the finances of public sector operations. The reporting by a government of actual results against such approved budgets is an essential part of the accountability process.

For example, fiscal discipline is a pivotal element of macroeconomic stability in the European Union. Therefore the level and composition of government expenditure and revenue, budget deficits and government debt have a significant impact on economic growth, macroeconomic stability, and inflation in the European Union. This is the reason why Member States' budgets have to be presented to the European Commission and have to be endorsed. Budget is one of the most important tools in the European Union.

"The fiscal compact" (as part of the Treaty on Stability, Coordination and Governance in the Economic and Monetary Union – Article 1) foresees the implementation of a balanced budget rule at the national level and a further strengthening of the excessive deficit procedure within the Stability and Growth Pact. President Herman Van Rompuy, during the signing ceremony of the Treaty on Stability, Coordination and Governance, stated that this "Treaty … constitutes an important step in re-establishing the confidence in … Economic and Monetary Union."

EXCESSIVE DEFICIT PROCEDURE

The basic rule of budgetary policy enshrined in the Treaty (the Treaty on Stability, Coordination and Governance in the Economic and Monetary Union) is that Member States shall avoid excessive government deficits. Compliance with this rule is to be examined on the basis of reference values for the general government deficit (3%) and gross debt (60%) in relation to GDP, whereby a number of qualifications can be applied.

In particular, only an exceptional and temporary excess of the deficit over the reference value can be exempt from being considered excessive, and then only if it remains close to the reference value. The decision as to whether a Member State is in a situation of excessive deficit lies with the ECOFIN Council, acting upon a proposal from the European Commission.

If the Council decides that a Member State is in a situation of excessive deficit, the excessive deficit procedure provides for the necessary steps to be taken. These could lead to imposing sanctions on the country concerned.

STABILITY AND GROWTH PACT

The Stability and Growth Pact provides an operational clarification of the Treaty's budgetary rules. It defines the procedures for multilateral budgetary surveillance (preventive arm) as well as the conditions under which to apply the excessive deficit procedure (corrective arm). The Pact is an essential part of the macroeconomic framework of the Economic and Monetary Union. By requesting Member States to coordinate their budgetary policies and to avoid excessive deficits, it contributes to achieving macroeconomic stability in the EU and plays a key role in securing low inflation and low interest rates, which are essential contributions for delivering sustainable economic growth and job creation.

The main rationale of the Stability and Growth Pact is to ensure sound budgetary policies on a permanent basis. The Pact lays down the obligation for Member States to adhere to the medium-term objectives for their budgetary positions of "close to balance or in surplus," as defined under country-specific considerations. Adjusting to such positions will allow Member States to deal with normal cyclical fluctuations without breaching the 3% of GDP reference value for the government deficit."[1]

In addition, some individual entities in the public sector may be required, or may elect, to make their approved budget(s) publicly available. For instance, intergovernmental organizations are mostly funded thanks to mandatory and/or voluntary contributions from their Member States. They are usually required to make their

---

[1] See http://www.ecb.europa.eu/mopo/eaec/fiscal/html/index.en.html.

approved budget(s) publicly available. In such cases, the entity will also be held publicly accountable for its compliance with, and performance against, its approved budget(s).

For instance, the OECD budget is funded as follows:

> The Organisation is funded primarily by assessed and voluntary contributions from its member countries, within the framework of a biennial Programme of Work and Budget.
>
> The Budget is the act whereby Council accords the necessary commitment authorisations and makes the necessary appropriations for the functioning of the Organisation and the carrying out of its activities. It determines the amount of contributions to be paid by members after taking into account other resources of the Organisation. All of the Organisation's member countries fund the Budget for Part I programmes, accounting for about 50% of the consolidated Budget. Their contributions are based on both a proportion that is shared equally and a scale proportional to the relative size of their economies. Part II Budgets include programmes of interest to a limited number of members and/or relating to sectors of activity not covered by Part I. Part II programmes are funded according to a scale of contributions or other financing arrangements agreed among the participating countries. Annex Budgets are established for certain specific activities such as the Pension, Investments and Publications. The pre-accession budget relates to nonrecurring costs associated with accession that are borne by the candidate countries. Note 23 gives further details of the income and expenditure budget and actual results for 2013.[2]

THE ROLE OF IPSAS 24 ON PRESENTATION OF BUDGET INFORMATION IN FINANCIAL STATEMENTS

IPSAS 24 Presentation of Budget Information in Financial Statements sets out reporting requirements for governments and other public sector entities to meet the need for accountability in the public sector. There is no International Financial Reporting Standard (IFRS) equivalent to IPSAS 24, as the private sector is not subject to the same accountability demands as the public sector. Where governments, such as the UK, have adopted IFRS as the basis of public sector financial reporting then, in addition to having regard to any relevant legislative or regulatory requirements to report on budget information, they may also have regard to IPSAS 24.

IPSAS 24, which is unique, is therefore a fundamental standard to consider for financial reporting and accountability under IPSAS in the public sector.

As described above, budget is one of the most important tools in the European Union. This is why Member States' budgets have to be presented to the European Commission and have to be endorsed. IPSAS 24 can be a supplementary tool allowing the European Commission to have an overview, not only of Member States' budgets, but also of the outturn of these budgets. It would therefore oblige Member States to present the outturn of their budget, and to be accountable for their budget outturn. This is a very powerful, very useful tool for stakeholders.

---

[2] OECD (2013) Financial Statements, see note 1: General information, p. 8.

APPLYING IPSAS 24 ON THE PRESENTATION OF BUDGET INFORMATION IN FINANCIAL STATEMENTS

IPSAS 24 applies to all entities which are required to, or choose to, make their approved budgets publicly available. IPSAS 24 does not require budgets to be made publicly available, nor does it require that financial statements disclose information about, or make comparison with, budgets which are not made publicly available.

For instance, the budget of the World Health Organization (WHO) is made publicly available. Under IPSAS, the WHO is to report the outturn of its budget in its financial statements according to IPSAS 24 (WHO, 2013a). See Example 14.1 for an illustration of this.

Example 14.1 WHO Proposed programme budget 2014–2015 to the 66th World Health Assembly

Table 1. Proposed programme budget 2014–2015 by category (US$ million)

Category	Programme budget 2012–2013[a]	Percentage of total	Proposed programme budget 2014–2015	Percentage of total	Change in proposed programme budget 2014–2015 to 2012–2013	Percentage change in proposed programme budget 2014–2015 to 2012–2013
1. Communicable diseases	913	23.1	841	21.1	−72	−7.9
2. Noncommunicable diseases	264	6.7	318	8.0	54	20.5
3. Promoting health through the life-course	353	8.9	388	9.8	35	9.9
4. Health systems	490	12.4	531	13.4	41	8.4
5. Preparedness, surveillance and response	218	5.5	287	7.2	69	31.7
6. Corporate services/enabling functions	622	15.7	684[c]	17.2	62	10.0
Emergencies						
Polio eradication	596	15.1	700	17.6	104	17.4
Outbreak and crisis response	469	11.8	228	5.7	−241	−51.4
Total	**3 959**[b]	*100*	**3 977**	**100**	**18**	**0.5**

[a] The programme budget was approved by the World Health Authority in resolution WHA64.3.

[b] The total for the Programme budget 2012–2013 includes US$ 28.8 million for the Stop TB Partnership and US$ 5 million for the European Observatory on Health Systems and Policies. For comparative purposes they have been removed from Categories 1 and 4 respectively.

[c] Category 6 represents the costs of the Organization for corporate services and enabling functions within the programme budget. In addition, US$ 139 million is charged directly to all Categories to recover the costs of administrative services directly attributable to these programmes through a Post Occupancy Charge as an integral component of standard staff costs. The full cost of Category 6 is therefore US$ 823 million.

IPSAS 24 is written primarily for governments and intergovernmental organizations which have a parliamentary or similar process for formal approval of budgets but may equally apply to other entities, such as local authorities whose budgets are made available to local taxpayers.

IPSAS 24 aims to ensure that public sector entities demonstrate accountability and enhance the transparency of their financial statements by showing how they have complied with the approved budget(s) for which they are held publicly accountable and therefore requires:

- A comparison of budget amounts and the actual amounts to be included in the financial statements of entities which are required to, or elect to, make their approved budget(s) publicly available and for which they are, therefore, held publicly accountable;
- As well as disclosure of an explanation of the reasons for material differences between the budget and actual amounts.

Where the budgets(s) and the financial statements are prepared on the same basis, entities will also demonstrate their financial performance in achieving the budgeted results.

Different terms are currently used to describe budgets. It is useful to define the following terms in Table 14.1:

Table 14.1 Budget reporting terminology

Term	Definition
Annual budget	An approved budget for one year. It does not include published forward estimates or projections for periods beyond the budget period.
Approved budget	The expenditure authority derived from laws, appropriation bills, government ordinances, and other decisions related to the anticipated revenue or receipts for the budgetary period.
Budgetary basis	The basis (e.g., accruals basis, cash basis, or modified cash basis) used in the budget.
Comparable basis	The actual amounts are presented on the same accounting basis, same classification basis, for the same entities, and for the same period as the approved budget.
Final budget	The original budget adjusted for all reserves, carry over amounts, transfers, allocations, supplemental appropriations, and other authorized legislative, or similar authority, changes applicable to the budget period.
Original budget	The initial approved budget for the budget period.
Multiyear budget	An approved budget for more than one year. It does not include published forward estimates or projections for periods beyond the budget period.

The Nature of Budgets

An approved budget may be derived from laws, appropriation bills, government ordinances, and/or other decisions:

- Generally for a government some form of legislation will set out the broad requirements for the content, timing, and approval process;
- For intergovernmental organizations, statutes and financial regulations will usually define the requirements for the content, timing, and approval process;
- For other entities the requirements are likely to be less formal, but a minimum requirement is likely to be approval by an authorized body.

An approved budget reflects the revenues or receipts expected to arise in the budget period based on current plans and expected economic conditions. For a government it generally provides authority to withdraw funds from the government treasury or similar body up to specified limits for agreed and identified purposes. A budget is not, in principle, simply a forecast of expected income and expenditure but frequently sets a formal legal limit within which an entity must operate. Entities other than a government may have other approaches or limitations (IPSAS 24.8, 24.9).

IPSAS 24 deals with all kinds of budgets which may be set:

- To cover expenditure only, income and expenditure, cash flows, and/or components of the statement of financial position;
- Generally for a period of one year or longer periods (multiyear budgets). Multiyear budgets may or may not be easily divisible into annual figures for comparison with actual annual financial results.

Governments and other entities may set a first or original budget(s) and a final budget(s). Adjustments to original budgets may be made for reserves, commitments, transfers between budget heads, expenditure not envisaged, or shortfalls in revenues. The final budget is taken to include all such authorized changes or amendments (IPSAS 24.12).

IPSAS 24 does not prescribe the form, approval process, period, legal status, adjustment process, or other requirements of a budget, which are beyond its power. IPSAS 24 deals with the presentation of the outturn of the budget (whatever format it may have) in order to provide users with useful information to assess performance of the entity in terms of its service cost, efficiency, and accomplishment in relation with the adopted budget.

Financial Statement Presentation

A comparison of the budget amounts and actual amounts should be presented:

- Either as a separate additional financial statement;
- Or as additional columns in the financial statements (IPSAS 24.14).

The choice of presentation may depend on how similar the form of the budget is to the required financial information to be presented.

The use of additional budget columns in the financial statements is only allowed where the financial statements and the budget are prepared on a comparable basis.

A comparable basis means the same basis of accounting (whether cash, accruals, or other), for the same entities and reporting period, and adoption of the same classification structure (IPSAS 24.21).

The standard stresses the importance of comparability. The inclusion of budget figures which are not directly comparable to the financial statement figures would be meaningless and confusing.

In many cases, budgets are not designed under IPSAS. Budget is therefore rarely presented on the face of the financial statements as an additional column. This may change in the coming years.

When the budget and financial statements are not prepared on a comparable basis (for example, where financial statements are prepared on an accruals basis but budgets are prepared on a cash basis), a separate statement must be presented. IPSAS 24 suggests "Statement of Comparison of Budget and Actual Amounts" as a title. This statement must follow the budget basis of reporting and may therefore be presented on a different basis of accounting from the financial statements; it may cover a different set of entities (for example excluding commercial and market entities in accordance with a statistical reporting system), or a different period. An explanation needs to be given of the differences in bases (IPSAS 24.23 and 24.31).

Where the budget and financial statements are not prepared on a comparable basis, the actual amounts presented on a comparable basis to the budget in the Statement of Comparison should be reconciled to the amounts in the financial statements, identifying separately any basis,[3] timing,[4] and entity differences.

Such reconciliation shall be made to the following actual amounts in the financial statements (IPSAS 24.47):

- If the accrual basis is adopted in the budget, total revenues, total expenses, and net cash flows from operating activities, investing activities, and financing activities;
- If a basis other than the accrual basis is adopted for the budget, net cash flows from operating activities, investing activities, and financing activities.

This information is required in order to demonstrate to a reader that the actual figures in the budget comparison are derived from the accounting records which underlie the official financial statements.

The reconciliation can be presented either on the face of the Statement of Comparison or in the notes to the financial statements. The reconciliation may be split into basis differences, where the accounting basis is different (for example cash and accrual), timing differences, when the budget period differs from the period reflected in the financial statements, or entity differences, when the budget omits certain entities included in the financial statements (IPSAS 24.47 and 24.48).

---

[3] This would be the basis on which the budget was prepared vis-à-vis the financial statement, for example, if the budget is prepared on a cash basis while the financial statements are prepared using accrual-based accounting standards.

[4] If there is a deviance between the timing of the budget vis-à-vis the financial statements. In some public sector entities, bi-annual budgets are prepared, while the financial statements are prepared on an annual basis. The other timing aspect is that of the financial year for the financial statements and the budget period.

WHO has chosen to split the reconciliation into basis differences, timing differences, and entity differences, as shown in IPSAS Financial Reporting in Practice 14.1.

IPSAS Financial Reporting in Practice 14.1. Budget Reporting at WHO, 2013 Financial Statements (p. 27)

World Health Organization

Statement V. Statement of Comparison of Budget and Actual Amounts

For the year ended 31 December 2013 (In US dollars)

	Programme budget 2012–2013	Expenses 2013	Expenses 2012	Total expenses 2012–2013	Difference – programme budget and expenses
Strategic objectives					
1. Communicable diseases	1 278 130 000	762 322 493	614 022 050	1 376 344 543	(98 214 543)
2. HIV/AIDS, tuberculosis and malaria	540 298 000	206 452 907	181 714 613	388 167 520	152 130 480
3. Chronic noncommunicable conditions	113 763 000	60 592 478	47 412 836	108 005 314	5 757 686
4. Child, adolescent, maternal, sexual and reproductive health, and ageing	218 306 000	123 729 088	97 672 590	221 401 678	(3 095 678)
5. Emergencies and disasters	382 028 000	184 685 626	144 162 271	328 847 897	53 180 103
6. Risk factors for health	122 255 000	48 660 814	44 776 525	93 437 339	28 817 661
7. Social and economic determinants of health	42 789 000	20 423 214	16 849 129	37 272 343	5 516 657
8. Healthier environment	86 825 000	43 581 261	38 854 554	82 435 815	4 389 185
9. Nutrition, food safety and food security	54 898 000	32 767 090	27 154 471	59 921 561	(5 023 561)
10. Health systems and services	348 093 000	168 408 576	134 846 988	303 255 564	44 837 436
11. Medical products and technologies	137 283 000	74 693 751	61 909 715	136 603 466	679 534
12. WHO leadership, governance, and partnerships	257 570 000	128 496 424	124 325 224	252 821 648	4 748 352
13. Enabling and support functions	376 741 000	180 190 310	159 979 398	340 169 708	36 571 292
Total	**3 958 979 000**	**2 035 004 032**	**1 693 680 363**	**3 728 684 425**	**230 294 605**

Basis differences		
In-kind/in-service expenses	38 562 107	44 681 506
Transfer from assessed contributions to Real Estate Fund	10 000 000	-
Tax Equalization Fund expenses	11 423 628	14 533 591
Other non-programme budget utilization	749 426	6 601 885
Common Fund activities	24 156 690	1 079 242
Total basis differences	**84 891 851**	**66 896 224**
Timing differences		
Programme budget expenses in prior periods	(4 805 730)	125 153 581
Total timing differences	**(4 805 730)**	**125 153 581**
Entity differences		
Expenses under Common Fund, Enterprise Fund, Special Purpose Fund, and Fiduciary Fund	145 908 175	194 947 377
Total entity differences	**145 908 175**	**194 947 377**
Total expenses as per the Statement of Financial Performance (Statement II)	**2 260 998 329**	**2 080 677 545**

On the face of the Statement of Comparison or in the notes to the financial statements of WHO for 2013, basis differences refer to the difference in scope between budget and accounting records. For instance, Common Fund Activities are not included in specific lines of the budget.

Timing differences are due to the fact that, for budget purposes, when the entity is committed to an agreement, it has to be deducted from the budget. However, the delivery of goods or services may take place later on. This is why Programme budget expenses which were expensed in the budget of prior periods have to be expensed in accounting the year the goods or the services are delivered. Budget recording and accounting records are different and it is therefore very important to communicate appropriately, whether in relation to budget outturn or to surplus/deficit of the year as stated on the statement of financial performance.

Both the original and final budget amounts should be shown, with an explanation of whether changes from the original budget to the final budget are a consequence of reallocation within the budget or other factors. The explanation can be shown in the notes to the financial statements or in a separate report, with a cross-reference to the report in the notes to the financial statements (IPSAS 24.29).

This requirement is particularly relevant where changes to budgets require a formal and public approval process. The explanation of differences between original and final budgets is considered important in terms of accountability and provides useful input for analysis of the financial effects of changing economic conditions and of policy shifts.

A simple example of a note disclosure is given in the Implementation Guidance to IPSAS 24:

"The original budget was approved by legislative action on [date] and a supplemental appropriation of XXX for disaster relief support was approved by legislative action on [date] due to the earthquake in the Northern Region on [date]. The original budget objectives and policies, and subsequent revisions, are explained more fully in the Operational Review and Budget Outcomes reports issued in conjunction with the financial statements". This example refers to the major difference in a footnote with cross-reference to other published documents for more detail.

Material differences between the budget and actual amounts need to be explained, either by way of note disclosure or in a separate report issued alongside the financial statements, with a cross-reference in the notes (IPSAS 24.14c). The explanation might be given in management discussion and analysis, operations review, or other public report.

This requirement is one of the most significant in terms of accountability, as it confirms, or otherwise, the robustness of the entity's budget process and may identify unexpected or unusual items of income or expenditure of which the public should be aware. Explanations need not be very detailed but should be sufficient to describe the nature and reasons for significant differences.

Where budgets are prepared in great detail, amounts will need to be aggregated for presentation in financial statements to avoid information overload (IPSAS 24.25–24.28). Readers of financial statements are not helped by excessive detail although such detail may be important in controlling expenditure at the operational level.

Where multiyear budgets are prepared, entities will need to use judgment in determining the allocation of budgets to particular years. Entities are encouraged to provide additional note disclosure about the relationship between budget and actual amounts during the budget period (IPSAS 24.37–24.38).

To summarize, Figure 14.1 helps to provide an overview of the presentation and disclosure requirements under IPSAS 24.

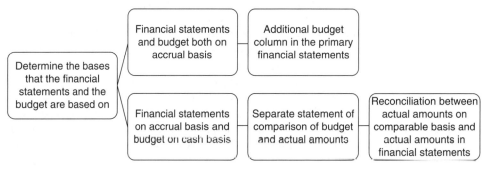

Figure 14.1   Presentation and disclosure of budget information

Disclosure Requirements

The notes to the financial statements should explain the budgetary basis and classification basis adopted in the approved budget (IPSAS 24.39).

There may be differences between the accounting basis used in preparation and presentation of the budget and the accounting basis used in the financial statements, for example the budget may be on a cash or modified cash basis. Formats and classifications may also differ, for example the budget may be based on the economic classification of expenses (e.g., employee costs, costs of goods and services, etc.) rather than the functional one (e.g., health, education, etc.), or be linked to performance outcome objectives (IPSAS 24.41).

The notes should:

- State the period of the approved budget (IPSAS 24.43). Generally, the period will match that of the financial statements, but if that is not the case, for example with multiyear budgets, this fact will need to be disclosed to make the statements understandable.
- Give details of the entities included in the approved budget (IPSAS 24.45). While the financial statements may include all resources controlled by an entity on a consolidated basis, approved budgets may not cover all such entities, for example entities operating on a commercial or market basis. Disclosure of the entities included in the budget is necessary for an understanding of the difference in scope.

WHO has, for example, disclosed the following note supporting information to the Statement of Comparison of Budget and Actual Amounts, and has even included reconciliation with the actual amounts in the Statement of Cash Flow.

IPSAS Financial Reporting in Practice 14.2. Supporting Note Disclosure to Statement of Comparison of Budget and Actual Amounts at WHO, 2013 Financial Statements (pp. 66–67).

7. Supporting information to the Statement of Comparison of Budget and Actual Amounts

In May 2011, the Health Assembly adopted resolution WHA64.3, the appropriation resolution for the financial period 2012–2013, in which it noted the total effective budget of US$ 3959 million. WHO's budget is adopted on a biennial basis by the Health Assembly. No revisions have been made to the Programme budget 2012–2013. As the Organization's methodology is based on a results-based framework, the approved programme budget is measured on expenses incurred during the programme budget period.

WHO's budget and financial statements are prepared using different accounting bases. The Statement of Financial Position, Statement of Financial Performance, Statement of Changes in Net Assets/Equity, and Statement of Cash Flow are prepared on a full accrual basis, whereas the budget is established on a modified cash basis (i.e. actual expenses are used to measure the budget utilization).

As per the requirements of IPSAS 24, the actual amounts presented on a comparable basis to the budget shall, where the financial statements and the budget are not prepared on a comparable basis, be reconciled to the actual amounts presented in the financial statements, identifying separately any differences in terms of basis, timing, entity and presentation. The General Fund, as per Note 2.17, represents the programme budget results, except for the Tax Equalization Fund expenses, other non-programme budget utilization and all in-kind/in-service expenses which are not included in the programme budget results.

Explanations of material differences between the final budget and the actual amounts are available in document A67/42, which describes the implementation of the Programme budget 2012–2013 and the results achieved.

As required by IPSAS 24, a reconciliation is provided on a comparable basis between the actual amounts as presented in Statement V and the actual amounts in the financial accounts identifying separately any basis, timing, entity and presentation differences.

Basis differences occur when the components of the approved programme budget are used for activities other than the implementation of technical programmes. Examples of this include Tax Equalization Fund expenses, in-kind/in-service expenses, other non-programme budget utilization and other Common Fund activities.

Timing differences represent the inclusion in WHO's financial accounts of programme budget expenses in other financial periods.

Entity differences represent the inclusion in WHO's financial accounts of the amounts against two funds, Member States – other and the Fiduciary Fund. These funds do not form part of the Organization's programme budget.

Presentation differences concern differences in the format and classification schemes in the Statement of Cash Flow and the Statement of Comparison of Budget and Actual Amounts.

A reconciliation between the actual amounts on a comparable basis in the Statement of Comparison of Budget and Actual Amounts (Statement V) and the actual amounts in the Statement of Cash Flow (Statement IV) for December 2013 is presented below.

	2013			
	Operating	**Investing**	**Financing**	**Total**
Actual amount on a comparable basis (Statement V)	(2 035 004 032)	–	–	(2 035 004 032)
Basis differences	84 891 851	(426 252 917)	(2 967 805)	(344 328 871)
Timing differences	(4 805 730)	–	–	(4 805 730)
Entity differences	145 908 175	9 177 217	–	155 085 392
Presentation differences	2 209 536 583	–	–	2 209 536 583
Actual amount in the Statement of Cash Flow (Statement IV)	**400 526 847**	**(417 075 700)**	**(2 967 805)**	**(19 516 658)**

WHO, in order to facilitate the understanding of the differences between amounts in the Statement of Comparison of Budget and Actual Amounts and amounts in the Statement of Cash Flow for 2013, explains that they are prepared using different accounting bases, and discloses how the reconciliation was settled, identifying basis, timing, entity, and presentation differences.

The disclosure of comparative information for the previous year in respect of the requirements of the standard is not required. A comparison of the budget amount and actual amount is only required for the period to which the financial statements relate (IPSAS 24.52). It is considered that budget reporting for previous periods would result in information overload and would not be in the interest of users of the financial statements. The focus of IPSAS 24 is rather on supporting the discharge of the entity's obligation to be accountable for its compliance with the approved budget for the current reporting period.

15 FINANCIAL INSTRUMENTS

Public sector entities can enter into complex financial transactions to reduce their exposure to risks. Recent financial crisis has led many governments to intervene in various ways, including by taking an investment in financial institutions that needed a capital injection or by purchasing "toxic" financial assets (Schumesh et al., 2012).

This means that public sector entities invest, directly or indirectly, significant amounts in financial assets. The nature of these complex financial transactions has led to entities adopting different accounting practices, with increased use of fair values and extensive application of hedge accounting techniques (i.e., offsetting).

As financial instruments become more complex and commonplace, clear and full disclosure becomes increasingly important.

Three standards have been published by the IPSASB to cover the accounting and financial reporting of financial instruments:

- IPSAS 28 Financial Instruments Presentation;
- IPSAS 29 Financial Instruments: Recognition and Measurement;
- IPSAS 30 Financial Instruments: Disclosures.

The underlying principle of these standards is to limit off balance sheet items, and therefore to record all financial instruments (including derivatives) on the balance sheet in order to show risks to stakeholders and readers of the financial statements.

WHAT IS A FINANCIAL INSTRUMENT?

A financial instrument is any contract that gives rise to a financial asset of one entity and a financial liability or equity instrument of another entity (see IPSAS 28.9) – Table 15.1.

Table 15.1 Definition of financial asset and financial liability

Definition	A **financial asset** is any asset that is: (a) cash; (b) an equity instrument of another entity; or (c) a contractual right to receive cash or another financial asset or to exchange financial assets or financial liabilities with another entity under conditions that are potentially favorable to the entity.	A **financial liability** is either: (a) a contractual obligation to deliver cash or another financial asset; or (b) a contractual obligation to exchange financial assets or liabilities with another entity on potentially unfavorable terms.	An equity instrument is a contract where an entity has an interest in the net assets (assets less liabilities) of another entity.
Examples	Cash, trade receivables, and equity investments	Trade payables and loans	

A financial asset is defined as shown in Figure 15.1:

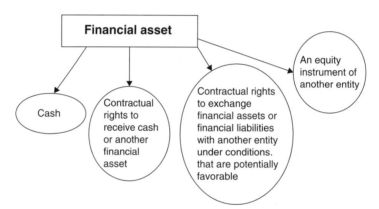

Figure 15.1 Definition of a financial asset

A financial liability is defined as shown in Figure 15.2:

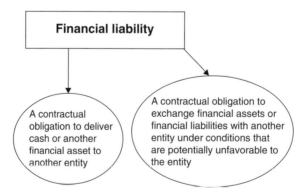

Figure 15.2 Definition of a financial liability

The definition of financial assets and liabilities is very broad since it includes loans, borrowings, derivatives, but also trade receivables, trade payables, cash and cash equivalents.

Financial assets and liabilities include cash and cash equivalents, which are defined as cash in current accounts at the bank and on hand, as well as short-term, highly liquid investments that are readily convertible to known amounts of cash and which are subject to an insignificant risk of change in value (IPSAS 2.8). This definition seems straightforward at first sight. However, it is worthwhile to understand what types of "highly liquid investments that are readily convertible to known amounts of cash and which are subject to an insignificant risk of changes in value" can be considered as cash equivalents. The scope of cash and cash equivalents is often a matter of judgment.

In its financial statements excerpted in Financial Reporting in Practice 15.1, IAEA describes what are considered to be cash and cash equivalents.

IPSAS Financial Reporting in Practice 15.1. Cash and Cash Equivalents, IAEA 2013 Financial Statements for 2013, Gov/2014/14 (p. 47)

Note 4: Cash and cash equivalents

	(expressed in euro '000)	
	31/12/2013	**31/12/2012**
Cash in current accounts at bank and on hand	19 101	10 889
Cash in call accounts	36 224	43 630
Term deposits with original maturities of 3 months or less	26 000	114 816
Treasury bills with original maturities of 3 months or less	9 996	–
Total cash and cash equivalents	**91 321**	**169 335**

81. The decrease of €78.014 million (46.1%) in the total cash and cash equivalents is due to a shift towards term deposits and other investments with original maturities between 3 and 12 months (refer to Note 5). This shift was mainly driven by the continued very low interest rates on term deposits with original maturities of less than three months. Despite this shift, the weighted average period to maturity of the total cash and cash equivalents and investments holdings of the Agency remained under three months as per Note 38.

82. Some cash is held in currencies which are either legally restricted or not readily convertible to euros. At 31 December 2013, the euro equivalent of these currencies was €1.006 million (€1.324 million at 31 December 2012), based on the respective United Nations operational rates of exchange.

Cash and cash equivalents, as disclosed in the IAEA financial statements above, include cash in current accounts at the bank and on hand, as well as term deposits with

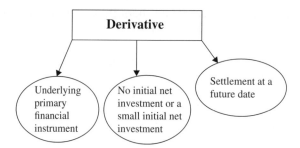

Figure 15.3   Definition of a derivative

original maturities of three months or less and treasury bills with original maturities of three months or less.

Moreover, IAEA, as recommended in IPSAS 2.61, describes the amount and nature of restricted cash balances: cash held in currencies which are either legally restricted or not readily convertible to euros. It is important to inform readers of the financial statements that some cash is of restricted use.

Assets that have physical substance, such as property and machinery, are not financial assets and neither are intangible assets, such as patents and brands. These assets generate future economic benefits for an entity although there is no contractual right to receive cash or another financial asset.

In addition, a financial asset arises where a contract may be settled in the entity's own equity instruments, for which the entity will receive either a variable number of its own equity instruments, or a derivative that may be settled other than by the exchange of a fixed amount of cash or another financial asset for a fixed number of its own equity instruments (IPSAS 28.9).

A financial liability arises where a contract may be settled in the entity's own equity instruments, for which the entity will deliver either a variable number of its own equity instruments, or a derivative that may be settled other than by the exchange of a fixed amount of cash or another financial asset for a fixed number of its own equity instruments (IPSAS 28.9).

Financial instruments include both primary instruments (e.g., receivables, payables and equity securities) and derivative financial instruments (e.g., financial options, futures and forwards, interest rate swaps, and currency swaps).

A derivative is a type of financial instrument (see Figure 15.3) that has specific characteristics, as set out below (IPSAS 29.10):

- Its value changes in response to the change in a specified interest rate, financial instrument price, commodity price, foreign exchange rate, index of prices or rates, credit rating or credit index, or other variable.
- It requires no initial net investment or an initial net investment that is smaller than would be required for other types of contracts that would be expected to have a similar response to changes in market factors.
- It is settled at a future date.

The underlying can be a specified interest rate, financial instrument price, commodity price, foreign exchange rate, index of prices or rates, credit rating or credit index, or other variable, provided in the case of a non-financial variable that the variable is not specific to a party to the contract (IPSAS 29.10).

FINANCIAL INSTRUMENTS: PRESENTATION

IPSAS 28 sets out the principles for presenting financial instruments as liabilities or net assets/equity, and for offsetting financial assets and financial liabilities. Their presentation requirements are consistent with, and complement, those of IPSAS 29, which addresses recognition and measurement criteria and IPSAS 30 which covers the disclosure requirements for financial instruments.

IPSAS 28 applies to all entities and to all types of financial instruments, except where another standard is more specific.

The main principle is that a financial instrument, or its components, should be classified, upon initial recognition by the issuer, as a financial liability, a financial asset, or an equity instrument according to the substance of the contract and the definitions of a financial liability, a financial asset, and an equity instrument (IPSAS 28.13).

According to IPSAS 28.14, some exceptions to this principle exist. This will lead to financial instruments that meet the definition of a financial liability being classified as equity because they represent the residual interest in the net assets of the entity. The two exceptions identified are:

- Puttable instruments meeting specific criteria:
    In case of a puttable financial instrument, the issuer has a contractual obligation to repurchase or redeem the instrument against cash or another financial asset on exercise of the put. As an exception to the definition of a financial liability, an instrument that includes such an obligation is classified as an equity instrument if it has all of the features as described in IPSAS 28.15.
- Obligations to deliver a pro rata share of the net assets of the entity on liquidation.

An issuer of a financial instrument may have a contractual obligation to deliver to another entity a pro rata share of its net assets only on liquidation. The obligation arises because liquidation either is certain to occur and outside the control of the entity (e.g., a limited life entity) or is uncertain to occur but is at the option of the instrument holder. As an exception to the definition of a financial liability, an instrument that includes such an obligation is classified as an equity instrument if it has all of the features as described in IPSAS 28.17.

A contract is not an equity instrument solely because it may result in the receipt or delivery of the entity's own equity instruments. A financial instrument is an equity instrument only when (IPSAS 28.14):

(a) The instrument includes no contractual obligation to:
    (i) Deliver cash or another financial asset to another entity;

      (ii) Exchange financial assets or financial liabilities with another entity under conditions that are potentially unfavorable to the issuer;

  (b) If the instrument will or may be settled in the issuer's own equity instruments, it is:

      (i) A non-derivative that includes no contractual obligation for the issuer to deliver a variable number of its own equity instruments;

      (ii) A derivative that will be settled only by the issuer exchanging a fixed amount of cash or another financial asset for a fixed number of its own equity instruments.

IPSAS 28 also applies to a contract to buy and sell non-financial items that can be settled by exchanging cash or another financial instrument (such as a commodities contract), provided the contract is not in accordance with the entity's expected purchase, sale, or usage requirements (i.e., the contract is of an investment nature) (IPSAS 28.49).

Financial instruments are classified as current or non-current assets/liabilities depending on their maturity (see IPSAS Financial Reporting in Practice 15.2).

IPSAS Financial Reporting in Practice 15.2. Financial instruments, IAEA, 2013 Financial Statements (p. 92)

NOTE 38: Financial Instrument Disclosures

216. All financial assets and liabilities are carried at their amortized cost. Given the short-term nature of the Agency's financial assets and liabilities, their carrying value represents a reasonable estimate of their fair value.

217. The Agency's activities expose it to credit risk, liquidity risk, currency risk and interest rate risk. Detailed information on the Agency's management of each of these risks and the related exposures is provided in the following sections. From an overall perspective, the Agency's investment management objective prioritizes capital preservation as its primary objective, ensuring sufficient liquidity to meet cash operating requirements, and then earning a competitive rate of return on its portfolio within these constraints. Capital preservation and liquidity are emphasized over the rate of return. Currently, no investment can be longer than one year.

The above example shows that IAEA has chosen to focus on capital preservation and liquidity risk rather than on the rate of return, and, therefore, to investment in instruments which cannot be longer than one year. All investments are classified as current assets, as disclosed in their note 5 below (see IPSAS Financial Reporting in Practice 15.3).

IPSAS Financial Reporting in Practice 15.3. Financial Instruments, IAEA, 2013 Financial Statements (p. 47)

NOTE 5: Investments

	(expressed in euro '000)	
	31/12/2013	**31/12/2012**
Term deposits with original maturities between 3 and 12 months	290 794	245 572
Treasury bills with original maturities between 3 and 12 months	65 854	57 681
Other discounted notes	18 123	–
Total investments	374 771	303 253

83. The increase of €71.518 million (23.6%) in investments is the result of a shift from investments in instruments with original maturities of three months or less (reported in cash and cash equivalents in Note 4 above) towards investments in instruments with original maturities between 3 and 12 months.

Compound Financial Instrument

A compound financial instrument is one that contains both a liability component and an equity component. Such components should be classified separately according to their substance (IPSAS 28.33).

A compound instrument should be split into its component parts at the date that it is issued. The split should not be revised for subsequent changes in market interest rates, share prices, or other events that change the likelihood that the conversion option will be exercised (IPSAS 28.34–28.35).

The initial carrying amount of a compound financial instrument should be split into its equity and liability components; after deducting from the fair value of the instrument as a whole the amount that was determined for the liability component, the residual is allocated as the net assets/equity component (IPSAS 28.37). A convertible bond is an example of a compound instrument, since it has a debt element and a potential equity element (on conversion).

The economic effect of issuing the convertible bond is the same as issuing a non-convertible bond and an option to purchase shares. The value of the convertible bond should therefore be split into its component parts to reflect the substance of the instrument. An entity should estimate the fair value of the component parts.

Interest, Dividends, Losses, and Gains

Interest, dividends or similar distributions, losses, and gains relating to a financial instrument or a component that is a financial liability shall be recognized as revenue or expense in surplus or deficit. Distributions to holders of an equity instrument shall be recognized directly in net assets/equity, net of any related income tax benefit. Transaction costs incurred on transactions in net assets/equity shall be accounted for as a deduction from net assets/equity, net of any related income tax benefit (IPSAS 28.40).

OFFSETTING

Financial assets and financial liabilities should be offset and presented net in the statement of financial position when the entity:

- Has a legally enforceable right to set off the amounts recognized;
- Intends either to settle on a net basis, or to realize the asset and settle the liability simultaneously (IPSAS 28.47).

FINANCIAL INSTRUMENTS: RECOGNITION AND MEASUREMENT

IPSAS 29 establishes principles for recognizing (and derecognizing) and measuring financial assets and financial liabilities and some contracts to buy or sell non-financial items. The scope of this standard is consistent with IPSAS 28. However there are a number of additional exceptions to their application. What is within and outside the scope is summarized in Table 15.2:

Table 15.2   IPSAS 29 scoping

Within scope	Out of scope
Subsidiaries, associates and joint ventures;	Debt and equity investments;
Employee benefits;	Originated loans;
Insurance contracts;	Own debt;
Financial instruments, contracts, and obligations under share-based payment transactions;	Derivatives;
	Interest rate swaps;
A contract in a business combination to buy or sell an entity at a future date;	Currency forwards/swaps;
	Purchased/written options; and
Certain loan commitments; and	Most commodity contracts
Rights to payment to reimburse an entity to settle a provision.	

Liabilities in relation to financial guarantee contracts are within the scope of IPSAS 29.

A financial guarantee contract is defined as being one that requires the issuer to make specified payments to reimburse any loss that the holder may make where the debtor has failed to make the required payments when they were due as set out in the terms of the debt instrument (IPSAS 29.10).

The principle of initial recognition of financial instruments is shown in Figure 15.4:

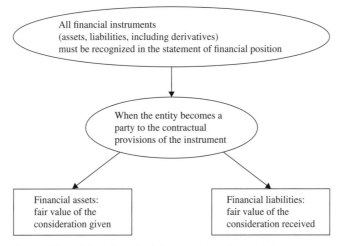

Figure 15.4 Principle of initial recognition of financial instruments

Financial Assets and Liabilities

A financial asset or financial liability should be recognized when an entity enters into the contractual provisions of the financial instrument (IPSAS 29.16). The value at which a financial asset or financial liability should originally be measured is its fair value plus, in certain circumstances, any directly attributable transaction costs, such as fees and commissions paid to brokers and advisers (IPSAS 29.45).

For subsequent measurement of financial assets, the treatment depends on the categorization of the financial asset, as explained below.

Where an entity holds investments in equity instruments that do not have a quoted price in an active market and it is not possible to calculate their fair values reliably, they should be measured at cost. Derivatives that are linked to such investments, or require the delivery of such an investment, should also be measured at cost (IPSAS 29.48).

An entity is required to consider whether financial assets are impaired (carried at more than their recoverable amount) at the end of each reporting period. Impairment is where an event has occurred after the initial recognition of a financial asset and that event results in a detrimental effect on the cash flows expected in relation to the item. No account is taken of losses that are expected to arise as a result of future events (IPSAS 29.67).

IPSAS 29 define four categories of financial instrument:

- A financial asset (or liability) at fair value through profit and loss/surplus or deficit;
- Held-to-maturity investments;
- Loans and receivables; and
- Available-for-sale (AFS) financial assets.

Table 15.3   Financial assets and liabilities measurement

Financial assets	Measurement	Change in value
Held-to-maturity investments (HTM)	Amortized cost	N/A (except when impaired)
Loans and receivables	Amortized cost	N/A (except when impaired)
Financial asset at fair value through profit and loss/surplus or deficit (FVTPL: fair value through profit and loss)	Fair value	Profit and loss
Available-for-sale financial assets (AFS)	Fair value	Net assets
Financial liabilities	**Measurement**	**Change in value**
Financial liability at fair value through profit and loss/surplus or deficit (FVTPL: fair value through profit and loss)	Fair value	Profit and loss
Other debts	Amortized cost	N/A

The classification of the instrument determines its subsequent measurement (amortized cost or fair value). Specific rules apply to embedded derivatives and hedging instruments.

Public sector bodies will mainly report on surplus or deficit and IPSAS 29 uses only these terms. However, in respect of the first of the four categories above, some references to the terms "profit" and "loss" can be found in IPSAS 29. This is partly because some instruments will reflect the results of entities which do report on profits or losses, and partly because the category of "at fair value through profit and loss" is extensively referenced in accounting literature on financial instruments.

Financial assets and liabilities are measured according to their classification (see Table 15.3).

The World Health Organization (WHO) presents the classification of its financial instruments as illustrated in IPSAS Financial Reporting in Practice 15.4.

IPSAS Financial Reporting in Practice 15.4. Financial Instruments at WHO, 2013 Financial Statements (pp. 28–29)

Financial instruments are recognized when WHO becomes party to the contractual provisions of the instrument until such time as the rights to receive cash flows from those assets have expired or have been transferred and the Organization has transferred substantially all the risks and rewards of ownership. Investments can be classified as being: (i) financial assets or financial liabilities at fair value through surplus or deficit; (ii) held-to-maturity; (iii) available-for-sale; or (iv) bank deposits and other receivables. All purchases and sales of investments are recognized on the basis of their trade date.

Financial assets or financial liabilities at fair value through surplus or defecit are financial instruments that meet either of the following conditions:

(i) they are held-for-trading; or (ii) they are designated by the entity upon initial recognition as at fair value through surplus or deficit.

Financial instruments in this category are measured at fair value and any gains or losses arising from changes in the fair value are accounted for through surplus or deficit and included within the Statement of Financial Performance in the period in which they arise. All derivative instruments, such as swaps, currency forward contracts or options are classified as held-for-trading except for designated and effective hedging instruments as defined under IPSAS 29. Financial assets in the externally managed portfolios designated upon initial recognition as at fair value through surplus or deficit are classified as current assets or non-current assets according to the time horizon of the investment objectives of each portfolio. If the time horizon is less than or equal to one year, they are classified as current assets, and if it is more than one year, they are classified as non-current assets.

Held-to-maturity investments are non-derivative financial assets with fixed or determinable payments and fixed maturity dates that WHO has both the intention and the ability to hold to maturity. Held-to-maturity investments are stated at amortized cost using the effective interest rate method, with interest revenue being recognized on an effective yield basis in the Statement of Financial Performance.

Available-for-sale investments are classified as being available-for-sale where WHO has not designated them either as held-for-trading or as held-to-maturity. Available-for-sale items are stated at fair value (including transaction costs that are directly attributable to the acquisition of the financial asset) with value changes recognized in net assets/equity. Impairment charges and interest calculated using the effective interest rate method are recognized in the Statement of Financial Performance. As at 31 December 2013, no available-for-sale financial assets were held by the organization.

Bank deposits and other receivables are non-derivative financial assets with fixed or determinable payments that are not quoted in an active market. Accrued revenue related to interest, dividends and pending cash to be received from investments are included herein. Bank deposits and other receivables are stated at amortized cost calculated using the effective interest rate method, less any impairments. Interest revenue is recognized on the effective interest rate basis, with the exception of short-term receivables for which the recognition of interest would be immaterial.

Other financial liabilities included payables and accruals relating to investments and are recognized initially at fair value and subsequently measured at amortized cost using the effective interest rate method, with the exception of short-term liabilities for which the recognition of interest would be immaterial.

WHO presents its classification of financial instruments. It can be seen that, even if WHO has presented its policy regarding available-for-sale investments, no available-for-sale financial assets were held by WHO at the end of the year. Investments are therefore either held for trading or held to maturity investments. In practice, it does mean that there is no reevaluation reserve in net assets at the end of the year because either investments are valued at fair value through surplus or deficit or at amortized cost.

One important and strategic question the management of an entity has to consider when classifying financial assets is: how long is the entity willing to keep these instruments? Is the entity intending to hold them to maturity? Or does it intend to sell them before maturity? In some instances, these types of question can be difficult to answer, as the longer term plan for the instruments may not have been decided upon. In such cases, for example, if a public sector holds bonds (state bonds for instance), then the entity should not classify them as held to maturity investments because if the entity needs/wants to sell them before maturity, it would have to declassify the whole category to fair value through surplus or deficit, which would affect the profit and loss of the period. Moreover, the entity would not be allowed to use this category for two years.

If the entity does not know whether these bonds will be kept to maturity (the problem exists only for bonds, because shares do not have maturity!), then they can be classified either as available-for-sale investments or financial assets at fair value through surplus or deficit. The choice of the category is not only linked to the impact on the surplus or deficit of the period. The choice is linked to the strategy of the entity. If it is chosen to classify them as financial assets at fair value through surplus or deficit, it typically conveys that the entity is holding these instruments for trading. There is no straightforward answer. It really depends on the management strategy and the choice of accounting policies is supposed to reflect the management approach. The entity has to remember this when there is no specific view on when to sell the bonds, because the entity may have to deal with many unknown parameters. The entity may simply want to classify them as available-for-sale investments, the most "neutral" category.

Financial Liabilities

An entity should measure financial liabilities at amortized cost using the effective interest method, except for:

- Financial liabilities at fair value through profit or loss/surplus or deficit (whether because the liability is held for trading or designated to the category by the entity, which an entity is permitted to do in certain circumstances) (IPSAS 29.49);
- Financial liabilities that arise when a transfer of financial assets does not qualify for derecognition (IPSAS 29.33, 29.49);
- Financial guarantee contracts (IPSAS 29.49);
- Commitments to provide a loan at a below-market interest rate (IPSAS 29.49);
- Where a derivative liability is linked to, or to be settled by, the transfer of an unquoted equity instrument whose fair value cannot be measured reliably – it should be measured at cost (IPSAS 29.49); and
- Financial liabilities designated as hedged items, which are subject to hedge accounting requirements (IPSAS 29.49).

Amortized Cost

The amortized cost of a financial liability is the initial amount recognized in respect of the financial liability, minus principal repayments, plus or minus the cumulative amortization using the effective interest method of any difference between the initial amount recognized and the amount payable on redemption (IPSAS 29.10).

The effective interest rate is the rate that exactly discounts the scheduled cash flows payable or receivable across the expected life of the financial instrument or, when appropriate, a shorter period to the net carrying amount of the financial asset or financial liability (IPSAS 29.10). This is a method of calculating the amortized cost of a financial asset or a financial liability (or group of financial assets or financial liabilities) and of allocating the interest revenue or interest expense over the relevant period.

When calculating the effective interest rate, an entity shall estimate cash flows considering all contractual terms of the financial instrument (e.g., prepayment, call, and similar options) but shall not consider future credit losses. The calculation includes all fees paid or received between parties to the contract that are an integral part of the effective interest rate, transaction costs, and all other premiums or discounts. There is a presumption that the cash flows and the expected life of a group of similar financial instruments can be estimated reliably. However, in those rare cases when it is not possible to estimate reliably the cash flows or the expected life of a financial instrument (or group of financial instruments), the entity shall use the contractual cash flows over the full contractual term of the financial instrument (or group of financial instruments).

If the entity revises the estimate of the expected cash flow on a borrowing, the entity shall adjust the amount recognized at amortized cost to reflect the new discounted expected cash flows, using the initial effective interest rate. The adjustment of the amount recognized at amortized cost shall be recognized in profit and loss (known as the "Cumulative catch up method").

For foreign currency receivables and debts, the effective interest rate method uses cash flows in foreign currency. At the end of the period, the amortized cost of the receivable or of the debt is converted using the foreign currency rate at the end of the period.

Example 15.1   Three-year loan

On 31 December N, FCEA was granted a three-year loan of €1 000 000, refundable in fine, with an 8% interest rate. FCEA has been charged €15 000 for loan fees and commissions.

The effective interest rate is calculates as follows, taking into account all cash flows in and out:

$$985°000 = \frac{80°000}{(1+r)} + \frac{80°000}{(1+r)^2} + \frac{1080°000}{(1+r)^3}$$

The effective interest rate r = 8.59% differs from the 8% interest rate of the loan.

Question and Answer

Question:

A €100K refundable in fine loan, with a 6% interest rate and a five-year maturity, was granted on 1 January N. It bears €20K of origination fees. Its effective interest rate is 11.48%.

The table below provides information about the amortized cost, interest expenses, and cash flows of the loan in each reporting period. (in €K):

Year	Cash flows	Discounted cash flows	Interest expense	Amortized cost of the period	Amortized cost
T0	80 (=100−20)				80.00
1	(6)	5.38	9.18	3.18	83.18
2	(6)	4.83	9.55	3.55	86.73
3	(6)	4.33	9.95	3.95	90.68
4	(6)	3.89	10.41	4.41	95.09
5	(106)	61.57	10.91	(95.09)	0
Total			50.00	(80.00)	

NB: The loan is initially recognized for its emission cost minus origination fees.

Determine the amount of the amortized cost as well as of the interest expenses during the five years of the loan.

Answer:

The amount of the amortized cost as well as of the interest expenses during the five years of the loan are as follows:

in €K	T0	1	2	3	4	5
Amortized cost (statement of financial position)	80.00	83.18	86.73	90.68	95.09	0
Interest expense (statement of financial performance)		(9.18)	(9.55)	(9.95)	(10.41)	(10.91)

Fair Value

In determining the fair value of a financial asset or a financial liability for the purpose of applying IPSAS 28, IPSAS 29, or IPSAS 30, an entity shall apply paragraphs AG101–AG115 of Appendix A of IPSAS 29 (IPSAS 29.50). Fair value of a financial instrument depends on the existence of an active market, which must be determined using the following methodology.

The best evidence of fair value is quoted prices in an active market. If the market for a financial instrument is not active, an entity establishes fair value by using a valuation technique. The objective of using a valuation technique is to establish what the transaction price would have been on the measurement date in an arm's length exchange motivated by normal operating considerations. Valuation techniques include using recent arm's length market transactions between knowledgeable, willing parties, if available, reference to the current fair value of another instrument that is substantially the same, discounted cash flow analysis, and option pricing models. If there is a valuation technique commonly used by market participants to price the instrument and that technique has been demonstrated to provide reliable estimates of prices obtained in actual market transactions, the entity uses that technique. The chosen valuation technique makes maximum use of market inputs and relies as little as possible on entity-specific inputs. It incorporates all factors that market participants would consider in setting a price and is consistent with accepted economic methodologies for pricing financial instruments. Periodically, an entity calibrates the valuation technique and tests it for validity using prices from any observable current market transactions in the same instrument (i.e., without modification or repackaging) or based on any available observable market data (IPSAS 29.51).

Impairment

At each reporting date an entity is required to assess whether objective evidence for impairment exists (IPSAS 29.67).

Impairment losses for a financial asset or group of assets are incurred only if there is objective evidence as a result of one or more events that occurred after the initial recognition of the asset (IPSAS 29.68). If such evidence exists, the entity is required to perform a detailed impairment analysis to determine whether and to what extent an impairment loss should be recognized (IPSAS 29.67).

For assets carried at amortized cost, the impairment loss is measured as the difference between the asset's carrying amount and the present value of estimated cash flows discounted at the financial asset's original effective interest rate (IPSAS 29.72). If, in a subsequent period, the amount of the impairment loss relating to a financial asset carried at amortized cost decreases due to an event occurring after the impairment was originally recognized, the previously recognized impairment loss is reversed through surplus or deficit (IPSAS 29.74). After the individual assessment of whether individual significant assets are impaired and for which no impairment exists, these assets are grouped with financial assets with similar credit risk characteristics and collectively assessed for impairment (IPSAS 29.73).

For assets carried at cost, the impairment loss is measured as the difference between the asset's carrying amount and the present value of estimated cash flows discounted at the current market rate of return. Impairment losses on assets carried at cost should not be reversed (IPSAS 29.75).

For available-for-sale financial assets, the impairment loss is calculated, after reversal of cumulative gains or losses in net asset/equity, as the difference between the current fair value and the acquisition cost (IPSAS 29.76). Impairments relating to investments in AFS equity instruments are not reversed through surplus or deficit, for debt instruments classified as AFS they are reversed through surplus or deficit if objectively related to an event after the recognition of the loss (IPSAS 29.79).

FINANCIAL INSTRUMENTS: DISCLOSURE

Disclosures should be made to provide users of the financial statements with an understanding of the effect that financial instruments have had on an entity's financial performance, position, and cash flows. IPSAS 30 Financial Instruments: disclosure requires a number of disclosures to be made that will help meet this objective.

The objective of IPSAS 30 is to require entities to provide disclosures in their financial statements that enable users to evaluate the significance of financial instruments for the entity's financial position and performance, and the nature and extent of risks arising from financial instruments to which the entity is exposed during the period and at the end of the reporting period, and how the entity manages those risks (IPSAS 30.1).

For instance, IPSAS 30 requires disclosing the following relating to fair value: fair value of each class of financial asset and financial liability (IPSAS 30.29) and for each class:

- Offsetting should only be performed to the extent that the carrying amounts are offset in the financial statements (IPSAS 30.30);
- Methods and valuation technique used and the assumptions applied should be disclosed.

IPSAS 30 specifies a fair value hierarchy with three levels of inputs based on input significance for the measurement of the overall fair value (IPSAS 30.32) – see Figure 15.5:

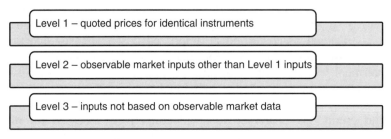

Level 1 – quoted prices for identical instruments

Level 2 – observable market inputs other than Level 1 inputs

Level 3 – inputs not based on observable market data

Figure 15.5   Fair value hierarchy

For each category of financial instruments, the following disclosures are required (IPSAS 30.33) – see Figure 15.6:

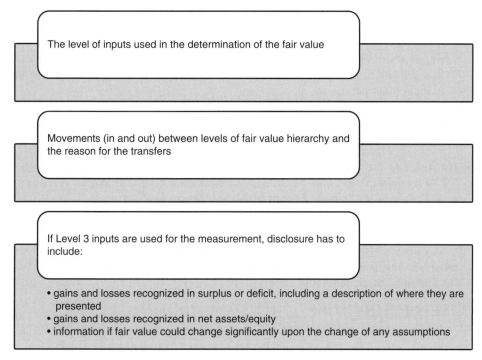

The level of inputs used in the determination of the fair value

Movements (in and out) between levels of fair value hierarchy and the reason for the transfers

If Level 3 inputs are used for the measurement, disclosure has to include:

• gains and losses recognized in surplus or deficit, including a description of where they are presented
• gains and losses recognized in net assets/equity
• information if fair value could change significantly upon the change of any assumptions

Figure 15.6 Fair value hierarchy and disclosures

This is only an example of how precise IPSAS 30 is in seeking useful information to understand the risks and the management of financial instruments.

IPSAS 30 focuses on risks and risk management. Information should be disclosed that enables users of the financial statements to evaluate the nature and extent of risks arising from financial instruments to which the entity is exposed at the end of the reporting period (IPSAS 30.38). The risks relating to financial instruments include but are not limited to (IPSAS 30.39):

• Credit risk;
• Liquidity risk;
• Market risk.

IPSAS 30 requires an entity to make both qualitative and quantitative disclosures.

For each type of risk related to financial instruments the following qualitative disclosures are required (IPSAS 30.40):

• Risk exposures and their source;
• Objectives, policies, and processes for managing those risks and how these risks are measured;
• Changes from the previous period.

For each type of risk related to financial instruments the following quantitative disclosures are required (IPSAS 30.41):

- Summary quantitative data about exposure to each risk at the reporting date; this information should be based on the information that is disclosed to key management personnel;
- Disclosures about credit risk, liquidity risk, and market risk, unless these risks are not material;
- Concentrations of risk.

See for instance the presentation of the financial instrument risks in the Note to the 2013 Financial Statements of the United Nations Relief and Works Agency for Palestine Refugees in the Near East in Financial Report in Practice 15.5.

IPSAS Financial Reporting in Practice 15.5. Management of Currency Risk, United Nations Relief and Works Agency for Palestine Refugees (UNWRA), 2013 Financial Statements (pp. 78–81)

Management of currency risks

2.8 The primary principle of the currency risk management policy of UNRWA is the preservation of the value of its financial resources in United States dollar terms. The Agency's currency risk can be identified mainly as a potential loss in the value of non-received non-United States dollar contributions and non-United States dollar cash assets as a result of a strengthening United States dollar. The risk arises from the date on which the contributions are pledged. To protect its assets and cash flow against adverse currency movements, UNRWA adopts a conservative risk management approach (e.g., hedging) to minimize its exposure to exchange rate fluctuations. To hedge the currency risk, UNRWA entered into several forward contracts in 2013 for expected non-United States dollar contributions in 2014 (see note 10).

2.9 Such hedges are consistent with the Agency's risk management objective and strategy, given that they remove the risk of an appreciation of the United States dollar and provide a fixed known income amount. The gain or loss from hedging will be offset by foreign exchange gain or loss from donor contributions.

2.10 UNRWA provides protection against local currencies (currency adjustment factor) to its area staff for their salaries. The Agency's currency risk management policies allow hedging against local currencies to reduce the exposure stemming from fluctuations in exchange rates between the United States dollar and local currencies. At the end of the year, there were no outstanding hedging investments for local currencies.

Financial instruments

2.21 UNRWA has applied the following new IPSAS, which have been issued and are effective from 1 January 2013: IPSAS 28: Financial instruments: presentation; IPSAS 29: Financial instruments: recognition and measurement; and IPSAS 30: Financial instruments: disclosure and presentation. They replaced IPSAS 15: Financial instruments: disclosure and presentation. They establish principles for recognizing and measuring financial assets and financial liabilities, presenting financial instruments as liabilities or net assets/equity, offsetting financial assets and financial liabilities, and requirements for disclosure.

2.22 Financial instruments are recognized when UNRWA becomes a party to the contractual provisions of the instrument until such time as the rights to receive cash flows from those assets have expired or have been transferred and UNRWA has transferred substantially all the risks and rewards of ownership.

2.23 Loans, receivables and payables are non-derivative financial instruments with fixed or determinable payments that are not quoted in active markets. These financial instruments comprise contributions receivable in cash, loans receivable as part of the credit facilities of the Microfinance Department, other receivables, cash in bank accounts and accounts payable. All non-derivative financial instruments are recognized in the statement of financial position at their fair values. The nominal value of receivables and payables approximates the fair value of the transaction.

2.24 UNRWA uses derivative financial instruments to hedge exchange risk. Foreign exchange forward contracts are revalued and the revaluation gain or loss is reported in the statement of financial performance if the contracts belong to the current year. For contracts relating to subsequent years, the revaluation gain or loss is reported in the statement of financial position. For revaluation at year-end, the market rate for the forward contract is obtained from the banks and these are compared against the United Nations operational rate of exchange to ascertain the gain or loss.

Financial risk management

2.25 The activities carried out by UNRWA expose it to various financial risks, primarily the effects of changes in foreign currency exchange rates. Consequently, the Agency's financial risk management policies are focused on the unpredictability of foreign exchange rates and are aimed at minimizing, where feasible, potential adverse effects on the financial performance of UNRWA. Financial risk management is carried out by a central treasury function using UNRWA technical guidelines covering areas of financial risk such as foreign exchange, the use of derivative financial instruments and the investment of excess liquidity.

Credit risk

10.4 UNRWA has limited credit risk, because its donors are generally of a high credit standing. Contributions receivable comprise primarily amounts due from sovereign nations. Details of contributions receivable, including allowances for reductions in contribution revenue, are provided in note 6.

10.5 The greatest area of credit risk arises from loans provided by the Microfinance Department. The Department manages credit risk by:

- Establishing ceilings on amounts of direct credit for each product linked to the cash flow of each client;
- Providing a range of products to different sectors and segments to spread credit and reduce concentrations;

- Formulating credit policies by product, covering collateral requirements and credit compliance with regulatory requirements in each jurisdiction;
- Establishing the authorization structure for the approval and renewal of credit facilities;
- Reviewing and assessing credit risk in excess of designated limits prior to facilities being committed to customers. Renewals of facilities are subject to the same process;
- Developing and maintaining a risk-grading system in order to categorize exposure according to when impairment provisions are required against specific credit exposures;
- Providing guidance and training to improve skills of staff in order to promote best practice in the management of credit risk.

10.6 In 2013, the credit risk in the Syrian Arab Republic and the Gaza Strip continued to increase as a result of conflict. The Microfinance Department manages this risk by increasing provisions as the portfolio at risk increases as a percentage of the full portfolio.

10.7 UNRWA has its cash deposited with various banks, and is therefore exposed to the risk that a bank will default in its obligations towards the Agency. However, UNRWA holds all significant cash deposits in banks that have a "P-1" credit rating.

10.8 There is no perceived risk that other receivables may not be liquidated when they fall due.

Interest rate risk

10.9 UNRWA deposits its funds in short-term fixed interest accounts, and therefore has no significant interest rate risk exposure.

Foreign currency risk

10.10 UNRWA receives contributions from donors in currencies other than the primary currency of the expenditures, United States dollars. In 2013, 38 per cent of contributions were denominated in the United States dollar base currency and 62 per cent were denominated in other currencies. The Microfinance Department lends in different currencies in each of the Agency's fields of operation, with the United States dollar used in the Gaza Strip, the Jordanian dinar used in Jordan and the West Bank, and the Syrian pound used in the Syrian Arab Republic.

10.11 Furthermore, some field office expenditures are incurred in non-United States dollar currencies. UNRWA is therefore exposed to foreign currency exchange risk arising from fluctuations of currency exchange rates. Foreign exchange forward contracts are used to hedge the non-United States dollar exchange exposure for donor contributions.

10.12 In order to protect its assets and cash flow against adverse currency movements, UNRWA adopts a conservative risk management approach, hedging to minimize its exposure to exchange rate fluctuations. In order to hedge the currency risk, UNRWA enters into forward contracts to remove the risk of an appreciation of the United States dollar and to provide a known, fixed income amount.

10.13 During the year ended 31 December 2013, three contracts were settled. As at 31 December 2013, UNRWA had two unrealized contracts. The realized losses are included in the currency exchange differences presented in the statement of financial performance.

10.14 As at 31 December 2013, 80 per cent of cash held in banks was denominated in the United States dollar base currency, 4 per cent was denominated in local currencies used by the UNRWA field offices to support operating activities, and the remaining cash at banks was held in other currencies. A full breakdown of cash held at banks in currencies other than the United States dollar is provided in note 4.

16 CONSOLIDATIONS AND STRATEGIC INVESTMENTS

This chapter focuses on a suite of IPSAS. Firstly it covers currently applicable IPSAS 6 Consolidated and Separate Financial Statements, IPSAS 7 Investments in Associates, and IPSAS 8 Interests in Joint Ventures.

However, as of 1 January 2017, IPSAS 6, 7, and 8 will be superseded by a new set of issued IPSAS, namely 34, 35, 36, 37, and 38.[1] This suite of "new" IPSAS were published in January 2015 with an effective date of 1 January 2017, with early adoption permitted. If an entity applies these "new" IPSAS for a period beginning before 1 January 2017, it shall disclose that fact and apply IPSAS 34, IPSAS 35, IPSAS 36, IPSAS 37, and IPSAS 38 at the same time.

This chapter therefore also includes coverage of the following:

- IPSAS 34 Separate Financial Statements
- IPSAS 35 Consolidated Financial Statements
- IPSAS 36 Investments in Associates and Joint Ventures
- IPSAS 37 Joint Arrangements
- IPSAS 38 Disclosure of Interests in Other Entities.

---

[1] The new IPSAS are based on IFRS 10 Consolidated Financial Statements, IFRS 11 Joint Arrangements, IFRS 12 Disclosure of Interests in Other Entities, IAS 27 Separate Financial Statements, and IAS 28 Investments in Associated and Joint Ventures. The standards align with the requirements of these equivalent IASB pronouncements, except where departure is considered justified due to public sector considerations.

In order to provide a complete picture of IPSAS as they stand today and forth-coming applicable IPSAS, this chapter will include coverage of currently applicable IPSAS (i.e., 6, 7, and 8) as well as highlighting the forthcoming changes in the "new" IPSAS that have to be applied at the latest in annual financial statements covering periods beginning on or after 1 January 2017.

In terms of IPSAS 33 First-time Adoption of Accrual Basis International Public Sector Accounting Standards and transitional provisions in IPSAS 6–8 versus IPSAS 34–36, it is important to note that the IPSASB considered whether IPSAS 33 should refer to IPSAS 6–8 *as well as* IPSAS 34–36. The IPSASB noted that as IPSAS 33 was published in January 2015, any entity adopting IPSAS 33 and electing to apply the three-year exemptions would be required to apply IPSAS 34–36 by the time the transitional period was complete. Consequently, the IPSASB formed the view that it was very unlikely that entities adopting IPSAS 33 prior to 1 January 2017 would adopt IPSAS 6–8 as this would require a further transition to IPSAS 34–36 shortly afterwards. *The IPSASB therefore concluded that IPSAS 33 should not include provisions relating to IPSAS 6–8.* This chapter therefore includes reference to transitional provisions as stipulated in IPSAS 33 in "note" boxes.

CONSOLIDATED AND SEPARATE FINANCIAL STATEMENTS (IPSAS 6)

IPSAS 6 Consolidated and Separate Financial Statements stipulates the account-ing and financial reporting requirements for consolidation. When a group of entities presents financial information about their activities as if it were a single economic entity, the financial statements are known as consolidated financial statements. Con-solidated financial statements are prepared on the basis that the group is a single economic entity, by aggregating the transactions and balances of the controlling entity and all its controlled entities. A group is simply a collection of entities, where one, the parent/controlling entity, controls the activities of the others, its controlled entities.

The preparation of single entity financial statements would not reflect the eco-nomic reality of the financial performance and position under the control of the parent entity. However the preparation of separate entity financial statements, whether for the parent/controlling entity or subsidiary/controlled entity, is often required for account-ability or legal reasons. The terms "controlling entity" and "controlled entity" are used in IPSAS 6.

A controlling entity can control another entity in a number of ways. The easiest control relationship to identify is where one entity has more than half the voting rights in another entity.

Economic entity	**Controlling entity**	**Controlled entity**
Economic entity means a group of entities comprising a controlling entity and one or more controlled entities.	Controlling entity is an entity that has one or more controlled entities.	Controlled entity is an entity that is controlled by another entity, known as the controlling entity.

Establishing Control

Control is the power to govern the financial and operating policies of another entity to benefit from its activities. Control consists of two parts: firstly, control of the financial and operating policies is necessary (power); and secondly, benefits must be obtained from that control. IPSAS 6 includes a number of examples where (power) control may exist even though the controlling entity does not hold a majority of the voting rights. Such situations include:

- Where the controlling entity has directly or indirectly through controlled entities, ownership of a majority voting interest in the other entity; or
- Where the controlling entity has the power, either granted by or exercised within existing legislation, to appoint or remove a majority of the members of the board of directors or equivalent governing body, and control of the other entity is by that board or by that body; or
- Where the controlling entity has the power to cast, or regulate the casting of, a majority of the votes that are likely to be cast at a general meeting of the other entity; or
- Where the controlling entity has the power to cast the majority of the votes at meetings of the board of directors or equivalent governing body, and control of the other entity is by that board or by that body.

IPSAS 6 provides a list of power indicators:

- The entity has the ability to veto operating and capital budgets of the other entity.
- The entity has the ability to veto, overrule, or modify governing body decisions of the other entity.
- The entity has the ability to approve the hiring, reassignment, and removal of key personnel of the other entity.
- The mandate of the other entity is established and limited by legislation.
- The entity holds a golden share (or equivalent) in the other entity that confers rights to govern the financial and operating policies of that other entity.

In addition to above "power conditions" IPSAS 6 also includes specific "benefit conditions" and suggests that control is likely to require the existence of one of the "power conditions" and one of the "benefit conditions." The benefit conditions are: (a) the power to dissolve the other entity and obtain a significant level of the residuary assets or bear significant obligations; and (b) the power to extract distributions of assets from the other entity, and/or possible liability for obligations of the other entity.

Within the public sector there are likely to be many different types of arrangements leading to the issue of consolidated financial statements and the application of IPSAS 6. These could include:

- Direct share ownership of a company by a public sector entity;
- Control by a government department of a separately constituted government agency;

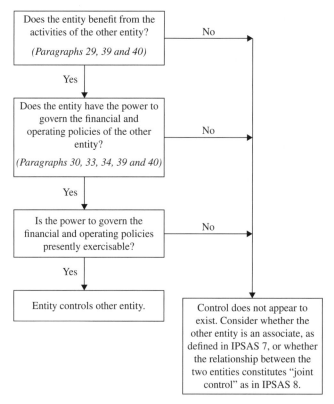

Figure 16.1   Establishment of control (IPSAS 6.41)

- The requirement, by law or practice, to prepare consolidated financial statements for a group of entities such as all local authorities; or
- The requirement, by law or practice, to prepare consolidated financial statements for the whole of the government.

IPSAS 6 provides a diagram (reproduced in Figure 16.1) (IPSAS 6.41) that summarizes how to establish control of another entity.

Example 16.1   Consolidation in South Africa (IPSAS-based Generally Recognised Accounting Practices (GRAP), see GRAP 6, Consolidated and Separate Financial Statements)

In the South African context, the government is divided into three spheres, namely the national, provincial, and local spheres of government. Although provinces and municipalities are responsible for executing its assigned functions in line with the overall policies and objectives set by the relevant national department, the autonomy of the different spheres is guaranteed in terms of the Constitution of South Africa and provinces and municipalities can therefore decide how they will achieve those objectives.

The national government does not **control** provinces or municipalities for accounting purposes, although funding may be received from the national government.

However, circumstances where one sphere of government intervenes in the administration of an entity in another sphere of government, if that entity cannot and does not fulfill its executive obligation, must be evaluated to establish whether the intervention meets the definition of control for consolidation purposes.

Regulatory and purchase powers do not constitute control for the purposes of financial reporting and GRAP 6 is the South African Standard equivalent to IPSAS 6.

Therefore, control does not extend to:

- The power of the legislature to establish the regulatory framework within which the entities operate and to impose conditions or sanctions on their operations; and
- Entities that are economically dependent on another entity. For example, where an entity is dependent on a department for funding. The department has some power, but not to govern the entity's financial and operating policies.

The treatment in the consolidated financial statements of arrangements giving rise to joint control (under IPSAS 8 Interests in Joint Ventures) and for those giving rise to significant influence (under IPSAS 7 Investments in Associates) is also included in this chapter.

Preparing Consolidated Financial Statements

The scope of IPSAS 6 is wide and it should be applied in the preparation and presentation of consolidated financial statements for a group of entities under the control of an economic entity (IPSAS 6.1).

IPSAS 6 also addresses the accounting requirements for investments in subsidiaries, jointly controlled entities, and associates in separate financial statements. Separate financial statements are those of an individual investing entity rather than those of the combined group (IPSAS 6.6). IPSAS 6 does not however cover the treatment of a business combination, for example the acquisition of a subsidiary, in the group financial statements. This topic is not covered by IPSAS for the time being, but should be in the near future.

Subject to limited exceptions, IPSAS 6 requires every controlling entity to prepare a set of consolidated financial statements (IPSAS 6.15). An exception to this requirement arises in circumstances where the shareholders of the controlling entity will gain limited benefit from the preparation of consolidated financial statements at this level.

Example 16.2   Consolidation mandatory only for the ultimate parent company

For example, a controlling entity, Entity B, is a wholly-owned controlled entity, controlled by Entity A. Entity B controls Entity C and Entity D.

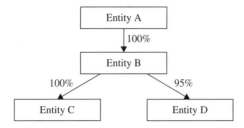

Entity B is a parent company, and, as such, should prepare consolidated financial statements of group B, including Entity B, Entity C, and Entity D.

However Entity B is wholly owned by Entity A. In this scenario, the only shareholder is the superior parent/ultimate controlling entity which is required to prepare its own consolidated financial statements. Entity is not required, under IPSAS 6, to prepare consolidated financial statements. It does not preclude the fact that Entity B could be required, for other reasons, to prepare consolidated financial statements, for instance, because it is obliged by some law or regulation.

The exception illustrated in the above example also applies where a partially-owned controlled entity has informed the other shareholders (i.e., the shareholders, or their equivalent, of the subsidiary/controlled entity other than the parent/controlling entity) of the proposal not to prepare consolidated financial statements and there were no objections. The ultimate parent/controlling entity (i.e., the top entity in the group), or the intermediate parent/controlling entity if one exists, is required to prepare consolidated financial statements that are publicly available and in accordance with IFRS or IPSAS for this exception to be available (IPSAS 6.16), since IFRS are recognized as equivalent to IPSAS.

This exception cannot be utilized where the parent/controlling entity has debt or equity instruments traded on any public market. In such circumstances its consolidated financial statements are likely to have a wider circulation and therefore should be prepared according to IPSAS 6 (IPSAS 6.16).

In the public sector, many controlling entities that are either wholly owned or partially owned represent key sectors or activities of a government and may by law or for purposes of accountability be required to prepare and make public their financial statements.

Consolidation Procedures

In preparing consolidated financial statements, an entity should combine the financial statements of the controlling entity and its controlled entities line by line, by adding together like items of assets, liabilities, net assets/equity, revenue, and expenses (IPSAS 6.43).

The following steps are then taken:

1. The carrying value of the controlling entity's investment in each controlled entity and the controlling entity's portion of the controlled entity's net assets/equity are eliminated. The relevant international or national accounting standard dealing with business combinations provides guidance on the treatment of any resultant goodwill. For instance, in South Africa, the difference between the consideration paid (if any) and the assets acquired or liabilities assumed as of acquisition date is recognized in surplus or deficit (in accordance with GRAP 106 Transfer of Functions between Entities Not under Common Control) or in accumulated surplus or deficit (under GRAP 105 Transfer of Functions between Entities under Common Control).
2. Non-controlling interest (minority interests) in the surplus or deficit of the controlled entity is identified.
3. Non-controlling interest (minority interests) in the net assets/equity of the controlled entity is identified, which consists of:
   (a) The amount of non-controlling interest (minority interests) at the date of the original combination. The relevant international or national accounting standard dealing with business combinations provides guidance on calculating this amount. For instance, in South Africa, transfer of functions is calculated in accordance with GRAP 105 or 106 – Transfer of functions between entities under/not under common control.
   (b) The amount of non-controlling interest (minority interests) in changes in net assets/equity since the date of combination (in South Africa, the initial transfer of functions date).

The following are some of the detailed requirements for consolidating controlled entities:

- Balances, transactions, revenues, and expenses between group entities should be eliminated in full (IPSAS 6.45).
- Consolidated financial statements should be prepared using the same reporting date across all entities. When a controlled entity has a reporting date different from that of the controlling entity then appropriate adjustments should be made for the effect of significant transactions between that date and the reporting date of the controlling entity. When the reporting dates of the controlling entity and a controlled entity are different, the controlled entity prepares, for consolidation purposes, additional financial statements as of the same date as the financial statements of the controlling entity, unless it is impracticable to do so (IPSAS 6.47).
- Consolidated financial statements should be prepared using the same accounting policies for similar transactions and other events across all entities. If the controlled entity uses different accounting policies than those adopted for the consolidated financial statements then appropriate adjustments should be made to its financial statements for consolidation purposes (IPSAS 6.49).

- Non-controlling interest (minority interests) should be presented separately from controlling interest in the consolidated statement of financial position (IPSAS 6.54).
- Non-controlling interest's (minority interest) share in surplus or deficit should be disclosed separately from the controlling interest's share in the surplus or deficit in the consolidated statement of financial performance (IPSAS 6.54).

Loss of Control

Loss of control of a controlled entity can happen with or without a change in absolute or relative ownership levels, for example, when the controlled entity becomes subject to control by another government, court, administrator, regulator, or by another entity. It could also occur because of a contractual arrangement or because a foreign government may sequester the operating assets of a foreign-controlled entity so that the controlling entity loses the power to govern the operating policies of the controlled entity (IPSAS 6.42).

If a controlling entity loses control of a controlled entity, it should follow the steps below:

1. Derecognize the assets and liabilities of the controlled entity at their carrying amounts at the date when control is lost.
2. Derecognize the carrying amount of any non-controlling interest (minority interests) at the date when control is lost.
3. Recognize:
   - The fair value of the consideration received (if any), for the loss of control;
   - The distribution, if the transaction that resulted in the loss of control involves a distribution of residual interests of the controlled entity to owners.
4. Recognize any investment retained at its fair value at the date when control is lost.
5. Reclassify amounts to surplus or deficit (as a reclassification adjustment). Therefore, any gains or losses will be reclassified from net assets to surplus and deficit, if the gains and losses previously recognized in net assets are required to be reclassified to surplus or deficit on the disposal of assets and liabilities.
6. Transfer amounts directly to accumulated surplus or deficit. Therefore, any reserves will be transferred directly to accumulated surplus or deficit, if the reserves previously recognized in net assets are required to be transferred directly to accumulated surplus or deficit on the disposal of the asset. For example, a revaluation surplus will be transferred directly to accumulated surplus or deficit and not to surplus or deficit as in the previous step.
7. Recognize any resulting difference as a gain or loss in surplus or deficit or in accumulated surplus or deficit attributable to the controlling entity.

Changes in ownership interest in a controlled entity that do not result in a loss of control should be accounted for as transactions that affect net assets; therefore the controlling interest and the non-controlling interest will be adjusted to reflect the changes in their relative interests. The difference between the amounts by which the non-controlling interest (minority interests) is adjusted and the fair value of the consideration paid or received should be recognized directly in net assets and attributed to the owner(s) of the controlling entity.

Any investment retained in the former controlled entity should be recognized at its fair value at the date when control is lost (refer to step 4 above). This fair value will be regarded as the fair value on initial recognition of a financial asset or, when appropriate, the cost on initial recognition of an investment in an associate or jointly controlled entity.

Impairment Losses

When separate financial statements are prepared, investments in controlled entities and in jointly controlled entities are accounted for:

(a) Using the equity method as described in IPSAS 7;
(b) At cost; or
(c) As a financial instrument in accordance with IPSAS 29 (IPSAS 6.58).

How the impairment of an investment in a controlled entity in the separate financial statements is determined depends on how it was initially recognized and measured.

To assess whether an investment in a controlled entity that is accounted for in the separate financial statements at cost is impaired, the controlling entity determines the recoverable amount of the asset in accordance with IPSAS 26 Impairment of Cash-generating Assets. In determining value in use, the controlling entity estimates future cash flows from the asset on the basis of continuing use of the asset and its ultimate disposal by the controlling entity.

To assess whether an investment in a controlled entity that is accounted for in the separate financial statements at fair value is impaired, the controlling entity determines the impairment loss of the asset in accordance with IPSAS 29 Financial Instruments. In determining the amount, the controlling entity estimates future cash flows (excluding future credit losses that have not been incurred) from the asset discounted at the asset's original effective interest rate.

Transitional Provisions

Controlling entities that adopt accrual accounting for the first time in accordance with IPSAS may have many controlled entities, with a significant number of transactions between these entities. Consequently, it may be challenging to identify some transactions and balances that need to be eliminated for the purpose of preparing the consolidated financial statements of the economic entity. Therefore, entities are not required to comply with the requirement for the elimination of balances and transactions between entities within the economic entity (cf. IPSAS 6.45) for reporting periods beginning on a date within three years following the date of first adoption of accrual accounting in accordance with IPSAS.

Where entities apply the transitional provision it is important to note that this is to be disclosed.

Note on Upcoming Changes. IPSAS 33 First-time Adoption of Accrual Basis International Public Sector Accounting Standards

The IPSASB agreed that a first-time adopter may elect to measure an investment in a controlled entity, joint venture, or associate at cost in its separate financial statements on the date of adoption of IPSAS at either cost as determined in accordance with IPSAS 6, or deemed cost. Deemed cost is determined as fair value in accordance with IPSAS 29 Financial Instruments: Recognition and Measurement (cf. IPSAS 33.BC85).

Therefore the transitional exemption or provision for IPSAS 35 (to supersede IPSAS 6) allows for the relief to recognize and/or measure interests in controlled entity:

- Elect to not eliminate inter-entity balances, transactions, revenue, and expenses;
- Controlled entity becomes first-time adopter later or earlier than its controlling entity;
- Not present financial statements as consolidated financial statements if three-year relief for recognition and/or measurement and/or elimination option was adopted;
- Assess if investment entity on date of adoption and determine fair value at that date.

Disclosure

Key required disclosures under IPSAS 6 (IPSAS 6.57) include:

- A list of significant controlled entities;
- The fact that a controlled entity is not consolidated as it meets the presentation exemption, if this is applicable;
- Summarized financial information of controlled entities that are not consolidated.

As noted under transitional provisions, if transitional provisions are applied, then this has to be disclosed.

Note on Upcoming Changes. IPSAS 35, Consolidated Financial Statements

IPSAS 35, Consolidated Financial Statements will supersede the requirements in IPSAS 6 regarding consolidated financial statements. IPSAS 35 still requires that control be assessed having regard to benefits and power, but the definition of control has changed. It focuses on an entity's ability to influence the nature and amount of benefits through its power over another entity. This new definition of control may impact previous assessments of control, and therefore whether certain entities should be consolidated. IPSAS 35 provides considerably more guidance on assessing control.

IPSAS 35 introduces the concept of "investment entities," which may be applicable to some sovereign wealth funds. Generally, an investment entity measures its investments in controlled entities at fair value through surplus or deficit. After thorough consultation, the IPSASB decided, for public sector specific reasons, that an entity which controls an investment entity should retain this method of accounting for an investment entity's investments in its consolidated financial statements, regardless of whether it is itself an investment entity.

IPSAS 35 no longer permits an exemption from consolidation for temporarily controlled entities (which was allowed in IPSAS 6). Consistent with the IPSASB's policy of reducing unnecessary differences between IPSASs and Government Finance Statistics reporting guidelines, the IPSASB has aligned the principles in IPSAS 35 with the Government Finance Statistics Manual 2014 (pre-publication draft) where feasible.

INVESTMENTS IN ASSOCIATES (IPSAS 7)

IPSAS 7 stipulates the accounting and financial reporting requirements for investments in associates. Investments by public sector entities can take a number of different forms. What is frequently seen is a situation where one entity has the majority of the voting rights of another, and as such it gains control. However, outright control is not always the most appropriate form of investment for an entity to have. There may be instances where although an entity does not control another entity, the activity in which it operates is still of significant importance to it. In such circumstances an investor may instead decide to maintain sufficient ownership of the entity to have the power to influence decisions of its governing body but not to have control over it. This is often the case when government have decided to privatize previous entities in strategic sectors, such as energy, defense, transport ..., but maintain some form of power/influence over these entities.

Investments that meet these criteria will typically be classed as associates. As the investor has what is described as significant influence over the investee, it is appropriate to report its share of the investee's results rather than just the dividends receivable; after all, it is partly answerable for the investee's performance.

Investments in associates are likely to be relatively infrequent. However there may be particular reasons for such holdings, for example:

- Strategic investment in essential industries, such as oil or energy;
- Holdings in entities involved in developing particular geographical areas; and
- Retention of holdings in activities previously owned and managed by government.

Identifying an Associate and Establishing Significant Influence

An associate is an entity over which the investor has significant influence and that is neither a controlled entity nor an interest in a joint venture. For an investment to meet the definition of an associate it should not be a subsidiary, where the investor has control, or a joint venture, where the investor has joint control (IPSAS 7.7).

Significant influence is defined as the power to participate in the financial and operating policy decisions of the investee without having control or joint control over those policies (IPSAS 7.7). The assessment of significant influence is a matter of professional judgment. However, IPSAS 7 includes practical guidance to assist management in making that assessment.

Where an investor has at least 20% of the voting power in another entity, IPSAS 7 presumes that this size of holding is enough to give rise to significant influence over that entity.

IPSAS 7 provides a list of factors that normally indicate that significant influence is present. These factors include:

- Where the investor has a representative on the board of directors or on an equivalent governing body;
- Where the investor actively participates in the policy-making processes of the entity, including the level of dividends or other distributions to be paid;
- Where a number of significant transactions take place between the investor and the investee;
- Where members of management move between the two entities; or
- Where the investor provides essential technical information to the entity.

Even when the investor holds less than 20% of the voting power, one or more of these factors in combination may indicate that significant influence exists.

Disclosure

Key disclosures include the following (IPSAS 7.43–7.46):

- The fair value of the investments (i.e., if published prices quotations are available);
- Summarized financial information of associates, including the aggregated amounts of assets, liabilities, revenues, and surplus or deficit;
- The unrecognized share of losses of an associate, both for the period and cumulatively, if the investor has discounted recognition of its share of losses of the associate.

Note on Upcoming Changes. IPSAS 33 First-time Adoption of Accrual Basis International Public Sector Accounting Standards

IPSAS 33 stipulates that the following transition relief will be applicable in IPSAS 36 (to supersede IPSAS 7):

- Elect to not eliminate share in associate's surplus and deficit;
- Associate becomes first-time adopter later or earlier than its controlling entity;
- Not present investment in associates in consolidated financial statements if three-year relief for recognition and/or measurement and/or elimination option was adopted.

> **Note on Upcoming Changes. IPSAS 36 Investments in Associates and Joint Ventures**
>
> IPSAS 36, Investments in Associates and Joint Ventures explains the application of the equity method of accounting, which is used to account for investments in associates and joint ventures. The requirements are very similar to the current guidance in IPSAS 7. Because equity accounting must now be used when accounting for joint ventures, the title of the standard now also refers to joint ventures.
>
> IPSAS 36 does not permit a different accounting treatment for temporary investments (which was allowed in IPSAS 7).

JOINT VENTURES (IPSAS 8)

IPSAS 8 Interests in Joint Ventures sets out the accounting requirements in relation to interests in joint ventures and the appropriate recognition of joint venture assets, liabilities, income, and expenses in the financial statements of venturers and investors (IPSAS 8.1).

Investments by public sector entities can take a number of different forms. Typically where one entity has the majority of the voting rights in another, it gains control. However, in particular circumstances, it is more beneficial to share such investments with other interested parties. By sharing the investment each investor contributes different skills; alternatively the arrangement benefits all parties through reduced costs. Such arrangements are commonly known as joint ventures.

Establishing Joint Control

A joint venture is where two, or more, parties (described as venturers) act together under contractual arrangements to carry out activities that are under their joint control. Joint control is the agreed sharing of control over an entity by a contractual arrangement, and exists only when the strategic financial and operating decisions relating to the activity require the unanimous consent of the parties sharing control (the venturers). The presence of a "contractual arrangement" to share control is the principal factor in determining whether a joint venture relationship exists. The existence of a contractual arrangement is the key distinguishing factor between interests that involve joint control from investments in associates where the investor has significant influence. This typically means that the parties agree to share control and to require unanimous agreement for all strategic decisions. Control is the power to govern the financial and operating activities of an economic activity so as to obtain benefits. An entity that invests in a joint venture but does not have joint control is known simply as an "investor."

The existence of a binding arrangement is usually evidenced in a number of ways, for example:

- A contract between the venturers;
- Minutes of discussions between the venturers; or

Table 16.1   Three types of joint ventures

Jointly controlled operations	Jointly controlled assets	Jointly controlled entities
The parties to the transaction share the activities that are to be carried out. Effectively, the venturers pool resources and provide expertise to the overall operations.	Jointly controlled assets are used to generate benefits to be shared by each of the venturers.	A separate legal entity is set up with ownership being shared by the venturers.

- Incorporation of a binding arrangement in enabling legislation, articles, or other by-laws of the joint venture (IPSAS 8.8).

It is important to note that a binding arrangement is usually in writing (although this is not a requirement) and deals with matters such as:

- The activity, duration, and reporting obligations of the joint venture;
- The appointment of the management of the joint venture and the voting rights of the venturers;
- Capital contributions by the venturers; and
- The sharing by the venturers of the output, revenue, expenses, surpluses or deficits, or cash flows of the joint venture (IPSAS 8.8).

The aim of a binding arrangement is to establish joint control over a joint venture to ensure that no single venturer is in a position to control an activity unilaterally.

Where one of the venturers is identified as the **operator or manager** of the joint venture which acts within the financial and operating policies that have been agreed by the venturers in accordance with the binding arrangement and delegated to the operator or manager, it will be a joint venture.

Conversely, if the operator or manager has the **power to govern the financial and operating policies** of the activity, it would constitute **control** over the joint venture. In such a case, the joint venture will be a controlled entity of the operator or manager and it should account for its interest in the controlled entity in accordance with IPSAS 6 Consolidated and Separate Financial Statements.

The Three Types of Joint Venture

In practical terms there are a number of forms a joint venture investment can take, but IPSAS 8 identifies only three broad types (see Table 16.1).

Jointly Controlled Operations

The parties to the transaction share the activities that are to be carried out. Effectively, the venturers pool resources and provide expertise to the overall operations. In a jointly controlled operation, a separate entity is not set up.

Each venturer will use its own property, plant, and equipment in carrying out the activities and will incur its own expenses and liabilities. Each venturer will also be responsible for raising its own finance. Therefore, each venture should recognize in their financial statements:

- The assets that it controls and the liabilities that it incurs; and
- The expenses that it incurs and the share of the revenue that it earns from the sale or provision of goods or services by the joint venture.

No further consolidation procedures will be required and it is not required that financial statements are prepared for the joint venture. However, management accounts can be prepared so that the performance of the joint venture can be separately assessed.

The contractual arrangements between the entities which create this form of joint venture investment will normally set out how the revenues and expenses will be shared. The substance of such an arrangement is that each venturer is carrying on its own activities as essentially a separate part of its own business, since there is no separate entity.

The accounting for the joint venture should therefore reflect the economic substance of this arrangement by recognizing the assets that the venturer controls. The venturer's own property, plant, and equipment which it uses to carry out activities of the jointly controlled operation, any liabilities for which it continues to have an obligation, and the expenses that it incurs should be recognized by the entity.

Each venturer should also recognize its share of income generated by the jointly controlled operations.

Recognition of these amounts should be included in the individual entity financial statements of each venturer because they are part of its activities. No further adjustment is therefore required in the preparation of the consolidated financial statements (IPSAS 8.20).

Example 16.3 Jointly controlled operations

University A from country A and University B from country B enter into a binding arrangement whereby they combine their operations, resources, and expertise to deliver a service on a common new campus in country C.

Each venturer is responsible for a specific activity (University A for science, University B for literature), bears its own costs, and takes a share of the revenue, such as government grants, as determined in accordance with the binding arrangement. Neither of the two universities would have had enough knowledge, expertise, and financial means to settle this new campus by itself.

Under IPSAS 8 the requirement for "held for sale" investments is to account for them in accordance with the relevant international or national accounting standard dealing with the recognition and measurement of financial instruments (IPSAS 8.3a and 8.47). Where the venturer is not required to prepare consolidated financial statements under IPSAS 6 Consolidated and Separate Financial Statements it should treat the joint venture in accordance with IPSAS 6, which means that it should be accounted for:

(a) Using the equity method as described in IPSAS 7;
(b) At cost; or
(c) As a financial instrument in accordance with IPSAS 29 (IPSAS 6.58).

In addition, an exemption applies where the venturer is a wholly owned subsidiary (or partially owned but the minority interest shareholders have been notified of the intention not to apply the requirements of IPSAS 8 and they have not objected) and the venturer does not have debt or equity instruments traded in a public market (nor is in the process of issuing debt or equity in a public market) and the venturer's parent prepares consolidated financial statements that are publicly available and are prepared in accordance with IPSAS (IPSAS 8.3).

Jointly Controlled Assets

Jointly controlled assets are used to generate benefits to be shared by each of the venturers. Such arrangements do not involve the creation of a separate entity and the assets may be jointly owned, although the important attribute of such an arrangement is that the assets in question are jointly controlled.

Typically each venturer receives an agreed share of the benefits generated by the operation of the assets and bears an agreed share of the expenses incurred.

Each venturer in such an arrangement is again essentially using the assets as part of its normal operating activities and should therefore report them as part of those activities in its individual financial statements. In particular, a venturer should recognize its share of the jointly controlled assets, any liabilities that the entity has an obligation to meet, and a share of the liabilities that are jointly incurred.

Jointly incurred expenses and a share of the relevant income and expenses that are earned or incurred jointly should also be recognized by each venture (IPSAS 8.25).

Example 16.4 Jointly controlled assets

For instance, in France in June 2012, public certifiers (all ministries and universities) of Rhône-Alpes and Agera (Association of Rhône-Alpes large schools) set up a unique regional platform designed to meet the demands of collective VAE (validation des acquis de l'expérience – official recognition of skills gained through work experience).[2]

This platform brings together AFPA, the Agera, National Education, Direccte, DRAAF the Rhône-Alpes DRJSCS, and universities.

It is a peculiarity of the Rhône-Alpes region, built to provide businesses, territories … a common service to all certifiers. It is funded by the Direccte and certifiers themselves, via the mobilization of staff in charge of VAE.

The platform is designed for applications involving different VAE certifiers, unlike the collective requests initiated by companies who decide to spend a collective VAE on a single certification as a CQP. Sponsors will no longer go through the various certifiers, but through a unique platform, which is a jointly controlled asset in the public sector.

> "This complex provision Interest is particular to reduce the response time for candidates in facilitating the work of companies or public sponsors," said Philippe Idelovici, Coordinator of VAE in the Academy of Grenoble.
>
> It is also to promote the use of VAE in the GPEC (forward management of jobs and skills), where applications for VAE may vary candidates aimed a particular degree within a particular ministry.

No additional adjustments are required in the preparation of the consolidated financial statements since the individual entity financial statements of each venturer already reflect the economic reality of the arrangements.

Jointly Controlled Entities

A separate legal entity is set up with ownership being shared by the venturers. The third type of joint venture arrangement is a jointly controlled entity. The identifying factor in this arrangement is that a separate legal entity is set up with ownership being shared by the venturers.

The separate entity may take a number of forms. It may be an incorporated entity, a corporation, or a partnership.

The importance of the establishment of a separate entity is that it is able to enter into contracts and raise finance in its own right. As a separate legal entity it will also have to maintain its own accounting records and prepare and present its own financial statements.

A jointly controlled entity controls its own assets, incurs its own expenses and liabilities, and generates its own income. Each venturer will typically be entitled to a predetermined proportion of the surpluses made by the joint venture entity.

Example 16.5 Jointly controlled entity

A common example of a jointly controlled entity is when two entities combine their activities in a particular line of service delivery by transferring the relevant assets and liabilities into a jointly controlled entity.

Where a venturer has an interest in a jointly controlled entity, it is required to recognize in its consolidated financial statements its share of the entity either by:

- Proportionate consolidation, which involves consolidating the venturer's share of the individual line items of the joint venture's financial statements (IPSAS 8.35); or
- Equity accounting, which involves reporting the change in the venturer's share of the joint venture entity each period (IPSAS 8.43).

---

[2] See http://www.inffolor.org/portail/public/fr/content/vae-collectives-en-rhône-alpes-une-plate-forme-commune.

Proportionate Consolidation

Proportionate consolidation is where the venturer's share of the joint venture's assets, liabilities, income and expenditure is combined line by line with the venturer's own items (IPSAS 8.6).

Proportionate consolidation employs the principles used in the full consolidation process required by IPSAS 6 for the reporting of subsidiaries (controlled entities). The different proportions that are consolidated in respect of a subsidiary (controlled entity) and a joint venture represent the different levels of control held by the parent entity (controlling entity). In a subsidiary, the parent has ultimate control and therefore 100% of a subsidiary's net assets and results are consolidated, whereas control is shared in a joint venture, so only the venturer's share is consolidated.

The venturer may present the effects of proportionate consolidation in one of two ways. The first is by combining the proportion of the joint venture results and financial position on a line by line basis with that of the venturer's financial statements. This method results in single figures being presented for each line item. The alternative method is to split each line item between that which relates to the venturer and that which represents the proportion of the joint venture entity.

IPSAS 8 permits the use of the equity accounting method although they recommend the use of proportionate consolidation.

A venturer should cease accounting for a joint venture entity under either method when it ceases to have joint control over the joint venture. If the venturer obtains complete control of the joint venture, then it should be accounted for in accordance with IPSAS 6 from that date (IPSAS 8.4, 8.46, 8.51).

Transitional Provisions

Transitional provisions are stipulated in IPSAS 8.65–8.68. Where the proportionate consolidation treatment set out in IPSAS 8 is adopted, venturers are not required to eliminate balances and transactions between themselves, their controlled entities, and entities that they jointly control for reporting periods beginning on a date within three years following the date of first adoption of accrual accounting in accordance with IPSAS. Where entities apply the transitional provision they shall disclose the fact that not all inter-entity balances and transactions have been eliminated.

Note on Upcoming Changes. IPSAS 33 First-time Adoption of Accrual Basis International Public Sector Accounting Standards

IPSAS 33 stipulates that the following transition relief will be applicable in IPSAS 37: Where a first-time adopter accounted for its investment in a joint venture under its previous basis of accounting using proportionate consolidation, the investment in the joint venture shall be measured on the date of adoption as the aggregate of the carrying amount of the assets and liabilities that the entity previously proportionately consolidated, including any purchased goodwill arising from acquisition transactions (IPSAS 33, para. 132).

Disclosures

Key disclosures (cf. IPSAS 8.61–8.64) include the following:

- The methods used to recognize the entity's interests in joint ventures;
- A listing and description of interests in significant joint ventures and the proportion of ownership interest held in jointly controlled entities;
- The aggregate amount of the contingent liabilities;
- A brief description of contingent assets and, where practicable, an estimate of their financial effect.

Note on Upcoming Changes. IPSAS 37 Joint Arrangements

IPSAS 37 Joint Arrangements establishes requirements for classifying joint arrangements and accounting for those different types of joint arrangements. They are classified as either joint operations or joint ventures:

- In a joint operation, the parties to the arrangement have rights to the assets and obligations for the liabilities relating to the arrangement.
- In a joint venture, the parties to the arrangement have rights to the net assets of the arrangement.

These classifications differ from IPSAS 8, which referred to three types of arrangements (jointly controlled entities, jointly controlled operations, and jointly controlled assets).

IPSAS 37 requires that an entity account for its interest in a joint operation by recognizing its share of the assets, liabilities, revenue, and expenses of the joint arrangement. It also requires that joint ventures be accounted for using the equity method. These requirements differ from those of IPSAS 8, which permitted jointly controlled entities to be accounted for using either the equity method or proportionate consolidation.

Note also that IPSAS 38 Disclosure of Interests in Other Entities brings together the disclosures previously included in the three former IPSAS 6–8. IPSAS 38 adds new disclosure requirements, including those related to structured entities that are not consolidated and controlling interests acquired with the intention of disposal.

SEPARATE FINANCIAL STATEMENTS (IPSAS 34)

The objective of IPSAS 34 is to prescribe the accounting and disclosure requirements for investments in controlled entities, joint ventures, and associates when an entity prepares separate financial statements. The requirements stipulated in IPSAS 34 are very similar to the current requirements for separate financial statements in IPSAS 6.

DISCLOSURE OF INTERESTS IN OTHER ENTITIES (IPSAS 38)

IPSAS 38 brings together the disclosures previously included in IPSAS 6–8. It also introduces new disclosure requirements, including those related to structured entities that are not consolidated and controlling interests acquired with the intention of disposal.

17 SPECIFIC STANDARDS: ACCOUNTING FOR AGRICULTURE AND ACCOUNTING IN HYPERINFLATION ECONOMIES

This chapter covers IPSAS 27 Agriculture and IPSAS 10 Financial Reporting in Hyperinflationary Economies. These are two specific IPSAS standards, one linked to the activity, the other one linked to the economical and monetary environment:

- IPSAS 27 relates to reporting on agricultural activity, which is of marginal relevance to most public sector entities; and
- IPSAS 10 is aimed at entities whose functional currency is the currency of a hyperinflationary economy.

AGRICULTURE (IPSAS 27)

Reporting on agricultural activity is of marginal relevance to most public sector accounts preparers, although significant in some jurisdictions, notably in countries where part or all of agricultural land and activities are state owned. An agricultural activity is the management by an entity of the biological transformation of biological assets: for sale, into agricultural produce, or into additional biological assets.

Farming and the agricultural sector have many unique aspects. For example, animals and plants, described as biological assets, have characteristics which are not present in other industries. Another significant feature is that government assistance in the agricultural sector is common and is often substantial. However assistance does not necessarily mean that IPSAS 27 is to be applied to these activities.

For instance, the mission of World Food Programme (WFP):

is to end global hunger. Every day, WFP works worldwide to ensure that no child goes to bed hungry and that the poorest and most vulnerable, particularly women and children, can access the nutritious food they need. WFP supports national, local and regional food security and nutrition plans. It partners with other United Nations agencies, international organizations, non-governmental organizations, civil society and the private sector to enable people, communities and countries to meet their own food needs (WFP, 2014)

Nevertheless, none of WFP activities are within the scope of IPSAS 27 on Agriculture. They fall in the scope of IPSAS 12 on Inventories.

Agricultural activity is described as the management by an entity of the biological transformation of living animals or plants (biological assets) for sale, or for distribution at no charge or for a nominal charge or for conversion into agricultural produce or into additional biological assets (IPSAS 27, IN1; para. 9). Biological assets are to be measured at fair value less costs to sell unless fair value measurement is unreliable. The standard presumes that the fair value of agricultural produce can be determined reliably, which serves as the costs basis for application of IPSAS 12 Inventories subsequently.

Agricultural produce is the harvested product of the entity's biological assets and a biological asset is a living animal or plant (IPSAS 27, para. 9). IPSAS 27 provides a table with examples of biological assets, agricultural produce, and products that are the result of processing after harvest – see Table 17.1 (IPSAS 27, para. 6):

IPSAS 27 applies to (IPSAS 27.2):

- Biological assets;
- Agricultural produce at the point of harvest, described as the detachment of produce from a biological asset or the cessation of a biological asset's life processes.

IPSAS 27 does not apply to:

- Land related to agricultural activity;
- Intangible assets related to agricultural activity;
- Biological assets held for the provision or supply of services.

Table 17.1 Biological assets, agricultural produce, and products that are the result of processing after harvest

Biological assets	Agricultural produce	Products that are the result of processing after harvest
Sheep	Wool	Yarn
Trees in a plantation forest	Felled trees	Logs
Plants	Cotton	Thread, clothing
Dairy cattle	Milk	Cheese
Pigs	Carcass	Sausage

IPSAS 27 does not establish any new principles for land related to agricultural activity. Instead, an entity follows IPSAS 16 Investment Property or IPSAS 17 Property, Plant and Equipment, depending on which standard is appropriate in the circumstances.

Recognition

A biological asset or agricultural produce is recognized in the statement of financial position when, and only when, the following three criteria are met:

- Past event has occurred and resulted in the entity having control over the asset;
- It is probable that the future economic benefits, or service potential, associated with the asset, will flow to the entity; and
- The fair value or cost of the asset can be measured reliably.[1]

Measurement

A biological asset shall be measured on initial recognition and at each reporting date at its fair value less costs to sell (see also footnote 1). Determining fair value is achieved by considering if there is, or is not, an active market. Figure 17.1 below illustrates the two options for determining fair value (see IPSAS 27.21 and 27.22).

Agricultural produce harvested from an entity's biological assets shall be measured at its fair value less costs to sell at the point of harvest. That measurement is the cost at that date when applying IPSAS 12, or another applicable standard. Establishing the fair value for a biological asset or agricultural produce may be facilitated by grouping biological assets or agricultural produce according to significant attributes; for example, by age or quality. An entity selects the attributes corresponding to the attributes used in the market as a basis for pricing (IPSAS 27.18, 27.19).

A gain or loss arising on initial recognition of a biological asset or agricultural produce at fair value less costs to sell is included in surplus or deficit for the period in which it arises. A change in fair value of a biological asset is also recognized in surplus or deficit.

Since all biological assets are valued at fair value, all costs (other than costs to purchase the biological asset) related to these assets are expensed when incurred. Therefore the purchase price approximates fair value.

IPSAS 27 includes the following guidance on determining the fair value of a biological asset or agricultural produce (IPSAS 27.21–27.22, 27.24–27.27):

- The quoted market price in an active market is a reliable and preferred basis for determining the fair value of that asset. The fair value of a biological asset is based on the current market price and is not adjusted to reflect the existence of a contract that stipulates delivery at a future date.

---

[1] Paragraph 34 of IPSAS 27 provides that in case the fair value can not be measured reliably, then the biological asset shall be measured at cost less any accumulated depreciation and any accumulated impairment losses.

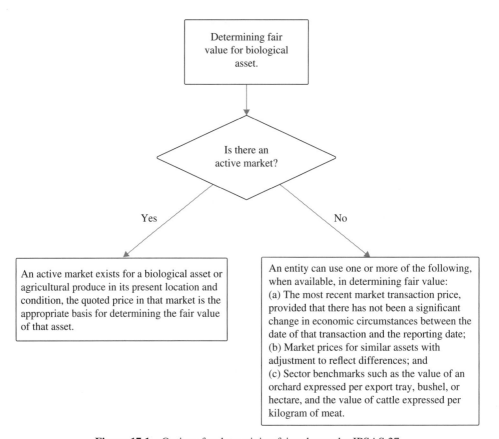

Figure 17.1   Options for determining fair value under IPSAS 27

- If an active market does not exist, a market-determined price such as the most recent market price for that type of asset, or market prices for similar or related assets, or sector benchmarks is to be used.
- If reliable market-determined prices are not available, the present value of expected net cash flows from the asset must be used, discounted at a current market-determined rate.

IPSAS 27.28 stipulates that the cost of the asset could be an indicator of its fair value, particularly when little biological transformation has taken place or the impact of biological transformation on price is not expected to be material.

IPSAS 27.34 presumes that fair value can be reliably measured for biological assets. However, this presumption can be rebutted when the biological asset does not have a market determined price and for which alternative methods of estimating fair value are clearly unreliable. In that case, the biological asset is measured at cost less accumulated depreciation and impairment losses. Afterwards, when the fair value becomes reliably measurable, the biological asset is to be measured at fair value less costs to sell.

Gains and Losses

On initial recognition of biological assets and agricultural produce, a gain may arise. One example could be when a calf is born, or as a result of harvesting. A loss may also arise on initial recognition, due to the fact that estimated point-of-sale costs are deducted in determining fair value less estimated point-of-sale costs of biological assets or agricultural produce. The gains and losses should be included in surplus or deficit in the period in which they arise.

Example 17.1   Gain on initial recognition of a biological asset

A public sector entity is engaged in cheese production and holds 500 cows that are able to produce milk for the cheese. On one particular day, the cows produced 500 liters of milk.

The fair value less estimated point-of-sale costs should be determined at the time of milking and included in surplus or deficit. If the fair value less point-of-sale costs is estimated at €1.20 per liter for that day, a gain of €600 (500 × 1.20) should be included in surplus or deficit.

Disclosure

IPSAS 27 requires the following disclosures:

- Aggregate gain or loss on biological assets and agricultural produce for changes in fair value;
- Description of each group of biological assets;
- The nature of the entity's activities involving each group of biological assets;
- Non-financial estimates of the physical quantities of each group of biological assets and the output of agricultural produce;
- Methods and assumptions in estimating fair value;
- Fair value of agricultural produce harvested during the period; and
- A reconciliation of changes in the carrying amount of the biological assets between the beginning and end of the period.

The entity should also disclose information on risks, commitments, and restrictions on biological assets which are important for the readers of the financial statements:

- Existence and carrying amount of biological assets whose title is restricted or that are pledged as security;
- Nature and extent of restrictions to use or sell biological assets;
- Commitments for development or acquisition of biological assets;
- Financial risk management strategies related to the agricultural activity.

When fair value cannot be measured reliably, the entity shall disclose the following:

- Description of the biological assets;
- The reason why fair value cannot measured reliably;
- If possible, a range of estimates within which fair value is highly likely to lie;
- Depreciation method used;
- Useful lives or depreciation rates applied;
- The gross carrying amount and the accumulated depreciation, at beginning and end of the reporting period.

In case biological assets are measured at cost less accumulated depreciation and impairment losses, the entity shall disclose:

- Gain or loss upon disposal of these assets;
- A reconciliation of the carrying amounts at the beginning and end of the period;
- Impairment losses, reversal of impairment losses, and depreciation included in surplus or deficit.

Moreover, in case the fair value of biological assets previously measured at cost becomes available, the entity is to disclose the following additional information:

- Description of the biological assets;
- Explanation of why fair value has become reliably measurable;
- Effect of the change.

All these disclosures are aimed at helping the readers of the financial statements to understand the value of biological assets, especially when they are not valued at fair value, which is the preferred treatment.

Below is an example of presentation of biological assets in the Biosev S.A. consolidated interim financial statements for the three-month period ended 30 June 2014, financial statements being prepared under IFRS.

Example 17.2   Disclosure on biological assets, Biosev (2014, pp. 11 and 28–29)

1. GENERAL INFORMATION

Biosev S.A. ("Company"), headquartered at Avenida Brigadeiro Faria Lima, 1355, 11° andar, Pinheiros, São Paulo, SP, and its subsidiaries (collectively "Group") are mainly engaged in the production, processing and sale of agricultural products, primarily sugarcane and its by-products; the agricultural operations in Company-owned or third-party land; the export, import and sale of petroleum by-products, lubricants, fuel, grease and hydrated ethyl alcohol; the purchase, sale, import and export of agricultural products and its by-products; and the generation and sale of electricity and its by-products.

The preparation of the individual and consolidated interim financial information in accordance with CPC 21(R1) and IAS 34 requires the adoption of certain accounting estimates by the Company's management. The interim financial statements have been prepared based on the historical cost, except for certain financial instruments, held-for-sale assets, and biological assets measured at their fair values. The historical cost is generally based on the fair value of the consideration paid in exchange for assets on the transaction date.

14. BIOLOGICAL ASSETS

	Company (BR GAAP)		Consolidated (BR GAAP and IFRS)	
	30/06/2014	31/03/2014	30/06/2014	31/03/2014
Opening balance	650 583	712 682	1 279 891	1 241 580
Increases arising from expenses on sugarcane crops and crop treatments	123 098	522 884	181 088	796 705
	773 681	**1 235 566**	**1 460 979**	**2 038 285**
Losses on changes in fair value less estimated costs to see	(47 506)	(524 919)	(81 676)	(570 327)
Write-off	–	(278)	–	(278)
Sugarcane harvest in the period at fair value	(17 193)	(59 786)	(55 004)	(187 789)
	708 982	**650 583**	**1 324 299**	**1 279 891**

When determining the fair value, the Company takes the following into consideration:

Valuation methodology

The discounted cash flow for the next six years was the method used for the economic and financial evaluation of sugarcane biological assets, which represents the average extraction period of sugarcane plantation.

Discount rate

The discount rate used to calculate the discounted cash flow was 5.5%, which represents the weighted average cost of capital (WACC), net of taxes. This rate is used as proper parameter to calculate the discount rate applicable to future cash flows of the biological assets.

Market overview

Own or third-party sugarcane is processed by the plant or ethanol distillery. Its own sugarcane has two different origins: (a) sugarcane grown in own land; and (b) sugarcane grown in leased land, where the plant leases the land from third parties and is responsible for all farming activities. These lease agreements are basically entered into for a six-year period (one cycle). The sugarcane from third parties (suppliers) is acquired by the plant under supply contracts. Either the supplier or the plant itself can be responsible for the transportation of sugarcane to the plant.

CONSECANA's formula calculates the consideration per ton of sugarcane based on:

(a) The volume of ATR/TR delivered by the sugarcane supplier.
(b) The share of the sugarcane production cost as a percentage of the sugar, ethanol residue, anhydrous ethanol and hydrated ethanol.
(c) The net prices of sugar in the domestic and foreign markets, and the prices of anhydrous ethanol and ethyl ethanol fuel, hydrated ethanol, and ethanol for other purposes.
(d) The plant's production mix for said crop.

CONSECANA's reference price is published on a monthly basis.
The following assumptions were used to determine the fair value:

	Company (BR GAAP)		Consolidated (BR GAAP and IFRS)	
	30/06/2014	31/03/2014	30/06/2014	31/03/2014
Estimated harvest area (in hectares)	195 804	186 950	303 536	291 605
Expected yields (in tonnes of sugarcane per hectare)	68.2	67.0	73.0	72.2
Total volume of recoverable sugar (in kilogram per tonne of sugarcane)	132.4	132.4	132.2	133.8
Value of a kilogram of total recoverable sugar (in R$) – CONSECANA	0.5125	0.5190	0.5125	0.5190
Discount rate	5.5%	5.5%	5.5%	5.5%

As at June 30, 2014, the Company provided as guarantee for the export prepayment 73 134 hectares (73 134 hectares as at March 31, 2014), equivalent to approximately 4 890 548 tons of sugarcane (4 890 548 as at March 31, 2014), in the amount of R$85 337, at fair value, as at June 30, 2014 (R$79 486 as at March 31, 2014). Such prepayment was disbursed on July 16, 2012 and falls due on January 31, 2015.

Biosev Group is mainly engaged in the production and sale of agricultural products, primarily sugar cane and its by-products. Sugar cane biological assets fair value is determined using discounted cash flows over six years, which represents the average extraction period of a sugar cane plantation. Fair value is not a market value. Moreover, in order to discount cash flows, Biosev Group uses the WACC (weighted average cost of capital) as discount rate, which is a common practice. Determination of sugar cane biological assets fair value is extremely important for the readers of the Biosev Group financial statements, especially assumptions used (such as discount rate, estimated harvest area, expected yields, total volume of recoverable sugar, value or a kilogram of total recoverable sugar) in order to form their own judgment.

FINANCIAL REPORTING IN HYPERINFLATIONARY ECONOMIES (IPSAS 10)

IPSAS 10 Financial Reporting in Hyperinflationary Economies prescribes the accounting treatment of financial statements of entities whose functional currency is the currency of a hyperinflationary economy to ensure that these financial statements are useful and meaningful to the readers of the financial statements. Therefore, the financial statements (including comparatives) should be restated to reflect the change in the purchasing power on the basis of a general price index. Hyperinflationary economies are those with very high rates of general inflation which have such a depreciating effect on the country's currency that it loses its purchasing power at a very fast rate. IPSAS 10 does not include any absolute rate or definition of hyperinflation. Professional judgment is needed to assess when restatement of financial statements is required.

IPSAS 10 includes characteristics of an economy, which are indicators that can assist in determining whether an economy is hyperinflationary. Figure 17.2 below outlines the key indicators.

Hyperinflation causes particular problems for entities operating in such economies since money loses its purchasing power at such a high rate that comparisons are at best unhelpful, and potentially misleading. This includes the comparison of results between accounting periods and for similar transactions within the same accounting period.

Thus, where an entity has operations in a hyperinflationary economy it is likely that without the restatement required by IPSAS 10 Financial Reporting in

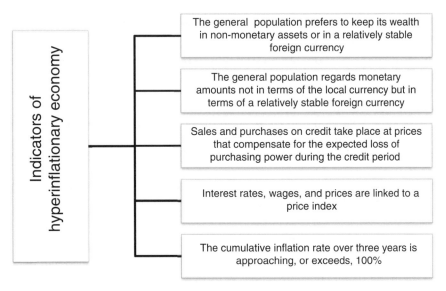

Figure 17.2 Indicators that can assist in determining whether an economy is hyperinflationary under IPSAS 10

Table 17.2 Restated financial statements and a functional currency in a hyperinflationary economy

Statement of financial position	Statement of financial performance	Statement of cash flows
Restatements are made by applying a general price index: • Monetary items that are already stated in the measuring unit at the reporting date are not restated. • Non-monetary items, not already carried at fair value or net realizable value, are restated based on the change in the general price index between the dates those items were acquired and the reporting date. • When a non-monetary item has been revalued at another date than the acquisition date, the price evolution between the revaluation date and the reporting date is taken into account based on the general price index.	Restatements are made by application of the change of a general price index to all revenues and expenses since the date they were actually recorded.	All items in the statements of cash flow are expressed in terms of the measuring unit current at the end of the reporting period. Corresponding figures for the previous reporting period are restated by applying a general price index.

Hyperinflationary Economies the reporting of operating results and the financial position in the local currency will become distorted over time.

Restatement of Financial Statements in Hyperinflationary Economies

The financial statements of an entity whose functional currency is the currency of a hyperinflationary economy are stated in terms of the measuring unit current at the end of the reporting period. Corresponding figures in relation to prior periods are also restated. The gain or loss on the net monetary position is included in surplus or deficit and separately disclosed.

It should be noted that the application of the restatement principles included in IPSAS 10 requires professional judgment. The objective is not to be accurate but rather to provide relevant information that can be compared over time (Schumesh et al., 2012).

Restated financial statements of an entity whose functional currency is the currency of a hyperinflationary economy are as follows:

Gain or Loss on the Net Monetary Position

The gain or loss on the net monetary position should be included and disclosed separately in the statement of financial performance. This gain or loss is an indicator of the purchasing power gain or loss as a consequence of the inflation and may be derived by different methods.

Consolidation

Controlling entities, reporting in the currency of a hyperinflationary economy themselves, when consolidating an entity in a hyperinflationary economy should restate the financial statements of this entity in the measuring unit current at the reporting date before consolidation.

Economies Ceasing to be Hyperinflationary

When an economy ceases to be hyperinflationary, the entity shall discontinue the preparation and presentation of financial statements prepared in accordance with IPSAS 10. It shall treat the amounts expressed in the measuring unit current at the end of the previous reporting period as the basis for the carrying amounts in its subsequent financial statements.

Disclosure

IPSAS 10 requires disclosure of the following:

- The fact that the financial statements and prior comparative figures are restated for changes in the general purchasing power of the functional currency, in terms of the measuring unit current at the reporting date;
- The identity and level of the price index at the reporting date and the movement in the index during the current and the previous reporting periods.

Moreover, the surplus or deficit on the net monetary position should be disclosed on the face of the statement of financial performance to inform the reader of the impact of hyperinflation on the value of the financial statements.

CONCLUSION

IPSAS 27 and IPSAS 10 are two very specific standards, the first because of the nature of the activities covered by IPSAS 27 Agriculture, the second because hyperinflationary economies are fortunately not so common, at least among entities applying accrual basis of accounting IPSAS.

18 RECOMMENDED PRACTICE GUIDELINES (RPGs)

Recommended practice guidelines (RPGs) are non-mandatory best practice. RPGs are a new type of publication that provides guidance on the broader aspects of financial reporting that are outside the financial statements. They are not IPSAS and are not mandatory.

The IPSASB has issued RPG 1 Reporting on the Long-Term Sustainability of an Entity's Finance;

RPG 2 Financial statement discussion and analysis and RPG 3 on Reporting Service Performance. This chapter will thus provide an overview of the three RPGs.

REPORTING ON THE LONG-TERM SUSTAINABILITY OF AN ENTITY'S FINANCES (RPG 1)

In July 2013, the IPSASB issued Recommended Practice Guidelines (RPG) 1 *Reporting on the Long-Term Sustainability of an Entity's Finances.* RPG 1 provides guidance on reporting on the long-term sustainability of a public sector entity's finances over a specified time horizon in accordance with stated assumptions on policy and demographic and economic variables.

RPG 1 explains that projections need to be based on current policy; not just supportable assumptions. In terms of scope, it applies to all public sector entities. It complements reporting of obligations to provide social benefits but the scope is much wider.

'RPG 1 provides straightforward guidance on presenting information about the capacity of an entity to provide social benefits at existing levels, to maintain existing

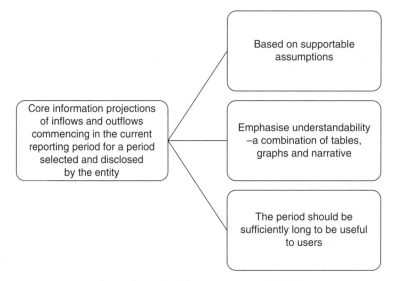

Figure 18.1   High-level overview of RPG 1

taxation revenues and to meet its financial commitments,' said IPSASB Chair Andreas Bergmann.[1] "By developing guidance on reporting information about the long-term sustainability of an entity's finances, RPG 1 reflects the IPSASB Conceptual Framework's position that, in order to meet users' needs, the scope of financial reporting is more comprehensive than the financial statements."

Objective of RPG 1

The objective of RPG 1 is to provide guidance on the reporting of the long-term sustainability of a public sector entity's finances (or the reporting of long-term fiscal sustainability information). The aim of such reporting is to provide an indication of the projected long-term sustainability of an entity's finances over a specified time span in accordance with stated assumptions.

The scope of RPG 1 includes an entity's projected inflows and outflows and is not limited to those flows related to programs providing social benefits. However, the RPG recognises that the flows relating to, for example, programs providing social benefits require contributions from participants. Such programs can be a highly significant component of reporting long-term fiscal sustainability information for many entities.

The reporting of environmental sustainability is not directly addressed in RPG 1, nevertheless, an entity should assess the financial impacts of environmental factors and take them into account when developing its projections.

Figure 18.1 provides a high-level overview of the focus in RPG as to how to report on core information projections of inflows and outflows. RPG 1 details that the

[1] See https://www.ifac.org/news-events/2013-07/ipsasb-publishes-first-recommended practice-guideline -long-term-sustainability-p (last accessed 31 July 2014).

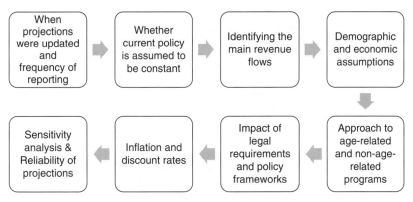

Figure 18.2 Encouraged disclosures

assumption need to be supportable; emphasises understandability of data presented and explains to the user of RPG 1 that the time period need to be sufficiently long to be useful to the reader of the financial statements.

RPG 1: Disclosures

RPG 1 encourages disclosure of the extent to which it is followed. The encouraged disclosures include descriptions of (see Figure 18.2):

Reporting Long-term Fiscal Sustainability Information

In deciding whether to report long-term fiscal sustainability information, an entity has to determine whether there are users and readers of the financial statements who would be using forward-looking financial information. Long-term fiscal sustainability information is more comprehensive than information derived from financial statements and includes projected inflows and outflows related to the provision of goods and services and programs providing social benefits using current policy assumptions over a specified time span.

As such, RPG 1 takes into account decisions made by the entity, on or before the reporting date, that will give rise to future outflows that do not meet the definition of and/or recognition criteria for liabilities at the reporting date. Correspondingly, it takes into account future inflows that do not meet the definition of and/or recognition criteria for assets at the reporting date.

Policies and decisions taken today have a long-term impact on future inflows and outflows of resources. Consequently there is a need for information on the impact of such policies and decisions that supplement information on liabilities, expenses, assets, and revenues in the financial statements. Long-term fiscal sustainability information prepared in accordance with the RPG 1 should enable users to understand and assess a wide range of aspects of the long-term fiscal sustainability of the entity, including the nature and extent of financial risks that the entity faces.

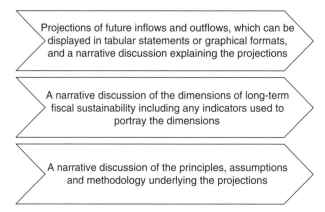

Figure 18.3   Components of information

Form and content of long-term fiscal sustainability information

The form and content of an entity's long-term fiscal sustainability information will differ depending on the nature of the entity and the regulatory environment in which it operates.

A single presentation approach is unlikely to satisfy the objectives of financial reporting. In general, long-term fiscal sustainability information would include the components listed in Figure 18.3.

Projections are to be prepared on the basis of current policy assumptions, and assumptions about future economic and other conditions. The suitable selection of time span is also critical. As time span increases, the assumptions underpinning the projections become less robust and potentially less verifiable. This, at the same time means, that exceptionally short time spans can increase the risk that the consequences of events outside the time horizon would be ignored, thus reducing the relevance of projections.

The Dimensions of Long-term Fiscal Sustainability

The reporting of long-term fiscal sustainability information should include a narrative discussion on each of its dimensions; service, revenue and debt (RPG 1 provides an illustration of this). The dimensions are inter-related as changes in one dimension affect the other dimensions. For example, future services and entitlements to beneficiaries (the service dimension) are funded by revenue and/or debt.

Service dimension

The service dimension focuses on the capacity of an entity to maintain (or vary) the volume and quality of the services it provides or the entitlement programs it delivers to beneficiaries over a certain period of time, under the current policy assumptions on revenue from taxation and other sources, and debt constraints. The entity is to consider its exposition to risk factors, such as the willingness of recipients and beneficiaries to accept reduction in services and entitlements.

An entity may be exposed because it does not have the ability to determine or vary service levels, for example, where another level of government determines the level of services to be provided. This is for instance the case of an intergovernmental organisation which is committed to serve pensions to its pensioners and active staff according to a pension fund system installed by its Member States. The intergovernmental organisation depends on the budget decided by its Member States and is therefore exposed to the risk factor of being unable to serve pensions on the long term despise its commitment. It is also quite unlikely that beneficiaries (active staff and pensioners) accept that the level of pensions served is reduced.

Revenue dimension

The revenue dimension focuses on the capacity of an entity to vary existing taxation levels or other revenue sources or introduce new revenue sources. It considers taxation levels and other revenue sources over a certain period of time, under the current policy assumptions on revenue from taxation and other sources, and debt constraints. The entity is to consider its exposure to risk factors, such as the unwillingness of taxpayers to accept increases in taxation levels, and the extent of its dependence upon revenue sources outside its control or influence.

Intergovernmental organisations are to consider risk factors such as the (un)willingness of Member States to accept increase in their annual contribution, either on global level, or on individual level. For instance, under the United Nations system, some Member States may see their annual contribution increase or decrease according to the evolution of their economy. Therefore a Member State is facing three constraints on the value of its contribution: first the evolution of the budget of the intergovernmental organisation, second its UN scale rating, and third the evolution of its currency compared to the currency used in the intergovernmental organisation to bill contribution (usually USD or euros). In order to assess the (un)willingness of Member States to accept increase in their annual contribution, intergovernmental organisations have to consider these risk factors, which are likely to be blocking elements in some cases.

Debt dimension

The debt dimension focuses on the capacity of the entity to meet its financial commitments as they are due, or to refinance, or increase debt as necessary. It considers debt levels over a certain period of time, under the current policy assumptions on the provision of services to recipients and entitlements for beneficiaries, and revenue from taxation and other sources, and debt constraints. The entity is to consider its exposition to risk factors, such as the entity's exposure to interest rate risk, market and lender confidence.

The level of net debt is important for an assessment of the debt dimension, as, at any reporting date, it represents the amount expended on the past provision of goods and services that has to be financed in the future.

Projected levels of net debt can be presented by projecting current policy assumptions for the provision of goods and services, and for revenue from taxation and other

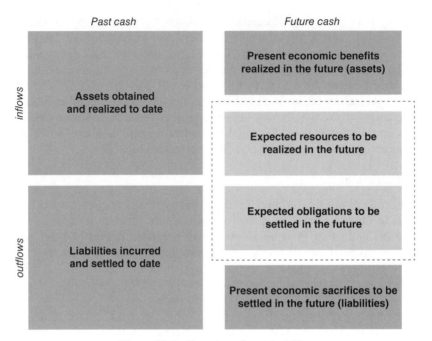

Figure 18.4   Overview of sustainability

sources. This information assists users in assessing the entity's ability to meet its financial commitments as they come due or to maintain, refinance or increase its levels of debt and thereby evaluate the sustainability of the entity's debt (see Figure 18.4).

This indicator is likely to be relevant for many entities as long as stake holders understand its meaning. Net debt does not give any indication on the level of cash flow needed for the coming year. However it gives an indication on the "business model" of the entity. Is this model sustainable on the long run? Or on the other hand, according to the current policy assumptions, will the net debt be out of control over the period of the projections, may be in 10 or 20 years from now? Many governments, tax payers, citizens and other stakeholders may be very interested in this indicator once they have understood its interest, notably the impact on the long term of net debt, either borrowings (bonds) or social commitments (welfare or pension commitments).

The following example, from Appendix B of RPG 1 illustrates the two aspects (capacity and vulnerability) of each of the three dimensions and the relationship between the three dimensions and shows relationships between the dimensions of long-term fiscal sustainability (see Figure 18.5).

FINANCIAL STATEMENT DISCUSSION AND ANALYSIS (RPG 2)

The objective of RPG 2 is to develop financial reporting guidance on narrative reporting in financial statements. In terms of scope, it covers all entities preparing general purpose financial statements in accordance with IPSAS 1.

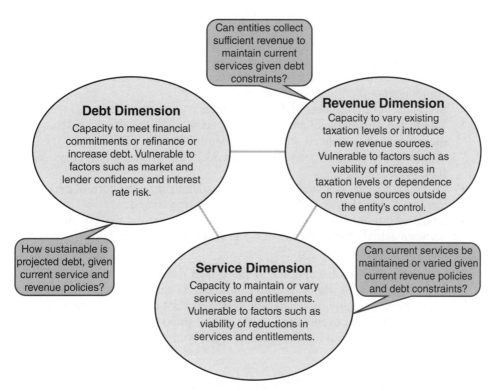

Figure 18.5 Relationships between the dimensions of long-term fiscal sustainability

"Financial statement discussion and analysis presented in accordance with RPG 2 represents good practice," explained IPSASB Chair Andreas Bergmann. "It sets out the status, scope, and reporting boundary for the information. RPG 2 is intended to encourage more public sector entities to provide users with financial statement discussion and analysis."[2]

Financial statement discussion and analysis should be issued by public sector entities at least annually, when they issue their financial statements.

Information presented in financial statement discussion should:

- Be consistent with the qualitative characteristics in the Conceptual Framework;
- Be consistent with the financial statements, being based on currently known facts and supportable assumptions;
- Be identified and clearly distinguished from the financial statements themselves;
- Include a specific compliance statement with the RPG.

---

[2] See EY (2013).

Analysis of financial statements should include:

- Description of significant events and activities impacting financial results;
- Brief discussion of the purpose and information and interrelationship of each component of the financial statements;
- Significant commitments and contingencies;
- Where the analysis includes financial performance measures which are not included in the financial statements themselves, the performance measures should be defined and explained and reconciled to information in the financial statements;
- Comparative analysis where relevant to understanding the current period;
- Explain and analyze significant changes and trends; and
- To extent not provided elsewhere in financial statements: analysis of variances between actual results and budget, and between current and prior years.

RPG 2 also addresses discussion and analysis of risk and uncertainties.

RPG 2 is introducing the equivalent of MD&A (management discussion and analysis) produced annually by listed companies, at least in the USA and in Europe, explaining the significant events of the year and all important information that management wants to share with market players, stock holders and other third parties.

REPORTING SERVICE PERFORMANCE INFORMATION (RPG 3)

RPG 3, Reporting Service Performance Information, was published 31 March 2015.

RPG 3 provides guidelines on reporting service performance information. RPG 3 provides principles applicable to the presentation of service performance information and definitions that aim to establish a standardised service performance information terminology. RPG 3 also provides guidance on the selection of performance indicators having regard to an entity's service performance objectives, disclosures about the basis of the reported information, and service performance related narrative discussion and analysis.

RPG 3 aims to support the provision of high-quality service performance information by entities, whether they are already reporting service performance information or plan to begin reporting such information in the future.

Service performance information covers a wide scope of activities, since public sector entities provide services, such as:

- Services provided directly to individuals and institutions, for example, health or education services or the provision of goods such as food or books;
- Services provided indirectly to individuals and institutions, for example, services which aim to develop, promote, protect or defend a community, institution, country, or community values and rights;

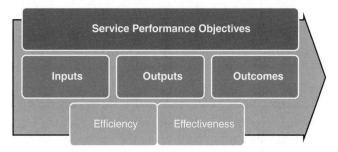

Figure 18.6   Big picture – reporting service performance

- Transfers to individuals and institutions;
- Provision of policies, regulations or legislation to achieve public policy goals; and
- Collection of taxes and other revenues.

This RPG, which reflects the IPSASB's position that the scope of financial reporting is more comprehensive than the financial statements, sets out good practice for reporting service performance information, by providing guidance on presentation decisions with respect to service performance information that will meet users' needs; and recommending minimum characteristics for reporting service performance information.

GBEs are excluded from the scope of this RPG. However it does not mean that this guideline could not be applied by GBEs. The IPSASB considers that where GBEs report service performance information, the guidance in this RPG would be useful for such reporting.

Where a controlling entity provides information on services provided by one or more controlled GBEs, information about the GBEs' services, reported by the controlling entity, needs to follow the RPG's requirements. In that case, GBEs are not excluded from the scope of the RPG, as controlled entities – see Figure 18.6.

RPG 3 Disclosures

RPG 3 stipulates below disclosures:

- Narrative discussion and analysis to support assessments of efficiency and effectiveness of services;
- Reconciliation or comparison between reported service related costs and the expenses reported in the financial statements, and;
- Sufficient information to understand *basis* of service performance information presented.

It emphasizes four dimensions:

Why? Information on entity's service performance objectives, including the need or demand for these objectives to be achieved

What? Performance indicators to show achievements

How? Comparisons of actual performance to planned (or targeted) results, including information on the factors that influence results.

When? Time-oriented information, including comparisons of actual results over time and to milestones.

CONCLUSION

In meeting its objective to serve the public interest by setting high-quality public sector accounting standards and by facilitating the adoption and implementation of these, thereby enhancing the quality and consistency of practice throughout the world and strengthening the transparency and accountability of public sector finances, the IPSASB sets International Public Sector Accounting Standards (IPSAS) as well as Recommended Practice Guidelines (RPGs) for use by public sector entities, including national, regional, and local governments, and related governmental agencies.

While IPSAS relate to the general purpose financial statements (financial statements) and are authoritative, RPGs are pronouncements that provide guidance on good practice in preparing general purpose financial reports (GPFRs) that are not financial statements.

Unlike IPSAS, RPGs do not establish requirements, and do not provide guidance on the level of assurance (if any) to which information should be subjected. However, their guidance is aimed at being useful on the broader aspects of financial reporting that are outside the financial statements.

PART 3

CASH-BASED IPSAS

19 CASH BASIS IPSAS

The IPSASB has in addition to its suite of accrual-based IPSAS issued a standard for financial reporting under the cash basis of accounting. This standard has been developed taking into account the circumstances and requirements of the public sector and as such there is no equivalent standard for the private sector within the IFRS/IAS suite of standards.

Compliance with the cash basis IPSAS supports public sector entities to enhance accountability in regards to cash receipts, cash payments, and cash balances at the reporting date. The measurement focus in cash-based financial statements is therefore on the balances of cash and fluctuations thereof. Sound cash-based accounting provides input for assessments of public sector entities' ability to generate adequate cash flows in the future as well as the sources and uses of cash.

Public sector entities that apply and comply with the cash-basis IPSAS will strengthen their financial reporting pertaining to cash receipts, cash payments, and cash balances. The disadvantage of cash accounting is that it tells only part of the financial story (see Table 19.1). Cash basis IPSAS will however serve as a sound starting point for public sector entities that do not have any accounting standards in place to strengthen their financial reporting practices.

The cash basis IPSAS contains two parts; Part 1 is mandatory and Part 2 is not mandatory (see Table 19.2).

Table 19.1   Cash accounting versus accrual accounting – a high-level overview

Cash Accounting	Accrual Accounting
Transactions are accounted for only at the point where there is a cash (which includes cash equivalents) receipt or cash payment.	Transactions are recognized as the underlying economic events occur, regardless of the timing of the related cash receipts and payments.
Revenues are recognized when cash is received.	Revenue is recognized when income is earned.
Expenses are recognized when cash payments are made.	Expenses are recognized when resources are consumed or liabilities are incurred.
Only cash assets and cash liabilities are recognized on the statement of cash balances (i.e., the cash basis balance sheet).	Assets and liabilities are recognized on the balance sheet. This includes non-cash assets and liabilities such as, for example, property, plant and equipment, intangible assets, and employee liabilities.

Table 19.2   Parts 1 and 2 of cash basis IPSAS

Part 1. Mandatory	Part 2. Non-Mandatory
Specifies the requirements which are applicable to all entities preparing general purpose financial statements under the cash basis of IPSAS. In order for a public sector entity to claim to report in accordance with the IPSAS Financial Reporting under the Cash Basis of Accounting, all requirements of Part 1 of the standard must be complied with.	Identifies additional accounting policies and disclosures that a public sector entity is encouraged to adopt with the objective of enhancing financial accountability and transparency in the financial statements.

The key definitions included in the IPSAS for Financial Reporting under the Cash Basis of Accounting include:

- Cash, which is defined as cash on hand, demand deposits, and cash equivalents.
- Cash equivalents, which are defined as short-term, highly-liquid investments that are readily convertible to known amounts of cash and which are subject to an insignificant risk of changes in value.
- Cash flows, which are defined as inflows and outflows of cash.

It should be noted that the definition of cash flows provided in the cash basis IPSAS differs from the one provided in IPSAS 2. In the cash basis IPSAS, cash flows are limited to in- and outflows of cash only, while in IPSAS 2 they also include cash equivalents.

Question and Answer

Question:

When would an investment qualify as a cash equivalent under cash basis IPSAS?

Answer:

An investment would normally be categorized as a cash equivalent if it has a short maturity. Paragraph 1.2.3 of cash basis IPSAS states that short term would typically be three months or less from the date of acquisition. It should be noted that equity investments are *not* included as cash equivalents unless, in substance, they would meet the definition of a cash equivalent.

Question and Answer

Question:

Are bank overdrafts always considered as a component of cash?

Answer:

Bank overdrafts, which are repayable on demand, form an integral part of an entity's cash management. In these circumstances, bank overdrafts are included as a component of cash. A characteristic of such banking arrangements is that the bank balance often fluctuates between being positive and being overdrawn. Otherwise, bank borrowings (bank overdrafts) are considered to give rise to cash inflows and are not considered as a component of cash. They are classified as proceeds from borrowings, which means that some proceeds from borrowings can be short-term borrowings as long as they are not repayable on demand.

CONTENT PART 1 CASH BASIS IPSAS (MANDATORY)

Part 1 of the cash basis IPSAS, Financial Reporting Under the Cash Basis of Accounting, is applicable to all public sector entities with the exception of Government Business Enterprises (GBEs) (see Chapters 1, 3–4 for definition and discussion on GBE). The cash basis IPSAS can be applied to the financial statements of separate public sector entities as well as to consolidated financial statements.

When is Cash Controlled?

Only controlled cash will appear on a public sector entity's statement of cash receipts and payments. Thus determining if and when cash is controlled is of importance. Cash basis IPSAS, paragraph 1.2.6, establishes that cash is controlled when a public sector entity can use the cash for the achievement of its own objectives or otherwise benefit from the cash as well as being able to exclude or regulate access of others to that benefit.

It should be noted that cash basis IPSAS specifies requirements for disclosures to be made on cash balances that are held by the public sector entity at the reporting date, but not controlled (cf. paragraph 1.4.9).

Question and Answer

Question:

Cash is deposited into the bank account of public sector entity A. Public sector entity A is to transfer this cash to a third party, on behalf of its government, 30 days later. Is the cash controlled by public sector entity A?

Answer:

Public sector entity A controls the cash for the period during which the cash resided in its bank account.

Question and Answer

Question:

The aid agency AA has agreed to help country C providing a grant to build a strategic bridge. The aid agency AA pays a construction company directly for building the strategic bridge for country C rather providing the funds to country C. Does country C have to record cash in and cash out for the construction of this bridge?

Answer:

Country C does not receive cash (or cash equivalent): the amount paid on its behalf to the construction company does not constitute cash. Therefore country C does not have to record cash in nor cash out for the construction of the bridge. Nevertheless, country C benefits from the cash payment made on its behalf.

Question and Answer

Question:

Under cash basis IPSAS, is it possible to present expenditure in the financial statements when they are posted to the public accounting system rather than when they are actually paid?

Answer:

No. Payments should be recognized when outflow of cash occurs, and receipts when cash is received to the entity.

Table 19.3   Required components in IPSAS cash basis financial statements

Required components in IPSAS cash basis financial statements

A statement of cash receipts and payments that (a) recognizes all cash receipts, payments, and balances controlled by the entity; and (b) separately identifies payments made by third parties on behalf of the entity.

Accounting policies and explanatory notes.

If the entity makes its approved budget publicly available, a comparison of budget and actual amounts, either as a separate additional financial statement or as a budget column in the statement of cash receipts and payments.

Cash Basis Financial Statements

Under cash basis IPSAS public sector entities are required to include the components shown in Table 19.3 in their financial statements (cf. paragraph 1.3.4).

In addition to the required components, cash basis IPSAS, also notes that additional statements may be included. Paragraph 1.3.9 provides examples on such supplementary statements.

What Information Should be Included in the Required Statement of Cash Receipts and Payments

Paragraph 1.3.12 of cash basis IPSAS specifies the information that is required to be included in the statement of cash receipts and payments. It includes the following:

(a) Total cash receipts of the public sector entity showing separately a sub-classification of total cash receipts using a classification basis appropriate to the entity's operations;
(b) Total cash payments of the entity showing separately a sub-classification of total cash payments using a classification basis appropriate to the entity's operations;
(c) Starting and closing cash balances of the entity.

The subsequent paragraph, 1.3.13 states that total cash receipts and total cash payments, and cash receipts and cash payments for each sub-classification of cash receipt and payment, should be reported on *a gross basis*. The standard, however, permits an exception from the gross basis, and allows for cash receipts and payments to be reported on a *net basis* when:

(a) They arise from transactions which the public sector entity administers on behalf of other parties and which are recognized in the statement of cash receipts and payments; or
(b) They are for items in which the turnover is quick, the amounts are large, and the maturities are short.

The standard allows for additional elaboration and examples of transactions where a presentation on a net basis of cash receipts and payments is allowed in paragraphs 1.3.19–1.3.20. See IPSAS Financial Reporting in Practice 19.1 for an example where transactions are reported on a net basis under the IPSAS cash basis standard. In the Maldives Civil Aviation Authority financial statements for the year 2013 there is a small part with a net reporting on "petty cash balance."

IPSAS Financial Reporting in Practice 19.1. Maldives Civil Aviation Authority Cash Basis Financial Statements for the year 2013

Maldives Civil Aviation Authority
Financial Statements for the year 2013 (in MVR)

Statement of Receipts and Payments for the year ended 31st December 2013

	Notes	Trust Account 2013	Grants 2013	Trust Account 2012	Grants 2012
Receipts					
Opening Balance	14	98 327	–	–	–
Amount drawn from the Approved Budget	3	17 675 827	–	7 266 530	–
Income received	4	5 087 715	–	2 794 571	–
Petty Cash Balance held at Year End	15	865	–	14	–
Grant and Donations	18	–	–	–	129 010
Travelling Expenses received for maintenance organisations' inspections	18	–	100 082	–	–
Total receipts		22 862 732	100 082	10 061 114	129 010
Payments					
Salaries and Wages	5	11 464 289	–	4 908 039	–
Pensions	6	266 924	–	141 699	–
Travelling Expenses	7, 18	949 807	94 486	286 432	27 839
Stationery and Office Requisites	8	⁻126 457	–	77 819	–
Administrative Supplies	9, 18	348 281	–	281 768	22 058
Training Expenses	10, 18	2 523 637	–	101 227	79 114
Repairs and Maintenance	11	22 732	–	2 014	–
Government, Grants and Subsidies	12	1 684 870	–	1 467 531	–
Capital Expenditure	13	252 844	–	–	–
Total Expenditure		17 675 841	94 486	7 266 530	129 010
Deposits to Public Bank Account (PBA)	14	–	–	1 967 401	–
Deposits to Civil Aviation Fund	14	5 125 278	–	728 857	–

Balance of Travelling Expenses received for maintenance organisations' inspections	18	–	5 596	–	–
Total Payments (including the amount deposited to PBA)		22 801 119	100 082	9 962 787	129 010
Balance		61 612	–	98 327	–

2.8 Cash Balance

Cash balances reported in the financial statements are petty cash balance, and income received to the Authority which is not deposited in the Trust Account (Civil Aviation Fund) at the end of the financial year.

Question and Answer

Question:

What are some examples of transactions for which a public sector entity can report on a net basis under cash basis IPSAS?

Answer:

Agency transactions may encompass a variety of transactions where a public sector entity administers transactions (i.e., acts as an agent) on behalf of others. Such agency transactions allow for net reporting under cash basis IPSAS. Examples of such transactions include:

(a) The collection of taxes by one level of government for another level of government not including taxes collected by a government for its own use as part of a tax sharing arrangement.
(b) Funds held for customers by an investment or trust entity.
(c) Funds administered by a central entity on the "single account" basis for management of government expenditure.

Note that paragraphs 1.3.20–1-3.23 of cash basis IPSAS provide further elaboration and examples on when net reporting is permitted.

It should be noted that the standard requires that line items, headings, and subtotals should be presented in the statement of cash receipts and payments when such presentation is necessary to provide fairly the entity's cash receipts, payments, and balances. Any sub-classifications (or classes) of total cash receipts and payments that a public sector entity discloses (cf. paragraphs 1.3.12 and 1.3.14) are a matter of professional judgment.

IPSAS Financial Reporting in Practice 19.2 provides an example of:

1. How cash receipts can be classified. For example, separately identifiable cash receipts from taxation, donations, borrowings etc.,
2. Cash payments: service delivery, debt reduction, etc., and
3. Alternative presentations are also possible.

IPSAS Financial Reporting in Practice 19.2. Municipality of Kline Cash Basis Financial Statements for the year ended 31 December 2011 (KOSOVO)

Kline Municipality
Section 12. Statement of Cash Receipts and Payments for the year ended 31 December 2011

	Notes	2011 Single treasury account KCB €'000	Payments from third parties €'000	2010 Single treasury account KCB €'000	Payments from third parties €'000	2009 Single treasury account KCB €'000	Payments from third parties €'000
Funds sources							
Government Grant	2	6 400	–	5 324	–	4 579	–
Revenues	3	621	–	827	–	1 081	–
Fund designated for specific purposes		–	–	–	–	–	–
Designated donor grants	4	46	–	18	–	232	–
Borrowed Funds	5	–	–	–	–	–	–
Other receipts	6	–	1 051	–	630	–	–
Total funds		**7 067**	**1 051**	**6 169**	**630**	**5 892**	**-**
Utilization of funds							
Operations							
Wages and Salaries	7	4 184	–	3 355	–	3 051	–
Goods and Services	8	622	–	517	–	514	–

Utilities	9	183	–	132	–	157	–
		4 989	–	**4004**	–	**3 722**	–
Transfers							
Transfers and subsidies	10	85	–	58	–	55	–
Capital expenditures		–	–	–	–	–	–
Property, Plant and Equipment	11	1993	–	2 107	–	2 115	–
Other payments	12	–	1 051	–	630	–	–
Return of Loan	13	–	–	–	–	–	–
Total		**7 067**	**1 051**	**6 169**	**630**	**5 892**	–

Reporting on Payments by Third Parties on Behalf of the Entity

In the public sector it is not unusual for payments to be carried out by third parties on behalf of a public sector entity. Thus, cash basis IPSAS covers these types of transactions in paragraphs 1.3.24–1.3.29. For transactions where a third party directly settles the obligations of an entity or purchases goods and services for the benefit of the entity, the entity should disclose this in a separate column on the face of the statement of cash receipts and payments. The standard requires that the public sector entity must distinguish between total payments that are made by third parties which are part of the economic entity and those that are made by third parties which are not part of the economic entity to which the reporting entity belongs.

Government banking arrangements are a critical factor in managing and controlling the cash resources of government (see Pattanayak and Fainboim, 2011).[1] Governments may opt to manage expenditure of its individual departments and entities through a centralized treasury function or a "single account" arrangement. For single account arrangements, payments are made on behalf of those government departments and entities by a central entity (e.g., treasury) after appropriate authorization and documentation from the department. For such transactions, the department, or entity, does not control cash in- and outflows and cash balances. As such, the department or entity shall report in a separate column on the face of the statement of cash receipts and payments the amounts of payments made by the central entity on its behalf and the

---

[1] They are important for ensuring that (i) all tax and non-tax revenues are collected and payments are made correctly in a timely manner; and (ii) government cash balances are optimally managed to reduce borrowing costs (or to maximize returns on surplus cash). Pattanayak and Fainboim (2011) detail how this is achieved by establishing a unified structure of government bank accounts via a treasury single account (TSA) system.

sources and uses of the amount expended sub-classified on a basis appropriate for the department or entity (see paragraph 1.3.25).

Question and Answer

Question:

What is a treasury single account?

Answer:

A treasury single account can be defined as a unified structure of government bank accounts supporting optimal utilization of government cash resources and enabling consolidation. It separates transaction-level control from overall cash management. A treasury single account is thus a bank account (or a set of linked bank accounts) through which the government transacts all its receipts and payments and gets a consolidated view of its cash position at the end of each day.

As explained by Pattanayak and Fainboim (2011), this banking arrangement for government transactions is based on the principle of fungibility of all cash irrespective of its end use. While it is necessary to distinguish individual cash transactions (e.g., a typical revenue and/or expenditure transaction of a government unit) for control and reporting purposes, these objectives are achieved through the accounting system and not by holding and/or depositing cash in transaction-specific individual bank accounts. This allows the Ministry of Finance/Treasury to delink management of cash from control at a transaction level.

As an example, the Government of Uganda (GoU) introduced a treasury single account (TSA) framework with effect from 1 October 2013. This reform was introduced in accordance with their Public Finance and Accountability Act (PFAA) 2003 (see Government of Uganda, 2013).

Disclosures

The IPSAS cash basis paragraphs detail requirements in terms of accounting policies and disclosure notes. They state that an entity following IPSAS cash basis shall ensure that the notes to the financial statements:

(a) Present information about the basis of preparation of the financial statements and the specific accounting policies[2] selected and applied for significant transactions and other events; and

(b) Provide additional information which is not presented on the face of the financial statements but is necessary for a fair presentation of the entity's cash receipts, cash payments, and cash balances (see paragraph 1.3.30).

---

[2] Note that paragraph 1.3.32 of IPSAS cash basis requires the development of accounting policies to ensure that the financial statements provide information that meets a number of qualitative characteristics.

The general purpose financial statements prepared under the cash basis IPSAS shall present information that is shown in Figure 19.1:

Figure 19.1   Nature of information under IPSAS cash basis

Financial statements are to be presented at least annually, and should be issued within six months of the reporting date.[3] If the reporting date of a public sector entity following cash basis IPSAS changes, and the financial statements are presented for a period other than one year, this must be disclosed. An entity shall also disclose the date when the financial statements were authorized for issue and who gave authorization. If another body has the power to amend the financial statements after issuance, the entity should disclose that fact (paragraph 1.4.5). In addition it should be noted that if an entity chooses to disclose information prepared on a different basis from the cash basis of accounting as defined in the cash basis IPSAS (or as required by paragraphs 1.3.4(a) or 1.3.4(c) of cash basis IPSAS), such information should be disclosed in the notes to the financial statements (paragraph 1.3.5).

Consolidation under IPSAS Cash Basis

Section 1.6 of IPSAS cash basis provides the necessary definitions and requirements for the preparation of cash basis consolidated financial statements. A controlling entity, other than a controlling entity identified in paragraphs 1.6.7 and 1.6.8, should issue consolidated financial statements which consolidate all controlled entities, foreign and domestic, other than controlled entities operating under severe external long-term restrictions which prevent the controlling entity from benefiting from its activities.

Cash basis IPSAS 1.6.7 stipulates that a controlling entity that is a wholly owned controlled entity does not have to present consolidated financial statements provided users of such financial statements are unlikely to exist or their information needs are met by the controlling entity's consolidated financial statements.

---

[3] A timeframe of three months is strongly encouraged under IPSAS cash basis (paragraph 1.4.4).

Cash basis IPSAS 1.6.8 provides that the same applies to a controlling entity that is virtually wholly owned, provided the controlling entity obtains the approval of the owners of the minority interest.

Cash basis IPSAS provides the procedure for consolidation shown in Table 19.4 (paragraph 1.6.16):

Table 19.4   IPSAS cash basis consolidation procedure

Consolidation procedure

Cash balances and cash transactions between entities within the economic entity should be eliminated in full.

When the financial statements used in a consolidation are drawn up to different reporting dates, adjustments should be made for the effects of significant cash transactions that have occurred between those dates and the date of the controlling entity's financial statements. In any case, the difference between the reporting dates should be no more than three months.

Consolidated financial statements should be prepared using uniform accounting policies for like cash transactions. If it is not practicable to use uniform accounting policies in preparing the consolidated financial statements, that fact should be disclosed together with the proportions of the items in the consolidated financial statements to which the different accounting policies have been applied.

The aim of consolidation is to reflect only transactions between the consolidating entity and other entities external to it, thus preventing double counting of transactions.

IPSAS Financial Reporting in Practice 19.3. South Africa Consolidated Financial Statements (National Departments, the National Revenue Fund, State Debt and Loan Accounts) for 2013

	Notes	2012/13 R'000	2011/12 R'000
CASH FLOWS FROM OPERATING ACTIVITIES			
Receipts disclosed by the National Revenue Fund		**812 776 365**	**755 777 618**
Revenue collected by SARS		776 676 313	726 751 938
Departmental Revenue collected		10 299 627	13 767 388
Direct Exchequer Receipts		14 743 552	7 954 491
CARA Receipts		35 341	17 333
Surrenders from departments		9 298 495	6 916 173
Other revenue received by the revenue fund		1 723 037	367 295
Receipts disclosed by National Departments		**12 227 443**	**13 447 688**
Annual appropriated funds received		(94 202)	(29 413)
Statutory appropriated funds received		173	–

Departmental revenue received	9 336 877	11 618 630
Direct Exchequer receipts	777 973	11 520
NRF Receipts	31 535	37 333
Aid assistance received	2 175 087	1 809 618
Payments disclosed by the National Revenue Fund	**424 591 816**	**396 512 016**
Statutory Appropriation	421 737 608	389 567 232
CARA Payments	157 827	–
Appropriation for unauthorised expenditure	60 917	–
Direct Exchequer Payments	2 587 197	6 944 784
Other	48 267	–
Net increase in working capital	(2 238 407)	(2 394 317)
Surrendered to Revenue Fund	(20 080 332)	(20 558 767)
Surrendered to RDP Fund/Donor	(885 245)	(583 222)
Current payments	(157 452 205)	(145 937 684)
Payments for financial assets	(1 691 014)	(1 167 773)
Transfers and subsidies paid	(380 372 298)	(353 485 329)

Net cash flows available from operating activities	29	**(162 307 509)**	**(151 413 802)**

CASH FLOWS FROM INVESTING ACTIVITIES

Payments for capital assets	(14 173 245)	(11 987 266)
Proceeds from sale of capital assets	94 226	115 052
Increase in loans	(446 634)	(359 157)
Increase in investments	(738 360)	20 667
Increase in other financial assets	(6 348)	(368)
Net cash flows from investing activities	**(15 270 361)**	**(12 211 072)**

CASH FLOWS FROM FINANCING ACTIVITIES

Distribution/dividend received	1 873 621	1 594 932
Increase in net assets	1 196 001	392 172
Increase in non-current payables	220 277	474 296
Increase in borrowings	149 414 494	189 893 543
Net cash flows from financing activities	**152 704 393**	**192 354 943**
Net decrease in cash and cash equivalents	(24 873 477)	28 730 069
Cash and cash equivalents at beginning of period	199 544 658	170 818 369
Cash and cash equivalents at end of period	**174 671 181**	**199 548 438**

"1. PRESENTATION OF THE FINANCIAL STATEMENTS

[…] All departments are controlled by Government. These consolidated financial statements include the financial results of the departments and Parliament.

> Government Departments apply uniform accounting policies as prescribed by the National Treasury except to the extent that a department has requested a deviation from the Treasury.
>
> Departmental revenue is allocated by SARS and directly deposited into the National Revenue Fund which forms part of the overall consolidation revenue, and is accounted for on a modified cash basis. [...]
>
> Inter-entity transactions and balances between the departments and the National Revenue Fund (NRF) are eliminated. PAYE is not eliminated as it is not considered as an interdepartmental transaction. VAT is not eliminated as government does not pay VAT directly to the NRF and government is not a VAT vendor. National Revenue Fund only recognised material provisions that will result in the potential cash outflow to government."

Transition relief for consolidation

IPSAS cash basis provides for transitional relief for consolidation. Paragraph 1.6.21 details that controlling entities that adopt cash basis IPSAS may have large numbers of controlled entities with significant volumes of transactions between those entities. As a result it can be difficult to identify all the transactions and balances that need to be eliminated for the purpose of preparing the consolidated financial statements of the economic entity.

Therefore, the standard provides transitional relief for the entity for reporting periods beginning on a date within three years following the date of first adoption of this standard, from the requirement to eliminate all cash balances and transactions between entities within the economic entity (paragraph 1.8.2). However, paragraph 1.8.3 requires that entities which apply the transitional provision should disclose the fact that not all balances and transactions between entities within the economic entity have been eliminated.

Foreign Currency Transactions and Balances

Cash basis IPSAS provides for the treatment of foreign currency cash receipts, payments, and balances. The treatment for cash receipts and payments arising from transactions in foreign currencies differs from that of cash balances held in a foreign currency (see Figure 19.2).

The cash receipts and cash payments of a foreign controlled entity are to be translated at the exchange rates between the reporting currency and the foreign currency at the dates of the receipts and payments (paragraph 1.7.4). An entity is to disclose the amount of exchange differences included as reconciling items between opening and closing cash balances for the period.

Presentation of Budget Information in the Financial Statements

A public sector entity that makes its approved budget publicly available is required to present a comparison of the budget amounts for which it is held publicly accountable and actual amounts either as a separate additional financial statement or as additional

Cash receipts and payments in foreign currency	Cash balances held in foreign currency
• Cash receipts and payments arising from transactions in foreign currencies should be recorded in the public sector entity's reporting currency. The exchange rate between the reporting currency and the foreign currency is applied to the foreign currency at the date of the receipts and payments	• Cash balances held in a foreign currency should be reported using the closing rate

Figure 19.2   Treatment of foreign currency transactions and balances

budget column in the statement of cash receipts and payments currently presented in accordance with cash basis IPSAS (cf. paragraph 1.9.8). Section 1.9 of IPSAS cash basis is devoted to defining the requirements for the presentation of budget information in the financial statements.

Distinguishing between the different definitions of budgets provided in cash basis IPSAS is essential in order to meet the presentation requirement of budget information. Table 19.5 provides an overview of the key budget definitions.

Cash basis IPSAS prescribes that if budget and actual amounts are prepared on a comparable basis then the public sector entity is required to present a comparison of these as an additional column in the statement of cash receipts and payments. If budget and actual amounts are not prepared on a comparable basis then a reconciliation statement is required by the standard. Comparable basis under the cash-based IPSAS means that the actual amounts are presented on the same accounting basis and classification basis for the same entities and for the same period as the approved budget.

Table 19.5   Key budget definitions (cf. paragraph 1.9.1)

Term	Definition
Annual budget	An approved budget for one year. It does not include published forward estimates or projections for periods beyond the budget period.
Approved budget	The expenditure authority derived from laws, appropriation bills, government ordinances, and other decisions related to the anticipated revenue or receipts for the budgetary period.
Final budget	The original budget adjusted for all reserves, carry over amounts, transfers, allocations, supplemental appropriations, and other authorized legislative or similar authority changes applicable to the budget period.
Original budget	The initial approved budget for the budget period.
Multiyear budget	A budget that is approved for more than one year. It does not include published forward estimates or projections for periods beyond the budget period.

The requirements for the comparison of budget and actual amounts, are that it must present separately, for each level of legislative oversight, the following:

(a) The original and final budget amounts;
(b) The actual amounts on a comparable basis; and
(c) The note disclosure of the entity must provide an explanation of material differences between the budget for which it is held publicly accountable and actual amounts unless such explanations are published in other public documents published in conjunction with the financial statements. If the latter is the case, then a reference to such related documents must be provided in the note disclosure of the entity.

Example. Note on Budget Disclosure. (South Africa Consolidated Financial Statements – Constitutional Institutions, Schedule 2, 3A and 3B Public Entities and Trading Accounts for the year ended 31 March 2013)

"BUDGET INFORMATION IN ACCORDANCE WITH GRAP 24

As there is no publically available budget that is reconcilable with the group of entities for the purposes of the National Government Department Consolidation, and National Public Entity Consolidation, it is deemed inappropriate to present a comparison between actual and budget information at this level of consolidation."

IPSAS Financial Reporting in Practice 19.4. Statement of Comparison of Budget and Actual Amounts, Cash Basis Financial Statements, Maldives Civil Aviation Authority, for the year 2013

Maldives Civil Aviation Authority
Financial Statements for the year 2013 (in MVR)

Statement of Comparison of Budget and Actual Amounts for the year ended 31st December 2013

	Notes	Approved Budget 2013	Budget deductions/ additions	Transfers within budget codes	Final Budget 2013	Income/ Expenses 2013	Balance
Budget/Receipts							
Approved Budget	3	31 022 341	–	–	31 022 341	17 675 841	13 346 500
Income Received	4	–	–	–	–	5 087 715	–
Total Receipts		**31 022 341**	**–**	**–**	**31 022 341**	**22 763 556**	**13 346 500**
Recurrent expenditure							
Salaries and Wages	5	18 280 298	–	–	18 280 298	11 464 289	6 816 008

Pensions	6	429 834	–	–	429 834	266 924	162 910
Travelling Expenses	7	1 761 453	–	–	1 761 453	949 807	811 646
Stationery and Office Requisites	8	166 090	–	–	166 090	126 457	39 633
Administrative Supplies	9	1 913 081	–	–	1 913 081	384 281	1 528 800
Training Expenses	10	5 040 082	–	–	5 040 082	2 523 637	2 516 445
Repairs and Maintenance	11	71 200	11 800	–	83 000	22 732	60 268
Government Grants and Subsidies	12	2 236 171	–	–	2 236 171	1 684 870	551 301
Total Recurrent Expenditure		**29 898 209**	**11 800**	**–**	**29 910 009**	**17 422 997**	**12 487 012**
Balance before Capital Expenditure		**1 124 132**		**–**	**1 112 332**	**5 340 559**	
Capital Expenditure							
Furniture, Machinery & Equipment	13	1 124 132	(11 800)	–	1 112 332	252 844	859 488
Total Capital Expenditure		**1 124 132**	**(11 800)**	**–**	**1 112 332**	**252 844**	**859 488**
Total Expenditure		**31 022 341**	**–**	**–**	**31 022 341**	**17 675 841**	**13 346 500**
Budget Balance							**13 346 500**

2.10 Budget Information

In the Statement of Comparison of Budget and Actual Amounts, the Authority's policy is to show the original budget as approved by its Board of Directors, budget additions and deductions by the Ministry of Finance and Treasury, transfers within various budget codes and the effect of any circumstances which led to the non-availability of the budget. The final budget shown in the Statement of Comparison and Actual Amounts reflects these adjustments.

6. Pensions

Details		Approved Budget 2013	Transfers within budget codes	Budget deductions/ additions	Final Budget 2013	Expenditure 2013	Expenditure 2012
213001	Pension	429 834	–	–	429 834	266 924	141 699
	Totals	**429 834**	**–**	**–**	**429 834**	**266 924**	**141 699**

> The Board of Director Allowances of MVR 28,000 for the month of December 2012 was paid from 2013 budget in the month of January because of the budget constraints. Also, a total increment of MVR 645 298 for August and September 2012, resulting from changes to the salary structure was paid in the year 2013.

In addition, if any entity has changes from original to final budget, cash basis IPSAS requires that an explanation of whether the changes between the original and the final budget are a consequence of reallocation within the budget or due to other factors (cf. paragraph 1.9.23).

Public Sector Entities Receiving External Assistance

Cash basis IPSAS provides for detailed disclosure requirements on external assistance including total external assistance paid by third parties during the period to directly settle obligations of the entity or purchase goods and services on behalf of the entity; the balance of undrawn external assistance loans; significant terms and conditions of external assistance loans or grant agreements or guarantees that have not been complied with during the period when non-compliance resulted in cancellation of the assistance or has given rise to an obligation to return assistance previously provided; the amount of external assistance cancelled or to be returned should also be disclosed.

Specifically, cash basis IPSAS requires that an entity disclose separately on the face of the statement of cash receipts and payments, the total external assistance received in cash during the reporting period (paragraph 1.10.8). External assistance is all official resources which the recipient can use or otherwise benefit from in pursuit of its objectives. However, it should be noted that it does not include assistance provided by non-governmental organizations (NGOs), even if such assistance is provided under a binding arrangement. NGO or other third party cash donations is to be presented in the financial statement and can be further explained in the note disclosures.

EXAMPLES OF USE OF CASH BASIS IPSAS

This section of Chapter 19 provides some insight into a few countries in which the IPSAS cash basis has played a role on the path towards strengthening financial accounting and reporting.

Liberia

With the funding support of African Development/World Bank technical assistance was provided to the Ministry of Finance in Liberia to adopt cash basis IPSAS. The adoption of cash basis IPSAS was carried out in order to support the implementation of the new Public Financial Management (PFM) Act of 2009 (ADF, 2011). The PFM Act calls for substantial public financial management reforms, so as to enhance the fiduciary environment in Liberia with the aim of supporting effective implementation of poverty reduction strategies. The ADF (2011) suggest that a public financial management reform will contribute to enhanced transparency and efficiency in the use of public resources as well as creating the fiscal space for improved "pro-poor expenditure" and service delivery in line with the priorities of the poverty reduction strategies.

India

In a GASAB (2008) publication it was explained that India had been maintaining accounts on a cash basis but not in accordance with cash basis IPSAS. It was stated that there was a need for changes in the existing cash system to comply with cash basis IPSAS. Except for a few items like accrual-based treatment of GPF interest and non-cash transfer entries, the basis accounting process in India is aligned to cash basis IPSAS. A few procedural issues like the inclusion of a statement of accounting policies, inclusion of information about the entity etc., can be easily incorporated into the system.

It was highlighted that "India may adopt cash basis IPSAS in the short or medium term in respect of budget sector accounting information alone (i.e., controlled entities consolidation may not be attempted for the present). Since adoption of cash basis IPSAS is primarily to facilitate eventual migration to accrual basis accounting, the existing non-cash items may be continued" (GASAB, 2008).

In 2010, it was highlighted that the "GASAB has developed an operational framework and detailed road map for migration from existing cash basis of accounting to accrual basis. To facilitate migration to accrual accounting, GASAB is in the process of developing Standards on accrual basis to be issued as Indian Government Financial Reporting Standards (IGFRS)" (IPAI, 2010).

Malaysia

The Malaysian Federal Government adopted the cash basis IPSAS from the year ended 31 December 2005 (IPSASB, 2013). Implementing cash basis IPSAS was very valuable in the Malaysian public sector for establishing discipline around their accounting procedures and was, as such, a positive transitional step for them (ibid.). The transition to accrual accounting was then embarked upon in 2011. The Federal Government of Malaysia is now set to adopt full accrual-based accounting for financial reporting by 1 January 2015, so as to converge[4] with the requirements of accrual-based IPSAS (Gomes, 2013) – see Figure 19.3.

It has been stated that "[a] major issue that may impede IPSAS is that output-based budgeting is still run on a cash-basis." "Therefore," said Er Beng Kiong, Deputy Director of Accountancy Development Section, Accountant-General's Department, "the new accounting system also known as '1 GFMAS' has the capability of maintaining two ledgers, namely, the cash ledger and accrual ledger to keep track of both accrual and cash transactions. In this regard, in addition to the accrual financial statements, a cash basis Statement of Budget Performance will be prepared in 2015. In the interim, staff competencies will have to be upgraded as public sector employees have, up to now, been applying cash-based accounting. Retraining will be necessary" (Gomes, 2013).

---

[4]The accrual-based Malaysia Public Sector Accounting Standards (MPSAS) are primarily based on IPSAS but do diverge in some areas in order to accommodate national circumstances (IPSASB, 2013).

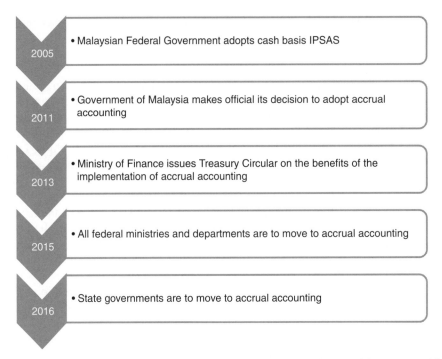

Figure 19.3 Adopting cash basis IPSAS is the first step in the Malaysian transition to accrual-based accounting (IPSASB, 2013)

Summary

The three countries included in this section illustrate that cash basis IPSAS can serve a beneficial role in a variety of ways, when countries seek to strengthen their financial reporting. Cash basis IPSAS has allowed them to present transparent and comprehensive financial reporting of cash payments, cash receipts, and balances and to compare their financial management over time. Most commonly we see that IPSAS cash basis can assist, as a milestone, in a longer process towards accrual accounting in the public sector. Adopting cash basis IPSAS enhances discipline around procedures, as well as public sector management, and can be considered not as a goal, but as a positive transitional step for countries wishing to transition to accrual basis IPSAS.

CONTENT PART 2 CASH BASIS IPSAS (NON-MANDATORY)

The non-mandatory section of cash basis IPSAS identifies additional accounting policies and disclosures that an entity is encouraged to adopt in order to enhance the transparency of its financial statements and its financial accountability. It contains explanations of alternative methods of presenting certain information.

The non-mandatory part of cash basis IPSAS provides the basis for the additional disclosures which are encouraged. Table 19.6 provides an overview of the key

Table 19.6 Overview of the key headings contained in Part 2 of IPSAS cash basis

Encouraged disclosures	Explanation
Going concern	An assessment of the entity's ability to continue as a going concern. In making such an assessment awareness of any material uncertainties related to events or conditions which could have an effect on the entity's going concern should be taken into account. A going concern assessment is mainly relevant for individual entities rather than for the government as a whole.
Extraordinary items	Provision of separate disclosure on the nature and amount of each extraordinary item is encouraged. The disclosure may be made on the face of the statement of cash receipts and payments, or in other financial statements, or in the notes to the financial statements. An extraordinary item is one that is distinctively different from the entity's ordinary items and activities. It is not expected to recur frequently and is outside the control of the entity.
Administered transactions (agency transactions)	An entity is encouraged to disclose in the notes to the financial statements, the amount and nature of cash flows and cash balances resulting from transactions administered by the entity as an agent on behalf of others where those amounts are outside the control of the entity.
Disclosing major classes of cash flows	Disclosure on the analysis of total cash payments and payments by third parties using a classification based on either nature or function, as appropriate; and proceeds from borrowings, which may also be classified into type and sources. Paragraphs 2.1.26–2.1.30 develop examples of classifications.
Related party disclosures	Application of IPSAS 20 on "Related party Disclosures" is encouraged.
Disclosure on assets, liabilities, and comparison with budget	Information on assets and liabilities controlled by the entity and used in the achievement of service delivery are encouraged to be disclosed. In addition, if an entity does not make publicly available its approved budget, then comparison with budgets is encouraged.
Consolidated financial statements	The key encouraged disclosures are: (a) The proportion of ownership interest in controlled entities and, where that interest is in the form of shares, the proportion of voting power held (only where this is different from the proportionate ownership interest); (b) Where applicable: • The name of any controlled entity in which the controlling entity holds an ownership interest and/or voting rights of 50% or less, together with an explanation of how control exists; and • The name of any entity in which an ownership interest of more than 50% is held but which is not a controlled entity, together with an explanation of why control does not exist; and • In the controlling entity's separate financial statements, a description of the method used to account for controlled entities.

headings contained in Part 2 of IPSAS cash basis and an introduction as to what they pertain to.

In addition to the encouraged disclosures described in Table 19.6, the non-mandatory Part 2 of IPSAS cash basis includes guidance for disclosures on joint ventures, financial reporting in hyperinflationary economies, assistance from NGOs, recipients of external assistance, and migration to accrual accounting.

PART 4

MAKING THE TRANSITION TO IPSAS AND CLOSING

20 MAKING THE TRANSITION TO IPSAS

Moving to accounting under International Public Sector Accounting Standards (IPSAS) can be a challenging endeavor. Ensuring proper convergence to IPSAS entails not only a vast amount of work in the accounting arena of any given public sector entity or government but also often implies major changes in business processes and practices.

By using a project management approach in adopting IPSAS an organization/government can make certain that, for example:

- The project gets necessary support from top management;
- A sound governance structure is put in place;
- Communication and training plans are developed and managed;
- New accounting policies are written; and
- Necessary alignment of business processes will take place in a timely manner.

Sound project management may facilitate cost-effective adoption of IPSAS and a broader strengthening of business practices across the implementing organization/government.

Transition to IPSAS covers a wide range of situations:

- Moving from IPSAS non-compliant cash accounting to IPSAS cash accounting;
- Moving from IPSAS cash accounting to full accrual accounting under IPSAS;
- Moving from modified accrual-based accounting or some accrual accounting standards to full accrual accounting under IPSAS.

The implementation of IPSAS is often seen as an integral part of public sector entities' quest to strengthen governance (see Chapter 2 of this book). Making the change to IPSAS in public entities and in particular within governments is dependent on political support and on the necessary legal provisions being made.

Acknowledging the importance and the difficulty of the adoption of accrual basis IPSAS, on 31 January 2015 the IPSASB released IPSAS 33 First-time Adoption of Accrual Basis International Public Sector Accounting Standards (IPSAS). The objective of IPSAS 33 is:

> to provide guidance to a first-time adopter that prepares and presents financial statements following the adoption of accrual basis IPSASs, in order to present high quality information (IPSAS 33.1):
>
> (a) That provides transparent reporting about a first-time adopter's transition to accrual basis IPSASs;
> (b) That provides a suitable starting point for accounting in accordance with accrual basis IPSASs irrespective of the basis of accounting the first-time adopter has used prior to the date of adoption; and
> (c) Where the benefits are expected to exceed the costs.

IPSAS 33 is mandatory for first-time adopters for a period beginning on or after 1 January 2017. Earlier application is permitted. IPSAS 33 is covered later in this chapter.

TRANSITIONING TO IPSAS

The successful adoption of IPSAS is seen as a step towards strengthening an entity's financial reporting and hence also the accountability and transparency of the implementing entity.

Example 20.1   IPSAS adoption within the United Nations

The adoption of IPSAS was seen as a key reform element within the United Nations System and it continues to receive support from governing bodies and senior management. Since 2006 United Nations system organizations have made headway in aligning themselves with IPSAS requirements. Yet they have become increasingly aware that this undertaking would be more arduous and complex than initially foreseen.

The adoption of IPSAS is beginning to have a major impact on United Nations system organizations, extending well beyond accounting. The conversion to IPSAS should allow for enhanced management of resources and business processes and improve results-based management across the United Nations system. Depending on the organizations' initial readiness for IPSAS requirements, the transition to IPSAS has been a major undertaking for most organizations as it is impacting accounting, financial reporting, and associated information technology systems and should lead to a new approach to planning, decision-making, budgeting, and financial reporting. It is expected that the reporting of assets, liabilities, revenue, and expenses in accordance with independent international standards will significantly improve the quality, comparability, and credibility of United Nations System financial statements to Member States, donors, and staff, enhancing accountability, transparency, and governance (see Aggestam-Pontoppidan, 2010).

The United Nations transition to IPSAS will be used in this chapter to illustrate the project management approach on the adoption of IPSAS. Studying the lessons learned from the United Nations organizations serves as an interesting example which may be considered as best practice for many first-time IPSAS adopters.

PROJECT MANAGEMENT PERSPECTIVE

IPSAS adoption will have the most significant impact on accounting and financial reporting functions, but it will also have an extended impact on other areas of an entity. Making the transition to IPSAS presents a number of major technical, administrative, cultural, and communicative challenges due to the complex nature of instituting accounting changes within the public sector. These challenges can be managed, in a practical context, through the use of project management methodology.

Two of the most substantial challenges, for most public sector entities seeking to adopt IPSAS, are those of keeping the implementation process within a reasonable timeframe and, relatedly, adopting the standards in a cost-effective manner. It is crucial that the change process entails senior management support, risk management, quality assurance, communication, and internal and external stakeholder involvement and support (see Figure 20.1).

The inherent political influences that are at play during the various stages of both the decision to implement IPSAS and the subsequent implementation process need to be recognized throughout the project management process. In addition, the success of IPSAS involves close integration of all practice areas (such as human resources, contracting, IT, and so forth) of the implementing entity. In fact, IPSAS adoption has impacts across people, process, and technology that will need to be factored into an entity's conversion to IPSAS.

Viewing the adoption of IPSAS simply as a financial reporting change can lead to costly rework at a later date and/or cumbersome and inefficient processes. As IPSAS conversion strategies are developed by an entity, changes required to existing systems and the ability to use technology to support IPSAS are important factors in determining the timing and costs of this effort.

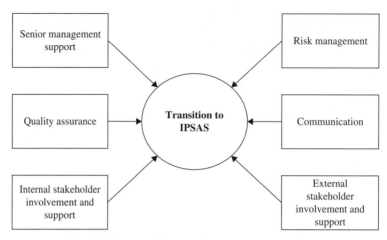

Figure 20.1   Transition to IPSAS – key success factors

The most notable and obvious changes in an entity adopting IPSAS are significant alterations to existing processes and technology. They include, but should definitely not be limited to, people, technology, and processes (see Figure 20.2):

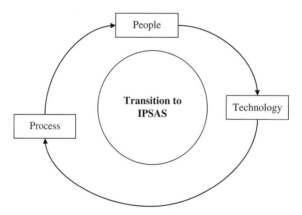

Figure 20.2   Critical components for the transition to IPSAS

Adopting IPSAS will often entail new accounting rules, new IT tools, and new work procedures as well as training for users within any implementing entity.

Figure 20.3 illustrates, at a high level, some of the key components of the IPSAS implementation process.

A sound project management approach assists entities in managing such challenges. The first step for any entity is naturally to select and define their project management methodology. Critical pre-implementation conditions are illustrated in Figure 20.4.

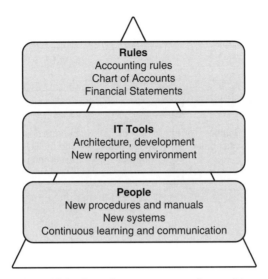

Figure 20.3   Some key components of a transition

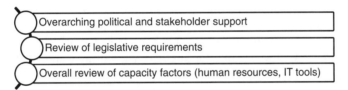

Figure 20.4   Critical pre-implementation conditions

Governing the Implementation Process

Once a public sector entity has considered and tackled critical pre-implementation conditions such as overarching political and stakeholder support, review of legislative requirements, implementation barriers, and an overall review of capacity factors such as IT, the entity may proceed to initiate an implementation project for the adoption of IPSAS. Such an implementation project may benefit from drawing on established project management methods.

A project management methodology should ensure that each process within a project is defined by specified key inputs and outputs, with specific goals to be achieved and activities to be carried out. Working with pre-defined inputs and expected deliverables ensures automatic control of any divergence from the plan. Prior to exploring the management of an implementation process of IPSAS, it is necessary to consider the importance of ensuring proper governance of that process. We will now consider a few key components of a healthy implementation process, as shown in Figure 20.5:

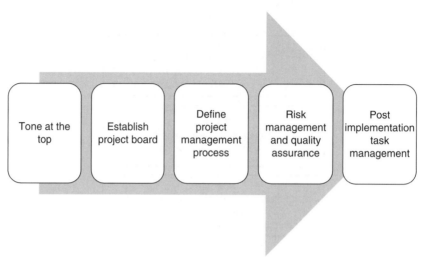

Figure 20.5   Key components of a healthy implementation process

Tone at the Top, Critical for Successful Implementation of IPSAS

Successful governance of the implementation process of IPSAS requires a sound and supportive tone at the top. An essential first step towards adopting IPSAS is to embed the support from top management. The tone at the top plays an important role in echoing the value and relevance of adopting new accounting standards throughout the public sector entity. The accounting literature has highlighted the fact that accounting innovations and changes in accounting systems are frequently subject to resistance (cf. Aggestam-Pontoppidan, 2010).

It may be beneficial, at an early stage in the implementation project, for management to frame and communicate to the entity not only their strong support for accrual accounting but also their commitment to managing the adoption of new accounting standards in a cost-effective manner and to managing the risks in the process.

Project Board: A Strategic Choice

The project board is a governing mechanism accountable for the success of a project. It is critical that the project board members have the necessary authority and responsibility to take decisions and commit resources to the project. It is also beneficial if some project board members have a sound understanding of accounting and financial reporting when implementing IPSAS.

The board essentially delegates the day-to-day running of the project to the dedicated project manager. The composition of the board will vary depending on the entity's operations, structure, geographical presence, and the nature of the entity's activities. The structure of a board commonly includes a project executive, senior users and suppliers, and the project manager.

The project manager has the authority to run the project on a day-to-day basis on behalf of the project board within the constraints laid down by the board. In the case of implementing accrual-based IPSAS the project manager will need a dual set of skills: an overarching understanding of IPSAS and accounting and an in-depth understanding of project management. Identifying an official with both sets of skills is often a challenging endeavor.

The responsibilities of each component of the project board can be summarized as follows:

Project executive	**Senior users**	**Senior suppliers**	**Project manager**
Accountable for the project	Responsible for specifying the needs of those who will use the final product(s), i.e., IPSAS-compliant financial statements	Accountable for the quality of products delivered by the supplier(s)	Responsible for the day-to-day management of and decision-making for the project.

Example 20.2   IPSAS implementation business case

The United Nations Children's Fund (UNICEF), for example, emphasized in its business case that the project board comprised UNICEF business process owners and representatives from various field offices (UNICEF, 2009).

The Food and Agriculture Organization (FAO), in reporting on their first IPSAS project board meeting note, similarly to UNICEF, that various business process owners are included. In the case of FAO their project board includes the Directors of Finance Division, Office of Programme, Budget and Evaluation, and the Information Technology Division (FAO, 2007). In moving towards accrual accounting, in particular if the implementing entity uses (modified) cash accounting as a starting point, it is crucial that it is communicated across the organization that the project is organization-wide and thus not limited to being an "accounting" project.

The nature of the project thus requires representatives from across business practices in any entity implementing accrual-based IPSAS. UNICEF further states in its business case that its project board is chaired by their Deputy Executive Director (UNICEF, 2009). The presence of senior management at the executive level is significant in conveying the importance of the project across the organization. For public entities that implement IPSAS it may also be important to consider appropriate geographical representation within the project board. In the case of UNICEF they have included representatives from various field offices. Considering inclusion of representatives from various geographical locations of the implementing entity will ensure consideration and coverage of business processes across the organization. In addition it will also ensure the motivation and involvement of staff across geographical boundaries. The establishment of an effective project board is crucial to ensure that the adoption of accrual-based IPSAS produces visibility and drives accountability throughout the implementing entity.

Project Management Process

The first step is to write a business case and project definition. The purpose of a business case is to describe the justification for establishing and continuing the project in question, making it the heart of any project. An integral part of defining the project is to establish a project resourcing strategy subject to approval by the project executive. The focus of the business case is thus on outlining the rationale for the implementation of IPSAS.

The business case will address critical issues such as:

- Why we need to implement new accounting standards/accounting methods;
- The benefits (both tangible and intangible) and risks;
- What are the potential costs; and
- An estimate of how long the project will take.

The business case will be updated throughout the project process. When using a project management approach to adopting IPSAS, the implementation project is divided into manageable components and phases as designed by the project manager.

From a high-level perspective, adopting IPSAS can be divided into a number of stages, for example, an initiation stage, a requirements stage, a design stage, and an implementation stage as shown in Table 20.1. The aim is the production of

Table 20.1   Stages of IPSAS adoption

1. Initiation stage	2. Requirement stage	3. Design stage
The purpose of the initiation stage is to complete the planning, scheduling, and organizational aspects of the IPSAS implementation project.	The requirements stage is then intended to work specifically with the impact of IPSAS on specific areas of financial activities and the respective change requirements that will be required.	The focus during the design stage is on data requirements and advancing new accounting policy within the implementing entity. The design stage is critical for the success of implementation and often includes numerous challenges.
The writing and approval of a business case will be an integral part of the initiation stage	The requirements stage is the time for the critical work of reviewing and establishing appropriate interpretations of IPSAS vis-à-vis the implementing entity concerned.	

4. Implementation stage

The implementation stage is the final formal stage, and the objective here is to finalize data cleansing and data gathering aspects of the transition plan and to execute the adoption of IPSAS-compliant financial statements. Getting the IT systems in place to "go live" with new accounting practices is often a long and challenging process that runs through all four stages of the implementation process and is finalized at the implementation stage. This is also the stage where the format of management reports is finalized. The specific tasks embedded in the implementation stage may include:

- A number of IPSAS transition tasks such as, for example, establishment of data entry tools; data gathering and cleansing; asset and liabilities valuation; and income data.
- Issuance of IPSAS-compliant financial reports.
- Adhering to IPSAS with a zero risk tolerance.

IPSAS-compliant annual financial statements and an entity in which business processes, practices, and regulations have been aligned with the new accounting environment.

Example 20.3   UNESCO, role of fit-gap analysis

UNESCO (2008), for example, emphasized that a gap analysis between current accounting practice and accrual-based IPSAS served as the basis for the project plans and the setting up of milestones. UNESCO added that gap analysis informed them that "some gaps have an impact on day-to-day operations within UNESCO entities and others relate more to accounting and financial reporting processes" (UNESCO, 2008: 2). The fit-gap analysis is thus a key component of the project management process and an apparent risk in adopting IPSAS is not to recognize gaps between current accounting practice and IPSAS. It is important at an early stage to identify and value assets as this is frequently one of the more challenging (and expensive) steps in moving to accrual accounting practices. Already, at the requirements stage, it is also important to address existing IT systems – will the accounting changes require the purchase of new computer systems, upgrades, or other changes?

Example 20.4   Examples of tasks in the requirement stage

Specific deliverables that may be produced during the requirement stage include, for example:

- An IPSAS policy review document with the purpose of detailing, by each [relevant] IPSAS standard, current accounting policy of the implementing entity versus IPSAS requirements. Based on such analysis the IPSAS policy decision document should make a preliminary high-level assessment of whether each standard is likely to have a significant impact on the business processes of the implementing entity.
- Establishment of a detailed training and communications strategy. While the business case in the initiation stage will have considered and established high-level training and communication plans, these plans should be further developed and deployed during the design stage.
- Reviewing IT and/or ERP systems readiness for IPSAS. The purpose is to establish a preliminary understanding of the changes that will be needed to meet new accounting requirements.
- Establishment of change management requirements and capability developments. The underlying business case and the IPSAS policy review document can assist an implementing entity in determining what new capabilities, in terms of, for example, human resources and technology, will need to be developed.

> • Establishment of a preliminary transition work plan. A transition work plan would typically cover required steps to converge from the current accounting practice of the implementing entity to IPSAS. The focus should be on operational aspects such as opening balances and data conversion.

Putting the Project Management Process into Practice

Putting the project management process into practice will depend on a number of factors, such as the governmental or entity context, size of the project, timeline, and budget.

For the purpose of adopting IPSAS the day-to-day project management is run by the project manager and governed through the project board. The project manager will frequently be employed in the finance/accounting area but will have a certain level of working knowledge in project management. Many of the tasks that are to be undertaken in the phases of the project management process can be sub-divided into thematic accounting work areas in order to make the overall process manageable and driven by subject-matter experts within the implementing government/entity. The thematic accounting work areas could include: revenue management; asset management; leases; foreign exchange; financial reporting; employee benefits; and so forth. This means that in practice, the project manager will often identify, in collaboration with the members of the project board and/or the CFO, one lead person for each of the accounting work areas.

Each of the thematic accounting work areas (such as PP&E or revenue) will be required to complete products required to ensure IPSAS compliance with the relevant IPSAS. One example is that of writing an IPSAS-compliant accounting policy. In this context it is crucial to re-emphasize that the project board must have enough power to be able to grant the necessary resources to the project. Adopting accrual-based IPSAS will require involvement from staff members across the entity, not only from accounting and finance.

Continuous Project Management Activities

In addition to the required tasks embedded in each of the steps in the project management and implementation of IPSAS, there are certain activities that are continuously ongoing throughout the implementation process.

These activities are:

- Communication;
- Training;
- Risk; and
- Quality management.

Communication and training

In managing an IPSAS implementation project it is essential to include communication and training as key project components. The project board meetings can serve as opportunities to bring up any and all issues that emerge throughout the adoption process and in this context also address and discuss communication and training needs as an iterative process. An entity that is implementing IPSAS will thus benefit from establishing a communication and training plan that becomes visible across the entity. The communication and training plan should include a stakeholder mapping against which the project manager can identify communication and training needs for each group of stakeholders.

It is essential that training is not provided too early in the project as staff may lose the knowledge gained before they can put it into practice. Training should thus be a continuous element in any accounting reform project and not a one-off exercise, and it should be carefully matched against progress in the project and the corresponding user needs. Training can be facilitated through the use of internal expert practitioners and external parties. It is beneficial for an entity to develop internal experts who can carry out training as this will facilitate the retention of this knowledge within the entity.

Example 20.5   The United Nations Economic and Social Commission for Asia and the Pacific (UNESCAP) explains its training plan[1]

"Following the decision by the United Nations to adopt IPSAS starting from 1 July 2013 for peacekeeping operations and from 1 January 2014 for non-peacekeeping entities (implementation date for ESCAP is 1 January 2014), plans are underway globally to prepare for this major change. The UN IPSAS Implementation Team commenced work on the IPSAS Training Plan and other preparatory activities to support the successful transitioning of the organization to the new accounting standards.

While the subject name may indicate that this relates to finance and accounting, I wish to point out that IPSAS will affect us all. Among the numerous changes that will be introduced, the timing of recording of expenditure will significantly impact us. In order to obtain a better understanding of IPSAS and its implications for each of you, all staff are encouraged to undertake training in IPSAS.

The training courses may be broadly classified as those designed to build awareness, and those designed for specialists who will need to apply IPSAS on a regular basis:

1. Awareness Training: Awareness training is a key component of the overall change management process. Its objective is to communicate the upcoming changes and its impact on the Organization to all stakeholders, and to encourage staff to start thinking about the implications for their own areas of work.
2. Conceptual Training: The objective of conceptual training is to develop understanding of IPSAS principles and requirements and to examine its impact on work processes as well as on the presentation of financial statements. Conceptual training is being done at three levels:
    (a) Working knowledge level – comprising Computer based training (CBTs),
    (b) Intermediate level – Instructor led courses (ILTs),
    (c) Advanced level – comprising ILTs."

---

[1] See http://www.unescap.org/asd/HRMS/odlu/staff_dev_prog/pro_expertise/ipsas.htm.

Risk and quality management

For the management of risk in the adoption of IPSAS, entities may choose to draw on principles of risk management often stipulated in project management methodologies. A quality plan is often closely interlinked with the risk management plan. Any implementing entity needs to address each IPSAS and analyze the risks associated with each standard for the entity. This will provide the basis for capturing the risks in the accounting arena. However, due to the wide scope of a project that aims to adopt accrual accounting it is important to recognize that the risks go beyond those in the accounting arena. Such risks include, but are not limited to:

- Lack of support from top management;
- Lack of cross-functional (across business practice) co-ordination and work efforts;
- Lack of targeted and cross-entity communication;
- Lack of resources; and
- Lack of targeted and customized training.

Post-implementation stage

Converging to IPSAS will usually increase the financial information produced by any implementing public sector entity. In the post-implementation phase there are critical communication and training factors to take into account in order to enable proper use to be made of the new financial information and to ensure that the accounting changes are understood across the implementing entity and its key stakeholders. This means that training in the new accounting practices, supporting business process and managerial benefits should not stop after the implementation phase, rather it may need to be escalated in order to reap any benefits of moving to accrual accounting. In addition, efforts to communicate with both internal and external stakeholders on the new financial information available in the financial reports are likely to be required in order to ensure that this information becomes meaningful and understandable by those who use it (see also Ouda, 2010).

Summarizing Implementation

Example 20.6   The JIU of the United Nations considers 16 best practices for implementing a smooth transition to IPSAS (see JIU, 2010)

1. Set up an inter-departmental IPSAS project steering committee or equivalent body tasked with ensuring that senior management understand the goals and vision driving the transition to IPSAS. The committee should have a multi-year mandate and include staff specialized in the pre-design, design and implementation of ERP systems.

2. Conduct an in-depth analysis of gaps between existing business processes, procedures, financial reporting and functionalities developed under UNSAS and the requirement and impact of each IPSAS standard.

3. In the case of a major shift in the project environment, reassess the initial IPSAS adoption strategy and adjust this as necessary.

4. Apply proven project planning and implementation methodologies including clearly defined strategic objectives, deliverables, timelines, milestones and monitoring procedures.

5. Develop a strategy for producing IPSAS-compliant opening balances for the targeted implementation date (first day of the first year of compliance) as well as the closing balance for the previous day, based on the previous accounting standard (UNSAS), but easily translatable into IPSAS terms for the opening balance of the targeted year.

6. With a view to ensuring continued engagement of governing bodies in the change process, regularly update the governing bodies on progress made in the implementation of IPSAS and request that they adopt the relevant decisions, in particular with regard to amendments required to financial regulations and allocation of resources for the project.

7. Determine and budget for the additional human resources required in the administrative, budgetary and finance areas to ensure not only effective implementation of the transition to IPSAS but also adequate capacity to maintain future IPSAS compliance.

8. Ensure that financial resources are made available for training, where feasible, of in-house experts in accounting, business and change management or for the recruitment of external experts.

9. Thoroughly analyze existing (legacy) information systems for compatibility and synergy with IPSAS requirements and, as a major element of the initial gap analysis, appreciate the changes that an ERP system must undergo to support IPSAS.

10. Communicate awareness on the transition to IPSAS through all available means of communication, training and documentation. This can be achieved through personal contact, presentations, and testimonies from persons involved in successful cases outside the entity, retreats, practical exercises and other training materials comparing present and new accounting policies.

11. Ensure that existing and future staff, in particular managers and supply chain and finance staff, are fully familiarized with the new procedures and requirements through the use of specific documentation (manuals) and training.

12. Adopt risk assessment, management and mitigation strategies and practices for project implementation in accordance with the project's objectives.

13. Plan and prepare interim financial statements for review by external auditor(s) well ahead of the final implementation date to avoid unpleasant surprises.

14. Establish and maintain, as soon as feasible, a bilateral dialogue between the organization and its external auditor(s) on the transition to IPSAS to help ensure that both external and internal auditors gain in-depth understanding of the new system and its impact on control procedures, as the implementation of IPSAS would require migration to accrual-based accounting.

15. Perform continuous testing of internal controls during the preliminary implementation stage of an IPSAS project to ensure the accuracy of the data.
16. Ensure that an independent and comprehensive validation and verification of the system is performed towards the end of its completion."

MINI CASE STUDY: OSCE's Strategy of Progressive Adoption of IPSAS Standards[2]

OSCE as an observer to the UN System

The Organization for Security and Co-operation in Europe (OSCE) is the world's largest regional security organization whose 57 participating States span the geographical area from Vancouver to Vladivostok. Although the OSCE is not a UN organization, the OSCE does operate under UN Charter, Chapter 8: "Regional Arrangements." As such, the OSCE was granted the status of observer to the United Nations System IPSAS co-ordination project in 2008. Prior to IPSAS compliance the OSCE was preparing its financial statements in accordance with the United Nations System Accounting Standards (UNSAS).

IPSAS adoption without a budget

The adoption of International Public Sector Accounting Standards (IPSAS) is seen as an essential component of good governance, accountability and transparency. The credibility of the OSCE financial statements relies on the quality of the accounting standards that regulate them and is important to ensure the confidence of participating States, donors, and the general public in the Organization. Comparability, harmonization, and continuous improvement of financial reporting are among the cornerstones of IPSAS.

Adoption of IPSAS was seen as a means of ensuring comparability with other international organizations, most notably the UN System. IPSAS supports the OSCE's position – its adoption of IPSAS showing stakeholders that they are exercising a level of financial and materials stewardship which complies with the internationally recognized accounting standards for public and non-profit organizations.

The IPSAS implementation project at OSCE faced a major obstacle: there was no approved budget for IPSAS adoption. Therefore the project had to be carried out using existing resources; staff had to undertake IPSAS related tasks in addition to their usual duties.

In order to progress with the project without losing momentum, it was decided to follow a strategy of progressive adoption of IPSAS standards and this strategy was formally approved by the participating States.

---

[2] Contributing author: Melissa Dias Buerbaumer, Ph.D., CPA, Chief of Accounts at the OSCE.

IPSAS adoption over a three-year period

The OSCE's IPSAS adoption strategy relied therefore on a risk mitigation methodology, whereby the main objective was not to accelerate change faster than could be absorbed or realistically achievable, but rather, taking a phased approach to IPSAS adoption, leveraging lessons learned and ultimately minimizing the scope for audit observations.

This is in line with the IPSAS standards themselves (through the so-called "transitional provisions" which, in certain cases, allow for a phase-out period) and even at the level of UNSAS. In fact, in the current version of IPSAS which dates from February 2010, it is stated that Organizations can adopt individual IPSAS standards and still be UNSAS-compliant:

> Where individual organizations find it necessary to depart from the practice set out in the standards they should disclose the reasons for doing so in the statement of significant accounting policies included in their financial statements. Where an organization departs from the practices set out below in order to apply IPSAS … the organization is deemed to comply with UNSAS so long the organization complies with the IPSAS individual standard in its entirety and all remaining UNSAS requirements. This allows organizations to gradually adopt IPSAS. (Extract from UNSAS revision IX, paragraph 3)

IPSAS implementation at the OSCE started before 2010, with an initial assessment of the impact of IPSAS and respective data requirements as well as simulation of IPSAS adjustments. The main task during 2010 was to put a process in place to identify and mitigate gaps that would pave the way for progressive IPSAS adoption. This included, during 2011, gap analysis and re-assessment of the gap mitigation strategy along with a variety of consultations with other organizations in the UN System adopting IPSAS and using Oracle as their ERP system.

In 2012 the OSCE was formally tasked by the Permanent Council to adopt IPSAS with a target deadline of 2014 (PC/DEC 1040), and to adopt the first four IPSAS standards while remaining under the UNSAS framework (see Figure 20.6).

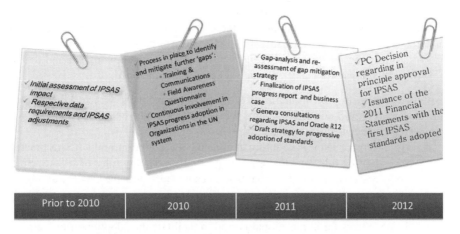

Figure 20.6 OSCE high level IPSAS adoption timeline

The adoption of IPSAS standards was achieved over a period of three years as depicted in Figure 20.7:

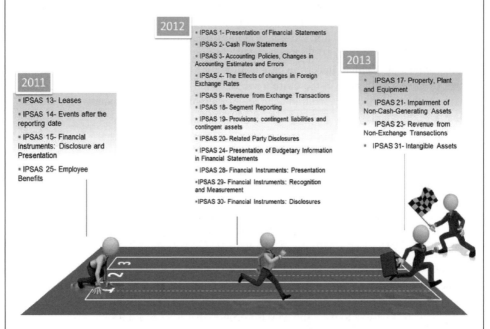

Figure 20.7 OSCE IPSAS adoption timeline per IPSAS

Gap analysis and mitigation

Understanding the gap in the requirements between UNSAS and IPSAS reporting requirements at OSCE was a key milestone in defining the scope of the project-related activities. A review of all the standards within IPSAS determined that of the existing 32 standards at the time, 12 did not apply to the OSCE's business model. For each of the standards that did apply, a "Gap Mitigation Strategy" was drafted, considering a variety of factors impacting the "gap" between the "status quo" current situation and the "to be" IPSAS adoption compliance end state. These factors included:

- The extent to which data is directly available from the Oracle IT system to support IPSAS-compliant figures for recognition in the financial statements and respective note disclosures;
- The difference in the accounting treatment between the current UNSAS practice of accounting rules and the required accrual accounting rules of IPSAS. Since UNSAS is on a modified accrual basis, in some instances the OSCE was already IPSAS-compliant;
- The existence or non-existence of transitional provisions. For certain standards IPSAS allows for a transitional period to facilitate the adoption of the requirements of the relevant standard;

- The extent which professional judgment is required (vs. a fully automated process) and complexity of business processes for obtaining IPSAS-compliant balances;
- The materiality of the specific item or type of transaction. During the exercise of the fit-gap analysis, the focus was on items with higher materiality, since the likelihood of affecting the audit opinion was higher;
- The level of ambiguity in terms of interpretation of each standard;
- The dependence/reliance on input from field missions.

For each of the IPSAS standards applicable to the OSCE, the abovementioned factors were considered and classified as "low," "medium," or "high," depending on their impact in the gap analysis. The sample guiding analysis matrix used for each standard is shown in Table 20.2 using the illustrative example of IPSAS 17 Property, Plant and Equipment:

Table 20.2   Analysis of factors impacting gap between "as is" current status and "to be" IPSAS

	Factors/Impact on "gap"	Low	Medium	High
1.	Unavailability of data directly from Oracle		x	
2.	Difference in accounting treatment: UNSAS vs. IPSAS			x
3.	(Non)Existence of transitional provisions	x		
4.	Professional judgment required		x	
5.	Business processes and variety of data sources			x
6.	Materiality			x
7.	Ambiguity in interpretation of standard	x		
8.	Dependence/reliance on input from field missions		x	

Probably the most important conclusion from the initial gap analysis is that the adopted strategy must build upon the different project dimensions, which make the IPSAS compliance exercise an ongoing, dynamic, and gradual process. Ultimately it is not the issuance of the first set of IPSAS-compliant financial statements that represents the finalization of the gap analysis/mitigation exercise. As new standards continue to be issued, and the business processes at the OSCE gradually change, it will be necessary to constantly review and eventually adapt the reporting framework to continue to ensure IPSAS compliance following formal adoption. Also it was understood that there could be new events and different realities every year which might have an impact on the level of IPSAS-compliant financial reporting.

What today can be considered negligible could become material in the future.

This reality is acknowledged and reflected in the level of the standards themselves (through the so called "transitional provisions" which allow, in certain cases, for a phase-out period) and even at the level of UNSAS. In fact, in the current version of IPSAS from February 2010, it is mentioned that organizations can adopt individual IPSAS and still be UNSAS-compliant:

> Where individual organizations find it necessary to depart from the practice set out in the standards they should disclose the reasons for doing so in the statement of significant accounting policies included in their financial statements. Where an organization departs from the practices set out below in order to apply IPSAS … the organization is deemed to comply with UNSAS so long the organization complies with the IPSAS individual standard in its entirety and all remaining UNSAS requirements. This allows organizations to gradually adopt IPSAS. (extract from UNSAS revision IX, paragraph 3)

Communication strategy

One of the common fallacies in the move to full accrual accounting is to underestimate the magnitude of the project by believing it is merely an accounting change that will only impact finance staff. Communication and training are also important for non-finance staff and have been identified as key components of a successful IPSAS adoption project.

Along with training, effective communication is a key component for successful IPSAS implementation. OSCE's aim is to deliver the right message from inception through post implementation, ensuring the following objectives:

- Building awareness and understanding of the project objectives, impacts, and benefits;
- Promoting individual responsibility/involvement and collective ownership of the process and results among key stakeholders and users;
- Obtaining resource commitment and validation of intermediate and final deliverables from key stakeholders and users;
- Providing detailed instructions, capacity building, and support to those users most impacted by IPSAS.

Identifying the key stakeholders and communicating the benefits of IPSAS to them is critical in ensuring their buy-in and cooperation for the IPSAS project. The following groups of stakeholders and the respective communication objectives were identified (see Table 20.3):

Table 20.3 Stakeholders and their communication objectives

Stakeholders Group	Inform	Involve	Invoke Action	Gain Buy-In
Project Team – working groups	✓	✓	✓	
Field Missions	✓	✓	✓	✓
Participating States	✓			✓
Key users in the Secretariat	✓	✓	✓	
Business Owners/Sponsors – Steering Committee	✓	✓	✓	✓
Internal and External Auditors	✓	✓	✓	✓

Communication milestones

The communication milestones are geared towards building a sense of collective ownership for the project along a continuum from simple awareness to a state of readiness to embark fully in the IPSAS project and deliver the expected outputs.

As depicted in Figure 20.8, involvement and awareness go hand-in-hand. A variety of "IPSAS communication awareness sessions" took place starting in 2010. Due to the absence of a dedicated IPSAS budget, the awareness venues were integrated within other regular scheduled events such as the Oracle Integrated Resource Management System Training (IRMA) sessions and other annual conferences.

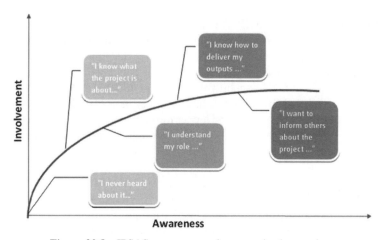

Figure 20.8 IPSAS awareness and communication sessions

The main objective of the IPSAS awareness sessions was to bring the stakeholders from what was frequently a common initial stage of: "I never heard about IPSAS" to the point where they understood the impact on the organization and their role and commitment to deliver results.

In particular for the group of field Chiefs of Finance and Administration and Finance Officers, specific feedback was requested from the target audience through "break-out" group exercises at the conferences that took place in 2011. For example, CFAs had the opportunity to "brainstorm" what they see as the major challenges and benefits of IPSAS adoption as well as ways to efficiently overcome those challenges. Finance Officers were requested to provide feedback on some key areas, such as Property, Plant and Equipment; Provisions and Contingencies; and Leases and Intangible Assets, and asked how they expect to cope with IPSAS requirements to ensure completeness and accuracy of reported data.

Throughout these sessions significant progress was noted in terms of understanding of IPSAS requirements and an increased willingness to engage in the required changes as compared to the sessions held in 2010.

Participating States, through a variety of presentations, have also been kept informed on a regular basis regarding the IPSAS project. These presentations have included providing background information on IPSAS and have highlighted the main impacts, benefits, risks, project governance, milestones, etc.

The OSCE External Auditors have also been identified as key stakeholders in the IPSAS implementation process. The External Auditors were briefed on the main impacts of IPSAS, the project pillars, and the key areas of focus. Moreover, the External Auditors were engaged in discussions regarding the IPSAS strategy and project plan, as well as the IPSAS pro-forma Financial Statements.

Training approach

The training approach towards IPSAS has two primary objectives: awareness training and specialist training. The idea behind awareness training is to communicate to all stakeholders the upcoming changes, benefits, and challenges and their impact on the OSCE and to encourage staff to start thinking about the implications for their own areas of work, and build support for the change to IPSAS. Specialist training is targeted towards stakeholders who will have a direct impact in the project and from whom specific deliverables are expected, either through their involvement in the various working groups during implementation and/or through additional activities related to post-implementation.

Measuring IPSAS training impact

Of paramount importance to efficient and effective training is a direct link to the practical tasks of IPSAS implementation. With this in mind, and in order to support the process of gap mitigation and analysis all locations were requested to complete an "IPSAS Awareness Questionnaire." As already mentioned, while the majority of IPSAS-related tasks are centralized in the Secretariat, all locations play a key role in bringing to the attention of the Secretariat/Accounts any matters that may have an impact on IPSAS-compliant reporting. To become better acquainted with IPSAS terminology and the Conceptual Framework, staff responsible for providing feedback in the questionnaire were strongly encouraged to complete the online training module corresponding to their specific area.

The major impacts of IPSAS implementation in the field missions are expected to occur in the larger, more complex missions. Nevertheless, the level of effort and dedication that these missions have shown in grasping key IPSAS concepts and their involvement in the implementation process was pleasing. This was most evident during the Annual Finance Meetings and the session dedicated to IPSAS.

Benefits from IPSAS Adoption

In addition to the lessons learned, 2010 implementers also shared the following key points in terms of IPSAS dividends:

- Strengthening financial management: clearer discussion and improved decision-making;
- The process leading to IPSAS adoption brought about a review of internal procedures, leading to enhanced controls and knowledge, in particular in the area of Property, Plant and Equipment, Inventories, and Revenue;
- Enhanced recognition of the organization's liabilities in connection with the measurement of the costs related to employee benefits, such as annual leave, after service health insurance, end of service allowance, and repatriation grants;
- Further development of metrics of key areas of financial risk management and performance;
- Corporate level information to senior management, presentation of quarterly key financial data and ratios based on high quality financial data, as well as the development of a common corporate view on financial performance and risk.

The materialization of the IPSAS dividends is not immediate, while organizations are busy focusing in the preparation of hard closures and adjusting balances before issuance of the first set of IPSAS-compliant financial statements. However, concerted efforts to instill the IPSAS culture within an organization, and debriefing on the process taken to reach IPSAS compliance, including the richness of the information available afterwards, is definitely an investment that will pay off.

> Higher confidence in the financial reports and increased assurance of efficient resource utilization, accountability and financial management
> Trust that OSCE is keeping up with international best practices on accounting and reporting
> Enhanced comparability of the OSCE's reporting with other international organizations

Participating States

> Better balanced comparisons between alternative disposition of resources and better oversight of assets and liabilities
> Increased transparency and stewardship with respect to assets and opportunity for improved internal controls and planning

Management

Figure 20.9   IPSAS benefits

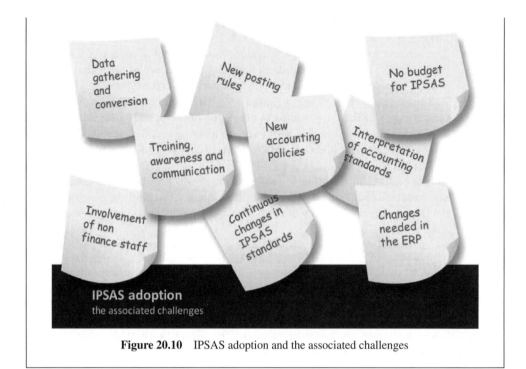

Figure 20.10   IPSAS adoption and the associated challenges

WHAT IS THE STARTING POINT FOR TRANSITION? DIFFERENT PATHS OF IPSAS ADOPTION

As pointed out earlier, transition to IPSAS covers a wide range of situations:

- Stage 1: Moving from non-IPSAS-compliant cash accounting to IPSAS cash accounting;
- Stage 2: Moving from IPSAS cash accounting to full accrual accounting under IPSAS;
- Stage 3: Moving from modified accrual-based accounting or some accrual accounting standards to full accrual accounting under IPSAS.

These three situations require proper project management, as described above. However, each of these three situations has its own specificities and needs a specific technical approach.

Let's review each of these three situations, step by step. The underlying idea is that:

- An entity may implement stage 1, then stage 2;
- Another "more advanced" entity may directly go for stage 3.

This chapter applies equally to any of the above situations. All adopting entities need to carefully manage their project, which may be segregated into sub-projects according to the political will and the financial and human capacities.

Stage 1: Moving from Non-IPSAS-compliant Cash Accounting to IPSAS Cash Accounting

Moving from non-IPSAS-compliant cash accounting to IPSAS cash accounting is the first stage of IPSAS adoption. It may concern several types of public sector entities. Governments from developing countries (among others) may want to structure their public reporting, implementing first the cash basis IPSAS (see Chapter 4).

Stage 1 is the most critical stage. Stage 2 and Stage 3 cannot be accomplished as long as Stage 1 is still pending. Cash accounting is not a well-developed accounting and reporting system, but it lays the foundations for accounting.

In order to implement IPSAS cash accounting it is necessary to implement procedures and systems (sometimes IT systems, but IT is not mandatory) to make sure that entity (usually a country) recognizes all cash in and all cash out. It means that the entity is building an internal control system to make sure that cash in and cash out are measured reliably, to prevent fraud and errors.

Implementing internal control and internal control culture can take time, but it is fundamental. The first step in enhancing transparency, for instance at the level of countries, is to ensure that all tax collected goes to the State, and that all payments by the State go to the designated beneficiaries.

Stage 1 implementation has very little to do with accounting, it is more about structuring an entity from an internal control point of view in order to permit the transition to full accrual-based IPSAS at a later stage.

Many African countries currently implementing cash accounting IPSAS have understood that it is a necessary stage before implementing accrual-based IPSAS, and a necessity to have access to international funding.

Example 20.7   Nigeria IPSAS adoption

The Accountant-General of the Federation (AGF) of Nigeria, Mr Jonah Otunla stated[3] that the implementation of IPSAS in Nigeria (in 2013) was long overdue as other countries of the world including African countries like Benin, Ghana and Kenya have long adopted the standards. The benefits of adopting IPSAS, he said, include better access to financing through either bond releases or international financing from organizations such as the International Monetary Fund (IMF) and the World Bank.

Stage 2: Moving from IPSAS Cash Accounting to Full Accrual Accounting under IPSAS

As explained above, Stage 1 is a necessary stage prior to implementing Stage 2, i.e., full accrual accounting under IPSAS.

---

[3] See NSE ANTHONY-UKO, 14 November 2012, available at www.allAfrica.com.

The transition from Stage 1 to Stage 2 may last for a long period of time because it is not easy to implement full accrual-based IPSAS. In order to prepare this transition, the IPSASB has included, in Part 2 of "Financial Reporting of Cash Basis of Accounting," recommended additional disclosures.

An entity may choose to add, period after period, more disclosures to its IPSAS cash accounting financial statements in order to prepare all necessary information for the adoption of full accrual IPSAS, and also to prepare stakeholders and other users of its financial statements for accrual-based accounts.

For instance, an entity may decide:

- To disclose the external assistance received during the period and the purpose for which this assistance was received,
- To present the statement of cash flow using the same format as defined in IPSAS 2,
- To report in the notes on its liabilities, starting with its employee benefits liabilities,
- To perform the inventory counting of its property, plant, and equipment items and disclose the information step by step, region by region, type of asset by type of asset …

All specific issues relating to accrual-based IPSAS described below in Stage 3 can be implemented, step by step, "off the record," disclosing information in the notes to the financial statements or changing the reporting format of the statement of cash flow to be IPSAS 2-compliant. And, when the entity is ready (technically, organizationally, and politically) to switch to full accrual accounting under IPSAS, transition is easier.

Stage 3: Moving from Modified Accrual-based Accounting or Some Accrual Accounting Standards to Full Accrual Accounting under IPSAS

Stage 3 is the most advanced stage. Moving from modified accrual-based accounting or some accrual accounting standards to full accrual accounting under IPSAS is still difficult (all these stages are difficult!) and the difficulty of this step of the transition should not be underestimated. Project management as described at the beginning of this chapter is an absolute necessity.

Sometimes, this stage is seen as a technical stage only, dealing with accounting differences between the former system and the accrual-based IPSAS. Viewing this stage as more a technical change than a complete entity/organizational change is the most common mistake. All the project management steps and prerequisites are fundamental and will not be repeated here. The remainder of this chapter will deal only with the specific technical approach for this stage.

The transition to full accrual-based IPSAS will impact operating procedures, reporting practices, and hence governance and relations with stakeholders. IPSAS will also expose managers to greater public scrutiny and therefore make them more accountable for the efficiency and effectiveness of their management. It is therefore crucial to select the appropriate accounting policies, not only for immediate results, but also for the long run.

Selecting accounting policies is a strategic issue, because accounting policies are supposed to be permanent, and should not generally be subject to future modification in the normal course of business. The adoption of IPSAS-compliant accounting policies requires additional commitment of time and effort from staff, as well as additional expertise. During the transition stage, depending on their available resources, the entity will either have to rely for an extended period of time on support from existing staff working in addition to their regular duties or recruit many additional staff or external contractors. These external contractors cannot be the external financial auditors of the entity because, under ISA (International Standards on Auditing), financial auditors are not allowed to implement accounting policies in an entity and then formulate an opinion on their own work. They would lose their independence. This applies to individual auditors, as well as to the entire audit firm they work for.

It is thus important to select expertise, internally and/or externally, and make sure that the amount of work is not underestimated. This technical accounting work is extensive and extremely time consuming. Moreover, once IPSAS compliance is achieved, new accounting areas will require permanent attention. It is a never-ending task because when new IPSAS are released there are organizational changes to account for, new transactions to record properly under IPSAS, a change in the information technology to implement. Depending on the size of the entity and its accounting complexity, it may be necessary to create a technical department in charge of accounting principles, following the model adopted by major listed European companies after the IFRS transition in 2005. For smaller entities, or, for instance, developing and emerging countries, this desk may be a shared desk. In other words, they may ask for the permanent assistance of external contractors.

On 31 January 2015 the IPSASB released IPSAS 33 First-time Adoption of Accrual Basis International Public Sector Accounting Standards (IPSAS). IPSAS 33 permits a first-time adopter to apply transitional exemptions and provisions that may impact fair presentation, but, at the end of the transitional period, the first-time adopter "must comply with the recognition, measurement, presentation and disclosure requirements in the other accrual basis IPSAS in order to assert compliance with accrual basis IPSASs as required in IPSAS 1, Presentation of Financial Statements" (IPSAS 33.5). IPSAS 33 transitional exemptions and provisions will be explained later in this chapter.

Some accounting changes have significant impacts at stage 3. Of course, the impact may vary according to the structure and activity of the entity. The following should not be considered as complete, and need to be adapted to every situation. It is intended to give clues to first-time adopters in order to help them anticipate the impacts of adoption of accrual-based IPSAS. Some IPSAS have major impacts, either financial or in terms of human resources and information systems.

Frequency of preparation of financial statements (IPSAS 1)

First of all, "financial statements shall be presented at least annually" (IPSAS 1.66). This appears simple, but for some entities applying modified accrual-based accounting, such as UNSAS (former accounting standards for the United Nations), it is a major change because financial statements were prepared on a biennial or multi-year basis. The change in frequency has a major impact on the staff who need to prepare financial statements in a timely manner.

It also has an impact on the frequency of meetings of the governing body approving the financial statements and on the mandate given to the financial auditors. This is the first element, and it should not be underestimated because it has some strategic, organizational, and financial impacts and should be anticipated in the budgeting process.

Assets: property, plant, and equipment (IPSAS 17)

Under modified accrual-based accounting, property, plant, and equipment (PP&E) items are usually charged to expenditure and not recorded on the face of the statement of financial position.

Example 20.8   Pre-IPSAS accounting standards in the United Nations

Under the pre-IPSAS accounting standards for the United Nations (which were basically modified accrual), PP&E items are immediately charged to expenditures, meaning that there was no track of PP&E inventory, nor PP&E depreciation over time.

For instance, under IPSAS 17, PP&E items controlled by an entity have to be recognized, measured, depreciated, and disclosed in notes to the financial statements. It looks easy, and in fact it is easy to understand, but it is one of the most difficult standards to apply in practice. This permanent control over PP&E requires the entity to perform an initial inventory counting, designate and train staff, and establish information systems to ensure a full accounting cycle for PP&E on an annual basis.

Inventory counting is particularly time and labor-intensive. Never underestimate the time necessary to perform the inventory counting. The first task is to track PP&E, to make sure that all items of PP&E are recorded. One issue is to determine what is a PP&E item – what the threshold should be for recognizing an item as PP&E, what the difference is between an expense and a PP&E item. Communication and training of staff in charge of the inventory counting is a heavy task because PP&E are everywhere. This training should not be too technical, but should present the consequences of recording PP&E items on the face of the statement of financial position. It is really a cultural change.

Example 20.9   Ecology Ministry for the French State, PP&E threshold[4]

The following thresholds to record PP&E items have been defined for the French State for the Ecology Ministry:

Books, CDRom > 80 euros

Other assets > 230 euros

It has been specified, in this text defining the rules applicable to record PP&E, that libraries may decide on a lower threshold to record books and CDRom.

For the United Nations, the recommended threshold is 5 000 USD: "The threshold level for PP&E recognition was a subject of heated debate among United Nations organizations, with some arguing for a higher threshold to reduce the administrative costs of capturing and maintaining data, and others advocating a lower one to ensure better control over PP&E. The level recommended by the IPSAS Task Force of the United Nations was US$5,000" (see JIU, 2010).

Once the counting is performed, the next question is what the value for each PP&E item counted should be. In theory, the entity must have kept track of the purchase of PP&E, but in practice, the information may not be easily available at an acceptable cost. IPSAS 17 allows entities to initially recognize PP&E items either at their historical cost or their fair value, which is then charged to expenses over the period of use of each PP&E item.

The use of fair value is sometimes justified by the difficulty of reliably substantiating the acquisition cost of PP&E items held by an entity for a long period of time, transferred between locations, etc.

Either method is possible to prepare the "opening balance sheet," but it has to be backed up by supporting documentation, thus entailing significant effort, including work to identify and classify all PP&E items using an appropriate valuation methodology. This step is even more difficult than ensuring that the inventory counting is complete.

For subsequent measurement of PP&E items, IPSAS 17 allows for a choice between the cost model and the revaluation model. This accounting option is different from the methods used for the initial recognition of PP&E items for the transition to IPSAS. In any case, it is an important question for the long run, and for the presentation of the financial situation of the entity to its stakeholders, as well as for budget purposes. The revaluation model will imply that some class of PP&E, defined in the accounting policies, will be revalued on a regular basis (to be defined; it could be, for instance, every two years, every five years ...) in order to ensure that the book value is never too different from its fair value. The consequence of its revaluation will be a regular "update" of the net assets of the entity, allowing its net assets not to decline as much as

---

[4] See Circulaire du 24 juillet 2013 relative à la tenue de l'inventaire physique des biens mobiliers, NOR: DEVK1318612C.

they would under historical cost, and even in some cases, to increase. It would present a better situation to the stakeholders. Is this what stakeholders care about? This option is interesting only for PP&E items with a fair value (usually a market value) which may increase over time, such as property. However, performing this revaluation on a regular basis has a cost. Experts, either internal staff or external contractors, would have to perform this revaluation measurement. It is therefore important to consider the cost/benefit ratio before selecting one of the two subsequent measurement options for PP&E items.

Under IPSAS 17, PP&E items must be depreciated over their useful lives, which also have to be determined, for the transition to IPSAS and later on routinely for new PP&E items. A depreciation charge is to be made periodically against an individual PP&E item to gradually decrease its value to its residual value (usually nil). The accounting treatment of depreciation under IPSAS 17 is useful to management in order to make informed decisions on matters such as construction and renovation works, sometimes years in advance. This depreciation gives information on the end of the useful life of a PP&E item, but does not give any information on the budget needed to replace the item because the amount recorded is usually the historical cost, not the expected replacement cost.

In practice, depreciation of PP&E items requires the acquisition and/or the development of an Enterprise Resource Planning (ERP) system module capable of automatically carrying out calculations and making corresponding records in the accounting system. In some cases, software dealing with PP&E is available in the country in which the entity operates and can be easily integrated into the accounting system. Usually, this software is not fully IPSAS-compliant and not adapted to the specifications of public sector entities. It is thus necessary to develop an ERP system, which is generally expensive and time consuming. The implementation of such an ERP system has many implications for the accounting software and the financial reporting. Since IPSAS 17 requires many disclosures, this ERP system must allow for the preparation of these notes to the financial statements, and also give useful management information to the managers and stakeholders.

Employee benefits (IPSAS 25)

Adoption of accrual-based IPSAS has a major impact on the recognition of liabilities, especially on full recognition of liabilities for employee benefits. Under modified accrual-based accounting such as LOLF (loi organique relative aux lois de finances – the French accrual-based accounting standards for the French State financial statements), no provision for employee benefits is recorded on the statement of financial position. Information on employee benefits is disclosed in the notes to the financial statements. This is the main difference between LOLF and accrual-based IPSAS. Technically, the employee benefits liabilities have been calculated since they are disclosed in the notes to the financial statements. The problem, in this case, is not technical, but rather political. The presentation of the statement of financial position would be very different. Adding these amounts of liabilities for employee benefits (pensions of active civil servants and pensioners) would reduce the net asset value. This would certainly have an impact on the presentation of the financial situation of the country. Adopting IPSAS would imply preparing readers of the financial statements to understand the meaning of these employee benefits liabilities, and explaining that these amounts are already disclosed in the notes to the financial statements. This transition might not be so simple from a communications point of view.

The issue of funding would have to be addressed with similarly urgent attention. Most liabilities to employees in the public sector (and in some countries) are paid out on a "pay-as-you-go" basis, with any unfunded portions being met from resources available in the period during which payments are made. This means that subsequent accounting periods generally bear some costs incurred in earlier periods for liabilities that had not been previously recognized and accrued for. In the IPSAS financial statements, liabilities for employee benefits would be recorded, but there would be no matching assets in the statement of financial position. It does not mean that there should be corresponding matching assets, because States may well pay future pensions with future cash in. However, careful long-term planning and estimates of cash in/cash out should be made to ensure that there will always be enough cash in to pay for pensions in the foreseeable future. These calculations and projections, as well as the political and strategic implications, are some of the most important issues of a transition to full accrual-based IPSAS. These decisions cannot be made at the project management level, but only at the top management level, seeking support from stakeholders.

Budget issue (IPSAS 24)

IPSAS 24 prescribes mandatory presentation of budget amounts against accounting data in the financial statements when the budget is made publicly available. It does mean that there should be a link between budgeting and accounting, and, of course, financial reporting. It is extremely complex to link the two. In Europe, only two countries who have officially adopted accrual-based accounting have taken up that double challenge: the United Kingdom (which has adopted IFRS) and Switzerland (which has adopted IPSAS). It took 13 years for the United Kingdom to complete this transition.

It is a little less difficult for non-profit intergovernmental organizations than for countries, but complexity remains.

Example 20.10   Budgets within the United Nations and IPSAS

For the time being, most non-profit intergovernmental organizations which have already moved to accrual-based accounting (including the EC) find it difficult to introduce accrual-based budgeting, at least in the short term. They will continue with cash-based budget presentation, arguing that accrual-based budgeting will not be easily accepted by their Member States. Cash-based budget presentations, however, have to be made on the basis of an annual financial period; while most United Nations system organizations have biennial or even multi-annual budgets. Another argument justifying that choice is that the implementation phase of IPSAS requires significant financial and human resources, affecting their ability to undertake another large-scale project.

> Additionally, accrual budgeting is more suitable for a stable environment such as that of the United Nations Secretariat, but less so for rapidly changing conditions, as in peacekeeping operations (JIU, 2010).

In practice, once the political issue has been settled, it is necessary to upgrade ERP systems to allow for simultaneous recording of each expense in the accrual and cash ledgers, to facilitate the comparison between actual and original amounts. The preparation of comparative schedules requires a joint effort by staff from accounting and budgeting departments, who may never have worked together before. It may be a real challenge to have these two populations working together, and "speaking the same language."

There are of course many other topics to deal with in a transition to full accrual-based IPSAS. We have simply tried to give an overview for those who are willing to implement full IPSAS in order to help them understand the most significant issues.

FIRST-TIME ADOPTION OF ACCRUAL BASIS IPSAS (IPSAS 33)

IPSAS 33 First-time Adoption of Accrual Basis International Public Sector Accounting Standards (IPSAS) is mandatory to first-time adopters for a period beginning on or after 1 January 2017. Earlier application is permitted. It does mean, in practice, that first-time adopters of accrual basis IPSAS, in 2015 and 2016 are not obliged to use IPSAS 33, but they are allowed to do so if they wish. The objective of IPSAS 33 is, as defined at the beginning of this chapter, "to provide guidance to a first-time adopter that prepares and presents financial statements following the adoption of accrual basis IPSASs, in order to present high quality information ..."

Since adopting accrual basis IPSAS is a long and difficult process, IPSAS 33 allows a transitional period of three years to give sufficient time to the first-time adopter to be fully IPSAS-compliant, i.e., to "comply with the recognition, measurement, presentation and disclosure requirements in the other accrual basis IPSAS in order to assert compliance with accrual basis IPSASs as required in IPSAS 1, Presentation of Financial Statements" (IPSAS 33.5).

During this transitional period, the first-time adopter cannot make an explicit and unreserved statement of compliance with accrual basis IPSAS. The first-time adopter is allowed to make an explicit and unreserved statement of compliance with accrual basis IPSAS only when the annual financial statements comply with all the requirements of all the applicable IPSAS. During the transitional period, a first-time may adopt exemptions that affect fair presentation and compliance with accrual basis IPSAS.

IPSAS 33.36 does not require recognizing and/or measuring the following assets and/or liabilities for reporting periods beginning on a date within three years following the date of transition to IPSAS:

- Inventories;
- Investment property;

- Property, plant and equipment;
- Defined benefit plans and other long-term employee benefits;
- Biological assets and agricultural produce;
- Intangible assets;
- Service concession assets and the related liabilities; and
- Financial instruments.

It does mean that first-time adopters have three years to conform to all IPSAS requirements relating to recognition and measurement of assets and liabilities, which seems to be a long transitional period, but which is in reality short when compared to the amount of work it is necessary to perform to adopt accrual basis IPSAS.

IPSAS 33.42 also permits a three-year transition period to recognize and measure non-exchange revenue according to IPSAS 23. During this transition period, first-time adopters may change their accounting policy in respect of revenue from non-exchange transactions on a class-by-class basis. The intention is to give some flexibility to first-time adopters. IPSAS 33 allows other exemptions relating to borrowing costs, leases, and related party disclosures.

When a first-time adopter presents its first IPSAS financial statements, these financial statements must be fully accrual basis IPSAS-compliant. On the date of adoption of accrual basis IPSAS, a first-time adopter shall apply the requirements of the IPSAS retrospectively except as required, or otherwise permitted, in IPSAS 33 (IPSAS 33.16).

Unless explicitly stated in IPSAS 33, in its opening statement of financial position, the first-time adopter shall:

(a) Recognize all assets and liabilities whose recognition is required by IPSAS;
(b) Not recognize items as assets or liabilities if IPSAS do not permit such recognition;
(c) Reclassify items that it recognized in accordance with the previous basis of accounting as one type of asset, liability, or component of net assets/equity, but which are a different type of asset, liability, or component of net assets/equity in accordance with IPSAS; and
(d) Apply IPSAS in measuring all recognized assets and liabilities (IPSAS 33.20).

For instance, IPSAS 33.77 encourages, but does not require, presentation of comparative information in the first IPSAS financial statements, which saves an enormous amount of time for the project team.

If reliable market-based evidence of fair value is not available for inventory, or investment property that is of a specialized nature, a first-time adopter may consider the following measurement alternatives in determining a deemed cost:

(a) For inventory, current replacement cost; and
(b) For investment property of a specialized nature, depreciated replacement cost. (IPSAS 33.70)

A first-time adopter may elect to use fair value when reliable cost information about the following assets and liabilities is not available:

- Inventory;
- Investment property, if the first-time adopter elects to use the cost model in IPSAS 16;
- Property, plant, and equipment;
- Intangible assets, other than internally generated intangible assets that meet:
    - (i) The recognition criteria in IPSAS 31 (excluding the reliable measurement criterion); and
    - (ii) The criteria in IPSAS 31 for revaluation (including the existence of an active market);
- Financial instruments; or
- Service concession assets.

Even though IPSAS 33 has not entered into force yet, it is recommended that first-time adopters anticipate the application of this standard intended to facilitate the transition to accrual-basis IPSAS.

CONCLUSION

Sound project management is invaluable when adopting IPSAS and this applies to any of the possible paths or stages of IPSAS adoption:

- Stage 1: Moving from a non-IPSAS-compliant cash accounting to IPSAS cash accounting;
- Stage 2: Moving from IPSAS cash accounting to full accrual accounting under IPSAS;
- Stage 3: Moving from modified accrual-based accounting or some accrual accounting standards to full accrual accounting under IPSAS.

A supportive "tone at the top" is necessary. In addition, appointing a project manager who has the necessary skills in both accrual accounting, more specifically IPSAS, and in project management will benefit the successful advancement of the project. Throughout the implementation process, continuous communication with all key stakeholders is essential. Training in combination with communication is critical to promote a positive view and establish the necessary knowledge for the entity to function with new accounting practices. It is thus important that a training program is designed to allow affected staff, and in some instances external stakeholders, to receive the necessary training and understanding of what changes will be introduced in the entity by the change in accounting practices. It should be highlighted that the training component does not end when the project ends but should rather be seen as a continuous process as the IPSAS are subject to changes and updates, and the entity may introduce new business processes that require new accounting processes to be established. See Annex 4 for an illustration of Iceland's IPSAS adoption plan.

CONCLUSION

In conclusion, we may refer to the recommendations made by IFAC to the G-20 for their 19–20 April 2012 meeting, focusing on the need for enhanced public sector financial management, transparency, and accountability:[1]

> In responding to the problems created by the global financial crisis and ensuing sovereign debt crisis, it is critical that the G-20 strives for reporting of high-quality, internationally consistent, relevant, and reliable financial and non-financial information by all sectors, including the public sector. For the last ten years IFAC has consistently promoted the need for enhanced transparency and accountability in the public sector, noting in particular the risk that a lack of transparency and accountability presents to the efficiency of capital markets, global financial stability, and long term sustainability.

The sovereign debt crisis has caused instability in the global financial system and is a significant threat to global financial stability. The failure of fiscal management in the public sector is unfortunately still widespread and has an economic impact that far exceeds the impact of losses incurred by corporate failures in the first decade of the 21st century. This global financial crisis (and ensuing sovereign debt crisis) demonstrates that the policies chosen to address the global financial crisis may have moved the problem from a corporate to a government sector problem.

The problems highlighted by the sovereign debt crisis include the lack of transparency and accountability of governments, as well as poor public finance management and public sector financial reporting, but they cannot be limited to these matters. Tax management structures are clearly not efficient in many countries, and do not create constraints or incentives for managing public finances in a manner that protects both the public interest and investors in government debt. This is why IFAC recommended the following institutional arrangements for public finances:

- High-quality and timely accrual-based financial reporting;
- Audited financial statements released within six months of year end;
- Budgeting, appropriations, and reporting on the same accrual basis;
- Full transparency in fiscal positions ahead of general elections, ensuring that voting is fully informed; and
- Limitations on deficit spending, or at least full transparency around the reasons for deficit spending and explanations of how, over an economic cycle, fiscal balance will be restored.

IFAC also recommended that "the G-20 actively encourage and facilitate the adoption of accrual-based accounting by governments and public sector institutions, which promotes greater transparency and accountability in public sector finances, and allows for monitoring of government debt and liabilities for their true economic

---

[1] See https://www.ifac.org/publications-resources/ifac-makes-recommendations-g-20.

implications." Global adoption of these standards would facilitate the comparability of such information on a global basis and assist in internal management decisions in resource allocation (planning and budgeting), monitoring, accountability, and long-term sustainability.

This book is intended to serve as a comprehensive guide on how to apply IPSAS, cash basis IPSAS as well as accrual accounting IPSAS, and to provide practical implementation examples for IPSAS practitioners, policy makers, academics, and students. The use of IPSAS alone would not solve the problems highlighted by the sovereign debt crisis, but the appropriate use of IPSAS financial information would assist public officials and other groups in assessing the implications of fiscal decisions proposed or made by government.

Application of IPSAS by governments worldwide can be a step towards improving the quality of financial information reported by public entities, which is critical for investors, taxpayers, and the general public to understand the full impact of decisions made by governments with respect to their financial performance, financial position, and cash flows. The move towards IPSAS adoption across nation states worldwide is still in its early stages but it is a development that is expected to continue.

This is just the beginning of a new era in public finances:

> Over the past five years there has been an increasing interest in the IPSASs and a strong trend towards their adoption; this trend is anticipated to continue. Currently over 80 jurisdictions have either fully or partly adopted IPSAS, or have processes in place to adopt IPSASs, directly or indirectly. This includes the government of New Zealand, South Asian countries like Thailand, Indonesia and Malaysia, African countries such as Nigeria, and South Africa, Latin and South American countries such as Peru and Brazil and some European countries, Switzerland, Austria, Lithuania and Estonia among them. A number of international organizations have also adopted IPSASs, for example, the United Nations Systems, the Organisation for Economic Co-operation and Development (OECD) and Interpol. The European Commission (EC) report issued during 2013 considered the suitability of IPSASs for the member states of the European Union and described the standards as an "indisputable reference" in the development of European Public Sector Accounting Standards. Other countries like Russia, India and China have also signaled their intention to adopt, though specific deadlines have not been set. (IPSASB, 2014)

ANNEX 1: BRIEF DESCRIPTION OF IPSAS

IPSAS 1 Presentation of Financial Statements sets out the overall considerations for the presentation of financial statements, guidance for their structure, and minimum requirements for the content of financial statements prepared under the accrual basis of accounting.

IPSAS 2 Cash Flow Statements requires the provision of information about the changes in cash and cash equivalents during the financial period from operating, investing, and financing activities.

IPSAS 3 Accounting Policies, Changes in Accounting Estimates and Errors specifies the accounting treatment for changes in accounting estimates, changes in accounting policies, and the correction of material errors.

IPSAS 4 The Effects of Changes in Foreign Exchange Rates deals with accounting for foreign currency transactions and foreign operations, sets out the requirements for determining which exchange rate to use for the recognition of certain transactions and balances, and prescribes how to recognize the financial effect of changes in exchange rates within the financial statements.

IPSAS 5 Borrowing Costs prescribes the accounting treatment for borrowing costs and requires either the immediate expensing of borrowing costs or, as an allowed alternative treatment, the capitalization of borrowing costs that are directly attributable to the acquisition, construction, or production of a qualifying asset.

IPSAS 6 Consolidated and Separate Financial Statements requires all controlling entities to prepare consolidated financial statements, which consolidate all controlled entities on a line-by-line basis.

IPSAS 7 Investments in Associates requires all such investments to be accounted for in the consolidated financial statements using the equity method of accounting.

IPSAS 8 Interests in Joint Ventures requires proportionate consolidation to be adopted as the benchmark treatment, and the equity method of accounting as an allowed alternative to account for joint ventures.

IPSAS 9 Revenue from Exchange Transactions establishes the conditions for the recognition of revenue arising from exchange transactions, and requires such revenue to be measured at the fair value of the consideration received or receivable.

IPSAS 10 Financial Reporting in Hyperinflationary Economies describes the characteristics of a hyperinflationary economy and requires financial statements of entities that operate in such economies to be restated so that the financial information provided is meaningful.

IPSAS 11 Construction Contracts defines construction contracts and establishes requirements for the recognition of revenues and expenses arising from such contracts.

IPSAS 12 Inventories establishes the measurement requirements for inventories (including those held for distribution at no or nominal charge), and provides guidance on the assignment of costs.

IPSAS 13 Leases establishes requirements for the accounting treatment of operating and finance leases by lessees and lessors.

IPSAS 14 Events After the Reporting Date establishes requirements for the treatment of certain events that occur after the reporting date, and distinguishes between adjusting and non-adjusting events.

IPSAS 15 Financial Instruments: Disclosure and Presentation *has been superseded* by IPSAS 28 Financial Instruments: Presentation, IPSAS 29 Financial Instruments: Recognition and Measurement, and IPSAS 30 Financial Instruments: Disclosures.

IPSAS 16 Investment Property establishes the accounting treatment and related disclosures for investment property, providing for application of either a fair value or historical cost model.

IPSAS 17 Property, Plant and Equipment (PPE) establishes the accounting treatment for property, plant, and equipment, including the basis and timing of their initial recognition, and the determination of their ongoing carrying amounts and related depreciation.

IPSAS 18 Segment Reporting establishes requirements for the disclosure of financial information of the distinguishable activities of reporting entities.

IPSAS 19 Provisions, Contingent Liabilities and Contingent Assets establishes requirements for the recognition and measurement of provisions, and the disclosure of contingent liabilities and contingent assets.

IPSAS 20 Related Party Disclosures establishes requirements for the disclosure of transactions with parties that are related to the reporting entity.

IPSAS 21 Impairment of Non-Cash-Generating Assets prescribes the procedures that apply to determine whether a non-cash-generating asset is impaired and to ensure that impairment losses are recognized.

IPSAS 22 Disclosure of Financial Information About the General Government Sector prescribes disclosure requirements for governments that elect to present information about the general government sector in their consolidated financial statements.

IPSAS 23 Revenue from Non-Exchange Transactions deals with issues that need to be considered in recognizing and measuring revenue from non-exchange transactions.

IPSAS 24 Presentation of Budget Information in Financial Statements sets out the requirement for a comparison of budget amounts and the actual amounts arising from execution of the budget to be included in the financial statements, and a reconciliation of the actual amounts in the budget to actual amounts in the financial statements.

IPSAS 25 Employee Benefits prescribes the accounting treatment and disclosure requirements of employee benefits, including the timing of recognition of liabilities and expenses.

IPSAS 26 Impairment of Cash-Generating Assets prescribes the procedures that apply to determine whether a cash-generating asset is impaired and to ensure that impairment losses are recognized.

IPSAS 27 Agriculture prescribes the accounting treatment and disclosures for biological assets and agricultural produce at the point of harvest when they relate to agricultural activity.

IPSAS 28 Financial Instruments: Presentation establishes principles for presenting financial instruments as liabilities or net assets/equity and for offsetting financial assets and financial liabilities.

IPSAS 29 Financial Instruments: Recognition and Measurement establishes principles for recognizing and measuring financial assets, financial liabilities, and some contracts to buy or sell non-financial items.

IPSAS 30 Financial Instruments: Disclosures requires entities to provide disclosures in their financial statements that enable users to evaluate (a) the significance of financial instruments for the entity's financial position and performance; and (b) the nature and extent of risks arising from financial instruments to which the entity is exposed during the period and at the end of the reporting period, and how the entity manages those risks.

IPSAS 31 Intangible Assets prescribes the accounting treatment for recognizing and measuring intangible assets.

IPSAS 32 Service Concession Arrangements prescribes the accounting for service concession arrangements by the grantor, a public sector entity.

IPSAS 33 First-Time Adoption of Accrual Basis IPSASs. An entity shall apply those amendments for annual financial statements covering periods beginning on or after 1 January 2017.

IPSAS 34 Separate Financial Statements. An entity shall apply this Standard for annual financial statements covering periods beginning on or after 1 January 2017.

IPSAS 35 Consolidated Financial Statements. An entity shall apply this Standard for annual financial statements covering periods beginning on or after 1 January 2017.

IPSAS 36 Investments in Associates and Joint Ventures. An entity shall apply this Standard for annual financial statements covering periods beginning on or after 1 January 2017.

IPSAS 37 Joint Arrangements. An entity shall apply this Standard for annual financial statements covering periods beginning on or after 1 January 2017.

IPSAS 38 Disclosure of Interests in Other Entities. An entity shall apply this Standard for annual financial statements covering periods beginning on or after 1 January 2017.

ANNEX 2: KEY CHARACTERISTICS OF PUBLIC SECTOR ENTITIES[1]

Characteristic	Description
Public accountability	Governments are elected through a democratic process to be granted constitutional or devolved rights, powers, and responsibilities. These responsibilities require broad accountability to the public and their elected representatives. Government and their institutions use public resources and may have been given delegated powers and responsibilities that also demand broad accountability to the public.
	Public accountability is an overriding feature of public sector entities and ensuring the availability of information to demonstrate such accountability is the primary objective of public sector reporting. Public accountability typically encompasses: • A conferred responsibility; • An obligation to report back on the discharge of that responsibility; • Monitoring to warrant accountability; and • Potential sanctions for non-performance.
Multiple objectives	The key aims of most public sector entities are not to generate a profit. Instead they are to: • Provide service; • Facilitate resource reallocation; and/or • Undertake policy development.
Rights and responsibilities	The rights and responsibilities of governments provide them with the ability to directly and indirectly affect the economy and society they operate in. The rights and responsibilities may vary by level of government. Governments can, for example: • Tax and set fiscal policy; • Penalize and fine; • Set monetary policy; • Make and enforce laws and regulations. In exchange, governments have the responsibility to, for example: • Meet their constitutional or devolved duties; • Set policies to manage the socio-economic issues of the jurisdiction in an efficient, effective, sustainable, and transparent manner through the stewardship and application of the public resources entrusted to them; • Deliver services and reallocate resources; • Be accountable for the efficient, effective, sustainable, and transparent stewardship and use of the public resources entrusted to them.
Lack of equity ownership	Public sector entities do not act to enhance the economic position of the entity for the benefit of owners.

[1]Content of table was laid out using PSAB (2011) and IPSASB (2011).

Operating and financial frameworks set by legislation	Public sector entities must operate within and illustrate their compliance with legal requirements.
	Transparent and public accountability against the policy objectives and policies set out in legislation underlies public sector reporting.
Importance and use of budgets	Most governments prepare and make publicly available their financial budgets. The budget documents are often extensively distributed and referenced.
	The budget mirrors the financial elements of the government's plans for the forthcoming period. It is the key tool for financial management and control, and is the central component of the process that provides for government and legislative oversight of the financial dimensions of operations.
Governance structures	Government's governance is provided by the legislature and comprises elected officials.
Nature of resources	Resources of public sector entities are generally held for service provision rather than for their ability to generate future cash flows. Examples include heritage and cultural resources and complex infrastructure systems. These resources may be held or managed by government organizations at various levels of government. These resources will often require continuous maintenance.
Non-exchange transactions	Some of the rights and responsibilities of public sector entities (see above under rights and responsibilities) give rise to non-exchange transactions (such as, taxes, fines and penalties, license and regulatory fees, social benefits). This means that a large share of transactions of many public sector entities is primarily non-exchange in nature (see Chapter 11 for IPSAS 23 on non-exchange revenue).

REFERENCES

IPSASB (2011). Key Characteristics of the Public Sector with Potential Implications for Financial Reporting, ED. (Available at: http://www.ifac.org/sites/default/files/publications/exposure-drafts/IPSASB_ED_Key-Characteristics-of-Public-Sector.pdf, last accessed 15 February 2015).

PSAB (2011). Consultation paper 1. (Available at: http://www.frascanada.ca/standards-for-public-sector-entities/documents-for-comment/item52207.pdf, last accessed 15 December 2014).

ANNEX 3: EMPLOYEE BENEFITS: AN OVERVIEW OF THE KEY PRINCIPLES

SHORT-TERM EMPLOYEE BENEFITS

Short-term employee benefits are those that fall due wholly within 12 months after the end of the period in which the employee renders the related service.

The expense and liability recognized should be the undiscounted amount.

POST-EMPLOYMENT BENEFITS

Post-employement benefits plans can be split between two types, namely defined contribution plan and defined benefit plan.

Defined contribution plan

With a defined contribution plan an entity makes fixed contributions into a separate entity and the entity will carry none of the actuarial or investment risks. The entity will only recognize a liability or asset if these contributions are in arrears or in advance respectively. The liability or asset is not discounted, except where it does not fall due wholly within 12 months.

Defined benefit plan[1]

With a defined benefit plan an entity provides employees with the agreed benefits of the plan and the entity carries all the actuarial and investment risks. The obligation is measured on a discounted basis because the liability may be settled many years after the employees render the related service. To simplify the measurement of the obligation for an entity, they will obtain a valuation from a qualified valuator. The valuation report will then be utilized for all the recognition and disclosure requirements.

The accounting treatment of multi-employer and state plans depends upon whether the entity has a legal or constructive obligation to pay future benefits.

- Should these plans be recognized as a defined benefit plan then only the entity's proportionate share of the defined benefit obligation, plan assets, and post-employment benefit cost associated with the plan should be recognized.
- If, however, the entity is unable to identify its share of the underlying financial position and performance of the plan with sufficient reliability, then an entity accounts for the plan as if it is a defined contribution plan. Additional disclosure is required by IPSAS25.

---

[1] A defined benefit plan is generally a plan whereby the amount of benefits that an employee will receive on retirement is specified in some way, for example as a proportion of an employee's final salary depending on the number of years' service worked (IAS 19.7; 25.10).

TERMINATION BENEFITS

For termination benefits, the past event that results in a present obligation for the entity to pay benefits is the termination itself, and not employee's service.

To recognize termination benefits an entity must demonstrate commitment to either: (a) terminating employment before normal retirement date; or (b) encouraging voluntary redundancy.

OTHER LONG-TERM EMPLOYEE BENEFITS

Other long-term employee benefits are recognized in the same fashion as defined benefit plans, except that there is much less uncertainty. The measurement of the amounts will therefore be less complex than for defined benefit plans.

Other long-term employee benefits also include, for example:

1. Bonus, incentive, and performance-related payments payable 12 months or more after the end of the reporting period in which the employees render the related service; and
2. Deferred compensation paid 12 months or more after the end of the reporting period in which it is earned.

ANNEX 4: APPENDIX TO CHAPTER 21. TRANSITION TO IPSAS. CASE EXAMPLE: ICELAND IPSAS IMPLEMENTATION PLAN [1]

Action	Phase I Jan–June 2014	Phase II July–Dec 2014	Phase II/Phase III 2015	Phase IV 2016	Phase V 2017
1a. Consolidation within class A, between A and B classes and A and C class (Transactions and balances between B and C classes aggregated)	– Identify relevant B and C entities – Inform accountants in agencies and line ministries – Agree method of capturing inter-entity transactions – Train staff who consolidate	– Develop form and content of separate (A entities) and consolidated financial statements – Document procedures for consolidation – Issue instructions to B and C entities to submit financial statements and supplementary information for 2014 by March 31, 2015; also other information requirements (e.g., for quarterly reporting) – Consolidate balance sheet as at January 1, 2014	– Prepare first trial consolidated financial statements for 2014 including notes according to IPSAS – Issue instructions to B and C entities to submit financial statements and supplementary information for 2014 by March 31, 2016		

(continued)

[1]See Khan et al. (2013).

Action	Phase I Jan–June 2014	Phase II July–Dec 2014	Phase II/Phase III 2015	Phase IV 2016	Phase V 2017
1b. Consolidation within class A, between A and B classes, A and C classes, and B and C classes			– Refine and improve accounting policies, processes, and data quality and completeness based on experience and comments of INAO	– Prepare second trial consolidated financial statements for 2015 including notes	
1c. Consolidation within class A, between A and B classes. A and C classes, and B and C classes				– Refine and improve accounting policies, processes, and data quality and completeness based on experience and comments of INAO	– Prepare official consolidated financial statements for 2016 including notes and submit for audit
2a. Land and buildings, roads and other infrastructure, other equipment (OBL effective 1.1 2015)	– Review quality and completeness of data in registers – Review existing valuation policies – Prepare technical requirements for Oracle – Specify useful lives for assets other than land – Establish cost or values – Impairment test	– Adapt Oracle asset module – Data transfer to Oracle (recording assets as both assets and expense in two parallel systems) – Prepare template for notes – Complete identification, recording, and valuation of any missing items	– Prepare information for IPSAS financial statements for 2014 – Calculate estimated depreciation for budget 2016 and future years, based on investment plans	– Refine and improve data for financial statements and estimates for budget and future years	– Record assets and related transactions in official system – Refine and improve data for financial statements and estimates for budget and future years

2b. Finance and operating leases	– Identify and review leases and classify as finance or operating leases – Prepare technical requirements for Oracle	– Adapt Oracle in a parallel system – Data transfer to Oracle – Prepare template for notes – Register in the system	– Prepare information for IPSAS statement for 2014 – Calculate amortization, depreciation for budget 2016 and subsequent years	– Refine and improve data for financial statements and estimates for budget and future years	– Record assets and related transactions in official system – Refine and improve data for financial statements and estimates for budget and future years
2c. Public-private partnerships	– Identify and review public–private partnerships arrangements – Treat as assets under appropriate categories and liabilities	– Adapt Oracle in a parallel system (record transactions as assets) – Data transfer to Oracle – Prepare of template for notes – Register within the system	– Prepare information for IPSAS statement for 2014 – Calculate depreciations under appropriate asset categories for budget 2016 and future years	– Refine and improve data for financial statements and estimates for budget and future years	– Record assets and related transactions in official system – Refine and improve data for financial statements and estimates for budget and future years

(continued)

Action	Phase I Jan–June 2014	Phase II July–Dec 2014	Phase II/Phase III 2015	Phase IV 2016	Phase V 2017
2d. Software and databases	– Collect and review any available data – Transfer data to Oracle (for available data) – Estimate useful lives	– Adapt Oracle in a parallel system – Transfer data to Oracle (record transactions as assets) – Prepare template for notes – Impairment test	– Prepare information for IPSAS statement for 2014 – Calculate depreciation for budget 2016 and future years	– Refine and improve data for financial statements and estimates for budget and future years	– Record assets and related transactions in official system – Refine and improve data for financial statements and estimates for budget and future years
2e. Inventories	– Review available data – In case of significant data gaps, register material inventories	– Adapt Oracle in a parallel system – Data transfer to Oracle (record transactions as assets) – Prepare template for notes	– Prepare information for IPSAS statements for 2014 and for budget 2016 and future years	– Refine and improve data for financial statements and estimates for budget and future years	– Record assets and related transactions in official system – Refine financial statements and estimates for budget and future years

2f. Accounting for associates	– Identify relevant entities – Develop methodology for equity accounting – Continue to account for associates at cost in separate financial statements of class A entities	– Identify missing entities – Include associates on equity basis in consolidated balance sheet as at January 1, 2014	– Include associates in first trial consolidated financial statements for 2014 including notes – Refine and improve accounting policies, processes, and data quality and completeness of associates based on experience and comments of INAO	– Include associates in second trial consolidated financial statements for 2015 including notes – Refine and improve accounting policies, processes, and data quality and completeness of associates based on experience and comments of INAO	– Include associates official consolidated financial statements for 2016 including notes and submit for audit
3a. Pension liabilities	– Specify accounting policy and new methodology for calculation – Recalculate according to new methodology	– Data transfer to Oracle – Record transactions as assets – Prepare template for notes	– Prepare information for IPSAS financial statements for 2014 – Prepare estimates for budget 2016 and future years	– Refine and improve data for financial statements and estimates for budget and future years	– Record revised liabilities and related transactions in official system – Refine and improve data for financial statements and estimates for budget and future years

(continued)

Action	Phase I Jan–June 2014	Phase II July–Dec 2014	Phase II/Phase III 2015	Phase IV 2016	Phase V 2017
3b. Other provisions	– Identify need for other provisions (e.g., leave entitlements, guarantees) – Analyze circumstances – Develop methodology	– Prepare template for notes – Recognize in opening balance sheet	– Improve methodologies – Supplement with additional material provisions not identified in opening balance sheet – Prepare input for budget 2016	– Refine and improve data for financial statements and estimates for budget and future years	– Record revised liabilities and related transactions in official system – Refine and improve data for financial statements and estimates for budget and future years
3c. Contingent liabilities	– Review completeness and quality of existing data	– Review probability of payments related to guarantees and other contingent liabilities, and if payments are probable, estimate provisions	– Recognize provisions as estimated – Revise presentation and disclose all contingent liabilities as a separate note, not as part of equity	– Continue to recognize and disclose according to IPSAS 19	
3d. Commitments	– Review completeness and quality of existing data		– Revise presentation and disclose significant commitments as a separate note, not as part of equity	– Continue to disclose as a separate note, not as part of equity	

4a. Financial assets and debt	– Categorization of financial assets according to IPSAS 28 – Analysis of arrangements – Develop accounting policy – Prepare revaluation – Analyze new requirements in the LIBRA debt management system	– Develop accounting policy – Prepare revaluation – Analyze new requirements in the LIBRA debt management system – Prepare template for notes	– Prepare information for IPSAS financial statements for 2014 – Prepare estimates for budget 2016 and future years	– Refine and improve data for financial statements and estimates for budget and future years – Prepare input for budget 2016	– Record revised assets and liabilities and related transactions in official system – Refine and improve data for financial statements and estimates for budget and future years
4b. Receivables and doubtful debts	– Analyze receivables to identify doubtful items – Revaluate receivables	– Prepare template for notes	– Prepare information for IPSAS financial statements for 2014 – Prepare estimates for budget 2016 and future years	– Refine and improve data for financial statements and estimates for budget and future years – Prepare input for budget 2016	– Record revised assets and provisions and related transactions in official system – Refine and improve data for financial statements and estimates for budget and future years

(continued)

Action	Phase I Jan–June 2014	Phase II July–Dec 2014	Phase II/Phase III 2015	Phase IV 2016	Phase V 2017
5a. Presentation of financial statements		– Develop template for revised statements – Develop statement of changes in net assets/equity – Develop template for direct method cash flow statement – Implement necessary IT-changes	– Use revised presentation for 2016 budget – Use revised budget for IPSAS 2014 financial statements	– Refine and improve presentation	– Prepare official IPSAS financial statements using new presentation
5b. Harmonized presentation of budget and accounts		– Develop common template for budget and ex-post operating statement, showing net lending/borrowings and operating result – Review other needs for harmonization	– Prepare 2016 budget using harmonized presentation – Prepare trial financial statement for 2014 using harmonized presentation	– Prepare 2017 budget using harmonized presentation – Prepare trial financial statement for 2015 using harmonized presentation	– Prepare official IPSAS financial statements using harmonized presentation and compare budget and actual
6a. Audit		– Review and comment on trial balance sheet as at January 1, 2014	– Review and report on first trial IPSAS financial statements for 2014	– Review and report on second trial IPSAS financial statements for 2014	– Audit official financial statements for 2016 and issue formal audit opinion and recommendations for improvements

BIBLIOGRAPHY

ADF (2011). Economic Governance and Competitiveness Support Program (EGCSP); Country: Liberia; Appraisal report. African Development Fund.

Adhémar, P. (2002). The Public Sector Committee (PSC) The Standards Project. In V. Montesinos and J.M. Vela (eds), *Innovations in Governmental Accounting* (Kluwer Academic Publishers), pp. 61–71.

Aggestam-Pontoppidan, C. (2010). A Project Management Perspective on the Adoption of Accrual-Based IPSAS, *International Journal of Governmental Financial Management*, December, pp. 49–66.

Alesani, D., Jensen, G., and Steccolini, I. (2012). IPSAS Adoption by the World Food Programme: An application of the contingency model to intergovernmental organisations. *International Journal of Public Sector Performance Management*, 2:1, pp. 61–80.

Alla, M. (2014). The Accounting for the Service Concession Arrangements in Albania. Conference of Informatics and Management Sciences, 24–28 March, pp. 222–225.

Accounting Standards Board (2012). Discussion paper on accounting for principal-agent activities in the public sector, July 2012.

Aversano, N. and Ferrone, C. (2012). The Accounting Problems of Heritage Assets. *Advanced Research in Scientific Areas 2012*, December, pp. 574–578.

Ball, I. (2012). New Development: Transparency in the public sector. *Public Money & Management*, 32:1, pp. 35–40.

Ball, I. (2014). IPSAS: the Greek elephant in the room. *Public Finance International*. (Available at http://opinion.publicfinanceinternational.org, last accessed 3 March 2015.)

Ball, I. and Pflugrath, G. (2012). Government Accounting—Making Enron look good. *World Economics*, 13:1, January–March, 1–18.

Bandy, G. (2014). *Financial Management and Accounting in the Public Sector* (Routledge).

Bandy, G. (2015). *Financial Management and Accounting in the Public Sector*, 2nd edn. (Routledge-Taylor & Francis Group).

Barth, M. E., and Schipper, K. (2008). Financial Reporting Transparency, *Journal of Accounting, Auditing and Finance*, 23:2, pp. 173–190.

Biosev, S.A. (2014). Consolidated interim financial statements for the three-month period ended 30 June 2014, financial statements prepared under IFRS.

Bjudding, T., Grossi, G., and Tagesson, T. (2014). *Public Sector Accounting* (Routledge).

Bovens, M. (2007, July). Analysing and Accessing Accountability: A Conceptual Framework, *European Law Journal*, 13:4, pp. 447–468.

Brusca, I., Caperchione, E., Cohen, S., and Manes Rossi, F. (2015). *Public Sector Accounting and Auditing in Europe—The Challenges of Harmonization* (Palgrave-Macmillan).

Bureau International des Poids et Mesures, Annual Report 2012. (Available at www.bipm.org/utils/common/pdf/rapport-annuel/Rapport-annuel-BIPM-2012.pdf, last accessed 1 March 2015.)

Cain, S. (2014). IPSAS: Coming of Age, *Public Finance*, November 2014. (Available at http://www.publicfinance.co.uk/2014/11/coming-of-age, last accessed 1 May 2015.)

Caperchione, E. (2015). Standard Setting in the Public Sector: State of the Art, in Brusca et al. (eds), *Public Sector Accounting and Auditing in Europe* (Palgrave-Macmillan), pp. 1–11.

Christiaens, J., Reyniers, B., and Rollé, C. (2010). Impact of IPSAS on Reforming Governmental Financial Information Systems: A comparative study, *International Review of Administrative Sciences*, 76:3, pp. 537–554.

Deloitte (2013). IPSASs in your Pocket. (Available at www.iasplus.com.)

Dye, K.M. (1988). International Harmonization of Governmental Accounting and Auditing Standards: Current Developments. In J.L. Chan and R. Jones (eds), *Governmental Accounting and Auditing International Comparisons* (Routledge), pp. 11–26.

Edgerton, D. (2013). Valuation and Depreciation: A guide for the not-for-profit and public sector under accrual based accounting standards. CPA Australia and the Australian Asset Management Collaborative Group (AAMCoG).

Elgie, R. (2001). Democratic Accountability and Central Bank Independence: A Reply to Various Critics, *West European Politics*, 24:1, pp. 217–221.

European Commission (2013). COM (2013) 114 Final Report from the Commission to the Council and the European Parliament. *Towards implementing harmonised public sector accounting standards in Member States*, Brussels.

European Union (2012). Treaty on Stability, Coordination and Governance of the Economic and Monetary Union (signed 2 March 2012, entry into force 1 January 2013).

Eurostat (2012). Public Consultation Assessment of the Suitability of the IPSAS for the Member States.

EY (2013). Changing tack, A new suite of accounting standards for public benefit entities. (Available at http://www.ey.com/Publication/vwLUAssets/Changing_Tack/$FILE/Changing%20tack%20FinalV.pdf, last accessed 22 January 2015.)

EY (2013). *IPSAS Outlook*, August 2013. (Available at http://www.ey.com/Publication/vwLUAssets/EY-Outlook-IPSAS/$FILE/EY-Outlook-IPSAS.pdf, last accessed 15 December 2015.)

EY (2013). Model public sector group, Illustrative financial statements for the year ended 31 December 2013, based on Intenational Public Sector Accounting Standards in issue at 30 June 2013. (Available at; http://www.ey.com/Publication/vwLUAssets/EY_Model_Public_Sector_Group_Illustrative_financial_statements/$FILE/EY-IPSAS-MG-YrEnd-Oct2013.pdf, last accessed 15 January 2015.)

EY (2014). *IPSAS Outlook*, November 2014. EY.com/IPSAS.

EY (2014). The conceptual framework – from start to finish. *IPSAS Outlook*, November 2014.

GASAB [India] (2008). A Study on Gap Analysis of Indian Government Accounting with International Standards. A Research Study by GASAB Secretariat. (Available at; http://www.gasab.gov.in/pdf/Gap_Analysis.pdf; accessed 5 August 2014.)

Gomes, M. (2013). Improving Public Sector Finance, *Accountants Today*, January–February, pp. 12–15.

GRAP (2014). GRAP 20 Related party disclosures Guideline. (Available at http://oag.treasury.gov.za/Publications/06.%20GRAP/02.%20Manuals/Approved%20and%20Not%20Effective/GRAP%20Guideline%2020%20-%20Related%20Partiey%20disclosures.pdf, last accessed 20 January 2015.)

Guthrie, J. and English, L. (1997). Performance information and programme evaluation in the Australian public sector. *International Journal of Public Sector Management*, 10:3, pp.154–164.

Hood, C. (1989). Public Administration and Public Policy: Intellectual challenges for the 1990s, *Australian Journal of Public Administration*, 48:4, pp. 346–358.

Hood, C. (1995). The 'New Public Management' in the 1980's: Variations on a theme, *Accounting, Organizations and Society*, 20:2/3, pp. 93–109.

Hoogervorst, H. (2011). Financial Reporting and Auditing—A Time for Change? The objectives of financial reporting. Speech by Hans Hoogervorst, Brussels, 9 February 2011, Conference organized by the European Commission. (Available at http://ec.europa.eu/internal_market/accounting/docs/conference20110209/speech_hoogervorst_en.pdf, last accessed 15 December 2014.)

Howard, R. J. (2001). Infrastructure Asset Management under Australian Accounting Standard 27 (AAS27): International development, Proceedings of the Institution of Civil Engineers, *Municipal Engineer* (ISSN 0965-0903), 145:4, pp. 305–310. (Available at http://www.ifac.org/publications-resources/process-reviewing-and-modifying-iasb-documents, last accessed 1 August 2014.)

Humphrey, C. and Loft, A. (2007). *IFAC – The First Fifteen Years: 1977–1992*. (Available at www.ifac.org, last accessed 1 August 2014.)

Humphrey, C. and Loft, A. (2008). *Setting Standards, Making History: The International Federation of Accountants (IFAC), 1977–2007* (OARnet, Sweden).

Humphrey, C., Jeppesen, K., Loft, A., and Turley, S. (2006). In Pursuit of Global Regulation: Changing governance and accountability structures at the International Federation of Accountants (IFAC), *Accounting, Auditing & Accountability Journal,* 19:3, pp. 428–451.

Humphrey, C., Loft, A., and Woods, M. (2009). The Global Audit Profession and the International Financial Architecture: Understanding regulatory relationships at a time of financial crisis, *Accounting, Organizations and Society,* 34:6–7, pp. 810–825.

Institute of Chartered Accountants Australia (ICAA) (2013). It's time … for global, high quality public sector financial reporting. (Available at www.charteredaccountants.com.au, last accessed 15 August 2014.)

Institute of Public Auditors of India (IPAI) (2010). Report on Pilot Study on Migration to Accrual Accounting, Forest and Health Departments of State Government of Madhya Pradesh (India). Sponsored by World Bank, New Delhi. (Available at; http://gasab.gov.in/gasab/pdf/IPAI-Final-Report-MPv2.pdf, last accessed 5 August 2014.)

International Atomic Energy Agency (IAEA) (2013). The Agency's Financial Statements for 2013, GOV/2014/14, 7 April 2014.

International Federation of Accountants (IFAC) (2004). Report of the Externally Chaired Review Panel on Governance, Role and Organisation of the International Federation of Accountants Public Sector Committee, June 2004. (Available at www.ifac.org/sites/default/files/downloads/PSCE xternalReviewReport.doc, last accessed 31 July 2014.)

International Monetary Fund (2014). Government Finance Statistics Manual 2014, pre-publication draft. (Available at http://www.imf.org/external/np/sta/gfsm/pdf/text14.pdf, last accessed 12 January 2015.)

International Standard on Auditing (ISA) 200, 'Overall objectives of the independent auditor and the conduct of an audit in accordance with international standards on auditing'.

International Standard on Auditing (ISA) 320. 'Materiality in planning and performing and audit'.

International Public Sector Accounting Standards Board (IPSASB) (2005). *International Public Sector Accounting Standards (IPSASs) and Statistical Bases of Financial Reporting: An Analysis of Differences and Recommendations for Convergence.* Research Report, January, 2005. (Available at http://www.auditorgeneral.gov.tt/sites/default/files/IPSAS%27s.pdf, last accessed 12 December 2014.)

IPSASB (2008). Process for Reviewing and Modifying IASB Documents, October 2008. (Available at

IPSASB (2011). Key Characteristics of the Public Sector with Potential Implications for Financial Reporting, ED. (Available at: http://www.ifac.org/sites/default/files/publications/exposure-drafts/IPSASB_ED_Key-Characteristics-of-Public-Sector.pdf, last accessed 15 February 2015.)

IPSASB (2013). International public sector accounting standards board fact sheet. April 2013. (Available at; http://www.ifac.org/sites/default/files/uploads/IPSASB/IPSASB-Fact-Sheet.pdf, last accessed 15 August 2014.)

IPSASB (2013). *IPSAS Adoption experience; A closer look at: Malaysia,* November 2013.

IPSASB (2014). *Handbook of International Public Sector Pronouncements,* 2014 edn, Vols I and II.

IPSASB (2014). IPSASB strategy consultation. (Available at https://www.ifac.org/sites/default/files/publications/files/IPSASB-Strategy-Consultation-2015-2019_0.pdf, last accessed 15 March 2015.)

IPSASB (2014). Strategy Consultation for the period from 2015 forward. (Available at http://www.ifac.org/sites/default/files/publications/files/IPSASB-Strategy-Consultation-2015-2019_0.pdf, last accessed 1 March 2015.)

IPSASB Governance Group (2014a). The Future Governance of the International Public Sector Accounting Standards Board (IPSASB). Public consultation, January 2014. Chairs; the International Monetary

Fund (IMF), the Organisation for Economic Co-operation and Development (OECD), and the World Bank.

IPSASB Governance Group (2014b). The Future Governance of the International Public Sector Accounting Standards Board (IPSASB) IPSASB Governance Review Group – Recommendations. (Available at http://www.oecd.org/gov/budgeting/IPSASB-Governance-Review.htm, last accessed 25 February 2015.)

IPSASB Governance Group (2014c). Public Consultation on the Future Governance of the International Public Sector Accounting Standards Board (IPSASB)- Summary of Responses. October 2014. (Available at http://www.oecd.org/gov/budgeting/IPSASB-Consultation-Summary.pdf, last accessed 15 January 2015.)

Jensen, G. and Smith, R. (2013). History of the IPSASB: growing influence—reduced control?. Paper to XII Permanent Study Group pf the EGPA, Salerno, Italy. May.

Joint Inspection Unit (2010). Preparedness of the United Nations system Organizations for the international public sector accounting standards (IPSAS), Prepared by Gérard Biraud, United Nations, Geneva 2010, JIU/REP/2010/6.

Jones, R. and Pendlebury, M. (2010). *Public Sector Accounting*, 6th edn (Pearson Education).

Khan, A., Seiwald, J., and van Schaik. F. (2014). *IPSAS in Iceland: Towards enhanced fiscal transparency*. IMF country report no. 14/353.

Kirk, N.E. (2001). 'True and fair view' versus 'present fairly' in conformity with Generally Accepted Accounting Principles. Discussion Paper Series 208, Massey University. (Available at http://www.massey.ac.nz/massey/fms/Colleges/College%20of%20Business/School%20of%20Accountancy/Documents/Discussion%20Papers/208.pdf, last accessed 7 January 2015.)

Lapsley, I., Mussari, R., and Paulsson, G. (2009). On Adoption of Accrual Accounting in the Public Sector: A self-evident and problematic reform, *European Accounting Review*, 18:4, pp. 719–723.

Mason, P. (2012). IPSAS: Coming to you soon? (Available at http://opinion.publicfinanceinternational.org/2012/05/ipsas-coming-to-you-soon/, last accessed 3 March 2015.)

Mulgan, R. (1997). Processes of Accountability, *Australian Journal of Public Administration*, 56, pp. 25–36.

Müller-Marques Berger, T. (2012). *IPSAS Explained, A Summary of International Public Sector Accounting Standards* (John Wiley & Sons and Ernst & Young).

New Zealand (2014). Financial Statements of the Government of New Zealand for the Year Ended 30 June 2014. (Available at http://www.treasury.govt.nz/government/financialstatements/yearend/jun14, last accessed 27 March 2015.)

New Zealand Treasury (2013). PBE IPSAS 23 Revenue from Non-Exchange Transactions – Differences to NZ IFRS (PBE). (Available at http://www.treasury.govt.nz/publications/guidance/reporting/ipsas/comparison-nzifrs/pdfs/tsy-pbe-ipsas-23.pdf, last accessed 1 June 2015.)

Nobes, C. (1991). Harmonization in Financial Reporting. In C. Nobes, and R. Parker, *Comparative International Accounting*, 3rd edn (Prentice Hall), pp. 70–91.

Norton, C.L. and Porter, G.A. (2011). *Introduction to Financial Accounting*, 7th edn (South-Western Cengage Learning).

NZASB (2013). Public Benefit Entity International Public Sector Accounting Standard 22 Disclosure of Financial Information about the General Government Sector. (Available at http://xrb.govt.nz/includes/download.aspx?ID=127888, last accessed 20 January 2015.)

OECD (2013). Financial statements of the Organization for Economic co-operation and development as at 31 December 2013. (Available at: http://www.oecd.org/officialdocuments/publicdisplaydocumentpdf/?cote=BC%282014%2914&docLanguage=en, last accessed 10 January 2015.)

OECD (2013). Financial statements at 31 December 2013. (Available at http://www.oecd.org/officialdocuments/publicdisplaydocumentpdf/?cote=BC(2014)14&docLanguage=en, last accessed 15 December 2014.)

Ouda, H. (2010) 'A Prescriptive Model for Successful Transition to Accrual Accounting in the Government Sector', *International Journal on Governmental Financial Management*, X:1, The International Consortium on Governmental Financial Management (ICGFM), Alexandria, VA, USA.

Parker, L.D. and Gould, G. (1999). Changing Public Sector Accountability: Critiquing New Directions, *Accounting Forum*, 23:2, pp. 109–135; Reproduced in R. Hodges (ed.), *Governance and the Public Sector* (Edward Elgar Publishing, 2005), pp. 229–255.

Pattanayak, S. and Fainboim, I. (2011). Treasury Single Account: An Essential Tool for Government Cash Management, Fiscal Affairs Department, IMF. (Available at http://www.imf.org/external/pubs/ft/tnm/2011/tnm1104.pdf, accessed 15 July 2014.)

Pollanen, R. and Pollanen, E. (2009). Financial Control and Accountability in Local Government: Recent initiatives in Ontario, *International Journal of Business and Public Administration*, 6:2, Summer, pp. 1–15.

Pollitt, C. (1993). *Managerialism and the Public Services*, 2nd edn (Blackwell).

Pownall, G. and Schipper, K. (1999). Implications of Accounting Research for the SEC's Consideration of International Accounting Standards for U.S. Securities Offerings, *Accounting Horizons*, 13:3, pp. 259–280.

PSAB (2011). Consultation paper 1. (Available at http://www.frascanada.ca/standards-for-public-sector-entities/documents-for-comment/item52207.pdf, last accessed 15 December 2014.)

PWC (2012). IPSAS in a nutshell – from principles to practice.

Rocher, S. (2010). «La genèse de la normalisation internationale de la comptabilité publique». *Revue Française de Comptabilité*, 438, pp. 38-41. (An English short version of the paper is available at http://www.univ-angers.fr/_attachments/mypage-sebastien-rocher-fr/ROCHER_Brief%2520History%2520IPSASB.pdf?download=true, last accessed 14 November 2014.)

Schumesch, P., De Laet, J., and De Greef, A. (2012). *IPSAS in a nutshell – from principles to practice*. PWC.UNWRA (2013). 2013 Financial Statements. A/69/5Add.4.

Sinclair, A. (1995). The Chameleon of Accountability: Forms and Discourses, *Accounting, Organisations and Society*, 20:2&3, pp. 219–237.

Soll (2015). Greece's accounting problem, 20 January 2015, *New York Times*. (Available at http://www.nytimes.com/2015/01/21/opinion/greeces-accounting-problem.html, last accessed 20 February 2015.)

Stanford, J. (2014). The Conceptual Framework – from start to finish. *IPSAS Outlook*, November 2014. EY.com/IPSAS.

Stanford, J. (2015). Social benefits. Presentation at the 15th Annual OECD accruals symposium, 26–27 February, Paris, France.

The Government of Uganda (2013). Guidelines on operation of a treasury single account – phase 1. Issued by the Permanent Secretary to the Treasury. (Available at www.finance.go.ug accessed 1 August 2014.)

Transparency International (2014). (Available at https://www.transparency.org/whoweare/organisation/faqs_on_corruption/2/.)

UK Ministry of Defence (2013). Annual Report and Accounts 2012–13 for the year ended 31 March 2013. (Available at http://www.gov.uk/government/uploads/system/uploads/attachment_data/file/222874/MOD_AR13_clean.pdf, last accessed 10 January 2015.)

UNAIDS (2012). Financial Report and Audited Financial Statements for the year ended 31 December 2012, UNAIDS/PCB (32)/13.6. (Available at: http://www.unaids.org/sites/default/files/sub_landing/files/20130516-Financial%20Reporting_En.pdf, last accessed 11 January 2015.)

UNDP (2012). United Nations Development Programme Financial Report and Audited Financial Statements for the year ended 31 December 2012 and Report of the Board of Auditors, A/68/5/Add.1. (Available at http://www.undp.org/content/dam/undp/library/corporate/Transparency/UNDP_2012_Financial_Report_and_audited_Fin_statements_%20and_Report_of_Board_of_auditors%20A_68_5_add1.pdf, last accessed 20 January 2015.)

UNDP (2015). Admininistrative services, Property, plant and equipment. (Available at; https://info.
undp.org/global/popp/asm/pages/property-plant-and-equipment.aspx, last accessed 15 February
2015.)

UNESCO (2013). Financial Report and Audited Financial Statements for the year ended 31 December 2013. (Available at http://unesdoc.unesco.org/images/0023/002302/230209e.pdf, last accessed 14
August 2015.)

UNICEF (2012). Financial Report and Audited Financial Statements for the year ended 31
December 2012. (Available at http://www.unicef.org/about/execboard/files/A-68-5-Add2-UNICEF_
Financial_Report-ODS-English.pdf, last accessed 7 January 2015.)

United Nations (2010). General Assembly Resolution A/RES/64/259. (Available at http://www.un.org/
ga/search/view_doc.asp?symbol=A/RES/64/259, last accessed 2 March 2015.)

UNOPS (2012), Financial Statements.

UNOPS (2014). IPSAS compliant accounting policies. Administrative Instruction, AI/FPG/2011/01
(rev.l). (Available at http://www.unops.org/SiteCollectionDocuments/Accountability/AI.FPG.2011.
01%20%28rev.%201%29.pdf, last accessed 7 January 2015.)

Valentinov, V. (2011). Accountability and the Public Interest in the Nonprofit Sector: A conceptual
framework, *Financial Accountability and Management*, 27, November 1: 32–42.

Van Rompuy (2012). Speech by President Herman Van Rompuy during the signing ceremony of the
Treaty on Stability, Coordination and Governance of the Economic and Monetary Union, EUCO 39/12,
2/03/2012. (Available at http://data.consilium.europa.eu/doc/document/ST-39-2012-INIT/en/pdf, last
accessed 27 March 2015.)

Wang, X. (2014). *Financial Management in the Public Sector – Tools, Applications and Cases*, 3rd edn
(M.E. Sharpe, Inc.).

WFP (2008). Audited Annual Accounts 2008. WFP/EB.A/2009/6-A/1. 11 May 2009. (Available at
www.wfp.org/eb, last accessed 15 November 2015.)

WFP (2013). Audited Annual Accounts 2013, WFP/EB.A/2014/6-A/1.

WFP (2014). Strategic Plan (2014-2017), WFP/EB.A/2013/5-A/1.

WHO (2012). Financial Report and Audited Financial Statements for the year ended 31 December 2012,
A66/29. (Available at http://www.who.int/about/resources_planning/A66_29-en.pdf, last accessed 1
May 2015.)

WHO (2012). Financial Statements.

WHO (2013a). Proposed Programme Budget 2014–2015 to the 66th World Health Assembly (A66/7) 19
April 2013. (Available at http://apps.who.int/gb/ebwha/pdf_files/WHA66/A66_7-en.pdf, last accessed
10 March 2015.)

WHO (2013b). Financial Report and Audited Financial Statements for the year ended 31 December
2013 to the 67th World Health Assembly (A67/43) 17 April 2014.

WHO (2013). World Health Organization Financial Report and Audited Financial Statements for the
year ended 31 December 2013, A67/43.

INDEX

Compiled by Marian Preston at INDEXING SPECIALISTS (UK) Ltd., Indexing House, 306A Portland Road, Hove, East Sussex BN3 5LP United Kingdom.